THE COMPLETE ILLUSTRATED
POEMS, SONGS & BALLADS

of

Robert Burns

Engraved by H. Robinson

Robert Burns

*Engraved by H. Robinson after
a drawing by Archibald
Skirving*

THE COMPLETE ILLUSTRATED
POEMS, SONGS & BALLADS

of

Robert Burns

with 80 black and white illustrations

LOMOND BOOKS

Consultant Editor: Samuel Carr

The text first published in Great Britain in 1905 by J.M. Dent & Co.
Selection of illustrations first published in various sources (see Note)

This illustrated edition first published in 1990 by
Chancellor Press exclusively for Lomond Books
Michelin House
81 Fulham Road
London SW3 6RB

Reprinted in 1991, 1992

ISBN 1 85152 018 X

Printed in Great Britain by The Bath Press, Avon

CONTENTS

POEMS

Contents

Contents

Contents

Contents

Contents

Contents

Contents

Contents

Contents

EARLY AND MINOR PIECES;
FRAGMENTS, EPIGRAMS AND EPITAPHS

Contents

Contents

Contents

Contents

A NOTE ON THE ILLUSTRATIONS

The pictures in this book have been reproduced from the following editions of the Poems: *The Works of the late celebrated Robert Burns*, illustrated from wood engravings by Thomas Bewick, 1807; *The Poetical Works of Robert Burns*, edited by A. Cunningham, 1834; *The Works of Robert Burns*, edited by Professor Wilson, 1865; *The Poetry of Robert Burns*, edited by W.E. Henley and T.F. Henderson, 1897; and *The National Burns*, edited by Rev. George Gilfillan, 1905. Many of the illustrations in these books are by anonymous or unattributed artists. The majority of those in the 1865 edition of the Works are engraved after originals by David Octavius Hill, an artist who is now better remembered as a pioneer Scottish photographer.

Robert Burns

From an etching by William Hole

ROBERT BURNS

—∿∿—

THE DEATH AND DYING WORDS
OF POOR MAILIE

THE AUTHOR'S ONLY PET YOWE

AN UNCO MOURNFU' TALE

As Mailie, an' her lambs thegither,
Was ae day nibbling on the tether,
Upon her cloot she coost a hitch,
An' owre she warsl'd in the ditch:
There, groaning, dying, she did lie,
When Hughoc he cam doytin by.

Wi' glowrin een, and lifted han's
Poor Hughoc like a statue stan's;
He saw her days were near-hand ended,
But, wae's my heart! he could na mend it!
He gapèd wide, but naething spak,
At length poor Mailie silence brak.

"O thou, whase lamentable face
Appears to mourn my woefu' case!
My dying words attentive hear,
An' bear them to my Master dear.

"Tell him, if e'er again he keep
As muckle gear as buy a sheep—

A

O, bid him never tie them mair,
Wi' wicked strings o' hemp or hair!
But ca' them out to park or hill,
An' let them wander at their will :
So may his flock increase, an' grow
To scores o' lambs, an' packs o' woo'!

"Tell him, he was a Master kin',
An' aye was guid to me an' mine;
An' now my dying charge I gie him,
My helpless lambs, I trust them wi' him.

"O, bid him save their harmless lives,
Frae dogs, an' tods, an' butchers' knives!
But gie them guid cow-milk their fill,
Till they be fit to fend themsel';
An' tent them duly, e'en an' morn,
Wi' taets o' hay an' ripps o' corn.

"An' may they never learn the gates,
Of ither vile, wanrestfu' pets—
To slink thro' slaps, an' reave an' steal
At stacks o' pease, or stocks o' kail!
So may they, like their great forbears,
For mony a year come thro' the shears :
So wives will gie them bits o' bread,
An' bairns greet for them when they're dead.

"My poor toop-lamb, my son an' heir,
O, bid him breed him up wi' care!
An' if he live to be a beast,
To pit some havins in his breast!
An' warn him—what I winna name—
To stay content wi' yowes at hame;

An' no to rin an' wear his cloots,
Like ither menseless, graceless brutes.

"An' neist, my yowie, silly thing,
Gude keep thee frae a tether string!
O, may thou ne'er forgather up,
Wi' ony blastit, moorland toop;
But aye keep mind to moop an' mell,
Wi' sheep o' credit like thysel'!

"And now, my bairns, wi' my last breath,
I lea'e my blessin wi' you baith:
An' when you think upo' your mither,
Mind to be kind to ane anither.

"Now, honest Hughoc, dinna fail,
To tell my master a' my tale;
An' bid him burn this cursed tether,
An' for thy pains thou'se get my blather."

This said, poor Mailie turn'd her head,
An' closed her een amang the dead!

POOR MAILIE'S ELEGY.

LAMENT in rhyme, lament in prose,
Wi' saut tears trickling down your nose;
Our bardie's fate is at a close,
                    Past a' remead!
The last, sad cape-stane o' his woes;
                    Poor Mailie's dead!

It's no the loss o' warl's gear,
That could sae bitter draw the tear,

Or mak our bardie, dowie, wear
        The mourning weed:
He's lost a friend an' neebor dear
        In Mailie dead.

  Thro' a' the town she trotted by him;
A lang half-mile she could descry him;
Wi' kindly bleat, when she did spy him,
        She ran wi' speed:
A friend mair faithfu' ne'er cam nigh him,
        Than Mailie dead.

  I wat she was a sheep o' sense,
An' could behave hersel' wi' mense:
I'll say't, she never brak a fence,
        Thro' thievish greed.
Our bardie, lanely, keeps the spence
        Sin' Mailie's dead.

  Or, if he wanders up the howe,
Her livin image in her yowe
Comes bleating till him, owre the knowe,
        For bits o' bread;
An' down the briny pearls rowe
        For Mailie dead.

  She was nae get o' moorland tips,
Wi' tauted ket, an' hairy hips;
For her forbears were brought in ships,
        Frae 'yont the Tweed.
A bonier fleesh ne'er cross'd the clips
        Than Mailie's dead.

  Wae worth the man wha first did shape
That vile, wanchancie thing—a raip!

It maks guid fellows girn an' gape,
        Wi' chokin dread ;
An' Robin's bonnet wave wi' crape
        For Mailie dead.

O, a' ye bards on bonie Doon !
An' wha on Ayr your chanters tune !
Come, join the melancholious croon
        O' Robin's reed !
His heart will never get aboon—
        His Mailie's dead !

EPISTLE TO JOHN RANKINE.

ENCLOSING SOME POEMS.

O ROUGH, rude, ready-witted Rankine,
The wale o' cocks for fun an' drinkin' !
There's mony godly folks are thinkin,
        Your dreams and tricks
Will send you, Korah-like, a-sinkin
        Straught to auld Nick's.

Ye hae sae mony cracks an' cants,
And in your wicked, drucken rants,
Ye mak a devil o' the saunts,
        An' fill them fou ;
And then their failings, flaws, an' wants,
        Are a' seen thro'.

Hypocrisy, in mercy spare it !
That holy robe, O dinna tear it !
Spare't for their sakes, wha aften wear it—
        The lads in black;
But your curst wit, when it comes near it,
        Rives 't aff their back.

Think, wicked Sinner, wha ye're skaithing :
It's just the Blue-gown badge and claithing
O' saunts ; tak that, ye lea'e them naething
          To ken them by
Frae ony unregenerate heathen,
          Like you or I.

I've sent you here some rhyming ware,
A' that I bargain'd for, an' mair ;
Sae, when you hae an hour to spare,
          I will expect,
Yon sang ye'll sen't, wi' cannie care,
          And no neglect.

Tho' faith, sma' heart hae I to sing !
My muse dow scarcely spread her wing ;
I've play'd mysel a bonie spring,
          An' danc'd my fill !
I'd better gaen an' sair't the king,
          At Bunker's Hill.

'Twas ae night lately, in my fun,
I gaed a rovin wi' the gun,
An' brought a paitrick to the grun'—
          A bonie hen ;
And, as the twilight was begun,
          Thought nane wad ken.

The poor, wee thing was little hurt ;
I straikit it a wee for sport,
Ne'er thinkin they wad fash me for't ;
          But, Deil-ma-care !
Somebody tells the poacher-court
          The hale affair.

Some auld, us'd hands had taen a note,
That sic a hen had got a shot;
I was suspected for the plot;
   I scorn'd to lie;
So gat the whissle o' my groat,
   An' pay't the fee.

But by my gun, o' guns the wale,
An' by my pouther an' my hail,
An' by my hen, an' by her tail,
   I vow an' swear!
The game shall pay, o'er muir an' dale,
   For this, neist year.

As soon's the clockin-time is by,
An' the wee pouts begun to cry,
Lord, I'se hae sporting by an' by
   For my gowd guinea,
Tho' I should herd the buckskin kye
   For't in Virginia.

Trowth, they had muckle for to blame!
'Twas neither broken wing nor limb,
But twa-three draps about the wame,
   Scarce thro' the feathers;
An' baith a yellow George to claim,
   An' thole their blethers!

It pits me aye as mad's a hare;
So I can rhyme nor write nae mair;
But pennyworths again is fair,
   When time's expedient:
Meanwhile I am, respected Sir,
   Your most obedient.

A POET'S WELCOME TO HIS LOVE-BEGOTTEN DAUGHTER.

THE FIRST INSTANCE THAT ENTITLED HIM TO THE VENERABLE APPELLATION OF FATHER.

Thou's welcome, wean; mishanter fa' me,
If thoughts o' thee, or yet thy mammie,
Shall ever daunton me or awe me,
                My sweet wee lady,
Or if I blush when thou shalt ca' me
                Tyta or daddie.

Tho' now they ca' me fornicator,
An' tease my name in countra clatter,
The mair they talk, I'm kend the better,
                E'en let them clash;
An auld wife's tongue's a feckless matter
                To gie ane fash.

Welcome! my bonie, sweet, wee dochter,
Tho' ye come here a wee unsought for,
And tho' your comin' I hae fought for,
                Baith kirk and queir;
Yet, by my faith, ye're no unwrought for,
                That I shall swear!

Sweet fruit o' monie a merry dint,
My funny toil is no a' tint,
Tho' thou cam to the warl' asklent,
                Which fools may scoff at;
In my last plack thy part's be in't
                The better ha'f o't.

Tho' I should be the waur bestead,
Thou's be as braw and bienly clad,
And thy young vears as nicely bred
      Wi' education,
As onie brat o' wedlock's bed,
      In a' thy station.

Wee image o' my bonie Betty,
As fatherly I kiss and daut thee,
As dear and near my heart I set thee
      Wi' as gude will
As a' the priests had seen me get thee
      That's out o' hell.

Lord grant that thou may aye inherit
Thy mither's person, grace, an' merit,
An' thy poor, worthless daddy's spirit,
      Without his failins,
'Twill please me mair to see thee heir it,
      Than stockit mailens.

For if thou be what I wad hae thee,
And tak the counsel I shall gie thee,
I'll never rue my trouble wi' thee—
      The cost nor shame o't,
But be a loving father to thee,
      And brag the name o't.

MAN WAS MADE TO MOURN—
A DIRGE.

When chill November's surly blast
  Made fields and forests bare,
One ev'ning, as I wandered forth
  Along the banks of Ayr,
    A*

I spied a man, whose aged step
　　Seem'd weary, worn with care ;
His face was furrow'd o'er with years,
　　And hoary was his hair.

" Young stranger, whither wand'rest thou ? "
　　Began the rev'rend sage ;
" Does thirst of wealth thy step constrain,
　　Or youthful pleasure's rage ?
Or haply, prest with cares and woes,
　　Too soon thou hast began
To wander forth, with me to mourn
　　The miseries of man.

" The sun that overhangs yon moors,
　　Out-spreading far and wide,
Where hundreds labour to support
　　A haughty lordling's pride ;—
I've seen yon weary winter-sun
　　Twice forty times return ;
And ev'ry time has added proofs,
　　That man was made to mourn.

" O man ! while in thy early years,
　　How prodigal of time !
Mis-spending all thy precious hours—
　　Thy glorious, youthful prime !
Alternate follies take the sway ;
　　Licentious passions burn ;
Which tenfold force gives Nature's law,
　　That man was made to mourn.

" Look not alone on youthful prime,
　　Or manhood's active might ;
Man then is useful to his kind,
　　Supported is his right :

But see him on the edge of life,
    With cares and sorrows worn ;
Then Age and Want—oh! ill-match'd pair—
    Shew man was made to mourn.

" A few seem favourites of fate,
    In pleasure's lap carest ;
Yet, think not all the rich and great
    Are likewise truly blest :
But oh ! what crowds in ev'ry land,
    All wretched and forlorn,
Thro' weary life this lesson learn,
    That man was made to mourn.

" Many and sharp the num'rous ills
    Inwoven with our frame !
More pointed still we make ourselves
    Regret, remorse, and shame !
And man, whose heav'n-erected face
    The smiles of love adorn,—
Man's inhumanity to man
    Makes countless thousands mourn !

" See yonder poor, o'erlabour'd wight,
    So abject, mean, and vile,
Who begs a brother of the earth
    To give him leave to toil ;
And see his lordly fellow-worm
    The poor petition spurn,
Unmindful, though a weeping wife
    And helpless offspring mourn.

" If I'm designed yon lordling's slave,
    By Nature's law design'd,
Why was an independent wish
    E'er planted in my mind ?

If not, why am I subject to
  His cruelty, or scorn?
Or why has man the will and pow'r
  To make his fellow mourn?

"Yet, let not this too much, my son,
  Disturb thy youthful breast:
This partial view of human-kind
  Is surely not the last!
The poor, oppressèd, honest man
  Had never, sure, been born,
Had there not been some recompense
  To comfort those that mourn!

"O Death! the poor man's dearest friend,
  The kindest and the best!
Welcome the hour my aged limbs
  Are laid with thee at rest!
The great, the wealthy fear thy blow,
  From pomp and pleasure torn;
But, oh! a blest relief for those
  That weary-laden mourn!"

THE TWA HERDS; OR, THE HOLY TULYIE.

AN UNCO MOURNFU' TALE.

"Blockheads with reason wicked wits abhor,
  But fool with fool is barbarous civil war."—POPE.

O a' ye pious godly flocks,
Weel fed on pastures orthodox,
Wha now will keep you frae the fox,
      Or worrying tykes?
O, wha will tent the waifs an' crocks,
      About the dykes?

The twa best herds in a' the wast,
That e'er ga'e gospel horn a blast
These five an' twenty simmers past—
      Oh, dool to tell !
Hae had a bitter black out-cast
      Atween themsel'.

O, Moodie, man, an' wordy Russell,
How could you raise so vile a bustle ;
Ye'll see how New-Light herds will whistle,
      An' think it fine !
The Lord's cause ne'er gat sic a twistle,
      Sin' I hae min'.

O, sirs ! whae'er wad hae expeckit
Your duty ye wad sae negleckit,
Ye wha were ne'er by lairds respeckit
      To wear the plaid ;
But by the brutes themselves eleckit,
      To be their guide.

What flock wi' Moodie's flock could rank ?—
Sae hale and hearty every shank !
Nae poison'd soor Arminian stank
      He let them taste ;
Frae Calvin's well aye clear they drank,—
      O, sic a feast !

The thummart, willcat, brock, an' tod,
Weel kend his voice thro' a' the wood,
He smell'd their ilka hole an' road,
      Baith out an' in ;
An' weel he lik'd to shed their bluid,
      An' sell their skin.

What herd like Russell tell'd his tale;
His voice was heard thro' muir and dale,
He kenn'd the Lord's sheep, ilka tail,
   Owre a' the height;
An' saw gin they were sick or hale,
  At the first sight.

He fine a mangy sheep could scrub,
Or nobly fling the gospel club,
And New-Light herds could nicely drub
   Or pay their skin;
Could shake them o'er the burning dub,
  Or heave them in.

Sic twa—O! do I live to see't?—
Sic famous twa should disagree't,
And names, like "villain," "hypocrite,"
   Ilk ither gi'en,
While New-Light herds, wi' laughin spite,
  Say neither's liein!

A' ye wha tent the gospel fauld,
There's Duncan deep, an' Peebles shauld,
But chiefly thou, apostle Auld,
   We trust in thee,
That thou wilt work them, het an' cauld,
  Till they agree.

Consider, sirs, how we're beset;
There's scarce a new herd that we get,
But comes frae 'mang that cursed set,
   I winna name;
I hope frae heav'n to see them yet
  In fiery flame.

Dalrymple has been lang our fae,
M'Gill has wrought us meikle wae,
An' that curs'd rascal ca'd M'Quhae,
   And baith the Shaws,
That aft hae made us black an' blae,
   Wi' vengefu' paws.

Auld Wodrow lang has hatch'd mischief;
We thought aye death wad bring relief;
But he has gotten, to our grief,
   Ane to succeed him,
A chield wha'll soundly buff our beef;
   I meikle dread him.

And mony a ane that I could tell,
Wha fain wad openly rebel,
Forby turn-coats amang oursel',
   There's Smith for ane;
I doubt he's but a grey nick quill,
   An' that ye'll fin'.

O! a' ye flocks o'er a' the hills,
By mosses, meadows, moors, and fells,
Come, join your counsel and your skills
   To cowe the lairds,
An' get the brutes the power themsel's
   To choose their herds.

Then Orthodoxy yet may prance,
An' Learning in a woody dance,
An' that fell cur ca'd Common-Sense,
   That bites sae sair,
Be banished o'er the sea to France:
   Let him bark there.

Then Shaw's an' D'rymple's eloquence,
M'Gill's close nervous excellence,
M'Quhae's pathetic manly sense,
          An' guid M'Math,
Wi' Smith, wha thro' the heart can glance,
          May a' pack aff.

EPISTLE TO DAVIE, A BROTHER POET

January

WHILE winds frae aff Ben-Lomond blaw,
An' bar the doors wi' driving snaw,
    An' hing us owre the ingle,
I set me down to pass the time,
An' spin a verse or twa o' rhyme,
    In hamely, westlin jingle :
While frosty winds blaw in the drift,
    Ben to the chimla lug,
I grudge a wee the great-folk's gift,
    That live sae bien an' snug :
        I tent less, and want less
            Their roomy fire-side ;
        But hanker, and canker,
            To see their cursed pride.

It's hardly in a body's pow'r
To keep, at times, frae being sour,
    To see how things are shar'd :
How best o' chiels are whiles in want,
While coofs on countless thousands rant,
    And ken na how to wair't ;

But, Davie, lad, ne'er fash your head,
  Tho' we hae little gear ;
We're fit to win our daily bread,
  As lang's we're hale and fier ;
    "Mair speir na nor fear na,"
      Auld age ne'er mind a feg ;
    The last o't, the warst o't,
      Is only but to beg.

To lie in kilns and barns at e'en,
When banes are craz'd, and bluid is thin,
  Is, doubtless, great distress !
Yet then content could make us blest ;
Ev'n then, sometimes, we'd snatch a taste
  Of truest happiness.
The honest heart that's free frae a'
  Intended fraud or guile,
However Fortune kick the ba',
  Has aye some cause to smile ;
    An' mind still, you'll find still,
      A comfort this nae sma' ;
    Nae mair then we'll care then,
      Nae farther we can fa'.

What tho', like commoners of air,
We wander out, we know not where,
  But either house or hal',
Yet nature's charms, the hills and woods,
The sweeping vales, and foaming floods,
  Are free alike to all.
In days when daisies deck the ground,
  And blackbirds whistle clear,
With honest joy our hearts will bound,
  To see the coming year :

On braes when we please then,
　We'll sit an' sowth a tune ;
Syne rhyme till't we'll time till't,
　An' sing't when we hae done.

It's no in titles nor in rank ;
It's no in wealth like Lon'on bank,
　To purchase peace and rest :
It's no in makin' muckle, mair ;
It's no in books, it's no in lear,
　To make us truly blest :
If happiness hae not her seat
　An' centre in the breast,
We may be wise, or rich, or great,
　But never can be blest ;
　　Nae treasures nor pleasures
　　　Could make us happy lang ;
　　The heart aye 's the part aye
　　　That makes us right or wrang.

Think ye, that sic as you and I,
Wha drudge an' drive thro' wet and dry,
　Wi' never-ceasing toil ;
Think ye, are we less blest than they,
Wha scarcely tent us in their way,
　As hardly worth their while ?
Alas ! how aft in haughty mood,
　God's creatures they oppress !
Or else, neglecting a' that's guid,
　They riot in excess !
　　Baith careless and fearless
　　　Of either heaven or hell ;
　　Esteeming and deeming
　　　It's a' an idle tale !

Then let us cheerfu' acquiesce,
Nor make our scanty pleasures less,
   By pining at our state :
And, even should misfortunes come,
I, here wha sit, hae met wi' some—
   An's thankfu' for them yet.
They gie the wit of age to youth ;
   They let us ken oursel' ;
They make us see the naked truth,
   The real guid and ill :
      Tho' losses and crosses
        Be lessons right severe,
      There's wit there, ye'll get there,
        Ye'll find nae other where.

But tent me, Davie, ace o' hearts !
(To say aught less wad wrang the cartes,
   And flatt'ry I detest)
This life has joys for you and I ;
An' joys that riches ne'er could buy,
   An' joys the very best.
There's a' the pleasures o' the heart,
   The lover an' the frien' ;
Ye hae your Meg, your dearest part,
   And I my darling Jean !
      It warms me, it charms me,
        To mention but her name :
      It heats me, it beets me,
        An' sets me a' on flame !

O all ye Pow'rs who rule above !
O Thou whose very self art love !
   Thou know'st my words sincere !

The life-blood streaming thro' my heart,
Or my more dear immortal part,
  Is not more fondly dear!
When heart-corroding care and grief
  Deprive my soul of rest,
Her dear idea brings relief,
  And solace to my breast.
    Thou Being, All-seeing,
      O hear my fervent pray'r!
    Still take her, and make her
      Thy most peculiar care!

All hail! ye tender feelings dear!
The smile of love, the friendly tear,
  The sympathetic glow!
Long since, this world's thorny ways
Had number'd out my weary days,
  Had it not been for you!
Fate still has blest me with a friend,
  In ev'ry care and ill;
And oft a more endearing band—
  A tie more tender still.
    It lightens, it brightens
      The tenebrific scene,
    To meet with, and greet with
      My Davie, or my Jean!

O, how that name inspires my style!
The words come skelpin, rank an' file,
  Amaist before I ken!
The ready measure rins as fine,
As Phœbus an' the famous Nine
  Were glowrin owre my pen.
My spaviet Pegasus will limp,
  Till ance he's fairly het;

And then he'll hilch, and stilt, an' jimp,
   And rin an unco fit :
      But least then the beast then
        Should rue this hasty ride,
      I'll light now, and dight now
        His sweaty, wizen'd hide.

HOLY WILLIE'S PRAYER.

"And send the godly in a pet to pray."—POPE.

O THOU, that in the heavens does dwell,
Wha, as it pleases best Thysel',
Sends ane to heaven an' ten to hell,
      A' for Thy glory,
And no for onie guid or ill
      They've done afore Thee!

I bless and praise Thy matchless might,
When thousands Thou hast left in night,
That I am here afore Thy sight,
      For gifts an' grace
A burning and a shining light
      To a' this place.

What was I, or my generation,
That I should get sic exaltation,
I wha deserv'd most just damnation
      For broken laws,
Sax thousand vears ere my creation,
      Thro' Adam's cause.

When from my mither's womb I fell,
Thou might hae plung'd me deep in hell,

To gnash my gooms, and weep and wail,
                In burnin lakes,
Where damnèd devils roar and yell,
                Chain'd to their stakes.

Yet I am here a chosen sample,
To show thy grace is great and ample;
I'm here a pillar o' Thy temple,
                Strong as a rock,
A guide, a buckler, and example,
                To a' Thy flock.

O Lord, Thou kens what zeal I bear,
When drinkers drink, an' swearers swear,
An' singing here, an' dancin there,
                Wi' great and sma';
For I am keepit by Thy fear
                Free frae them a'.

But yet, O Lord! confess I must,
At times I'm fash'd wi' fleshly lust:
An' sometimes, too, in warldly trust,
                Vile self gets in;
But Thou remembers we are dust,
                Defil'd wi' sin.

O Lord! yestreen, Thou kens, wi' Meg—
Thy pardon I sincerely beg;
O! may't ne'er be a livin plague
                To my dishonour,
An' I'll ne'er lift a lawless leg
                Again upon her.

Besides, I farther maun allow,
Wi' Leezie's lass, three times I trow—

Holy Willie

From an etching by William Hole

Holy Willie

"But yet, O Lord! confess I must
At times I'm fashed wi' fleshly lust:
And sometimes, too, in wardly trust,
   Vile self gets in;
But thou remembers we are dust,
   Defil'd wi' sin."

But Lord, that Friday I was fou,
    When I cam near her;
Or else, Thou kens, Thy servant true
    Wad never steer her.

Maybe Thou lets this fleshly thorn
Buffet Thy servant e'en and morn,
Lest he owre proud and high shou'd turn,
    That he's sae gifted:
If sae, Thy han' maun e'en be borne,
    Until Thou lift it.

Lord, bless Thy chosen in this place,
For here Thou has a chosen race:
But God confound their stubborn face,
    An' blast their name,
Wha bring Thy elders to disgrace
    An' public shame.

Lord, mind Gaw'n Hamilton's deserts;
He drinks, an' swears, an' plays at cartes,
Yet has sae mony takin arts,
    Wi' great and sma',
Frae God's ain priest the people's hearts
    He steals awa.

An' when we chasten'd him therefor,
Thou kens how he bred sic a splore,
An' set the warld in a roar
    O' laughing at us;—
Curse Thou his basket and his store,
    Kail an' potatoes.

Lord, hear my earnest cry and pray'r,
Against that Presbyt'ry o' Ayr;
Thy strong right hand, Lord make it bare
    Upo' their heads;

Lord visit them, an' dinna spare,
      For their misdeeds.

O Lord, my God! that glib-tongu'd Aiken,
My vera heart and flesh are quakin,
To think how we stood sweatin, shakin,
      An' p—'d wi' dread,
While he, wi' hingin lip an' snakin,
      Held up his head.

Lord, in Thy day o' vengeance try him,
Lord, visit them wha did employ him,
And pass not in Thy mercy by them,
      Nor hear their pray'r,
But for Thy people's sake destroy them,
      An' dinna spare.

But, Lord, remember me an' mine
Wi' mercies temporal and divine,
That I for grace an' gear may shine,
      Excell'd by nane,
And a' the glory shall be thine,
      Amen, Amen!

EPITAPH ON HOLY WILLIE.

HERE Holy Willie's sair worn clay
    Taks up its last abode;
His saul has ta'en some other way,
    I fear, the left-hand road.

Stop! there he is, as sure's a gun,
    Poor, silly body, see him;
Nae wonder he's as black's the grun,
    Observe wha's standing wi' him.

Your brunstane devilship, I see,
  Has got him there before ye;
But haud your nine-tail cat a wee,
  Till ance you've heard my story.

Your pity I will not implore,
  For pity ye have nane;
Justice, alas! has gi'en him o'er,
  And mercy's day is gane.

But hear me, Sir, deil as ye are,
  Look something to your credit;
A coof like him wad stain your name,
  If it were kent ye did it.

DEATH AND DOCTOR HORNBOOK

A TRUE STORY

SOME books are lies frae end to end,
And some great lies were never penn'd:
Ev'n ministers they hae been kenn'd,
          In holy rapture,
A rousing whid at times to vend,
          And nail't wi' Scripture.

But this that I am gaun to tell,
Which lately on a night befell,
Is just as true's the Deil's in hell
          Or Dublin city:
That e'er he nearer comes oursel'
          'S a muckle pity.

The clachan yill had made me canty,
I was na fou, but just had plenty;

I stacher'd whiles, but yet took tent aye
        To free the ditches;
An' hillocks, stanes, an' bushes, kenn'd aye
        Frae ghaists an' witches.

The rising moon began to glowre
The distant Cumnock hills out-owre:
To count her horns, wi' a' my pow'r,
        I set mysel';
But whether she had three or four,
        I cou'd na tell.

I was come round about the hill,
An' todlin down on Willie's mill,
Setting my staff wi' a' my skill,
        To keep me sicker;
Tho' leeward whiles, against my will,
        I took a bicker.

I there wi' *Something* does forgather,
That pat me in an eerie swither;
An awfu' scythe, out-owre ae shouther,
        Clear-dangling, hang;
A three-tae'd leister on the ither
        Lay, large an' lang.

Its stature seem'd lang Scotch ells twa,
The queerest shape that e'er I saw,
For fient a wame it had ava';
        And then its shanks,
They were as thin, as sharp an' sma'
        As cheeks o' branks.

'Guid-een,' quo' I; 'Friend! hae ye been mawin,
'When ither folk are busy sawin!'

It seem'd to make a kind o' stan'
    But naething spak ;
At length, says I, ' Friend ! whare ye gaun ?
    ' Will ye go back ? '

It spak right howe,—' My name is *Death*,
' But be na fley'd.'—Quoth I, ' Guid faith,
' Ye're maybe come to stap my breath ;
    ' But tent me, billie ;
' I red ye weel, tak care o' skaith,
    ' See, there's a gully ! '

' Gudeman,' quo' he, ' put up your whittle,
' I'm no designed to try its mettle ;
' But if I did, I wad be kittle
    ' To be mislear'd ;
' I wad na mind it, no that spittle
    ' Out-owre my beard.'

' Weel, weel ! ' says I, ' a bargain be't ;
' Come, gie's your hand, an' sae we're gree't ;
' We'll ease our shanks an' tak a seat—
    ' Come, gie's your news ;
' This while ye hae been mony a gate,
    ' At mony a house.'

' Ay, ay ! ' quo' he, and shook his head,
' It's e'en a lang, lang time indeed
' Sin' I began to nick the thread,
    ' An' choke the breath :
' Folk maun dae something for their bread,
    ' An' sae maun *Death*.

' Sax thousand years are near-hand fled
' Sin' I was to the butching bred,

'An' mony a scheme in vain's been laid,
       'To stap or scar me;
'Till ane Hornbook's ta'en up the trade,
       'And faith! he'll waur me.

'Ye ken Jock Hornbook i' the Clachan;
'Deil mak his king's-hood in a spleuchan!
'He's grown sae weel acquaint wi' Buchan
       'And ither chaps,
'The weans haud out their fingers laughin,
       'An' pouk my hips.

'See, here's a scythe, an' there's a dart,
'They hae pierc'd mony a gallant heart;
'But Doctor Hornbook wi' his art
       'An' cursed skill,
'Has made them baith no worth a f—t,
       'D—n'd haet they'll kill!

''Twas but yestreen, nae farther gane,
'I threw a noble throw at ane;
'Wi' less, I'm sure, I've hundreds slain;
       'But deil-ma-care,
'It just play'd dirl on the bane,
       'But did nae mair.

'Hornbook was by, wi' ready art,
'An' had sae fortified the part,
'That when I lookèd to my dart,
       'It was sae blunt,
Fient haet o't wad hae pierc'd the heart
       'Of a kail-runt.

'I drew my scythe in sic a fury,
'I near-hand cowpit wi' my hurry,

' But yet the bauld Apothecary
   ' Withstood the shock ;
' I might as weel hae tried a quarry
   ' O' hard whin rock.

' Ev'n them he canna get attended,
' Altho' their face he ne'er had kend it,
' Just ——— in a kail-blade, an' send it,
   ' As soon's he smells 't,
' Baith their disease, and what will mend it,
   ' At once he tells 't.

' And then a' doctor's saws an' whittles,
' Of a' dimensions, shapes, an' mettles,
' A' kinds o' boxes, mugs, an' bottles,
   ' He's sure to hae ;
' Their Latin names as fast he rattles
   ' As A B C.

' Calces o' fossils, earths, and trees ;
' True *sal-marinum* o' the seas ;
' The *farina* of beans and pease,
   ' He has't in plenty ;
' *Aqua-fontis*, what you please,
   ' He can content ye.

' Forbye some new, uncommon weapons,
' *Urinus spiritus* of capons ;
' Or mite-horn shavings, filings, scrapings,
   ' Distill'd *per se ;*
' *Sal-alkali* o' midge-tail clippings,
   ' And mony mae.'

' Waes me for Johnie Ged's-Hole now,'
Quoth I, ' if that thae news be true !

'His braw calf-ward whare gowans grew,
   'Sae white and bonie,
'Nae doubt they'll rive it wi' the plew;
    'They'll ruin Johnie!'

The creature grain'd an eldritch laugh,
And says 'Ye needna yoke the pleugh;
'Kirkyards will soon be till'd eneugh,
    'Tak ye nae fear:
'They'll a' be trench'd wi' mony a sheugh,
    'In twa-three year.

'Whare I kill'd ane, a fair strae-death,
'By loss o' blood or want of breath,
'This night I'm free to tak my aith,
    'That Hornbook's skill
'Has clad a score i' their last claith,
    'By drap an' pill.

'An honest wabster to his trade,
'Whase wife's twa nieves were scarce weel-bred,
'Gat tippence-worth to mend her head,
    'When it was sair;
'The wife slade cannie to her bed,
    'But ne'er spak mair.

'A country laird had ta'en the batts,
'Or some curmurring in his guts,
'His only son for Hornbook sets,
    'An' pays him well:
'The lad, for twa guid gimmer-pets,
    'Was laird himsel'.

'A bonie lass—ye kend her name—
'Some ill-brewn drink had hov'd her wame;

Death and Dr Hornbook

From an etching by Robert Bryden

Death and Dr Hornbook

"A bonie lass — ye kend her name —
Some ill-brew'n drink had hoved her wame;
She trusts hersel; to hide the shame,
        In Hornbook's care;
Horn sends her aff to her lang hame
        To hide it there."

' She trusts hersel', to hide the shame,
            In Hornbook's care ;
' Horn sent her aff to her lang hame,
            ' To hide it there.

' That's just a swatch o' Hornbook's way ;
' Thus goes he on from day to day,
' Thus does he poison, kill, an' slay,
            ' An's weel paid for't ;
' Yet stops me o' my lawful prey,
            ' Wi' his d—n'd dirt :

' But, hark ! I'll tell you of a plot,
' Tho' dinna ye be speakin o't ;
' I'll nail the self-conceited sot,
            ' As dead's a herrin ;
' Neist time we meet, I'll wad a groat,
            ' He get's his fairin ! '

But just as he began to tell,
The auld kirk-hammer strak the bell
Some wee short hour ayont the twal',
            Which rais'd us baith :
I took the way that pleas'd mysel',
            And sae did *Death*.

EPISTLE TO J. LAPRAIK.

AN OLD SCOTTISH BARD.—APRIL 1, 1785.

WHILE briers an' woodbines budding green,
An' paitricks scraichin loud at e'en,
An' morning poussie whiddin seen,
            Inspire my muse,
This freedom, in an unknown frien',
            I pray excuse.

On Fasten-e'en we had a rockin,
To ca' the crack and weave our stockin;
And there was muckle fun and jokin,
         Ye need na doubt;
At length we had a hearty yokin
         At sang about.

There was ae sang, amang the rest,
Aboon them a' it pleas'd me best,
That some kind husband had addrest
         To some sweet wife;
It thirl'd the heart-strings thro' the breast,
         A' to the life.

I've scarce heard ought describ'd sae weel,
What gen'rous, manly bosoms feel;
Thought I "can this be Pope, or Steele,
         Or Beattie's wark?"
They tauld me 'twas an odd-kind chiel
         About Muirkirk.

It pat me fidgin-fain to hear't,
An' sae about him there I speir't;
Then a' that kent him round declar'd
         He had ingine;
That nane excell'd it, few cam near't,
         It was sae fine:

That, set him to a pint of ale,
An' either douce or merry tale,
Or rhymes an' sangs he'd made himsel,
         Or witty catches—
'Tween Inverness an' Teviotdale,
         He had few matches.

Then up I gat, an' swoor an aith,
Tho' I should pawn my pleugh an' graith,
Or die a cadger pownie's death,
           At some dyke-back,
A pint an' gill I'd gie them baith,
           To hear your crack.

But, first an' foremost, I should tell,
Amaist as soon as I could spell,
I to the crambo-jingle fell;
           Tho' rude an' rough—
Yet crooning to a body's sel'
           Does weel eneugh.

I am nae poet, in a sense;
But just a rhymer like by chance,
An' hae to learning nae pretence;
           Yet, what the matter?
Whene'er my muse does on me glance,
           I jingle at her.

Your critic-folk may cock their nose,
And say, "How can you e'er propose,
You wha ken hardly verse frae prose,
           To mak a sang?"
But, by your leaves, my learnèd foes,
           Ye're maybe wrang.

What's a' your jargon o' your schools—
Your Latin names for horns an' stools?
If honest Nature made you fools,
           What sairs your grammars?
Ye'd better taen up spades and shools,
           Or knappin-hammers.

A set o' dull, conceited hashes
Confuse their brains in college-classes!
They gang in stirks, and come out asses,
      Plain truth to speak ;
Au' syne they think to climb Parnassus
      By dint o' Greek!

Gie me ae spark o' nature's fire,
That's a' the learning I desire ;
Then tho' I drudge thro' dub an' mire
      At pleugh or cart,
My muse, tho' hamely in attire,
      May touch the heart.

O for a spunk o' Allan's glee,
Or Fergusson's, the bauld an' slee,
Or bright Lapraik's, my friend to be,
      If I can hit it!
That would be lear enough for me,
      If I could get it.

Now, sir, if ye hae friends enow,
Tho' real friends I b'lieve are few ;
Yet, if your catalogue be fu',
      I'se no insist :
But, gif ye want ae friend that's true,
      I'm on your list.

I winna blaw about mysel,
As ill I like my fauts to tell ;
But friends, an' folk that wish me well,
      They sometime roose me ;
Tho' I maun own, as mony still
      As far abuse me.

Robert Burns – *From the statue by John Flaxman*

There's ae wee faut they whiles lay to me,
I like the lasses—Gude forgie me!
For mony a plack they wheedle frae me
          At dance or fair;
Maybe some ither thing they gie me,
          They weel can spare.

But Mauchline Race or Mauchline Fair,
I should be proud to meet you there:
We'se gie ae night's discharge to care,
          If we forgather;
An' hae a swap o' rhymin-ware
          Wi' ane anither.

The four-gill chap, we'se gar him clatter,
An' kirsen him wi' reekin water;
Syne we'll sit down an' tak our whitter,
          To cheer our heart;
An' faith, we'se be acquainted better
          Before we part.

Awa ye selfish, war'ly race,
Wha think that havins, sense, an' grace,
Ev'n love an' friendship should give place
          To catch-the-plack!
I dinna like to see your face,
          Nor hear your crack.

But ye whom social pleasure charms,
Whose hearts the tide of kindness warms,
Who hold your being on the terms,
          "Each aid the others,"
Come to my bowl, come to my arms,
          My friends, my brothers!

But, to conclude my lang epistle,
As my auld pen's worn to the gristle,
Twa lines frae you wad gar me fissle,
          Who am most fervent,
While I can either sing or whistle,
          Your friend and servant.

SECOND EPISTLE TO J. LAPRAIK

APRIL 21, 1785

While new-ca'd kye rowt at the stake
An' pownies reek in pleugh or braik,
This hour on e'enin's edge I take,
          To own I'm debtor‿
To honest-hearted, auld Lapraïk,
          For his kind letter.

Forjesket sair, with weary legs,
Rattlin the corn out-owre the rigs,
Or dealing thro' amang the naigs
          Their ten-hours' bite,
My awkart Muse sair pleads and begs
          I would na write.

The tapetless, ramfeezl'd hizzie,
She's saft at best an' something lazy:
Quo' she, " ye ken we've been sae busy
          This month an' mair,
That trowth, my head is grown right dizzie,
          An' something sair."

Her dowff excuses pat me mad;
"Conscience!" says I, "ye thowless jade!
I'll write, an' that a hearty blaud,
          This vera night;
So dinna ye affront your trade,
          But rhyme it right.

" Shall bauld Lapraik, the king o' hearts,
Tho' mankind were a pack o' cartes,
Roose you sae weel for your deserts,
       In terms sae friendly ;
Yet ye'll neglect to shaw your parts
       An' thank him kindly ? "

Sae I gat paper in a blink,
An' down gaed stumpie in the ink :
Quoth I, " before I sleep a wink,
       I vow I'll close it ;
An' if ye winna mak it clink,
       By Jove, I'll prose it ! "

Sae I've begun to scrawl, but whether
In rhyme, or prose, or baith thegither ;
Or some hotch-potch that's rightly neither,
       Let time mak proof ;
But I shall scribble down some blether
       Just clean aff-loof.

My worthy friend, ne'er grudge an' carp,
Tho' fortune use you hard an' sharp ;
Come, kittle up your moorland harp
       Wi' gleesome touch !
Ne'er mind how fortune waft and warp ;
       She's but a bitch.

She's gien me mony a jirt an' fleg,
Sin' I could striddle owre a rig ;
But, by the Lord, tho' I should beg
       Wi' lyart pow,
I'll laugh an' sing, an' shake my leg,
       As lang's I dow.

Now comes the sax-an-twentieth simmer
I've seen the bud upon the timmer,
Still persecuted by the limmer
   Frae year to year;
But yet, despite the kittle kimmer,
   I, Rob, am here.

Do ye envy the city gent,
Behint a kist to lie an' sklent;
Or purse-proud, big wi' cent. per cent.
   An' muckle wame,
In some bit brugh to represent
   A bailie's name?

Or is't the paughty feudal thane,
Wi' ruffl'd sark an' glancing cane,
Wha thinks himsel nae sheep-shank bane,
   But lordly stalks;
While caps an' bonnets aff are taen,
   As by he walks?

" O Thou wha gies us each guid gift!
Gie me o' wit an' sense a lift,
Then turn me, if Thou please, adrift
   Thro' Scotland wide;
Wi' cits nor lairds I wadna shift,
   In a' their pride! "

Were this the charter of our state,
" On pain o' hell be rich an' great,"
Damnation then would be our fate,
   Beyond remead;
But, thanks to heaven, that's no the gate
   We learn our creed.

For thus the royal mandate ran,
When first the human race began ;
" The social, friendly, honest man,
            Whate'er he be—
'Tis *he* fulfils great Nature's plan,
            And none but he."

O mandate glorious and divine !
The followers o' the ragged Nine,
Poor, thoughtless devils ! yet may shine
            In glorious light,
While sordid sons o' Mammon's line
            Are dark as night !

Tho' here they scrape, an' squeeze, an' growl,
Their worthless nievefu' of a soul
May in some future carcase howl,
            The forest's fright ;
Or in some day-detesting owl
            May shun the light.

Then may Lapraik and Burns arise,
To reach their native, kindred skies,
And sing their pleasures, hopes an' joys,
            In some mild sphere ;
Still closer knit in friendship's ties,
            Each passing year !

EPISTLE TO WILLIAM SIMSON

SCHOOLMASTER, OCHILTREE.—MAY 1785

I GAT your letter, winsome Willie ;
Wi' gratefu' heart I thank you brawlie ;
Tho' I maun say't, I wad be silly,
            And unco vain,
Should I believe, my coaxin' billie
            Your flatterin strain.

But I'se believe ye kindly meant it:
I sud be laith to think ye hinted
Ironic satire, sidelins sklented
        On my poor Musie;
Tho' in sic phraisin terms ye've penn'd it,
        I scarce excuse ye.

My senses wad be in a creel,
Should I but dare a hope to speel
Wi' Allan, or wi' Gilbertfield,
        The braes o' fame;
Or Fergusson, the writer-chiel,
        A deathless name.

(O Fergusson! thy glorious parts
Ill suited law's dry, musty arts!
My curse upon your whunstane hearts,
        Ye E'nbrugh gentry!
The tithe o' what ye waste at cartes
        Wad stow'd his pantry!)

Yet when a tale comes i' my head,
Or lassies gie my heart a screed—
As whiles they're like to be my dead,
        (O sad disease!)
I kittle up my rustic reed;
        It gies me ease.

Auld Coila now may fidge fu' fain,
She's gotten poets o' her ain;
Chiels wha their chanters winna hain,
        But tune their lays,
Till echoes a' resound again
        Her weel-sung praise.

Nae poet thought her worth his while,
To set her name in measur'd style ;
She lay like some unkenn'd-of-isle
    Beside New Holland,
Or whare wild-meeting oceans boil
    Besouth Magellan.

Ramsay an' famous Fergusson
Gied Forth an' Tay a lift aboon ;
Yarrow an' Tweed, to monie a tune,
    Owre Scotland rings
While Irwin, Lugar, Ayr, an' Doon
    Naebody sings.

Th' Illissus, Tiber, Thames, an' Seine,
Glide sweet in monie a tunefu' line :
But, Willie, set your fit to mine,
    An' cock your crest ;
We'll gar our streams an' burnies shine
    Up wi' the best !

We'll sing auld Coila's plains an' fells,
Her moors red-brown wi' heather bells,
Her banks an' braes, her dens and dells,
    Whare glorious Wallace
Aft bure the gree, as story tells,
    Frae Suthron billies.

At Wallace' name, what Scottish blood
But boils up in a spring-tide flood !
Oft have our fearless fathers strode
    By Wallace' side,
Still pressing onward, red-wat-shod,
    Or glorious died !

O sweet are Coila's haughs an' woods,
When lintwhites chant amang the buds,
And jinkin hares, in amorous whids,
   Their loves enjoy;
While thro' the braes the cushat croods
  With wailfu' cry!

Ev'n winter bleak has charms to me,
When winds rave thro' the naked tree;
Or frosts on hills of Ochiltree
   Are hoary gray;
Or blinding drifts wild-furious flee,
  Dark'ning the day!

O Nature! a' thy shews and forms
To feeling, pensive hearts hae charms!
Whether the summer kindly warms,
   Wi' life an' light;
Or winter howls, in gusty storms,
  The lang, dark night!

The muse, nae poet ever fand her,
Till by himsel he learn'd to wander,
Adown some trottin burn's meander,
   An' no think lang:
O sweet to stray, an' pensive ponder
  A heart-felt sang!

The war'ly race may drudge an' drive,
Hog-shouther, jundie, stretch, an' strive;
Let me fair Nature's face descrive;
   And I, wi' pleasure,
Shall let the busy, grumbling hive
  Bum owre their treasure.

Fareweel, " my rhyme-composing" brither!
We've been ower lang unkenn'd to ither!
Now let us lay our heads thegither,
    In things fraternal:
May envy wallop in a tether,
      Black fiend, infernal!

While Highlandmen hate tolls and taxes;
While moorlan' herds like guid, fat braxies;
While terra firma, on her axis,
    Diurnal turns;
Count on a friend, in faith an' practice,
      In Robert Burns.

POSTSCRIPT.

My memory's no worth a preen;
I had amaist forgotten clean,
You bade me write you what they mean
    By this ' new-light,'
'Bout which our herds sae aft hae been
    Maist like to fight.

In days when mankind were but callans
At grammar, logic, an' sic talents,
They took nae pains their speech to balance,
    Or rules to gie;
But spak their thoughts in plain, braid lallans,
    Like you or me.

In thae auld times, they thought the moon,
Just like a sark, or pair o' shoon,
Wore by degrees, till her last roon
    Gaed past their viewin;
An' shortly after she was done
    They gat a new ane.

This passed for certain, undisputed ;
It ne'er cam i' their heads to doubt it,
Till chiels gat up an' wad confute it,
          An' ca'd it wrang ;
An' muckle din there was about it,
          Baith loud an' lang.

Some herds, weel learn'd upo' the beuk ;
Wad threap auld folk the thing misteuk ;
For 'twas the auld moon turn'd a neuk
          An' out o' sight,
An' backlins-comin to the leuk
          She grew mair bright.

This was denied, it was affirm'd ;
The herds and hissels were alarm'd,
The rev'rend gray-beards rav'd and storm'd,
          That beardless laddies
Should think they better were inform'd,
          Than their auld daddies.

Frae less to mair, it gaed to sticks ;
Frae words an' aiths to clours an' nicks ;
An monie a fallow gat his licks,
          Wi' hearty crunt ;
An' some, to learn them for their tricks,
          Were hang't an' brunt.

This game was play'd in mony lands,
An' auld-light caddies bure sic hands,
That faith, the youngsters took the sands
          Wi' nimble shanks ;
Till lairds forbad, by strict commands,
          Sic bluidy pranks.

But new-light herds gat sic a cowe,
Folk thought them ruin'd stick-an'-stowe;
Till now, amaist on ev'ry knowe
      Ye'll find ane plac'd;
An' some their new-light fair avow,
      Just quite barefac'd.

Nae doubt the auld-light flocks are bleatin;
Their zealous herds are vex'd an' sweatin;
Mysel', I've even seen them greetin
      Wi' girnin spite,
To hear the moon sae sadly lied on
      By word an' write.

But shortly they will cowe the louns!
Some auld-light herds in neebor touns
Are mind't, in things they ca' balloons,
      To tak a flight;
An' stay ae month amang the moons
      An' see them right.

Guid observation they will gie them;
An' when the auld moon's gaun to lea'e them,
The hindmaist shaird, they'll fetch it wi' them,
      Just i' their pouch;
An' when the new-light billies see them,
      I think they'll crouch!

Sae, ye observe that a' this clatter
Is naething but a "moonshine matter;"
But tho' dull prose-folk Latin splatter
      In logic tulyie,
I hope we bardies ken some better
      Than mind sic brulyie.

EPISTLE TO JOHN GOLDIE, IN KILMARNOCK.

AUTHOR OF THE GOSPEL RECOVERED.
AUGUST 1785.

O GOWDIE, terror o' the whigs,
Dread o' blackcoats and reverend wigs!
Sour Bigotry on his last legs
   Girns an' looks back,
Wishing the ten Egyptian plagues
   May seize you quick.

Poor gapin, glowrin Superstition!
Wae's me, she's in a sad condition:
Fye: bring *Black Jock*, her state physician,
   To see her water:
Alas, there's ground for great suspicion
   She'll ne'er get better.

Enthusiasm's past redemption,
Gane in a gallopin consumption:
Not a' her quacks, wi' a' their gumption,
   Can ever mend her;
Her feeble pulse gies strong presumption,
   She'll soon surrender.

Auld Orthodoxy lang did grapple,
For every hole to get a stapple;
But now she fetches at the thrapple,
   An' fights for breath;
Haste, gie her name up in the chapel,
   Near unto death.

The Cottage in which Burns was born

From an engraving after David Octavius Hill

It's you an' *Taylor* are the chief
To blame for a' this black mischief;
But, could the Lord's ain folk get leave,
    A toom tar barrel
An' twa red peats wad bring relief,
    And end the quarrel.

For me, my skill's but very sma',
An' skill in prose I've nane ava';
But quietlenwise, between us twa,
    Weel may you speed!
And tho' they sud you sair misca',
    Ne'er fash your head.

E'en swinge the dogs, and thresh them sicker!
The mair they squeel aye chap the thicker;
And still 'mang hands a hearty bicker
    O' something stout;
It gars an owthor's pulse beat quicker,
    And helps his wit.

There's naething like the honest nappy;
Whare'll ye e'er see men sae happy,
Or women sonsie, saft an' sappy,
    'Tween morn and morn,
As them wha like to taste the drappie,
    In glass or horn?

I've seen me dazed upon a time,
I scarce could wink or see a styme;
Just ae half-mutchkin does me prime,—
    Ought less is little—
Then back I rattle on the rhyme,
    As gleg's a whittle.

THE HOLY FAIR.

A robe of seeming truth and trust
  Hid crafty observation ;
And secret hung, with poison'd crust,
  The dirk of defamation :
A mask that like the gorget show'd,
  Dye-varying on the pigeon ;
And for a mantle large and broad,
  He wrapt him in *Religion*.
                      HYPOCRISY A-LA-MODE.

UPON a simmer Sunday morn,
  When Nature's face is fair,
I walkèd forth to view the corn,
  An' snuff the caller air.
The rising sun owre Galston muirs
  Wi' glorious light was glinting ;
The hares were hirplin down the furrs,
  The lav'rocks they were chantin
                Fu' sweet that day.

As lightsomely I glowr'd abroad,
  To see a scene sae gay,
Three hizzies, early at the road,
  Cam skelpin up the way.
Twa had manteeles o' dolefu' black,
  But ane wi' lyart lining ;
The third, that gaed a wee a-back,
  Was in the fashion shining
                Fu' gay that day.

The twa appear'd like sisters twin,
  In feature, form, an' claes ;
Their visage wither'd, lang an' thin,
  An' sour as ony slaes :

The third cam up, hap-stap-an'-lowp,
  As light as ony lambie,
An' wi' a curchie low did stoop,
  As soon as e'er she saw me,
              Fu' kind that day.

Wi' bonnet aff, quoth I, " Sweet lass,
  I think ye seem to ken me;
I'm sure I've seen that bonie face,
  But yet I canna name ye."
Quo' she, an' laughin as she spak,
  An' taks me by the han's,
" Ye, for my sake, hae gien the feck
  Of a' the ten comman's
              A screed some day."

" My name is Fun—your cronie dear,
  The nearest friend ye hae;
An' this is Superstition here,
  An' that's Hypocrisy.
I'm gaun to Mauchline ' holy fair,'
  To spend an hour in daffin:
Gin ye'll go there, yon runkl'd pair,
  We will get famous laughin
              At them this day."

Quoth I, " Wi' a' my heart, I'll do't;
  I'll get my Sunday's sark on,
An' meet you on the holy spot;
  Faith, we'se hae fine remarkin! "
Then I gaed hame at crowdie-time,
  An' soon I made me ready;
For roads were clad, frae side to side,
  Wi' mony a weary body
              In droves that day.

Here farmers gash, in ridin graith,
　　Gaed hoddin by their cotters ;
There swankies young, in braw braid-claith,
　　Are springing owre the gutters.
The lasses, skelpin barefit, thrang,
　　In silks an' scarlets glitter ;
Wi' sweet-milk cheese, in mony a whang,
　　An' farls, bak'd wi' butter,
　　　　　　　Fu' crump that day.

When by the plate we set our nose,
　　Weel heapèd up wi' ha'pence,
A greedy glow'r black-bonnet throws,
　　An' we maun draw our tippence.
Then in we go to see the show :
　　On ev'ry side they're gath'rin ;
Some carrying dails, some chairs an' stools,
　　An' some are busy bleth'rin
　　　　　　　Right loud that day.

Here stands a shed to fend the show'rs,
　　An' screen our countra gentry ;
There ' Racer Jess,' an' twa-three whores,
　　Are blinking at the entry.
Here sits a raw o' tittlin jads,
　　Wi' heaving breast an' bare neck ;
An' there a batch o' wabster lads,
　　Blackguarding frae Kilmarnock,
　　　　　　　For fun this day.

Here some are thinkin on their sins,
　　An' some upo' their claes ;
Ane curses feet that fyl'd his shins,
　　Anither sighs an' prays :

On this hand sits a chosen swatch,
  Wi' screw'd-up, grace-proud faces;
On that a set o' chaps, at watch,
  Thrang winkin on the lasses
            To chairs that day.

O happy is that man, an' blest!
  Nae wonder that it pride him?
Whase ain dear lass, that he likes best,
  Comes clinkin down beside him!
Wi' arm repos'd on the chair back,
  He sweetly does compose him;
Which, by degrees, slips round her neck,
  An's loof upon her bosom,
            Unkend that day.

Now a' the congregation o'er
  Is silent expectation;
For Moodie speels the holy door,
  Wi' tidings o' damnation:
Should *Hornie*, as in ancient days,
  'Mang sons o' God present him,
The vera sight o' Moodie's face,
  To 's ain het hame had sent him
            Wi' fright that day.

Hear how he clears the points o' Faith
  Wi' rattlin and wi' thumpin!
Now meekly calm, now wild in wrath,
  He's stampin, an' he's jumpin!
His lengthen'd chin, his turned-up snout,
  His eldritch squeel an' gestures,
O how they fire the heart devout,
  Like cantharidian plaisters
          On sic a day!

But hark ! the tent has chang'd its voice
    There's peace an' rest nae langer ;
For a' the real judges rise,
    They canna sit for anger ;
Smith opens out his cauld harangues,
    On practice and on morals ;
An' aff the godly pour in thrangs,
    To gie the jars an' barrels
                    A lift that day.

What signifies his barren shine,
    Of moral powers an' reason ?
His English style, an' gesture fine,
    Are a' clean out o' season.
Like Socrates or Antonine,
    Or some auld pagan heathen,
The *moral man* he does define,
    But ne'er a word o' *faith* in
                    That's right that day.

In guid time comes an antidote
    Against sic poison'd nostrum ;
For Peebles, frae the water-fit,
    Ascends the holy rostrum :
See, up he's got the word o' God,
    An' meek an' mim has view'd it,
While Common-sense has taen the road,
    An' aff, an' up the Cowgate
                    Fast, fast that day.

Wee Miller neist the guard relieves,
    An' Orthodoxy raibles,
Tho' in his heart he weel believes
    An' thinks it auld wives' fables :

But faith! the birkie wants a manse,
 So, cannilie he hums them;
Altho' his carnal wit an' sense
 Like hafflins-wise o'ercomes him
                At times that day.

Now butt an' ben the change-house fills,
 Wi' yill-caup commentators;
Here 's crying out for bakes and gills,
 An' there the pint-stowp clatters;
While thick an' thrang, an' loud an' lang,
 Wi' logic and wi' scripture,
They raise a din, that in the end
 Is like to breed a rupture
                O' wrath that day.

Leeze me on drink! it gies us mair
 Than either school or college;
It kindles wit, it waukens lear,
 It pangs us fou o' knowledge:
Be't whisky-gill or penny wheep,
 Or ony stronger potion,
It never fails, on drinkin deep,
 To kittle up our notion,
                By night or day.

The lads and lassies, blythely bent
 To mind baith saul an' body,
Sit round the table, weel content,
 An' steer about the toddy:
On this ane's dress, an' that ane's leuk,
 They're makin observations;
While some are cozy i' the neuk,
 An' forming assignations
                To meet some day.

But now the Lord's ain trumpet touts,
  Till a' the hills are rairin,
And echoes back return the shouts;
  Black Russell is na sparin:
His piercin words, like Highlan' swords,
  Divide the joints an' marrow:
His talk o' Hell, where devils dwell,
  Our vera "sauls does harrow"
           Wi' fright that day!

A vast, unbottom'd, boundless pit,
  Fill'd fou o' lowin brunstane,
Whase raging flame, an' scorching heat,
  Wad melt the hardest whun-stane!
The half-asleep start up wi' fear,
  An' think they hear it roarin;
When presently it does appear,
  'Twas but some neibor snorin
           Asleep that day.

'Twad be owre lang a tale to tell,
  How monie stories past;
An' how they crouded to the yill,
  When they were a' dismist;
How drink gaed round, in cogs and caups,
  Amang the furms and benches;
An' cheese an' bread, frae women's laps,
  Was dealt about in lunches
           An' dawds that day.

In comes a gawsie, gash guidwife,
  An' sits down by the fire,
Syne draws her kebbuck an' her knife;
  The lasses they are shyer:

The auld guidmen, about the grace,
  Frae side to side they bother ;
Till some ane by his bonnet lays,
  An' gies them't, like a tether,
          Fu' lang that day.

Waesucks ! for him that gets nae lass,
  Or lasses that hae naething !
Sma' need has he to say a grace,
  Or melvie his braw claithing !
O wives, be mindfu' ance yoursel'
  How bonie lads ye wanted ;
An' dinna for a kebbuck-heel
  Let lasses be affronted
          On sic a day!

Now Clinkumbell, wi' rattlin tow,
  Begins to jow an' croon ;
Some swagger hame the best they dow,
  Some wait the afternoon.
At slaps the billies halt a blink,
  Till lasses strip their shoon :
Wi' faith an' hope, an' love an' drink,
  They're a' in famous tune
          For crack that day.

How mony hearts this day converts
  O' sinners and o' lasses !
Their hearts o' stane, gin night, are gane
  As saft as ony flesh is :
There's some are fou o' love divine ;
  There's some are fou o' brandy ;
An' mony jobs that day begin,
  May end in houghmagandie
          Some ither day.

THIRD EPISTLE TO J. LAPRAIK

Guid speed and furder to you, Johnie,
Guid health, hale han's an' weather bonie;
Now, when ye're nickin down fu' cannie
      The staff o' bread,
May ye ne'er want a stoup o' bran'y
      To clear your head.

May Boreas never thresh your rigs,
Nor kick your rickles aff their legs,
Sendin the stuff o'er muirs and haggs
      Like drivin wrack;
But may the tapmost grain that wags
      Come to the sack.

I'm bizzie too, an' skelpin at it,
But bitter, daudin showers hae wat it;
Sae my auld stumpie pen I gat it
      Wi' muckle wark,
An' took my jocteleg an' whatt it,
      Like ony clark.

It's now twa month that I'm your debtor,
For your braw, nameless, dateless letter,
Abusin me for harsh ill-nature
      On holy men,
While deil a hair yoursel' ye're better,
      But mair profane.

But let the kirk-folk ring their bells,
Let's sing about our noble sel's:
We'll cry nae jads frae heathen hills
      To help, or roose us;
But browster wives an' whisky stills,
      They are the muses.

Your friendship, sir, I winna quat it,
An' if ye mak' objections at it,
Then hand in neive some day we'll knot it,
  An' witness take,
An' when wi' usquabae we've wat it,
  It winna break.

But if the beast an' branks be spar'd
Till kye be gaun without the herd,
And a' the vittel in the yard,
  An' theekit right,
I mean your ingle-side to guard
  Ae winter night.

Then muse-inspirin aquavitæ
Shall make us baith sae blythe and witty,
Till ye forget ye're auld an' gutty,
  An' be as canty
As ye were nine years less than thretty—
  Sweet ane an' twenty!

But stooks are cowpit wi' the blast,
And now the sinn keeks in the west,
Then I maun rin amang the rest,
  An' quat my chanter ;
Sae I subscribe mysel' in haste,
  Yours, Rab the Ranter.

Sept. 13, 1785.

EPISTLE TO THE REV. JOHN M'MATH,

INCLOSING A COPY OF "HOLY WILLIE'S PRAYER,"
WHICH HE HAD REQUESTED. SEPT. 17, 1785.

WHILE at the stook the shearers cow'r
To shun the bitter blaudin show'r,

Or in gulravage rinnin scowr
        To pass the time,
To you I dedicate the hour
        In idle rhyme.

My musie, tir'd wi' mony a sonnet
On gown, an' ban', an' douce black bonnet,
Is grown right eerie now she's done it,
        Lest they should blame her,
An' rouse their holy thunder on it
        And anathem her.

I own 'twas rash, an' rather hardy,
That I a simple, country bardie,
Should meddle wi' a pack sae sturdy,
        Wha, if they ken me,
Can easy, wi' a single wordie,
        Lowse hell upon me.

But I gae mad at their grimaces,
Their sighin, cantin, grace-proud faces,
Their three-mile prayers, an' half-mile graces,
        Their raxin conscience,
Whase greed, revenge, an' pride disgraces
        Waur nor their nonsense.

There's Gaw'n, misca'd waur than a beast,
Wha has mair honour in his breast
Than mony scores as guid's the priest
        Wha sae abus'd him :
And may a bard no crack his jest
        What way they've us'd him ?

See him, the poor man's friend in need,
The gentleman in word an' deed—

An' shall his fame an' honour bleed
      By worthless skellums,
An' not a muse erect her head
      To cowe the blellums?

O Pope, had I thy satire's darts
To gie the rascals their deserts,
I'd rip their rotten, hollow hearts,
      An' tell aloud
Their jugglin hocus-pocus arts
      To cheat the crowd.

God knows, I'm no the thing I should be,
Nor am I even the thing I could be,
But twenty times I rather would be
      An atheist clean,
Than under gospel colours hid be
      Just for a screen.

An honest man may like a glass,
An honest man may like a lass,
But mean revenge, and malice fause
      He'll still disdain,
An' then cry zeal for gospel laws,
      Like some we ken.

They take religion in their mouth;
They talk o' mercy, grace an' truth,
For what?—to gie their malice skouth
      On some puir wight,
An' hunt him down, owre right and ruth,
      To ruin straight.

All hail, Religion! maid divine!
Pardon a muse sae mean as mine,

Who in her rough imperfect line
       Thus daurs to name thee ;
To stigmatise false friends of thine
       Can ne'er defame thee.

Tho' blotch't and foul wi' mony a stain,
An' far unworthy of thy train,
With trembling voice I tune my strain,
       To join with those
Who boldly dare thy cause maintain
       In spite of foes :

In spite o' crowds, in spite o' mobs,
In spite o' undermining jobs,
In spite o' dark banditti stabs
       At worth an' merit,
By scoundrels, even wi' holy robes,
       But hellish spirit.

O Ayr ! my dear, my native ground,
Within thy presbyterial bound
A candid liberal band is found
       Of public teachers,
As men, as christians too, renown'd,
       An' manly preachers.

Sir, in that circle you are nam'd ;
Sir, in that circle you are fam'd ;
An' some, by whom your doctrine's blam'd
       (Which gies you honour)
Even, sir, by them your heart's esteem'd,
       An' winning manner.

Pardon this freedom I have ta'en,
An' if impertinent I've been,

Impute it not, good sir, in ane
        Whase heart ne'er wrang'd ye,
But to his utmost would befriend
        Ought that belang'd ye.

SECOND EPISTLE TO DAVIE

A BROTHER POET

AULD NEIBOUR,
  I'm three times doubly o'er your debtor,
For your auld-farrant, frien'ly letter;
Tho' I maun say't, I doubt ye flatter,
        Ye speak sae fair;
For my puir, silly, rhymin clatter
        Some less maun sair.

Hale be your heart, hale be your fiddle,
Lang may your elbuck jink an' diddle,
To cheer you thro' the weary widdle
        O' war'ly cares;
Till bairns' bairns kindly cuddle
        Your auld grey hairs.

But Davie, lad, I'm red ye're glaikit;
I'm tauld the muse ye hae negleckit;
An' gif it's sae, ye sud be lickit
        Until ye fyke;
Sic haun's as you sud ne'er be faikit,
        Be hain't wha like.

For me, I'm on Parnassus brink,
Rivin the words to gar them clink;
Whiles dazed wi' love, whiles dazed wi' drink,
        Wi' jads or masons;
An' whiles, but aye owre late, I think
        Braw sober lessons.

Of a' the thoughtless sons o' man,
Commen' to me the bardie clan;
Except it be some idle plan
       O' rhymin clink,
The devil-haet,—that I sud ban—
       They ever think.

Nae thought, nae view, nae scheme o' livin,
Nae cares to gie us joy or grievin,
But just the pouchie put the neive in,
       An' while ought's there,
Then, hiltie, skiltie, we gae scrievin,
       An' fash nae mair.

Leeze me on rhyme! it's aye a treasure,
My chief, amaist my only pleasure;
At hame, a-fiel', at wark, or leisure,
       The muse, poor hizzie!
Tho' rough an' raploch be her measure,
       She's seldom lazy.

Haud to the muse, my daintie Davie:
The warl' may play you mony a shavie;
But for the muse, she'll never leave ye,
       Tho' e'er sae puir,
Na, even tho' limpin wi' the spavie
       Frae door to door.

HALLOWEEN

" Yes! let the rich deride, the proud disdain,
The simple pleasures of the lowly train;
To me more dear, congenial to my heart,
One native charm, than all the gloss of art."—GOLDSMITH.

Upon that night, when fairies light
On Cassilis Downans dance,

Colean Castle with the Fairy Coves

From an engraving after David Octavius Hill

Or owre the lays, in splendid blaze,
  On sprightly coursers prance ;
Or for Colean the rout is ta'en,
  Beneath the moon's pale beams ;
There, up the Cove, to stray and rove,
  Among the rocks and streams
          To sport that night ;

Amang the bonie winding banks,
  Where Doon rins, wimplin, clear ;
Where Bruce ance rul'd the martial ranks,
  An' shook his Carrick spear ;
Some merry, friendly, countra-folks
  Together did convene,
To burn their nits, an' pou their stocks,
  An' haud their Halloween
          Fu' blythe that night.

The lasses feat, an' cleanly neat,
  Mair braw than when they're fine ;
Their faces blythe, fu' sweetly kythe,
  Hearts leal, an' warm, an' kin' :
The lads sae trig, wi' wooer-babs
  Weel-knotted on their garten ;
Some unco blate, an' some wi' gabs
  Gar lasses' hearts gang startin
          Whiles fast at night.

Then, first an' foremost, thro' the kail,
  Their stocks maun a' be sought ance ;
They steek their een, and grape an' wale
  For muckle anes, an' straught anes.

Poor hav'rel Will fell aff the drift,
  An' wandered thro' the 'bow-kail,'
An' pou't for want o' better shift
  A runt, was like a sow-tail
      Sae bow't that night.

Then, straught or crooked, yird or nane,
  They roar an' cry a' throw'ther;
The vera wee-things, toddlin, rin,
  Wi' stocks out owre their shouther:
An' gif the custock's sweet or sour,
  Wi' joctelegs they taste them;
Syne coziely, aboon the door,
  Wi' cannie care, they've plac'd them
      To lie that night.

The lassies staw frae 'mang them a',
  To pou their stalks o' corn;
But Rab slips out, an' jinks about,
  Behint the muckle thorn:
He grippit Nelly hard and fast:
  Loud skirl'd a' the lasses;
But her tap-pickle maist was lost,
  Whan kiutlin in the fause-house
      Wi' him that night.

The auld guidwife's weel-hoordit nits
  Are round an' round divided,
An' mony lads an' lassies' fates
  Are there that night decided:
Some kindle couthie side by side,
  And burn thegither trimly;
Some start awa wi' saucy pride,
  An' jump out owre the chimlie
      Fu' high that night.

Jean slips in twa' wi' tentie e'e ;
  Wha 'twas, she wadna tell ;
But this is *Jock*, an' this is *me*,
  She says in to hersel' :
He bleez'd owre her, an' she owre him,
  As they wad never mair part :
Till fuff! he started up the lum,
  An' Jean had e'en a sair heart
      To see't that night.

Poor Willie, wi' his bow-kail runt,
  Was brunt wi' primsie Mallie ;
An' Mary, nae doubt, took the drunt,
  To be compar'd to Willie :
Mall's nit lap out, wi' pridefu' fling,
  An' her ain fit, it brunt it ;
While Willie lap, and swoor by jing,
  'Twas just the way he wanted
      To be that night.

Nell had the tause-house in her min',
  She pits hersel an' Rob in ;
In loving bleeze they sweetly join,
  Till white in ase they're sobbin :
Nell's heart was dancin at the view ;
  She whisper'd Rob to leuk for't :
Rob, stownlins, prie'd her bonie mou',
  Fu' cozie in the neuk for't,
      Unseen that night.

But Merran sat behint their backs,
  Her thoughts on Andrew Bell ;
She lea'es them gashin at their cracks,
  An' slips out by hersel' ;

c

She thro' the yard the nearest taks,
  An' for the kiln she goes then,
An' darklins grapit for the bauks,
  And in the blue clue throws then,
      Right fear't that night.

An' ay she win't, an' ay she swat—
  I wat she made nae jaukin;
Till something held within the pat,
  Good Lord! but she was quaukin!
But whether 'twas the deil himsel',
  Or whether 'twas a bauk-en',
Or whether it was Andrew Bell,
  She did na wait on talkin
      To spier that night.

Wee Jenny to her graunie says,
  "Will ye go wi' me, graunie?
I'll eat the apple at the glass,
  I gat frae uncle Johnie:"
She fuff't her pipe wi' sic a lunt,
  In wrath she was sae vap'rin,
She notic't na an aizle brunt
  Her braw new worset apron
      Out thro' that night.

"Ye little skelpie-limmer's-face!
  I daur you try sic sportin,
As seek the foul thief ony place,
  For him to spae your fortune:
Nae doubt but ye may get a sight!
  Great cause ye hae to fear it;
For mony a ane has gotten a fright,
  An' liv'd an' died deleerit,
      On sic a night,

" Ae hairst afore the Sherra-moor,
    I mind't as weel's yestreen—
I was a gilpey then, I'm sure
    I was na past fyfteen :
The simmer had been cauld an' wat,
    An' stuff was unco green ;
An' aye a rantin kirn we gat,
    An' just on Halloween
        It fell that night.

" Our stibble-rig was Rab M'Graen,
    A clever, sturdy fallow ;
His sin gat Eppie Sim wi' wean,
    That lived in Achmacalla :
He gat hemp-seed, I mind it weel,
    An' he made unco light o't ;
But mony a day was by himsel',
    He was sae sairly frighted
        That vera night."

Then up gat fechtin Jamie Fleck,
    An' he swoor by his conscience,
That he could saw hemp-seed a peck ;
    For it was a' but nonsense :
The auld guidman raught down the pock,
    An' out a handfu' gied him ;
Syne bad him slip frae 'mang the folk,
    Sometime when nae ane see'd him,
        An' try't that night.

He marches thro' amang the stacks,
    Tho' he was something sturtin ;
The graip he for a harrow taks,
    An' haurls at his curpin :

And ev'ry now an' then, he says,
  "Hemp-seed I saw thee,
An' her that is to be my lass
  Come after me, an' draw thee
        As fast this night."

He whistl'd up Lord Lennox' March,
  To keep his courage cheery;
Altho' his hair began to arch,
  He was sae fley'd an' eerie:
Till presently he hears a squeak,
  An' then a grane an' gruntle;
He by his shouther gae a keek,
  An' tumbled wi' a wintle
        Out-owre that night.

He roar'd a horrid murder-shout,
  In dreadfu' desperation!
An' young an' auld come rinnin out,
  An' hear the sad narration:
He swoor 'twas hilchin Jean M'Craw,
  Or crouchie Merran Humphie—
Till stop! she trotted thro' them a';
  An' wha was it but grumphie
        Asteer that night?

Meg fain wad to the barn gaen,
  To win three wechts o' naething;
But for to meet the deil her lane,
  She pat but little faith in:
She gies the herd a pickle nits,
  An' twa red-cheekit apples,
To watch, while for the barn she sets,
  In hopes to see Tam Kipples
        That vera night.

She turns the key wi' cannie thraw,
  An' owre the threshold ventures ;
But first on Sawnie gies a ca',
  Syne bauldly in she enters :
A ratton rattl'd up the wa',
  An' she, cried Lord preserve her !
An' ran thro' midden-hole an a',
  An' pray'd wi' zeal and fervour,
        Fu' fast that night.

They hoy't out Will, wi' sair advice ;
  They hecht him some fine braw ane ;
It chanc'd the stack he faddom't thrice
  Was timmer-propt for thrawin :
He taks a swirlie auld moss-oak
  For some black, grousome carlin ;
An' loot a winze, and drew a stroke,
  Till skin in blypes cam haurlin
        Aff's nieves that night.

A wanton widow Leezie was,
  As cantie as a kittlen ;
But och ! that night, amang the shaws,
  She gat a fearfu' settlin !
She thro' the whins, an' by the cairn,
  An' owre the hill gaed scrievin ;
Whare three lairds' lan's met at a burn,
  To dip her left sark-sleeve in
        Was bent that night.

Whiles owre a linn the burnie plays,
  As thro' the glen it wimpl't ;
Whiles round a rocky scaur it strays,
  Whiles in a wiel it dimpl't ;

Whiles glitter'd to the nightly rays,
  Wi' bickerin, dancin dazzle ;
Whiles cookit underneath the braes,
  Below the spreading hazel
        Unseen that night.

Amang the brachens, on the brae,
  Between her an' the moon,
The deil, or else an outler quey,
  Gat up, an' gae a croon :
Poor Leezie's heart maist lap the hool ;
  Near lav'rock-height she jumpit,
But mist a fit, an' in the pool
  Out-owre the lugs she plumpit,
        Wi' a plunge that night.

In order, on the clean hearth-stane,
  The luggies three are ranged ;
An' ev'ry time great care is ta'en
  To see them duly changed :
Auld uncle John, wha wedlock's joys
  Sin' Mar's-year did desire,
Because he gat the toom dish thrice,
  He heav'd them on the fire,
        In wrath that night.

Wi' merry sangs, an' friendly cracks,
  I wat they did na weary ;
And unco tales, an' funnie jokes—
  Their sports were cheap an' cheery :
Till butter'd sowens, wi' fragrant lunt,
  Set a' their gabs a-steerin ;
Syne, wi' a social glass o' strunt,
  They parted aff careerin
        Fu' blythe that night.

Halloween

Halloween

"Poor Leezie's heart maist lap the hool;
Near lav'rock height she jumpit . . . "

TO A MOUSE

ON TURNING HER UP IN HER NEST WITH THE
PLOUGH, NOVEMBER 1785

WEE, sleekit, cowrin, tim'rous beastie,
O, what a panic's in thy breastie!
Thou need na start awa sae hasty,
    Wi' bickering brattle!
I wad be laith to rin an' chase thee,
    Wi' murd'ring pattle!

I'm truly sorry man's dominion,
Has broken nature's social union,
An' justifies that ill opinion,
    Which makes thee startle
At me, thy poor, earth-born companion,
    An' fellow-mortal!

I doubt na, whiles, but thou may thieve;
What then? poor beastie, thou maun live!
A daimen icker in a thrave
    'S a sma' request;
I'll get a blessin wi' the lave,
    An' never miss't!

Thy wee bit housie, too, in ruin!
It's silly wa's the win's are strewin!
An' naething, now, to big a new ane,
    O' foggage green!
An' bleak December's winds ensuin,
    Baith snell an' keen!

Thou saw the fields laid bare an' waste,
An' weary winter comin fast,

An' cozie here, beneath the blast,
        Thou thought to dwell—
Till crash! the cruel coulter past
        Out thro' thy cell.

That wee bit heap o' leaves an' stibble,
Has cost thee mony a weary nibble!
Now thou's turn'd out, for a' thy trouble,
        But house or hald,
To thole the winter's sleety dribble,
        An' cranreuch cauld!

But Mousie, thou art no thy lane,
In proving foresight may be vain;
The best-laid schemes o' mice an' men
        Gang aft agley,
An' lea'e us nought but grief an' pain,
        For promis'd joy!

Still thou art blest, compar'd wi' me;
The present only toucheth thee:
But och! I backward cast my e'e,
        On prospects drear!
An' forward, tho' I canna see,
        I guess an' fear!

ADAM ARMOUR'S PRAYER

Gude pity me, because I'm little!
For though I am an elf o' mettle,
An' can, like ony wabster's shuttle,
        Jink there or here,
Yet, scarce as lang's a gude kail-whittle,
        I'm unco queer.

An' now Thou kens our waefu' case ;
For Geordie's jurr we're in disgrace,
Because we stang'd her through the place,
        An' hurt her spleuchan ;
For whilk we daurna show our face
        Within the clachan.

An' now we're dern'd in dens and hollows,
And hunted, as was William Wallace,
Wi' constables—thae blackguard fallows,
        An' sodgers baith ;
But Gude preserve us frae the gallows,
        That shamefu' death !

Auld grim black-bearded Geordie's sel'—
O shake him owre the mouth o' hell !
There let him hing, an' roar, an' yell
        Wi' hideous din,
And if he offers to rebel,
        Then heave him in.

When Death comes in wi' glimmerin blink,
An' tips auld drucken Nanse the wink,
May Sautan gie her doup a clink
        Within his yett,
An' fill her up wi' brimstone drink,
        Red-reekin het.

Though Jock an' hav'rel Jean are merry—
Some devil seize them in a hurry,
An' waft them in th' infernal wherry
        Straught through the lake,
An' gie their hides a noble curry
        Wi' oil of aik !

c*

As for the jurr—puir worthless body!
She's got mischief enough already;
Wi' stangèd hips, and buttocks bluidy,
                She's suffer'd sair;
But may she wintle in a woody,
                If she whore mair!

THE JOLLY BEGGARS.—A CANTATA.

Recitativo.

WHEN lyart leaves bestrow the yird,
Or wavering like the bauckie-bird,
    Bedim cauld Boreas' blast;
When hailstanes drive wi' bitter skyte,
And infant frosts begin to bite,
    In hoary cranreuch drest;
Ae night at e'en a merry core
    O' randie, gangrel bodies,
In Poosie-Nansie's held the splore,
    To drink their orra duddies;
        Wi' quaffing an' laughing,
            They ranted an' they sang,
        Wi' jumping an' thumping,
            The vera girdle rang,

First, neist the fire, in auld red rags,
Ane sat, weel brac'd wi' mealy bags,
    And knapsack a' in order;
His doxy lay within his arm;
Wi' usquebae an' blankets warm
    She blinkit on her sodger;

An' aye he gies the tozie drab
The tither skelpin kiss,
While she held up her greedy gab,
Just like an aumous dish ;
   Ilk smack still did crack still,
   Just like a cadger's whip ;
Then staggering an' swaggering.
He roar'd this ditty up—

Air.

Tune—" Soldier's Joy."

I am a son of Mars who have been in many wars,
   And show my cuts and scars wherever I come ;
This here was for a wench, and that other in a
   trench,
   When welcoming the French at the sound of
   the drum.
            Lal de daudle, &c.

My prenticeship I past where my leader breath'd
   his last,
   When the bloody die was cast on the heights
   of Abram :
And I servèd out my trade when the gallant
   game was play'd,
   And the Moro low was laid at the sound of
   the drum.

I lastly was with Curtis among the floating
   batt'ries,
   And there I left for witness an arm and a limb ;
Yet let my country need me, with Elliot to head
   me,
   I'd clatter on my stumps at the sound of a drum.

And now tho' I must beg, with a wooden arm
    and leg,
  And many a tatter'd rag hanging over my bum,
I'm as happy with my wallet, my bottle and my
    callet,
  As when I used in scarlet to follow a drum.

What tho', with hoary locks, I must stand the
    winter shocks,
  Beneath the woods and rocks oftentimes for a
    home,
When the tother bag I sell, and the tother bottle
    tell,
  I could meet a troop of hell, at the sound of a
    drum.

Recitativo.

He ended ; and the kebars sheuk,
    Aboon the chorus roar ;
While frighted rattons backward leuk,
    An' seek the benmost bore :
A fairy fiddler frae the neuk,
    He skirl'd out, encore !
But up arose the martial chuck,
    An' laid the loud uproar.

Air.

Tune---" Sodger Laddie."

I once was a maid, tho' I cannot tell when,
And still my delight is in proper young men :
Some one of a troop of dragoons was my daddie,
No wonder I'm fond of a sodger laddie.
            Sing, lal de lal, &c.

The first of my loves was a swaggering blade,
To rattle the thundering drum was his trade;
His leg was so tight, and his cheek was so ruddy,
Transported I was with my sodger laddie.

But the godly old chaplain left him in the lurch;
The sword I forsook for the sake of the church:
He ventur'd the soul, and I riskèd the body,
'Twas then I proved false to my sodger laddie.

Full soon I grew sick of my sanctified sot,
The regiment at large for a husband I got;
From the gilded spontoon to the fife I was ready,
I askèd no more but a sodger laddie.

But the peace it reduc'd me to beg in despair,
Till I met my old boy in a Cunningham fair;
His rags regimental, they flutter'd so gaudy,
My heart it rejoic'd at a sodger laddie.

And now I have liv'd—I know not how long,
And still I can join in a cup and a song;
But whilst with both hands I can hold the glass
    steady,
Here's to thee, my hero, my sodger laddie.

Recitativo.

Poor Merry-Andrew, in the neuk,
    Sat guzzling wi' a tinkler-hizzie;
They mind't na wha the chorus teuk,
    Between themselves they were sae busy:
    At length, wi' drink an' courting dizzy,
He stoiter'd up an' made a face;
    Then turn'd an' laid a smack on Grizzie,
Syne tun'd his pipes wi' grave grimace.

Air.

Tune—" Auld Sir Symon."

Sir Wisdom's a fool when he's fou;
   Sir Knave is a fool in a session;
He's there but a prentice I trow,
   But I am a fool by profession.

My grannie she bought me a beuk,
   An' I held awa to the school;
I fear I my talent misteuk,
   But what will ye hae of a fool?

For drink I would venture my neck;
   A hizzie's the half of my craft;
But what could ye other expect
   Of ane that's avowedly daft?

I ance was tied up like a stirk,
   For civilly swearing and quaffin;
I ance was abus'd i' the kirk,
   For towsing a lass i' my daffin.

Poor Andrew that tumbles for sport,
   Let naebody name wi' a jeer;
There's ev'n, I'm tauld, i' the Court
   A tumbler ca'd the Premier.

Observ'd ye yon reverend lad
   Mak faces to tickle the mob;
He rails at our mountebank squad,—
   It's rivalship just i' the job.

And now my conclusion I'll tell,
   For faith I'm confoundedly dry;
The chiel that's a fool for himsel',
   Guid Lord! he's far dafter than I.

Recitativo.

Then niest out spak a raucle carlin,
Wha kent fu' weel to cleek the sterlin;
For monie a pursie she had hooked,
An' had in mony a well been douked:
Her love had been a Highland laddie,
But weary fa' the waeful woodie!
Wi' sighs and sobs she thus began
To wail her braw John Highlandman.

Air.

Tune—" O an ye were dead, Guidman."

A Highland lad my love was born,
The Lalland laws he held in scorn;
But he still was faithfu' to his clan,
My gallant, braw John Highlandman.

Chorus.

Sing hey my braw John Highlandman!
Sing ho my braw John Highlandman!
There's not a lad in a' the lan'
Was match for my John Highlandman.

With his philibeg an' tartan plaid,
An' guid claymore down by his side,
The ladies' hearts he did trepan,
My gallant, braw John Highlandman.
    Sing hey, &c.

We rangèd a' from Tweed to Spey,
An' liv'd like lords an' ladies gay;
For a Lalland face he fearèd none,—
My gallant, braw John Highlandman.
    Sing hey, &c.

They banish'd him beyond the sea.
But ere the bud was on the tree,
Adown my cheeks the pearls ran,
Embracing my John Highlandman.
                    Sing hey, &c.

But, och ! they catch'd him at the last,
And bound him in a dungeon fast :
My curse upon them every one,
They've hang'd my braw John Highlandman !
                    Sing hey, &c.

And now a widow, I must mourn
The pleasures that will ne'er return :
No comfort but a hearty can,
When I think on John Highlandman.
                    Sing hey, &c.

Recitativo.

A pigmy scraper wi' his fiddle,
Wha us'd at trystes an' fairs to driddle,
Her strappin limb and gausy middle
                    (He reach'd nae higher)
Had hol'd his heartie like a riddle,
                    An' blawn't on fire.

Wi' hand on hainch, and upward e'e,
He croon'd his gamut, one, two, three,
Then in an arioso key,
                    The wee Apollo
Set off wi' allegretto glee
                    His giga solo.

Air.
Tune—"Whistle owre the lave o't."

Let me ryke up to dight that tear,
An' go wi' me an' be my dear ;

An' then your every care an' fear
May whistle owre the lave o't.

Chorus.

I am a fiddler to my trade,
An' a' the tunes that e'er I played,
The sweetest still to wife or maid,
Was whistle owre the lave o't.

At kirns an' weddins we'se be there,
An' O sae nicely's we will fare!
We'll bowse about till Daddie Care
Sing whistle owre the lave o't.
I am, &c.

Sae merrily's the banes we'll pyke,
An' sun oursel's about the dyke;
An' at our leisure, when ye like,
We'll whistle owre the lave o't.
I am, &c.

But bless me wi' your heav'n o' charms,
An' while I kittle hair on thairms,
Hunger, cauld, an' a' sic harms,
May whistle owre the lave o't.
I am, &c.

Recitativo.

Her charms had struck a sturdy caird,
As weel as poor gut-scraper;
He taks the fiddler by the beard,
An' draws a roosty rapier—

He swoor by a' was swearing worth,
To speet him like a pliver,
Unless he would from that time forth
Relinquish her for ever.

Wi' ghastly e'e, poor tweedle-dee
  Upon his hunkers bended,
An' pray'd for grace wi' ruefu' face,
  An' so the quarrel ended.
But tho' his little heart did grieve
  When round the tinkler prest her,
He feign'd to snirtle in his sleeve,
  When thus the caird address'd her:

Air.

Tune—" Clout the Cauldron."

My bonie lass, I work in brass,
  A tinkler is my station:
I've travell'd round all Christian ground
  In this my occupation;
I've taen the gold, an' been enrolled
  In many a noble squadron;
But vain they search'd when off I march'd
  To go an' clout the cauldron.
                    I've taen the gold, &c.

Despise that shrimp, that wither'd imp,
  With a' his noise an' cap'rin;
An' take a share with those that bear
  The budget and the apron!
And by that stowp! my faith an' houp,
  And by that dear Kilbaigie,
If e'er ye want, or meet wi' scant,
  May I ne'er weet my craigie.
                    And by that stowp, &c.

Recitativo.

The caird prevail'd—th' unblushing fair
  In his embraces sunk;
Partly wi' love o'ercome sae sair,
  An' partly she was drunk:

Sir Violino, with an air
　　That show'd a man o' spunk,
Wish'd unison between the pair,
　　An' made the bottle clunk
　　　　To their health that night.

But hurchin Cupid shot a shaft,
　　That play'd a dame a shavie—
The fiddler rak'd her, fore and aft,
　　Behint the chicken cavie.
Her lord, a wight of Homer's craft,
　　Tho' limpin wi' the spavie,
He hirpl'd up, an' lap like daft,
　　An' shor'd them *Dainty Davie*
　　　　O' boot that night.

He was a care-defying blade
　　As ever Bacchus listed!
Tho' Fortune sair upon him laid,
　　His heart, she ever miss'd it.
He had no wish but—to be glad,
　　Nor want but—when he thirsted;
He hated nought but—to be sad,
　　An' thus the muse suggested
　　　　His sang that night.

Air.

Tune—"For a' that, an' a' that."

I am a Bard of no regard,
　　Wi' gentle folks an' a' that;
But Homer-like, the glowrin byke,
　　Frae town to town I draw that.

Chorus.

For a' that, an' a' that,
　　An' twice as muckle's a' that;

I've lost but ane, I've twa behin',
I've wife eneugh for a' that.

I never drank the Muses' stank,
Castalia's burn, an' a' that;
But there it streams an' richly reams,
My Helicon I ca' that.
　　　For a' that, &c.

Great love I bear to a' the fair,
Their humble slave an' a' that;
But lordly will, I hold it still
A mortal sin to thraw that.
　　　For a' that, &c.

In raptures sweet, this hour we meet,
Wi' mutual love an' a' that;
But for how lang the flie may stang,
Let inclination law that.
　　　For a' that, &c.

Their tricks an' craft hae put me daft,
They've taen me in, an' a' that;
But clear your decks, and here's—'The Sex!'
I like the jads for a' that.

Chorus.

For a' that, an' a' that,
An' twice as muckle's a' that;
My dearest bluid, to do them guid,
They're welcome till't for a that.

Recitativo.

So sang the bard—and Nansie's wa's
Shook with a thunder of applause,
Re-echo'd from each mouth!

They toom'd their pocks, they pawn'd their duds,
They scarcely left to co'er their fuds,
    To quench their lowin drouth:
Then owre again, the jovial thrang
    The poet did request
To lowse his pack an' wale a sang,
    A ballad o' the best;
        He rising, rejoicing,
            Between his twa Deborahs,
        Looks round him, an' found them
            Impatient for the chorus.

Air.

Tune—"Jolly Mortals, fill your Glasses."
See the smoking bowl before us,
    Mark our jovial ragged ring!
Round and round take up the chorus,
    And in raptures let us sing—

Chorus.

A fig for those by law protected!
    Liberty's a glorious feast!
Courts for cowards were erected,
    Churches built to please the priest.

What is title, what is treasure,
    What is reputation's care?
If we lead a life of pleasure,
    'Tis no matter how or where!
        A fig for, &c.

With the ready trick and fable,
    Round we wander all the day;
And at night in barn or stable,
    Hug our doxies on the hay.
        A fig for, &c.

Does the train-attended carriage
  Thro' the country lighter rove?
Does the sober bed of marriage
  Witness brighter scenes of love?
      A fig for, &c.

Life is all a variorum,
  We regard not how it goes;
Let them cant about decorum,
  Who have character to lose.
      A fig for, &c.

Here's to budgets, bags and wallets!
  Here's to all the wandering train.
Here's our ragged brats and callets,
  One and all cry out, Amen!

Chorus.

A fig for those by law protected!
  Liberty's a glorious feast!
Courts for cowards were erected,
  Churches built to please the priest.

THE COTTER'S SATURDAY NIGHT.

INSCRIBED TO R. AIKEN, ESQ.

"Let not Ambition mock their useful toil,
  Their homely joys, and destiny obscure;
Nor Grandeur hear, with a disdainful smile,
  The short and simple annals of the poor."
                                        GRAY.

My lov'd, my honour'd, much respected friend!
  No mercenary bard his homage pays;
With honest pride, I scorn each selfish end,
  My dearest meed, a friend's esteem and praise;
  To you I sing, in simple Scottish lays,

The Cotter's Saturday Night

The Cotter's Saturday Night

"But hark! a rap comes gently to the door;
Jenny, wha kens the meaning o' the same,
Tells how a neibor lad comes o'er the moor
To do some errands and convey her name."

The lowly train in life's sequester'd scene,
  The native feelings strong, the guileless ways,
What Aiken in a cottage would have been ;
Ah ! tho' his worth unknown, far happier there
    I ween !

November chill blaws loud wi' angry sugh ;
  The short'ning winter-day is near a close ;
The miry beasts retreating frae the pleugh ;
  The black'ning trains o' craws to their repose :
  The toil-worn Cotter frae his labour goes,—
This night his weekly moil is at an end,
  Collects his spades, his mattocks, and his hoes,
Hoping the morn in ease and rest to spend,
And weary, o'er the moor, his course does hame-
    ward bend.

At length his lonely cot appears in view,
  Beneath the shelter of an aged tree ;
Th' expectant wee - things, toddlin, stacher
    through
  To meet their dad, wi' flichterin noise and glee.
  His wee bit ingle, blinkin bonilie,
His clean hearth-stane, his thrifty wifie's smile,
  The lisping infant, prattling on his knee,
Does a' his weary kiaugh and care beguile,
And makes him quite forget his labour and his
    toil.

Belyve, the elder bairns come drapping in,
  At service out, amang the farmers roun' ;
Some ca' the pleugh, some herd, some tentie rin
  A cannie errand to a neibor town ;
  Their eldest hope, their Jenny, woman-grown,

In youthfu' bloom—love sparkling in her e'e—
  Comes hame, perhaps to shew a braw new gown,
Or deposite her sair-won penny-fee,
To help her parents dear, if they in hardship be.

With joy unfeign'd, brothers and sisters meet,
  And each for other's weelfare kindly speirs :
The social hours, swift-wing'd, unnotic'd fleet ;
  Each tells the uncos that he sees or hears.
The parents partial eye their hopeful years ;
Anticipation forward points the view ;
  The mother, wi' her needle and her shears,
Gars auld claes look amaist as weel's the new ;
The father mixes a' wi' admonition due.

Their master's and their mistress's command,
  The younkers a' are warned to obey ;
And mind their labors wi' an eydent hand,
  And ne'er, tho' out o' sight, to jauk or play ;
" And O ! be sure to fear the Lord alway,
And mind your duty, duly, morn and night ;
  Lest in temptation's path ye gang astray,
Implore His counsel and assisting might :
They never sought in vain that sought the Lord
    aright."

But hark ! a rap comes gently to the door ;
  Jenny, wha kens the meaning o' the same,
Tells how a neibor lad came o'er the moor,
  To do some errands, and convoy her hame.
The wily mother sees the conscious flame
Sparkle in Jenny's e'e, and flush her cheek ;
  With heart-struck anxious care, enquires his
    name,

While Jenny hafflins is afraid to speak ;
Well-pleased the mother hears, it's nae wild,
    worthless rake.

Wi' kindly welcome Jenny brings him ben ;
    A strappin youth, he takes the mother's eye ;
Blythe Jenny sees the visit's no ill taen ;
    The father cracks of horses, pleughs, and kye.
The youngster's artless heart o'erflows wi' joy,
But blate an' laithfu', scarce can weel behave ;
    The mother, wi' a woman's wiles, can spy
What makes the youth sae bashfu' and sae grave,
Weel-pleas'd to think her bairn's respected like
    the lave.

O happy love ! where love like this is found :
    O heart-felt raptures ! bliss beyond compare !
I've pacèd much this weary, mortal round,
    And sage experience bids me this declare,—
    " If Heaven a draught of heavenly pleasure
        spare—
One cordial in this melancholy vale,
    'Tis when a youthful, loving, modest pair
In other's arms, breathe out the tender tale,
Beneath the milk-white thorn that scents the
    evening gale."

Is there, in human form, that bears a heart,
    A wretch ! a villain ! lost to love and truth !
That can, with studied, sly, ensnaring art,
    Betray sweet Jenny's unsuspecting youth ?
    Curse on his perjur'd arts ! dissembling smooth !
Are honour, virtue, conscience, all exil'd ?
    Is there no pity, no relenting ruth,

Points to the parents fondling o'er their child ?
Then paints the ruin'd maid, and their distraction
    wild ?

But now the supper crowns their simple board,
    The halesome parritch, chief of Scotia's food ;
The sowp their only hawkie does afford,
    That 'yont the hallan snugly chows her cood :
    The dame brings forth, in complimental mood,
To grace the lad, her weel-hain'd kebbuck, fell ;
    And aft he's prest, and aft he ca's it guid :
The frugal wifie, garrulous, will tell
How 'twas a towmond auld, sin' lint was i' the
    bell.

The cheerfu' supper done, wi' serious face,
    They, round the ingle, form a circle wide ;
The sire turns o'er, with patriarchal grace,
    The big ha'-bible, ance his father's pride :
    His bonnet rev'rently is laid aside,
His lyart haffets wearing thin and bare ;
    Those strains that once did sweet in Zion glide,
He wales a portion with judicious care ;
And "Let us worship God!" he says with
    solemn air.

They chant their artless notes in simple guise,
    They tune their hearts, by far the noblest aim ;
Perhaps 'Dundee's' wild-warbling measures rise,
    Or plaintive 'Martyrs,' worthy of the name ;
    Or noble 'Elgin' beets the heaven-ward flame,
The sweetest far of Scotia's holy lays :
    Compar'd with these, Italian trills are tame :
The tickl'd ears no heart-felt raptures raise ;
Nae unison hae they with our Creator's praise.

The Cotter's Saturday Night

The Cotter's Saturday Night

"The sire turns o'er, with patriarchal grace,
The big ha'-bible, ance his father's pride . . . "

The priest-like father reads the sacred page,
    How Abram was the friend of God on
        high;
Or Moses bade eternal warfare wage
    With Amalek's ungracious progeny;
    Or how the royal bard did groaning lie
Beneath the stroke of Heaven's avenging ire;
    Or Job's pathetic plaint, and wailing cry;
Or rapt Isaiah's wild, seraphic fire;
Or other holy seers that tune the sacred lyre.

Perhaps the Christian volume is the theme,
    How guiltless blood for guilty man was
        shed;
How He, who bore in Heaven the second
        name,
    Had not on earth whereon to lay His head:
    How His first followers and servants sped;
The precepts sage they wrote to many a land:
    How he, who lone in Patmos banishèd,
Saw in the sun a mighty angel stand,
And heard great Bab'lon's doom pronounc'd by
        Heaven's command.

Then kneeling down to Heaven's Eternal King,
    The saint, the father, and the husband prays:
Hope "springs exulting on triumphant wing,"
    That thus they all shall meet in future days,
    There ever bask in uncreated rays,
No more to sigh, or shed the bitter tear,
    Together hymning their Creator's praise,
In such society, yet still more dear;
While circling Time moves round in an eternal
        sphere.

Compar'd with this, how poor Religion's pride,
　In all the pomp of method, and of art;
When men display to congregations wide
　Devotion's ev'ry grace, except the heart!
The Power, incens'd, the pageant will desert,
The pompous strain, the sacerdotal stole;
　But haply, in some cottage far apart,
May hear, well-pleas'd, the language of the soul;
And in His Book of Life the inmates poor enroll.

Then homeward all take off their sev'ral way;
　The youngling cottagers retire to rest:
The parent-pair their secret homage pay,
　And proffer up to Heaven the warm request,
　That He who stills the raven's clam'rous nest,
And decks the lily fair in flow'ry pride,
　Would, in the way His wisdom sees the best,
For them and for their little ones provide;
But chiefly, in their hearts with grace divine preside.

From scenes like these, old Scotia's grandeur
　　springs,
　That makes her lov'd at home, rever'd abroad:
Princes and lords are but the breath of kings,
　"An honest man's the noblest work of God;"
　And certes, in fair virtue's heavenly road,
The cottage leaves the palace far behind;
　What is a lordling's pomp? a cumbrous load,
Disguising oft the wretch of human kind,
Studied in arts of hell, in wickedness refin'd!

O Scotia! my dear, my native soil!
　For whom my warmest wish to Heaven is sent,
Long may thy hardy sons of rustic toil
　Be blest with health, and peace, and sweet content!
　And O! may Heaven their simple lives prevent

From luxury's contagion, weak and vile !
  Then, howe'er crowns and coronets be rent,
A virtuous populace may rise the while,
And stand a wall of fire around their much-lov'd
    isle.

O Thou ! who pour'd the patriotic tide,
  That stream'd thro' great unhappy Wallace'
    heart,
Who dar'd to nobly stem tyrannic pride,
  Or nobly die, the second glorious part :
(The patriot's God peculiarly thou art,
His friend, inspirer, guardian, and reward !)
  O never, never Scotia's realm desert ;
But still the patriot, and the patriot-bard
In bright succession raise, her ornament and
    guard !

ADDRESS TO THE DEIL.

  " O Prince ! O chief of many thronéd pow'rs
  That led th' embattl'd seraphim to war—"
                    MILTON.

O Thou ! whatever title suit thee—
Auld Hornie, Satan, Nick, or Clootie,
Wha in yon cavern grim an' sootie,
           Clos'd under hatches,
Spairges about the brunstane cootie,
        To scaud poor wretches !

Hear me, auld Hangie, for a wee,
An' let poor damnèd bodies be ;
I'm sure sma' pleasure it can gie,
          Ev'n to a deil,
To skelp an' scaud poor dogs like me,
        An' hear us squeel !

Great is thy pow'r an' great thy fame;
Far ken'd an' noted is thy name;
An' tho' yon lowin' heuch's thy hame,
                 Thou travels far;
An' faith! thou's neither lag nor lame,
                 Nor blate, nor scaur.

Whiles, ranging like a roarin lion,
For prey, a' holes and corners tryin;
Whiles, on the strong-wing'd tempest flyin,
                 Tirlin the kirks;
Whiles, in the human bosom pryin,
                 Unseen thou lurks.

I've heard my rev'rend graunie say,
In lanely glens ye like to stray;
Or where auld ruin'd castles grey
                 Nod to the moon,
Ye fright the nightly wand'rer's way,
                 Wi' eldritch croon.

When twilight did my graunie summon,
To say her pray'rs, douse, honest woman!
Aft 'yont the dyke she's heard you bummin,
                 Wi' eerie drone;
Or, rustlin, thro' the boortrees comin,
                 Wi' heavy groan.

Ae dreary, windy, winter night,
The stars shot down wi' sklentin light,
Wi' you mysel' I gat a fright,
                 Ayont the lough;
Ye, like a rash-buss, stood in sight,
                 Wi' wavin sough.

The cudgel in my nieve did shake,
Each bristl'd hair stood like a stake,

Address to the Deil

Address to the Deil

"Wi' you mysel' I gat a fright
Ayont the lough;
Ye, like a rash-buss, stood in sight,
Wi' waving sough."

When wi' an eldritch, stoor "quaick, quaick,"
　　　　Amang the springs,
Awa ye squatter'd like a drake,
　　　　On whistling wings.

Let warlocks grim, an' wither'd hags,
Tell how wi' you, on ragweed nags,
They skim the muirs an' dizzy crags,
　　　　Wi' wicked speed;
And in kirk-yards renew their leagues,
　　　　Owre howkit dead.

Thence countra wives, wi' toil and pain,
May plunge an' plunge the kirn in vain;
For oh! the yellow treasure's ta'en
　　　　By witchin skill;
An' dawtit, twal-pint hawkie's gane
　　　　As yell's the bill.

Thence mystic knots mak great abuse
On young guidmen, fond, keen an' crouse
When the best wark-lume i' the house,
　　　　By cantrip wit,
Is instant made no worth a louse,
　　　　Just at the bit.

When thowes dissolve the snawy hoord,
An' float the jinglin icy boord,
Then water-kelpies haunt the foord,
　　　　By your direction,
And 'nighted trav'lers are allur'd
　　　　To their destruction.

And aft your moss-traversin Spunkies
Decoy the wight that late an' drunk is:
The bleezin, curst, mischievous monkies
　　　　Delude his eyes,

Till in some miry slough he sunk is,
   Ne'er mair to rise.

When masons' mystic word an' grip
In storms an' tempest raise you up,
Some cock or cat your rage maun stop,
   Or, strange to tell!
The youngest brither ye wad whip
   Aff straught to hell.

Lang syne in Eden's bonie yard,
When youthfu' lovers first were pair'd,
An' all the soul of love they shar'd,
   The raptur'd hour,
Sweet on the fragrant flow'ry swaird,
   In shady bower;

Then you, ye auld, snick-drawing dog!
Ye cam to Paradise incog,
An' play'd on man a cursèd brogue,
   (Black be your fa'!,
An' gied the infant warld a shog,
   'Maist ruin'd a'.

D'ye mind that day when in a bizz
Wi' reekit duds, an' reestit gizz,
Ye did present your smoutie phiz
   'Mang better folk
An' sklented on the man of Uzz
   Your spitefu' joke?

An' how ye gat him i' your thrall,
An' brak him out o' house an hal',
While scabs and botches did him gall,
   Wi' bitter claw;
An' lows'd his ill-tongu'd wicked scaul',
   Was warst ava?

But a' your doings to rehearse,
Your wily snares an' fechtin fierce,
Sin' that day Michael did you pierce,
    Down to this time,
Wad ding a Lallan tongue, or Erse,
    In prose or rhyme.

An' now auld Cloots, I ken ye're thinkin,
A certain bardie's rantin, drinkin,
Some luckless hour will send him linkin
    To your black pit;
But faith! he'll turn a corner jinkin,
    An' cheat you yet.

But fare-you-weel, auld Nickie-ben!
O wad ye tak a thought an' men'!
Ye aiblins might—I dinna ken—
    Still hae a stake:
I'm wae to think upo' yon den,
    Ev'n for your sake!

SCOTCH DRINK

 Gie him strong drink until he wink,
  That's sinking in despair;
 An' liquor guid to fire his bluid,
  That's prest wi' grief and care:
 There let him bouse, an' deep carouse
  Wi' bumpers flowing o'er,
 Till he forgets his loves or debts,
  An' minds his griefs no more.
    SOLOMON'S PROVERBS, xxxi. 6, 7.

Let other poets raise a frácas
'Bout vines, an' wines, an' drucken Bacchus,
An' crabbit names an' stories wrack us,
    An' grate our lug:
I sing the juice Scotch bear can mak us,
    In glass or jug.

D

O thou, my muse! guid auld Scotch drink!
Whether thro' wimplin worms thou jink,
Or, richly brown, ream owre the brink,
   In glorious faem,
Inspire me, till I lisp an' wink,
    To sing thy name!

Let husky wheat the haughs adorn,
An' aits set up their awnie horn,
An' pease and beans, at e'en or morn,
   Perfume the plain:
Leeze me on thee, John Barleycorn,
    Thou king o' grain!

On thee aft Scotland chows her cood,
In souple scones, the wale o' food!
Or tumblin in the boiling flood
   Wi' kail an' beef;
But when thou pours thy strong heart's blood,
    There thou shines chief.

Food fills the wame, an' keeps us leevin;
Tho' life's a gift no worth receivin,
When heavy-dragg'd wi' pine an' grievin;
   But, oil'd by thee,
The wheels o' life gae down-hill, scrievin,
    Wi' rattlin glee.

Thou clears the head o' doited Lear;
Thou cheers the heart o' drooping Care;
Thou strings the nerves o' Labour sair
   At's weary toil;
Thou even brightens dark Despair
    Wi' gloomy smile.

Aft, clad in massy siller weed,
Wi' gentles thou erects thy head;
Yet, humbly kind in time o' need,
   The poor man's wine;
His wee drap parritch, or his bread,
   Thou kitchens fine.

Thou art the life o' public haunts;
But thee, what were our fairs and rants?
Ev'n godly meetings o' the saunts,
   By thee inspired,
When gaping they besiege the tents,
   Are doubly fir'd.

That merry night we get the corn in,
O sweetly, then, thou reams the horn in!
Or reekin on a New-year mornin
   In cog or bicker,
An' just a wee drap sp'ritual burn in,
   An' gusty sucker!

When Vulcan gies his bellows breath,
An' ploughmen gather wi' their graith,
O rare! to see thee fizz an freath
   I' th' luggit caup!
Then Burnewin comes on like death
   At every chap.

Nae mercy then, for airn or steel,
The brawnie, banie, ploughman chiel,
Brings hard owrehip, wi' sturdy wheel,
   The strong forehammer,
Till block an' studdie ring an reel
   Wi' dinsome clamour.

When skirling weanies see the light,
Thou maks the gossips clatter bright,
How fumblin cuifs their dearies slight;
        Wae worth the name!
Nae howdie gets a social night,
        Or plack frae them.

When neibors anger at a plea,
An' just as wud as wud can be,
How easy can the barley brie
        Cement the quarrel!
It's aye the cheapest lawyer's fee,
        To taste the barrel.

Alake! that e'er my muse has reason,
To wyte her countrymen wi' treason!
But mony daily weet their weason
        Wi' liquors nice,
An' hardly, in a winter season,
        E'er spier her price.

Wae worth that brandy, burnin trash!
Fell source o' mony a pain an' brash!
Twins mony a poor, doylt, drucken hash,
        O' half his days;
An' sends, beside, auld Scotland's cash
        To her warst faes.

Ye Scots, wha wish auld Scotland well!
Ye chief, to you my tale I tell,
Poor, plackless devils like mysel'!
        It sets you ill,
Wi' bitter, dearthfu' wines to mell,
        Or foreign gill.

May gravels round his blather wrench,
An' gouts torment him, inch by inch,
Wha twists his gruntle wi' a glunch
      O' sour disdain,
Out owre a glass o' whisky-punch
        Wi' honest men!

O whisky! soul o' plays and pranks!
Accept a bardie's gratefu' thanks!
When wanting thee, what tuneless cranks
      Are my poor verses!
Thou comes—they rattle in their ranks,
      At ither's arses!

Thee, Ferintosh! O sadly lost!
Scotland, lament frae coast to coast!
Now colic grips, an' barkin hoast
      May kill us a';
For loyal Forbes' charter'd boast
      Is ta'en awa?

Thae curst horse-leeches o' th' Excise,
Wha mak the whisky stells their prize!
Haud up thy han', Deil! ance, twice, thrice!
      There, seize the blinkers!
An' bake them up in brunstane pies
      For poor damn'd drinkers.

Fortune! if thou'll but gie me still
Hale breeks, a scone, an' whisky gill,
An' rowth o' rhyme to rave at will,
      Tak a' the rest,
An' deal't about as thy blind skill
      Directs thee best.

THE AULD FARMER'S NEW-YEAR-
MORNING SALUTATION TO HIS
AULD MARE, MAGGIE,

On giving her the accustomed ripp of corn to hansel in
the New-Year.

A Guid New-year I wish thee, Maggie!
Hae, there's a ripp to thy auld baggie :
Tho' thou's howe-backit now, an' knaggie,
    I've seen the day
Thou could hae gaen like ony staggie,
     Out-owre the lay.

Tho' now thou's dowie, stiff an' crazy,
An' thy auld hide as white's a daisie,
I've seen the dappl't, sleek an' glaizie,
    A bonie gray :
He should been tight that daur't to raize thee,
    Ance in a day.

Thou ance was i' the foremost rank,
A filly buirdly, steeve an' swank ;
An' set weel down a shapely shank,
    As e'er tread yird ;
An' could hae flown out-owre a stank,
    Like ony bird.

It's now some nine-an'-twenty year,
Sin' thou was my guid-father's mear ;
He gied me thee, o' tocher clear,
    An' fifty mark ;
Tho' it was sma', 'twas weel-won gear,
    An' thou was stark.

The Auld Farmer's Salutation

The Auld Farmer's Salutation

"It's now some nine-an'-twenty year
Sin thou was my guid-father's mear . . . "

When first I gaed to woo my Jenny,
Ye then was trotting wi' your minnie:
Tho' ye was trickie, slee, an funnie,
        Ye ne'er was donsie;
But hamely, tawie, quiet, an' cannie,
      An' unco sonsie.

That day, ye pranc'd wi' muckle pride,
When ye bure hame my bonie bride:
An' sweet an' gracefu' she did ride,
        Wi' maiden air!
Kyle-Stewart I could bragged wide
      For sic a pair.

Tho' now ye dow but hoyte and hobble,
An' wintle like a saumont coble,
That day, ye was a jinker noble,
        For heels an' win'!
An' ran them till they a' did wauble,
      Far, far, behin'!

When thou an' I were young an' skeigh
An' stable-meals at fairs were dreigh,
How thou wad prance, and snore, an' skreigh
        An' tak the road!
Town's-bodies ran, an' stood abeigh,
      An' ca't thee mad.

When thou was corn't, an' I was mellow,
We took the road aye like a swallow:
At brooses thou had ne'er a fellow,
        For pith an' speed;
But ev'ry tail thou pay't them hollow,
      Whare'er thou gaed.

The sma', droop-rumpl't, hunter cattle
Might aiblins waurt thee for a brattle;
But sax Scotch mile, thou try't their mettle,
   An' gar't them whaizle:
Nae whip nor spur, but just a wattle
   O' saugh or hazel.

Thou was a noble fittie-lan',
As e'er in tug or tow was drawn!
Aft thee an' I, in aught hours' gaun,
   In guid March-weather,
Hae turn'd sax rood beside our han',
   For days thegither.

Thou never braing't, an' fetch't; an' fliskit;
But thy auld tail thou wad hae whiskit,
An' spread abreed thy weel-fill'd brisket,
   Wi' pith an' power;
Till sprittie knowes wad rair't an' riskit
   An' slypet owre.

When frosts lay lang, an' snaws were deep,
An' threaten'd labour back to keep,
I gied thy cog a wee bit heap
   Aboon the timmer:
I ken'd my Maggie wad na sleep,
   For that, or simmer.

In cart or car thou never reestit;
The steyest brae thou wad hae fac't it;
Thou never lap, an' sten't, and breastit,
   Then stood to blaw;
But just thy step a wee thing hastit,
   Thou snoov't awa.

My pleugh is now thy bairn-time a',
Four gallant brutes as e'er did draw;
Forbye sax mae I've sell't awa,
    That thou hast nurst:
They drew me thretteen pund an' twa,
    The vera warst.

Mony a sair daurk we twa hae wrought,
An' wi' the weary warl' fought!
An' mony an anxious day, I thought
    We wad be beat!
Yet here to crazy age we're brought,
    Wi' something yet.

An' think na', my auld trusty servan',
That now perhaps thou's less deservin,
An' thy auld days may end in starvin;
    For my last fow,
A heapit stimpart, I'll reserve ane
    Laid by for you.

We've worn to crazy years thegither;
We'll toyte about wi' ane anither;
Wi' tentie care I'll flit thy tether
    To some hain'd rig,
Whare ye may nobly rax your leather,
    Wi' sma' fatigue.

THE TWA DOGS:

A TALE.

'Twas in that place o' Scotland's isle,
That bears the name o' auld King Coil,
Upon a bonie day in June,
When wearin thro' the afternoon,

D*

Twa dogs, that were na thrang at hame,
Forgather'd ance upon a time.
   The first I'll name, they ca'd him Cæsar,
Was keepit for His Honour's pleasure :
His hair, his size, his mouth, his lugs,
Shew'd he was nane o' Scotland's dogs ;
But whalpit some place far abroad,
Whare sailors gang to fish for cod.
   His lockèd, letter'd, braw brass collar
Shew'd him the gentleman an' scholar ;
But though he was o' high degree,
The fient a pride na pride had he ;
But wad hae spent an hour caressin,
Ev'n wi' a tinkler-gipsy's messan :
At kirk or market, mill or smiddie,
Nae tawted tyke, tho' e'er sae duddie,
But he wad stan't, as glad to see him,
An' stroan't on stanes an' hillocks wi' him.
   The tither was a ploughman's collie—
A rhyming, ranting, raving billie,
Wha for his friend an' comrade had him,
And in his freaks had Luath ca'd him,
After some dog in Highland sang,
Was made lang syne—Lord knows how lang.
   He was a gash an' faithfu' tyke,
As ever lap a sheugh or dyke.
His honest, sonsie, baws'nt face
Aye gat him friends in ilka place ;
His breast was white, his touzie back
Weel clad wi' coat o' glossy black ;
His gawsie tail, wi' upward curl,
Hung owre his hurdies wi' a swirl.
   Nae doubt but they were fain o' ither,
And unco pack an' thick thegither ;

The Twa Dogs

The Twa Dogs

"Twas in that place o' Scotland's isle,
That bears the name o' auld King Coil,
Upon a bonie day in June,
When wearing thro' the afternoon,
Twa dogs, that were na thrang at hame,
Foregather'd ance upon a time."

Wi' social nose whiles snuff'd an' snowkit;
Whiles mice an' moudieworts they howkit;
Whiles scour'd awa' in lang excursion,
An' worry'd ither in diversion;
Till tir'd at last wi' mony a farce,
They set them down upon their arse,
An' there began a lang digression
About the "lords o' the creation."

CÆSAR.

I've aften wonder'd, honest Luath,
What sort o' life poor dogs like you have;
An' when the gentry's life I saw,
What way poor bodies liv'd ava.
Our laird gets in his rackèd rents,
His coals, his kane, an' a' his stents:
He rises when he likes himsel';
His flunkies answer at the bell;
He ca's his coach; he ca's his horse;
He draws a bonie silken purse,
As lang's my tail, where, thro' the steeks,
The yellow letter'd Geordie keeks.
Frae morn to e'en it's nought but toiling
At baking, roasting, frying, boiling;
An' tho' the gentry first are stechin,
Yet ev'n the ha' folk fill their pechan
Wi' sauce, ragouts, an' sic like trashtrie,
That's little short o' downright wastrie.
Our whipper-in, wee, blasted wonner,
Poor, worthless elf, it eats a dinner,
Better than ony tenant-man
His Honour has in a' the lan':
An' what poor cot-folk pit their painch in,
I own it's past my comprehension.

LUATH.

Trowth, Cæsar, whiles they're fash't eneugh;
A cottar howkin in a sheugh,
Wi' dirty stanes biggin a dyke,
Baring a quarry, an' sic like;
Himsel', a wife, he thus sustains,
A smytrie o' wee duddie weans,
An' nought but his han'-daurk, to keep
Them right an' tight in thack an' rape.

An' when they meet wi' sair disasters,
Like loss o' health or want o' masters,
Ye maist wad think, a wee touch langer,
An' they maun starve o' cauld an' hunger:
But how it comes, I never kent yet,
They're maistly wonderfu' contented;
An' buirdly chiels, an' clever hizzies,
Are bred in sic a way as this is.

CÆSAR.

But then to see how ye're negleckit,
How huff'd, an' cuff'd, an' disrespeckit!
Lord man, our gentry care as little
For delvers, ditchers, an' sic cattle;
They gang as saucy by poor folk,
As I wad by a stinkin brock.

I've notic'd, on our laird's court-day,—
An' mony a time my heart's been wae,—
Poor tenant bodies, scant o' cash,
How they maun thole a factor's snash;
He'll stamp an' threaten, curse an' swear,
He'll apprehend them, poind their gear;
While they maun stan', wi' aspect humble,
An' hear it a', an' fear an' tremble!

I see how folk live that hae riches;
But surely poor-folk maun be wretches!

LUATH.

They're no sae wretched 's ane wad think.
Tho' constantly on poortith's brink,
They're sae accustom'd wi' the sight,
The view o't gies them little fright.
  Then chance and fortune are sae guided,
They're aye in less or mair provided :
An' tho' fatigued wi' close employment,
A blink o' rest's a sweet enjoyment.
  The dearest comfort o' their lives,
Their grushie weans an' faithfu' wives ;
The prattling things are just their pride,
That sweetens a' their fire-side.
  An' whiles twalpennie worth o' nappy
Can mak the bodies unco happy :
They lay aside their private cares,
To mind the Kirk and State affairs ;
They'll talk o' patronage an' priests,
Wi' kindling fury i' their breasts,
Or tell what new taxation's comin,
An' ferlie at the folk in Lon'on.
  As bleak-fac'd Hallowmass returns,
They get the jovial, rantin kirns,
When rural life, of ev'ry station,
Unite in common recreation ;
Love blinks, Wit slaps, an' social Mirth
Forgets there's Care upo' the earth.
  That merry day the year begins,
They bar the door on frosty win's ;
The nappy reeks wi' mantling ream,
An' sheds a heart-inspiring steam ;
The luntin pipe, an' sneeshin mill,
Are handed round wi' right guid will :
The cantie auld folks crackin crouse,

The young anes rantin thro' the house—
My heart has been sae fain to see them,
That I for joy hae barkit wi' them.
    Still it's ower true that ye hae said,
Sic game is now ower aften play'd ;
There's mony a creditable stock
O' decent, honest, fawsont folk,
Are riven out baith root an' branch,
Some rascal's pridefu' greed to quench,
Wha thinks to knit himsel the faster
In favour wi' some gentle master,
Wha, aiblins thrang a parliamentin,
For Britain's guid his saul indentin—

CÆSAR.

    Haith, lad, ye little ken about it :
For Britain's guid ! guid faith ! I doubt it.
Say rather, gaun as Premiers lead him :
An' saying ay or no 's they bid him :
At operas an' plays parading,
Mortgaging, gambling, masquerading :
Or maybe, in a frolic daft,
To Hague or Calais takes a waft,
To mak a tour an' tak a whirl,
To learn *bon ton* an' see the worl'.
    There, at Vienna, or Versailles,
He rives his father's auld entails ;
Or by Madrid he takes the rout,
To thrum guitars an' fecht wi' nowt ;
Or down Italian vista startles,
Whore-hunting amang groves o' myrtles :
Then bowses drumlie German-water,
To mak himsel look fair an' fatter,
An' clear the consequential sorrows,

Love-gifts of Carnival signoras.
　For Britain's guid ! for her destruction !
Wi' dissipation, feud an' faction.

LUATH.

　Hech man ! dear sirs ! is that the gate
They waste sae mony a braw estate !
Are we sae foughten an' harass'd
For gear to gang that gate at last ?
　O would they stay aback frae courts,
An' please themsels wi' country sports,
It wad for ev'ry ane be better,
The laird, the tenant, an' the cotter !
For thae frank, rantin, ramblin billies,
Feint haet o' them's ill-hearted fellows ;
Except for breakin o' their timmer,
Or speakin lightly o' their limmer,
Or shootin of a hare or moor-cock,
The ne'er-a-bit they're ill to poor folk.
　But will ye tell me, master Cæsar,
Sure great folk's life's a life o' pleasure ?
Nae cauld nor hunger e'er can steer them,
The very thought o't need na fear them.

CÆSAR.

　Lord, man, were ye but whiles whare I am,
The gentles, ye wad ne'er envy them !
　It's true, they need na starve or sweat,
Thro' winter's cauld, or simmer's heat :
They've nae sair wark to craze their banes,
An' fill auld age wi' grips an' granes :
But human bodies are sic fools,
For a' their colleges an' schools,
That when nae real ills perplex them,
They mak enow themsel's to vex them ;

An' aye the less they hae to sturt them,
In like proportion, less will hurt them.
   A country fellow at the pleugh,
His acre's till'd, he's right eneugh;
A country girl at her wheel,
Her dizzen's dune, she's unco weel;
But gentlemen, an' ladies warst,
Wi' ev'n-down want o' wark are curst.
They loiter, lounging, lank an' lazy;
Tho' deil-haet ails them, yet uneasy;
Their days insipid, dull an' tasteless;
Their nights unquiet, lang an' restless.
   An' ev'n their sports, their balls an' races,
Their galloping through public places,
There's sic parade, sic pomp an' art,
The joy can scarcely reach the heart.
   The men cast out in party-matches,
Then sowther a' in deep debauches.
Ae night they're mad wi' drink an' whoring,
Neist day their life is past enduring.
   The ladies arm-in-arm in clusters,
As great an' gracious a' as sisters;
But hear their absent thoughts o' ither,
They're a' run-deils an' jads thegither.
Whiles, ower the wee bit cup an' platie,
They sip the scandal-potion pretty;
Or lee-lang nights, wi' crabbit leuks
Pore ower the devil's pictur'd beuks;
Stake on a chance a farmer's stackyard,
An' cheat like ony unhanged blackguard.
   There's some exceptions, man an' woman;
But this is gentry's life in common.
   By this, the sun was out of sight,
An' darker gloamin brought the night;

The bum-clock humm'd wi' lazy drone;
The kye stood rowtin i' the loan;
When up they gat an' shook their lugs,
Rejoic'd they werena *men* but *dogs* ;
An' each took aff his several way,
Resolv'd to meet some ither day.

THE AUTHOR'S EARNEST CRY
AND PRAYER

TO THE RIGHT HONOURABLE AND HONOURABLE
SCOTCH REPRESENTATIVES IN THE
HOUSE OF COMMONS

Dearest of distillation! last and best——
——How art thou lost!——
PARODY ON MILTON.

YE Irish lords, ye knights an' squires,
Wha represent our brughs an' shires,
An' doucely manage our affairs
In parliament,
To you a simple poet's pray'rs
Are humbly sent.

Alas! my roupit muse is hearse!
Your Honours' hearts wi' grief 'twad pierce,
To see her sittin on her arse
Low i' the dust,
And scriechin out prosaic verse,
An' like to brust!

Tell them wha hae the chief direction,
Scotland an' me's in great affliction,
E'er sin' they laid that curst restriction
On aqua-vitæ;
An' rouse them up to strong conviction,
An' move their pity

Stand forth an' tell yon Premier youth
The honest, open, naked truth:
Tell him o' mine an' Scotland's drouth,
   His servants humble:
The muckle deevil blaw you south
   If ye dissemble!

Does ony great man glunch an' gloom?
Speak out, an' never fash your thumb!
Let posts an' pensions sink or soom
   Wi' them wha grant them;
If honestly they canna come,
   Far better want them.

In gath'rin votes you were na slack;
Now stand as tightly by your tack:
Ne'er claw your lug, an' fidge your back,
   An' hum an' haw;
But raise your arm, an' tell your crack
   Before them a'.

Paint Scotland greetin owre her thrissle;
Her mutchkin stowp as toom's a whissle;
An' damn'd excisemen in a bussle,
   Seizin a stell,
Triumphant crushin't like a mussel,
   Or limpet shell!

Then, on the tither hand present her—
A blackguard smuggler right behint her,
An' cheek-for-chow, a chuffie vintner
   Colleaguing join,
Picking her pouch as bare as winter
   Of a' kind coin.

Is there, that bears the name o' Scot,
But feels his heart's bluid rising hot,
To see his poor auld mither's pot
          Thus dung in staves,
An' plunder'd o' her hindmost groat
          By gallows knaves?

Alas! I'm but a nameless wight,
Trod i' the mire out o' sight?
But could I like Montgomeries fight,
          Or gab like Boswell,
There's some sark-necks I wad draw tight,
          An' tie some hose well.

God bless your Honours! can ye see't—
The kind, auld, cantie carlin, greet,
An' no get warmly to your feet,
          An' gar them hear it,
An' tell them wi' a patriot-heat
          Ye winna bear it?

Some o' you nicely ken the laws,
To round the period an' pause,
An' with rhetóric clause on clause
          To mak harangues;
Then echo thro' Saint Stephen's wa's
          Auld Scotland's wrangs.

Dempster, a true blue Scot I'se warran';
Thee, aith-detesting, chaste Kilkerran;
An' that glib-gabbit Highland baron,
          The Laird o' Graham;
An' ane, a chap that's damn'd auldfarran',
          Dundas his name:

Erskine, a spunkie Norland billie ;
True Campbells, Frederick and Ilay ;
An' Livistone, the bauld Sir Willie ;
   An' mony ithers,
Whom auld Demosthenes or Tully
   Might own for brithers.

See, sodger Hugh, my watchman stented,
If poets e'er are represented ;
I ken if that your sword were wanted,
   Ye'd lend a hand ;
But when there's ought to say anent it,
   Ye're at a stand.

Arouse, my boys ! exert your mettle,
To get auld Scotland back her kettle ;
Or faith ! I'll wad my new pleugh-pettle,
   Ye'll see't or lang,
She'll teach you, wi' a reekin whittle,
   Anither sang.

This while she's been in crankous mood,
Her lost Militia fir'd her bluid ;
(Deil na they never mair do guid,
   Play'd her that pliskie !)
An' now she's like to rin red-wud
   About her whisky.

An' Lord ! if ance they pit her till't,
Her tartan petticoat she'll kilt,
An' durk an' pistol at her belt,
   She'll tak the streets,
An' rin her whittle to the hilt,
   I' the first she meets !

For God-sake, sirs! then speak her fair,
An' straik her cannie wi' the hair,
An' to the muckle house repair,
      Wi' instant speed,
An' strive, wi' a' your wit an' lear,
      To get remead.

Yon ill-tongu'd tinkler, Charlie Fox,
May taunt you wi' his jeers and mocks;
But gie him't het, my hearty cocks!
      E'en cowe the cadie!
An' send him to his dicing box
      An' sportin lady.

Tell yon guid bluid o' auld Boconnock's,
I'll be his debt twa mashlum bonnocks,
An' drink his health in auld Nance Tinnock's
      Nine times a-week,
If he some scheme, like tea an' winnocks,
      Wad kindly seek.

Could he some commutation broach,
I'll pledge my aith in guid braid Scotch,
He needna fear their foul reproach
      Nor erudition,
Yon mixtie-maxtie, queer hotch-potch,
      The Coalition.

Auld Scotland has a raucle tongue;
She's just a devil wi' a rung;
An' if she promise auld or young
      To tak their part,
Tho' by the neck she should be strung,
      She'll no desert.

And now, ye chosen Five-and-Forty,
May still your mither's heart support ye ;
Then, tho' a minister grow dorty,
           An' kick your place,
Ye'll snap your fingers, poor an' hearty,
           Before his face.

God bless your Honours, a' your days,
Wi' sowps o' kail and brats o' claise,
In spite o' a' the thievish kaes,
           That haunt St Jamie's !
Your humble poet sings an' prays,
           While Rab his name is.

POSTSCRIPT

Let half-starv'd slaves in warmer skies
See future wines, rich-clust'ring, rise ;
Their lot auld Scotland ne'er envies,
           But, blythe and frisky,
She eves her freeborn, martial boys
           Tak aff their whisky.

What tho' their Phœbus kinder warms,
While fragrance blooms and beauty charms,
When wretches range, in famish'd swarms,
           The scented groves ;
Or, hounded forth, dishonour arms
           In hungry droves !

Their gun's a burden on their shouther ;
They downa bide the stink o' powther ;
Their bauldest thought's a hank'ring swither
           To stan' or rin,
Till skelp—a shot—they're aff, a' throw'ther,
           To save their skin.

But bring a Scotchman frae his hill,
Clap in his cheek a Highland gill,
Say, such is royal George's will,
   An' there's the foe!
He has nae thought but how to kill
   Twa at a blow.

Nae cauld, faint-hearted doubtings tease him;
Death comes, wi' fearless eye he sees him;
Wi' bluidy hand a welcome gies him;
   An' when he fa's,
His latest draught o' breathin lea'es him
   In faint huzzas.

Sages their solemn een may steek,
An' raise a philosophic reek,
An' physically causes seek
   In clime an' season;
But tell me whisky's name in Greek,
   I'll tell the reason.

Scotland, my auld, respected mither!
Tho' whiles ye moistify your leather,
Till, whare ye sit on craps o' heather,
   Ye tine your dam;
Freedom an' whisky gang thegither!
   Tak aff your dram.

THE ORDINATION

" For sense, they little owe to frugal Heav'n—
To please the mob they hide the little giv'n."

KILMARNOCK wabsters, fidge an' claw,
 An' pour your creeshie nations;
An' ye wha leather rax an' draw,
 Of a' denominations;

Swith to the Laigh Kirk, ane an' a'
　An' there tak up your stations;
Then aff to Begbie's in a raw,
　An' pour divine libations
　　　　　For joy this day.

Curst "Common-sense," that imp o' hell,
　Cam in wi' Maggie Lauder;
But Oliphant aft made her yell,
　An' Russell sair misca'd her:
This day Mackinlay taks the flail,
　An' he's the boy will blaud her!
He'll clap a shangan on her tail,
　An' set the bairns to daud her
　　　　　Wi' dirt this day.

Mak haste an' turn King David owre,
　And lilt wi' holy clangor;
O' double verse come gie us four,
　An' skirl up the Bangor:
This day the kirk kicks up a stour,
　Nae mair the knaves shall wrang her,
For Heresy is in her pow'r,
　And gloriously she'll whang her
　　　　　Wi' pith this day.

Come, let a proper text be read,
　An' touch it aff wi' vigour,
How graceless Ham leugh at his dad,
　Which made Canaan a nigger;
Or Phineas drove the murdering blade,
　Wi' whore-abhorring rigour;
Or Zipporah, the scauldin jad,
　Was like a bluidy tiger
　　　　　I' th' inn that day.

There, try his mettle on the creed,
  And bind him down wi' caution,
That stipend is a carnal weed
  He taks but for the fashion;
And gie him o'er the flock to feed,
  And punish each transgression;
Especial, rams that cross the breed,
  Gie them sufficient threshin;
        Spare them nae day.

Now, auld Kilmarnock, cock thy tail,
  An' toss thy horns fu' canty;
Nae mair thou'lt rowt out-owre the dale,
  Because thy pasture's scanty;
For lapfu's large o' gospel kail
  Shall fill thy crib in plenty,
An' runts o' grace the pick an' wale,
  No gi'en by way o' dainty,
        But ilka day.

Nae mair by Babel's streams we'll weep,
  To think upon our Zion;
And hing our fiddles up to sleep,
  Like baby-clouts a-dryin!
Come, screw the pegs wi' tunefu' cheep,
  And o'er the thairms be tryin;
Oh, rare to see our elbucks wheep,
  And a' like lamb-tails flyin
        Fu' fast this day.

Lang, Patronage, with rod o' airn,
  Has shor'd the Kirk's undoin;
As lately Fenwick, sair forfairn,
  Has proven to its ruin:

Our patron, honest man ! Glencairn,
  He saw mischief was brewin ;
An' like a godly, elect bairn,
  He's waled us out a true ane,
           And sound, this day.

Now Robertson harangue nae mair,
  But steek your gab for ever ;
Or try the wicked town of Ayr,
  For there they'll think you clever :
Or, nae reflection on your lear,
  Ye may commence a shaver ;
Or to the Netherton repair,
  An' turn a carpet weaver
           Aff-hand this day.

Mu'trie and you were just a match,
  We never had sic twa drones ;
Auld Hornie did the Laigh Kirk watch,
  Just like a winkin baudrons,
And aye he catch'd the tither wretch,
  To fry them in his caudrons ;
But now his Honour maun detach,
  Wi' a' his brimstone squadrons,
           Fast, fast this day.

See, see auld Orthodoxy's faes
  She's swingein thro' the city !
Hark, how the nine-tail'd cat she plays !
  I vow it's unco pretty :
There, Learning, with his Greekish face,
  Grunts out some Latin ditty ;
And Common-sense is gaun, she says,
  To mak to Jamie Beattie
           Her plaint this day.

But there's Morality himsel',
　　Embracing all opinions;
Hear, how he gies the tither yell,
　　Between his twa companions!
See, how she peels the skin an' fell,
　　As ane were peelin onions!
Now there, they're packèd aff to hell,
　　An' banish'd our dominions,
　　　　　　　　Henceforth this day.

O happy day! rejoice, rejoice!
　　Come bouse about the porter!
Morality's demure decoys
　　Shall here nae mair find quarter:
Mackinlay, Russell, are the boys
　　That heresy can torture;
They'll gie her on a rape a hoyse,
　　And cowe her measure shorter
　　　　　　　By th' head some day

Come, bring the tither mutchkin in,
　　And here's—for a conclusion—
To ev'ry New-light mother's son,
　　From this time forth, confusion!
If mair they deave us wi' their din,
　　Or patronage intrusion,
We'll light a spunk, and ev'ry skin,
　　We'll rin them aff in fusion
　　　　　　　Like oil, some day.

EPISTLE TO JAMES SMITH

"Friendship, mysterious cement of the soul!
Sweet'ner of Life, and solder of Society!
I owe thee much——" BLAIR.

DEAR SMITH, the slee'st, pawkie thief,
That e'er attempted stealth or rief!

Ye surely hae some warlock-brief
          Owre human hearts ;
For ne'er a bosom yet was prief
          Against your arts.

For me, I swear by sun an' moon,
An' ev'ry star that blinks aboon,
Ye've cost me twenty pair o' shoon,
          Just gaun to see you ;
An' ev'ry ither pair that's done,
          Mair taen I'm wi' you.

That auld, capricious carlin, Nature.
To mak amends for scrimpit stature,
She's turn'd you off, a human creature
          On her first plan,
And in her freaks, on ev'ry feature
          She's wrote the Man.

Just now I've taen the fit o' rhyme,
My barmie noddle's working prime,
My fancy yerkit up sublime,
          Wi' hasty summon ;
Hae ye a leisure-moment's time
          To hear what's comin ?

Some rhyme a neibor's name to lash ;
Some rhyme (vain thought!) for needfu' cash ;
Some rhyme to court the countra clash,
          An' raise a din ;
For me, an aim I never fash ;
          I rhyme for fun.

The star that rules my luckless lot,
Has fated me the russet coat,

An' damn'd my fortune to the groat;
       But, in requit,
Has blest me with a random-shot
       O' countra wit.

This while my notion's taen a sklent,
To try my fate in guid, black prent;
But still the mair I'm that way bent,
       Something cries "Hoolie!
I red you, honest man, tak tent?
       Ye'll shaw your folly;

There's ither poets, much your betters,
Far seen in Greek, deep men o' letters,
Hae thought they had ensur'd their debtors,
       A' future ages;
Now moths deform, in shapeless tatters,
       Their unknown pages."

Then farewell hopes of laurel-boughs,
To garland my poetic brows!
Henceforth I'll rove where busy ploughs
       Are whistlin thrang,
An' teach the lanely heights an' howes
       My rustic sang.

I'll wander on, wi' tentless heed
How never-halting moments speed,
Till fate shall snap the brittle thread;
       Then, all unknown,
I'll lay me with th' inglorious dead,
       Forgot and gone!

But why o' death begin a tale?
Just now we're living sound and hale;

Then top and maintop crowd the sail,
      Heave Care o'er-side!
And large, before Enjoyment's gale,
      Let's tak the tide.

This life, sae far's I understand,
Is a' enchanted fairy-land,
Where Pleasure is the magic-wand,
      That, wielded right,
Maks hours like minutes, hand in hand,
      Dance by fu' light.

The magic-wand then let us wield;
For ance that five-an'-forty's speel'd,
See, crazy, weary, joyless eild,
      Wi' wrinkl'd face,
Comes hostin, hirplin owre the field,
      Wi' creepin pace.

When ance life's day draws near the gloamin,
Then fareweel vacant, careless roamin;
An' fareweel cheerfu' tankards foamin,
      An' social noise:
An' fareweel dear, deluding woman,
      The joy of joys!

O Life! how pleasant, in thy morning,
Young Fancy's rays the hills adorning!
Cold-pausing Caution's lesson scorning,
      We frisk away,
Like school-boys, at th' expected warning,
      To joy an' play.

We wander there, we wander here,
We eye the rose upon the brier,

Unmindful that the thorn is near,
                Among the leaves;
And tho' the puny wound appear,
                Short while it grieves.

Some, lucky, find a flow'ry spot,
For which they never toil'd nor swat;
They drink the sweet and eat the fat,
                But care or pain;
And haply eye the barren hut
                With high disdain.

With steady aim, some fortune chase;
Keen hope does ev'ry sinew brace;
Thro' fair, thro' foul, they urge the race,
                An' seize the prey:
Then cannie, in some cozie place,
                They close the day.

And others, like your humble servan',
Poor wights! nae rules nor roads observin,
To right or left eternal swervin,
                They zig-zag on;
Till, curst with age, obscure an' starvin,
                They aften groan.

Alas! what bitter toil an' straining—
But truce with peevish, poor complaining!
Is fortune's fickle *Luna* waning?
                E'en let her gang!
Beneath what light she has remaining,
                Let's sing our sang.

My pen I here fling to the door,
And kneel, ye Pow'rs! and warm implore,

"Tho' I should wander *Terra* o'er,
      In all her climes,
Grant me but this, I ask no more,
      Aye rowth o' rhymes.

"Gie dreepin roasts to countra lairds,
Till icicles hing frae their beards;
Gie fine braw claes to fine life-guards,
      And maids of honour;
An' yill an' whisky gie to cairds,
      Until they sconner.

"A title, Dempster merits it;
A garter gie to Willie Pitt;
Gie wealth to some be-ledger'd cit,
      In cent. per cent.;
But give me real, sterling wit,
      And I'm content.

"While ye are pleas'd to keep me hale,
I'll sit down o'er my scanty meal,
Be't water-brose or muslin-kail,
      Wi' cheerfu' face,
As lang's the Muses dinna fail
      To say the grace."

An anxious e'e I never throws
Behint my lug, or by my nose;
I jouk beneath Misfortune's blows
      As weel's I may;
Sworn foe to sorrow, care, and prose,
      I rhyme away.

O ye douce folk that live by rule,
Grave, tideless-blooded, calm an' cool,

Compar'd wi' you—O fool! fool! fool!
　　　　How much unlike!
Your hearts are just a standing pool,
　　　　Your lives, a dyke!

Nae hair-brain'd, sentimental traces
In your unletter'd, nameless faces!
In *arioso* trills and graces
　　　　Ye never stray;
But *gravissimo*, solemn basses
　　　　Ye hum away.

Ye are sae grave, nae doubt ye're wise;
Nae ferly tho' ye do despise
The hairum-scairum, ram-stam boys,
　　　　The rattling squad:
I see ye upward cast your eyes—
　　　　Ye ken the road!

Whilst I—but I shall haud me there,
Wi' you I'll scarce gang ony where—
Then, Jamie, I shall say nae mair,
　　　　But quat my sang,
Content wi' you to mak a pair.
　　　　Whare'er I gang.

THE VISION

DUAN FIRST

The sun had clos'd the winter day,
The curlers quat their roarin play,
And hunger'd maukin taen her way,
　　　　To kail-yards green,
While faithless snaws ilk step betray
　　　　Whare she has been.

E

The thresher's weary flinging-tree,
The lee-lang day had tirèd me;
And when the day had clos'd his e'e
            Far i' the west,
Ben i' the spence, right pensivelie,
            I gaed to rest.

There, lanely by the ingle-cheek,
I sat and ey'd the spewing reek,
That fill'd, wi' hoast-provoking smeek,
            The auld clay biggin;
An' heard the restless rattons squeak
            About the riggin.

All in this mottie, misty clime,
I backward mus'd on wasted time,
How I had spent my youthfu' prime,
            An' done nae thing,
But stringing blethers up in rhyme,
            For fools to sing.

Had I to guid advice but harkit,
I might, by this, hae led a market,
Or strutted in a bank and clarkit
            My cash-account;
While here, half-mad, half-fed, half-sarkit,
            Is a' th' amount.

I started, mutt'ring "blockhead! coof!"
And heav'd on high my waukit loof,
To swear by a' yon starry roof,
            Or some rash aith,
That I henceforth wad be rhyme-proof
            Till my last breath—

When click! the string the snick did draw;
An' jee! the door gaed to the wa';

The Vision

The Vision

"When click! the string the snick did draw;
And jee' the door gaed to the wa';
An' by my ingle-lowe I saw,
   Now bleezin bright,
A tight, outlandish hizzie, braw,
   Come full in sight."

An' by my ingle-lowe I saw,
        Now bleezin bright,
A tight, outlandish hizzie, braw,
        Come full in sight.

Ye need na doubt, I held my whisht;
The infant aith, half-form'd, was crusht;
I glowr'd as eerie's I'd been dusht
        In some wild glen;
When sweet, like honest Worth, she blusht,
        An' steppèd ben.

Green, slender, leaf-clad holly-boughs
Were twisted, gracefu', round her brows;
I took her for some Scottish Muse,
        By that same token;
And come to stop those reckless vows,
        Would soon be broken.

A "hair-brain'd, sentimental trace"
Was strongly markèd in her face;
A wildly-witty, rustic grace
        Shone full upon her;
Her eye, ev'n turn'd on empty space,
        Beam'd keen with honour.

Down flow'd her robe, a tartan sheen,
Till half a leg was scrimply seen;
An' such a leg! my bonie Jean
        Could only peer it;
Sae straught, sae taper, tight an' clean—
        Nane else came near it.

Her mantle large, of greenish hue,
My gazing wonder chiefly drew:
Deep lights and shades, bold-mingling, threw
        A lustre grand;

And seem'd, to my astonish'd view,
          A well-known land.

Here, rivers in the sea were lost;
There, mountains to the skies were toss't :
Here, tumbling billows mark'd the coast,
          With surging foam ;
There, distant shone Art's lofty boast,
          The lordly dome.

Here, Doon pour'd down his far-fetch'd floods ;
There, well-fed Irwine stately thuds :
Auld hermit Ayr staw thro' his woods,
          On to the shore ;
And many a lesser torrent scuds,
          With seeming roar.

Low, in a sandy valley spread,
An ancient borough rear'd her head ;
Still, as in Scottish story read,
          She boasts a race
To ev'ry nobler virtue bred,
          And polish'd grace.

By stately tow'r, or palace fair,
Or ruins pendent in the air,
Bold stems of heroes, here and there,
          I could discern ;
Some seem'd to muse, some seem'd to dare,
          With feature stern.

My heart did glowing transport feel,
To see a race heroic wheel,
And brandish round the deep-dyed steel,
          In sturdy blows ;

While, back-recoiling, seem'd to reel
      Their Suthron foes.

His Country's Saviour, mark him well !
Bold Richardton's heroic swell ;
The chief, on Sark who glorious fell,
      In high command ;
And he whom ruthless fates expel
      His native land.

There, where a sceptr'd Pictish shade
Stalk'd round his ashes lowly laid,
I mark'd a martial race, pourtray'd
      In colours strong :
Bold, soldier-featur'd, undismay'd,
      They strode along.

Thro' many a wild, romantic grove,
Near many a hermit-fancied cove
(Fit haunts for friendship or for love,
      In musing mood),
An aged Judge, I saw him rove,
      Dispensing good.

With deep-struck, reverential awe,
The learned Sire and Son I saw :
To Nature's God, and Nature's law,
      They gave their lore ;
This, all its source and end to draw,
      That, to adore.

Brydon's brave ward I well could spy,
Beneath old Scotia's smiling eye :
Who call'd on Fame, low standing by,
      To hand him on.

Where many a patriot-name on high,
   And hero shone.

DUAN SECOND.

With musing-deep, astonish'd stare,
I view'd the heavenly-seeming Fair;
A whispering throb did witness bear
   Of kindred sweet,
When with an elder sister's air
   She did me greet.

" All hail! my own inspirèd bard!
In me thy native Muse regard;
Nor longer mourn thy fate is hard,
   Thus poorly low;
I come to give thee such reward,
   As we bestow!

" Know, the great genius of this land
Has many a light aerial band,
Who, all beneath his high command,
   Harmoniously,
As arts or arms they understand,
   Their labours ply.

" They Scotia's race among them share:
Some fire the soldier on to dare;
Some rouse the patriot up to bare
   Corruption's heart:
Some teach the bard—a darling care—
   The tuneful art.

" 'Mong swelling floods of reeking gore,
They, ardent, kindling spirits pour;
Or, 'mid the venal senate's roar,
   They, sightless, stand,

To mend the honest patriot-lore,
   And grace the hand.

" And when the bard, or hoary sage,
Charm or instruct the future age,
They bind the wild poetic rage
   In energy,
Or point the inconclusive page
   Full on the eye.

" Hence, Fullarton, the brave and young ;
Hence, Dempster's zeal-inspirèd tongue ;
Hence, sweet, harmonious Beattie sung
   His ' Minstrel ' lays ;
Or tore, with noble ardour stung,
   The sceptic's bays.

" To lower orders are assign'd
The humbler ranks of human-kind,
The rustic bard, the lab'ring hind,
   The artisan ;
All choose, as various they're inclin'd,
   The various man.

" When yellow waves the heavy grain,
The threat'ning storm some strongly rein ;
Some teach to meliorate the plain
   With tillage-skill ;
And some instruct the shepherd-train,
   Blythe o'er the hill.

" Some hint the lover's harmless wile ;
Some grace the maiden's artless smile ;
Some soothe the lab'rer's weary toil
   For humble gains,

And make his cottage-scenes beguile
His cares and pains.

" Some, bounded to a district-space,
Explore at large man's infant race,
To mark the embryotic trace
Of rustic bard;
And careful note each opening grace,
A guide and guard.

" Of these am I—Coila my name:
And this district as mine I claim,
Where once the Campbells, chiefs of fame,
Held ruling pow'r:
I mark'd thy embryo-tuneful flame,
Thy natal hour.

" With future hope I oft would gaze
Fond, on thy little early ways,
Thy rudely caroll'd, chiming phrase,
In uncouth rhymes;
Fir'd at the simple, artless lays
Of other times.

" I saw thee seek the sounding shore,
Delighted with the dashing roar;
Or when the North his fleecy store
Drove thro' the sky,
I saw grim Nature's visage hoar
Struck thy young eye.

" Or when the deep green-mantled earth
Warm cherish'd ev'ry floweret's birth,
And joy and music pouring forth
In ev'ry grove;

I saw thee eye the general mirth
        With boundless love.

"When ripen'd fields and azure skies
Call'd forth the reapers' rustling noise,
I saw thee leave their ev'ning joys,
        And lonely stalk,
To vent thy bosom's swelling rise,
        In pensive walk.

"When youthful love, warm-blushing, strong,
Keen-shivering, shot thy nerves along,
Those accents grateful to thy tongue,
        Th' adorèd *Name*,
I taught thee how to pour in song,
        To soothe thy flame.

"I saw thy pulse's maddening play,
Wild send thee Pleasure's devious way,
Misled by Fancy's meteor-ray,
        By passion driven;
But yet the light that led astray
        Was light from Heaven.

"I taught thy manners-painting strains,
The loves, the ways of simple swains,
Till now, o'er all my wide domains
        Thy fame extends;
And some, the pride of Coila's plains,
        Become thy friends.

"Thou canst not learn, nor I can show,
To paint with Thomson's landscape glow;
Or wake the bosom-melting throe,
        With Shenstone's art;

E*

Or pour, with Gray, the moving flow
　　　Warm on the heart.

" Yet, all beneath th' unrivall'd rose,
The lowly daisy sweetly blows;
Tho' large the forest's monarch throws
　　　　His army shade,
Yet green the juicy hawthorn grows,
　　　Adown the glade.

" Then never murmur nor repine;
Strive in thy humble sphere to shine;
And trust me, not Potosi's mine,
　　　　Nor king's regard,
Can give a bliss o'ermatching thine,
　　　A rustic bard.

" To give my counsels all in one,
Thy tuneful flame still careful fan:
Preserve the dignity of Man,
　　　　With soul erect;
And trust the Universal Plan
　　　Will all protect.

" And wear thou *this* "—she solemn said,
And bound the holly round my head:
The polish'd leaves and berries red
　　　　Did rustling play;
And, like a passing thought, she fled
　　　In light away.

THE INVENTORY

IN ANSWER TO A MANDATE BY THE SURVEYOR
OF THE TAXES

Sir, as your mandate did request,
I send you here a faithfu' list,

O' gudes an' gear, an' a' my graith,
To which I'm clear to gi'e my aith.

Imprimis, then, for carriage cattle,
I hae four brutes o' gallant mettle,
As ever drew before a pettle.
My *hand-afore* 's a guid auld ' has been,'
An' wight an' wilfu' a' his days been:
My *hand-ahin* 's a weel gaun fillie,
That aft has borne me hame frae Killie,
An' your auld borough mony a time
In days when riding was nae crime.
But ance, when in my wooing pride
I, like a blockhead, boost to ride,
The wilfu' creature sae I pat to,
(Lord pardon a' my sins, an' that too!)
I play'd my fillie sic a shavie,
She's a' bedevil'd wi' the spavie.
My *furr-ahin* 's a wordy beast,
As e'er in tug or tow was traced.
The fourth's a Highland Donald hastie,
A damn'd red-wud Kilburnie blastie!
Forby a cowt, o' cowts the wale,
As ever ran before a tail:
Gin he be spar'd to be a beast,
He'll draw me fifteen pund at least.
Wheel-carriages I hae but few,
Three carts, an' twa are feckly new;
An auld wheelbarrow, mair for token,
Ae leg an' baith the trams are broken;
I made a poker o' the spin'le,
An' my auld mither brunt the trin'le.

For men, I've three mischievous boys,
Run-deils for rantin an' for noise;

A gaudsman ane, a thrasher t' other :
Wee Davock hauds the nowt in fother.
I rule them as I ought, discreetly,
An' aften labour them completely ;
An' aye on Sundays duly, nightly,
I on the " Questions " targe them tightly ;
Till, faith ! wee Davock's grown sae gleg,
Tho' scarcely langer than your leg,
He'll screed you aff ' Effectual calling,'
As fast as ony in the dwalling.

I've nane in female servant station,
(Lord keep me aye frae a' temptation !)
I hae nae wife—and that my bliss is,
An' ye have laid nae tax on misses ;
An' then, if kirk folks dinna clutch me,
I ken the deevils darena touch me.
Wi' weans I'm mair than weel contented,
Heav'n sent me ane mae than I wanted !
My sonsie, smirking, dear-bought Bess,
She stares the daddy in her face,
Enough of ought ye like but grace ;
But her, my bonie, sweet wee lady,
I've paid enough for her already ;
An' gin ye tax her or her mither,
By the Lord, ye'se get them a' thegither !

And now, remember, Mr Aiken,
Nae kind of licence out I'm takin :
Frae this time forth, I do declare
I'se ne'er ride horse nor hizzie mair ;
Thro' dirt and dub for life I'll paidle,
Ere I sae dear pay for a saddle ;

To a Louse

To a Louse

"O wad some Power the giftie gie us
To see oursels as ithers see us!"

My travel a' on foot I'll shank it,
I've sturdy bearers, Gude be thankit !
The kirk and you may tak you that,
It puts but little in your pat ;
Sae dinna put me in your beuk,
Nor for my ten white shillings leuk.

This list, wi' my ain hand I wrote it,
The day and date as under noted ;
Then know all ye whom it concerns,
Subscripsi huic,   ROBERT BURNS.
MOSSGIEL, *February* 22, 1786.

TO A LOUSE

ON SEEING ONE ON A LADY'S BONNET AT CHURCH

HA ! whaur ye gaun, ye crowlin ferlie ?
Your impudence protects you sairly ;
I canna say but ye strunt rarely,
          Owre gauze and lace ;
Tho', faith ! I fear ye dine but sparely
          On sic a place.

Ye ugly, creepin, blastit wonner,
Detested, shunn'd by saunt an' sinner,
How daur ye set your fit upon her—
          Sae fine a lady ?
Gae somewhere else and seek your dinner
          On some poor body.

Swith ! in some beggar's haffet squattle ;
There ye may creep, and sprawl, and sprattle,
Wi' ither kindred, jumping cattle,
          In shoals and nations ;

Whaur horn nor bane ne'er daur unsettle
          Your thick plantations.

Now haud you there, ye're out o' sight,
Below the fatt'rels, snug and tight;
Na, faith ye yet! ye'll no be right,
          Till ye've got on it—
The verra tapmost, tow'rin height
          O' Miss's bonnet.

My sooth! right bauld ye set your nose out,
As plump an' grey as ony groset:
O for some rank, mercurial rozet,
          Or fell, red smeddum,
I'd gie you sic a hearty dose o't,
          Wad dress your droddum.

I wad na been surpris'd to spy
You on an auld wife's flainen toy;
Or aiblins some bit duddie boy,
          On's wyliecoat;
But Miss's fine Lunardi! fye!
          How daur ye do't?

O Jeany, dinna toss your head,
An' set your beauties a' abread!
Ye little ken what cursed speed
          The blastie's makin:
Thae winks an' finger-ends, I dread,
          Are notice takin.

O wad some Power the giftie gie us
To see oursels as ithers see us!
It wad frae mony a blunder free us,
          An' foolish notion:
What airs in dress an' gait wad lea'e us,
          An' ev'n devotion!

TO A MOUNTAIN DAISY

ON TURNING ONE DOWN WITH THE PLOUGH, IN
APRIL 1786

WEE, modest, crimson-tippèd flow'r,
Thou's met me in an evil hour ;
For I maun crush amang the stour
   Thy slender stem :
To spare thee now is past my pow'r
   Thou bonie gem.

Alas ! it's no thy neibor sweet,
The bonie lark, companion meet,
Bending thee 'mang the dewy weet,
   Wi' spreckl'd breast !
When upward-springing, blythe, to greet
   The purpling east.

Cauld blew the bitter-biting north
Upon thy early, humble birth ;
Yet cheerfully thou glinted forth
   Amid the storm,
Scarce rear'd above the parent-earth
   Thy tender form.

The flaunting flow'rs our gardens yield,
High shelt'ring woods and wa's maun shield ;
But thou, beneath the random bield
   O' clod or stane,
Adorns the histie stibble field,
   Unseen, alane.

There, in thy scanty mantle clad,
Thy snawie bosom sun-ward spread,
Thou lifts thy unassuming head
   In humble guise ;
But now the share uptears thy bed,
   And low thou lies '

Such is the fate of artless maid,
Sweet flow'ret of the rural shade !
By love's simplicity betray'd,
   And guileless trust ;
Till she, like thee, all soil'd, is laid
   Low i' the dust.

Such is the fate of simple bard,
On life's rough ocean luckless starr'd !
Unskilful he to note the card
   Of prudent lore,
Till billows rage, and gales blow hard,
   And whelm him o'er !

Such fate to suffering worth is giv'n,
Who long with wants and woes has striv'n,
By human pride or cunning driv'n
   To mis'ry's brink ;
Till wrench'd of ev'ry stay but Heav'n,
   He, ruin'd, sink !

Ev'n thou who mourn'st the Daisy's fate,
That fate is thine—no distant date ;
Stern Ruin's plough-share drives elate,
   Full on thy bloom,
Till crush'd beneath the furrow's weight,
   Shall be thy doom !

TO RUIN

All hail, inexorable lord !
At whose destruction-breathing word,
 The mightiest empires fall !
Thy cruel, woe-delighted train,
The ministers of grief and pain,
 A sullen welcome, all !

To a Mountain Daisy

To a Mountain Daisy

"Wee, modest, crimson-tippèd
flower,
Thou's met me in an evil hour
For I maun crush amang the stour
Thy slender stem . . . "

With stern-resolv'd, despairing eye,
　I see each aimèd dart;
For one has cut my dearest tie,
　And quivers in my heart.
　　Then low'ring, and pouring,
　　　The storm no more I dread;
　　Tho' thick'ning, and black'ning,
　　　Round my devoted head.

And thou grim Pow'r by life abhorr'd,
While life a pleasure can afford,
　Oh! hear a wretch's pray'r!
No more I shrink appall'd, afraid;
I court, I beg thy friendly aid,
　To close this scene of care!
When shall my soul, in silent peace,
　Resign life's joyless day—
My weary heart its throbbings cease,
　Cold mould'ring in the clay?
　　No fear more, no tear more,
　　　To stain my lifeless face,
　　Enclaspèd, and graspèd,
　　　Within thy cold embrace!

THE LAMENT,

OCCASIONED BY THE UNFORTUNATE ISSUE OF A
FRIEND'S AMOUR.

" Alas! how oft does goodness wound itself,
And sweet affection prove the spring of woe!"
　　　　　　　　　　　　　　　　HOME.

O THOU pale orb that silent shines
　While care-untroubled mortals sleep!
Thou seest a wretch who inly pines,
　And wanders here to wail and weep!

With woe I nightly vigils keep,
Beneath thy wan, unwarming beam;
    And mourn, in lamentation deep,
How life and love are all a dream!

I joyless view thy rays adorn
    The faintly-markèd, distant hill;
I joyless view thy trembling horn,
    Reflected in the gurgling rill:
    My fondly-fluttering heart, be still!
Thou busy pow'r, remembrance, cease!
    Ah! must the agonizing thrill
For ever bar returning peace!

No idly-feign'd, poetic pains,
    My sad, love-lorn lamentings claim:
No shepherd's pipe—Arcadian strains;
    No fabled tortures, quaint and tame.
    The plighted faith, the mutual flame,
The oft-attested pow'rs above,
    The promis'd father's tender name;
These were the pledges of my love!

Encircled in her clasping arms,
    How have the raptur'd moments flown!
How have I wish'd for fortune's charms,
    For her dear sake, and her's alone!
    And, must I think it! is she gone,
My secret heart's exulting boast?
    And does she heedless hear my groan?
And is she ever, ever lost?

Oh! can she bear so base a heart,
    So lost to honour, lost to truth,
As from the fondest lover part,
    The plighted husband of her youth?

Alas! life's path may be unsmooth!
Her way may lie thro' rough distress!
　　Then, who her pangs and pains will soothe,
Her sorrows share, and make them less?

Ye wingèd hours that o'er us pass'd,
　　Enraptur'd more, the more enjoy'd,
Your dear remembrance in my breast
　　My fondly-treasur'd thoughts employ'd:
　　That breast, how dreary now, and void,
For her too scanty once of room!
　　Ev'n every ray of hope destroy'd,
And not a wish to gild the gloom!

The morn, that warns th' approaching day,
　　Awakes me up to toil and woe;
I see the hours in long array,
　　That I must suffer, lingering slow:
　　Full many a pang, and many a throe,
Keen recollection's direful train,
　　Must wring my soul, ere Phœbus, low,
Shall kiss the distant western main.

And when my nightly couch I try,
　　Sore harass'd out with care and grief,
My toil-beat nerves, and tear-worn eye,
　　Keep watchings with the nightly thief:
　　Or if I slumber, fancy, chief,
Reigns, haggard-wild, in sore affright:
　　Ev'n day, all-bitter, brings relief
From such a horror-breathing night.

O thou bright queen, who o'er th' expanse
　　Now highest reign'st, with boundless sway!
Oft has thy silent-marking glance
　　Observ'd us, fondly-wand'ring, stray!

The time, unheeded, sped away,
While love's luxurious pulse beat high,
    Beneath thy silver-gleaming ray,
To mark the mutual-kindling eye.

Oh! scenes in strong remembrance set!
    Scenes, never, never to return!
Scenes, if in stupor I forget,
    Again I feel, again I burn!
    From ev'ry joy and pleasure torn,
Life's weary vale I'll wander thro';
    And hopeless, comfortless, I'll mourn
A faithless woman's broken vow!

DESPONDENCY—AN ODE

Oppress'd with grief, oppress'd with care,
A burden more than I can bear,
    I set me down and sigh;
O life! thou art a galling load,
Along a rough, a weary road,
    To wretches such as I!
Dim-backward as I cast my view,
    What sick'ning scenes appear!
What sorrows yet may pierce me through,
    Too justly I may fear!
        Still caring, despairing,
            Must be my bitter doom;
        My woes here shall close ne'er
            But with the closing tomb!

Happy! ye sons of busy life,
Who, equal to the bustling strife,
    No other view regard!
Ev'n when the wishèd end's denied,
Yet while the busy means are plied,

They bring their own reward :
Whilst I, a hope-abandon'd wight,
   Unfitted with an aim,
Meet ev'ry sad returning night,
   And joyless morn the same !
     You, bustling and justling,
       Forget each grief and pain ;
     I, listless, yet restless,
       Find ev'ry prospect vain.

How blest the solitary's lot,
Who, all-forgetting, all forgot,
   Within his humble cell,
The cavern, wild with tangling roots,
Sits o'er his newly-gather'd fruits,
   Beside his crystal well !
Or haply, to his ev'ning thought,
   By unfrequented stream,
The ways of men are distant brought,
   A faint-collected dream ;
     While praising, and raising
       His thoughts to heav'n on high,
     As wand'ring, meand'ring,
       He views the solemn sky.

Than I, no lonely hermit plac'd
Where never human footstep trac'd,
   Less fit to play the part,
The lucky moment to improve,
And just to stop, and just to move,
   With self-respecting art :
But ah ! those pleasures, loves, and joys,
   Which I too keenly taste,
The solitary can despise,
   Can want, and yet be blest !

He needs not, he heeds not,
Or human love or hate;
Whilst I here must cry here
At perfidy ingrate!
O enviable early days,
When dancing thoughtless pleasure's maze,
To care, to guilt unknown!
How ill exchang'd for riper times,
To feel the follies, or the crimes,
Of others, or my own!
Ye tiny elves that guiltless sport,
Like linnets in the bush,
Ye little know the ills ye court,
When manhood is your wish!
The losses, the crosses,
That active man engage;
The fears all, the tears all,
Of dim declining Age!

EPISTLE TO A YOUNG FRIEND

May——, 1786.

I LANG hae thought, my youthfu' friend,
A something to have sent you,
Tho' it should serve nae ither end
Than just a kind memento:
But how the subject-theme may gang,
Let time and chance determine;
Perhaps it may turn out a sang:
Perhaps turn out a sermon.

Ye'll try the world soon my lad;
And, Andrew dear, believe me,
Ye'll find mankind an unco squad,
And muckle they may grieve ye:

For care and trouble set your thought,
  Ev'n when your end's attained;
And a' your views may come to nought,
  Where ev'ry nerve is strained.

I'll no say, men are villains a';
  The real, harden'd wicked,
Wha hae nae check but human law,
  Are to a few restricked;
But, och! mankind are unco weak,
  An' little to be trusted;
If *self* the wavering balance shake,
  It's rarely right adjusted!

Yet they wha fa' in fortune's strife,
  Their fate we shouldna censure;
For still, th' important end of life
  They equally may answer;
A man may hae an honest heart,
  Tho' poortith hourly stare him;
A man may tak a neibor's part,
  Yet hae nae cash to spare him.

Aye free, aff-han', your story tell,
  When wi' a bosom crony;
But still keep something to yoursel',
  Ye scarcely tell to ony:
Conceal yoursel' as weel's ye can
  Frae critical dissection;
But keek thro' ev'ry other man,
  Wi' sharpen'd, sly inspection.

The sacred lowe o' weel-plac'd love,
  Luxuriantly indulge it;
But never tempt th' illicit rove,
  Tho' naething should divulge it:

I waive the quantum o' the sin,
  The hazard of concealing;
But, och! it hardens a' within,
  And petrifies the feeling!

To catch dame Fortune's golden smile,
  Assiduous wait upon her;
And gather gear by ev'ry wile
  That's justified by honour;
Not for to hide it in a hedge,
  Nor for a train attendant;
But for the glorious privilege
  Of being independent.

The fear o' hell's a hangman's whip,
  To haud the wretch in order;
But where ye feel your honour grip,
  Let that aye be your border;
Its slightest touches, instant pause—
  Debar a' side-pretences;
And resolutely keep its laws,
  Uncaring consequences.

The great Creator to revere,
  Must sure become the creature;
But still the preaching cant forbear,
  And ev'n the rigid feature:
Yet ne'er with wits profane to range,
  Be complaisance extended;
An atheist-laugh's a poor exchange
  For Deity offended!

When ranting round in pleasure's ring,
  Religion may be blinded;
Or if she gie a random sting,
  It may be little minded;

But when on life we're tempest-driv'n—
 A conscience but a canker,
A correspondence fix'd wi' Heav'n,
 Is sure a noble anchor!

Adieu, dear, amiable youth!
 Your heart can ne'er be wanting!
May prudence, fortitude, and truth,
 Erect your brow undaunting!
In ploughman phrase, "God send you speed,"
 Still daily to grow wiser;
And may ye better reck the rede,
 Than ever did th' adviser!

ADDRESS OF BEELZEBUB

TO THE EARL OF BREADALBANE, PRESIDENT OF THE HIGHLAND SOCIETY

Long life, my lord, an' health be yours,
Unskaithed by hunger'd Highland boors;
Lord grant nae duddie, desperate beggar,
Wi' dirk, claymore, and rusty trigger,
May twin auld Scotland o' a life
She likes—as lambkins like a knife.

Faith you and Applecross were right
To keep the Highland hounds in sight:
I doubt na! they wad bid nae better,
Than let them ance out owre the water,
Then up among thae lakes and seas,
They'll mak what rules and laws they please:
Some daring Hancock, or a Franklin,
May set their Highland bluid a-ranklin;
Some Washington again may head them,
Or some Montgomery, fearless, lead them;

Till (God knows what may be effected
When by such heads and hearts directed)
Poor dunghill sons of dirt and mire
May to Patrician rights aspire!
Nae sage North now, nor sager Sackville,
To watch and premier o'er the pack vile,—
An' whare will ye get Howes and Clintons
To bring them to a right repentance—
To cowe the rebel generation,
An' save the honour o' the nation?
They, an' be damn'd! what right hae they
To meat, or sleep, or light o' day?
Far less to riches, pow'r, or freedom,
But what your lordship likes to gie them?

But hear, my lord! Glengary hear!
Your hand's owre light on them, I fear;
Your factors, grieves, trustees, and bailies,
I canna say but they do gaylies;
They lay aside a' tender mercies,
An' tirl the hullions to the birses;
Yet while they're only poind and herriet,
They'll keep their stubborn Highland spirit:
But smash them! crush them a' to spails,
An' rot the dyvors i' the jails!
The young dogs, swinge them to the labour;
Let wark an' hunger mak them sober!
The hizzies, if they're aughtlins fawsont,
Let them in Drury-Lane be lesson'd!
An' if the wives an' dirty brats
Come thiggin at your doors an' yetts,
Flaffin wi' duds, an' grey wi' beas',
Frightin away your ducks an' geese;
Get out a horsewhip or a jowler,

The langest thong, the fiercest growler,
An' gar the tatter'd gypsies pack
Wi' a' their bastards on their back!
Go on, my Lord! I lang to meet you,
An' in my house at hame to greet you;
Wi' common lords ye shanna mingle,
The benmost neuk beside the ingle,
At my right han' assigned your seat,
'Tween Herod's hip an' Polycrate:
Or (if you on your station tarrow),
Between Almagro and Pizarro,
A seat, I'm sure ye're weel deservin't;
An' till ye come—your humble servant,
                              BEELZEBUB.

HELL, *June 1st, Anno Mundi* 5790.

A DREAM

Thoughts, words, and deeds, the Statute blames with
  reason;
But surely *Dreams* were ne'er indicted Treason.

GUID-MORNIN' to your Majesty!
  May Heaven augment your blisses
On ev'ry new birth-day ye see,
  A humble poet wishes.
My bardship here, at your Levee
  On sic a day as this is,
Is sure an uncouth sight to see,
  Amang thae birth-day dresses
              Sae fine this day.

I see ye're complimented thrang,
  By mony a lord an' lady;
"God save the King" 's a cuckoo sang
  That's unco easy said aye:

The poets, too, a venal gang,
  Wi' rhymes weel-turn'd an' ready,
Wad gar you trow ye ne'er do wrang,
  But aye unerring steady,
          On sic a day.

For me! before a monarch's face,
  Ev'n there I winna flatter;
For neither pension, post, nor place,
  Am I your humble debtor:
So, nae reflection on your Grace,
  Your Kingship to bespatter;
There's mony waur been o' the race,
  And aiblins ane been better
          Than you this day.

'Tis very true, my sovereign King,
  My skill may weel be doubted;
But facts are chiels that winna ding,
  An' downa be disputed:
Your royal nest, beneath your wing,
  Is e'en right reft and clouted,
And now the third part o' the string,
  An' less, will gang about it
          Than did ae day.

Far be't frae me that I aspire
  To blame your legislation,
Or say, ye wisdom want, or fire,
  To rule this mighty nation:
But faith! I muckle doubt, my sire,
  Ye've trusted ministration
To chaps wha in a barn or byre
  Wad better fill'd their station
          Than courts yon day.

And now ye've gien auld Britain peace,
  Her broken shins to plaister,
Your sair taxation does her fleece,
  Till she has scarce a tester:
For me, thank God, my life's a lease,
  Nae bargain wearin faster,
Or faith! I fear, that, wi' the geese,
  I shortly boost to pasture
            I' the craft some day.

I'm no mistrusting Willie Pitt,
  When taxes he enlarges,
(An' Will's a true guid fallow's get,
  A name not envy spairges),
That he intends to pay your debt,
  An' lessen a' your charges;
But, God-sake! let nae saving fit
  Abridge your bonie barges
            An' boats this day.

Adieu, my Liege! may freedom geck
  Beneath your high protection;
An' may ye rax Corruption's neck,
  An' gie her for dissection!
But since I'm here, I'll no neglect,
  In loyal, true affection,
To pay your Queen, wi' due respect,
  My fealty an' subjection
            This great birth-day.

Hail, Majesty most Excellent!
  While nobles strive to please ye,
Will ye accept a compliment,
  A simple poet gies ye?

Thae bonie bairntime, Heav'n has lent,
 Still higher may they heeze ye
In bliss, till fate some day is sent,
 For ever to release ye
 Frae care that day.

For you, young Potentate o' Wales,
 I tell your highness fairly,
Down Pleasure's stream, wi' swelling sails,
 I'm tauld ye're driving rarely;
But some day ye may gnaw your nails,
 An' curse your folly sairly,
That e'er ye brak Diana's pales,
 Or rattl'd dice wi' Charlie
 By night or day.

Yet aft a ragged cowt's been known,
 To mak a noble aiver;
So, ye may doucely fill the throne,
 For a' their clish-ma-claver:
There, him at Agincourt wha shone,
 Few better were or braver:
And yet, wi' funny, queer Sir John,
 He was an unco shaver
 For mony a day.

For you, right rev'rend Osnaburg,
 Nane sets the lawn-sleeve sweeter,
Altho' a ribbon at your lug
 Wad been a dress completer:
As ye disown yon paughty dog,
 That bears the keys of Peter,
Then swith! an' get a wife to hug,
 Or trowth, ye'll stain the mitre
 Some luckless day!

Young, royal tarry-breeks, I learn,
  Ye've lately come athwart her—
A glorious galley, stem and stern,
  Weel rigg'd for Venus' barter;
But first hang out, that she'll discern,
  Your hymeneal charter;
Then heave aboard your grapple airn,
  An', large upon her quarter,
            Come full that day.

Ye, lastly, bonie blossoms a',
  Ye royal lasses dainty,
Heav'n mak you guid as weel as braw,
  An' gie you lads a-plenty!
But sneer na British boys awa!
  For kings are unco scant aye,
An' German gentles are but sma',
  They're better just than want aye
            On ony day.

God bless you a'! consider now,
  Ye're unco muckle dautit;
But ere the course o' life be through,
  It may be bitter sautit:
An' I hae seen their coggie fou,
  That yet hae tarrow't at it.
But or the day was done, I trow,
  The laggen they hae clautit
            Fu' clean that day.

A DEDICATION

TO GAVIN HAMILTON, ESQ.

EXPECT na, sir, in this narration,
A fleechin, fleth'rin Dedication,

To roose you up, an' ca' you guid,
An' sprung o' great an' noble bluid,
Because ye're surnam'd like His Grace—
Perhaps related to the race :
Then, when I'm tir'd and sae are ye
Wi' mony a fulsome, sinfu' lie,
Set up a face how I stop short,
For fear your modesty be hurt.

This may do—maun do, sir, wi' them wha
Maun please the great folk for a wamefou ;
For me ! sae laigh I need na bow,
For, Lord be thankit, I can plough ;
And when I downa yoke a naig,
Then, Lord be thankit, I can beg ;
Sae I shall say—an' that's nae flatt'rin—
It's just sic poet an' sic patron.

The Poet, some guid angel help him,
Or else, I fear, some ill ane skelp him !
He may do weel for a' he's done yet,
But only—he's no just begun yet.

The Patron (sir, ye maun forgie me ;
I winna lie, come what will o' me),
On ev'ry hand it will allow'd be,
He's just—nae better than he should be.

I readily, and freely grant,
He downa see a poor man want ;
What's no his ain, he winna tak it ;
What ance he says, he winna break it ;
Ought he can lend he'll no refus't,
Till aft his guidness is abus'd ;
And rascals whiles that do him wrang,
Ev'n that, he does na mind it lang ;

As master, landlord, husband, father,
He does na fail his part in either.

But then, nae thanks to him for a' that;
Nae godly symptom ye can ca' that;
It's naething but a milder feature
Of our poor, sinfu', corrupt nature:
Ye'll get the best o' moral works,
'Mang black Gentoos, and pagan Turks,
Or hunters wild on Ponotaxi,
Wha never heard of orthodoxy.
That he's the poor man's friend in need,
The gentleman in word and deed,
It's no thro' terror of damnation,
It's just a carnal inclination.

Morality, thou deadly bane,
Thy tens o' thousands thou hast slain!
Vain is his hope, whase stay an' trust is
In moral mercy, truth, and justice!

No—stretch a point to catch a plack:
Abuse a brother to his back;
Steal through the winnock frae a whore,
But point the rake that taks the door;
Be to the poor like ony whunstane,
And haud their noses to the grunstane;
Ply ev'ry art o' legal thieving;
No matter—stick to sound believing.

Learn three-mile pray'rs, an' half-mile graces,
Wi' weel-spread looves, an' lang, wry faces;
Grunt up a solemn, lengthen'd groan,
And damn a' parties but your own;
I'll warrant, then ye're nae deceiver,
A steady, sturdy, staunch believer

F

O ye wha leave the springs o' Calvin,
For gumlie dubs of your ain delvin!
Ye sons of Heresy and Error,
Ye'll some day squeel in quaking terror,
When Vengeance draws the sword in wrath,
And in the fire throws the sheath;
When Ruin, with his sweeping besom,
Just frets till Heav'n commission gies him;
While o'er the harp pale Misery moans,
And strikes the ever-deep'ning tones,
Still louder shrieks, and heavier groans!

Your pardon, sir, for this digression:
I maist forgat my Dedication;
But when divinity comes 'cross me,
My readers still are sure to lose me.

So, sir, you see 'twas nae daft vapour;
But I maturely thought it proper,
When a' my works I did review,
To dedicate them, sir, to you:
Because (ye need na tak it ill),
I thought them something like yoursel'.

Then patronize them wi' your favor,
And your petitioner shall ever——
I had amaist said, ever pray,
But that's a word I need na say;
For prayin, I hae little skill o't,
I'm baith dead-sweer, an' wretched ill o't;
But I'se repeat each poor man's pray'r,
That kens or hears about you, sir.——

"May ne'er Misfortune's gowling bark,
Howl thro' the dwelling o' the clerk!

May ne'er his gen'rous, honest heart,
For that same gen'rous spirit smart!
May Kennedy's far-honour'd name
Lang beet his hymeneal flame,
Till Hamiltons, at least a dizzen,
Are frae their nuptial labours risen :
Five bonie lasses round their table,
And sev'n braw fellows, stout an' able,
To serve their king an' country weel,
By word, or pen, or pointed steel!
May health and peace with mutual rays,
Shine on the ev'ning o' his days ;
Till his wee, curlie John's ier-oe,
When ebbing life nae mair shall flow,
The last, sad, mournful rites bestow! "

    I will not wind a lang conclusion,
With complimentary effusion;
But, whilst your wishes and endeavours
Are blest with Fortune's smiles and favours,
I am, dear sir, with zeal most fervent,
Your much indebted, humble servant.

    But if (which Pow'rs above prevent)
That iron-hearted carl, Want,
Attended, in his grim advances,
By sad mistakes, and black mischances,
While hopes, and joys, and pleasures fly him,
Make you as poor a dog as I am,
Your 'humble servant' then no more ;
For who would humbly serve the poor?
But, by a poor man's hopes in Heav'n!
While recollection's pow'r is giv'n—
If, in the vale of humble life,
The victim sad of fortune's strife,

I, thro' the tender-gushing tear,
Should recognise my master dear;
If friendless, low, we meet together,
Then, sir, your hand—my friend and brother!

ON A SCOTCH BARD

GONE TO THE WEST INDIES

A' ye wha live by sowps o' drink,
A' ye wha live by crambo-clink,
A' ye wha live and never think,
          Come, mourn wi' me!
Our billie's gien us a' a jink,
          An' owre the sea!

Lament him a' ye rantin' core,
Wha dearly like a random splore;
Nae mair he'll join the merry roar,
          In social key;
For now he's taen anither shore,
          An' owre the sea!

The bonie lasses weel may wiss him,
And in their dear petitions place him;
The widows, wives, an' a' may bless him
          Wi' tearfu' e'e;
For weel I wat they'll sairly miss him
          That's owre the sea!

O Fortune, they hae room to grumble!
Hadst thou taen aff some drowsy bummle,
Wha can do nought but fyke an' fumble,
          'Twad been nae plea;
But he was gleg as ony wumble,
          That's owre the sea!

Auld, cantie Kyle may weepers wear,
An' stain them wi' the saut, saut tear;
'Twill mak her poor auld heart, I fear,
      In flinders flee:
He was her Laureat mony a year,
        That's owre the sea!

He saw Misfortune's cauld nor-west
Lang mustering up a bitter blast;
A jillet brak his heart at last,
      Ill may she be!
So, took a berth afore the mast,
        An' owre the sea.

To tremble under Fortune's cummock,
On scarce a bellyfu' o' drummock,
Wi' his proud, independent stomach,
      Could ill agree;
So, row't his hurdies in a hammock,
        An' owre the sea.

He ne'er was gien to great misguidin,
Yet coin his pouches wad na bide in;
Wi' him it ne'er was under hidin;
      He dealt it free:
The Muse was a' that he took pride in,
        That's owre the sea.

Jamaica bodies, use him weel,
An' hap him in a cozie biel:
Ye'll find him aye a dainty chiel,
      An' fou o' glee:
He wad na wrang'd the vera deil,
        That's owre the sea.

Fareweel, my rhyme-composing billie!
Your native soil was right ill-willie;
But may ye flourish like a lily,
          Now bonilie!
I'll toast you in my hindmost gillie,
          Tho' owre the sea!

A BARD'S EPITAPH

Is there a whim-inspirèd fool,
Owre fast for thought, owre hot for rule,
Owre blate to seek, owre proud to snool,
          Let him draw near;
And owre this grassy heap sing dool,
          And drap a tear.

Is there a bard of rustic song,
Who, noteless, steals the crowds among,
That weekly this area throng,
          O, pass not by!
But, with a frater-feeling strong,
          Here heave a sigh.

Is there a man, whose judgment clear
Can others teach the course to steer,
Yet runs, himself, life's mad career,
          Wild as the wave,
Here pause—and, thro' the starting tear,
          Survey this grave.

The poor inhabitant below
Was quick to learn and wise to know,
And keenly felt the friendly glow,
          And softer flame;
But thoughtless follies laid him low,
          And stain'd his name!

Reader, attend ! whether thy soul
Soars fancy's flights beyond the pole,
Or darkling grubs this earthly hole,
    In low pursuit :
Know, prudent, cautious, self-control
    Is wisdom's root.

ADDRESS TO THE UNCO GUID

OR THE RIGIDLY RIGHTEOUS

My Son, these maxims make a rule,
  An' lump them aye thegither ;
The *Rigid Righteous* is a fool,
  The *Rigid Wise* anither :
The cleanest corn that ere was dight
  May hae some pyles o' caff in ;
So ne'er a fellow creature slight
  For random fits o' daffin.
    Solomon.—Eccles. ch. vii. verse 16.

O ye wha are sae guid yoursel',
  Sae pious and sae holy,
Ye've nought to do but mark and tell
  Your neibours' fauts and folly !
Whase life is like a weel-gaun mill,
  Supplied wi' store o' water ;
The heapèd happer's ebbing still,
  An' still the clap plays clatter.

Hear me, ye venerable core,
  As counsel for poor mortals
That frequent pass douce Wisdom's door
  For glaikit Folly's portals :
I, for their thoughtless, careless sakes,
  Would here propone defences—
Their donsie tricks, their black mistakes,
  Their failings and mischances.

Ye see your state wi' theirs compared,
  And shudder at the niffer;
But cast a moment's fair regard,
  What maks the mighty differ?
Discount what scant occasion gave,
  That purity ye pride in;
And (what's aft mair than a' the lave)
  Your better art o' hidin.

Think, when your castigated pulse
  Gies now and then a wallop,
What ragings must his veins convulse,
  That still eternal gallop!
Wi' wind and tide fair i' your tail,
  Right on ye scud your sea-way;
But in the teeth o' baith to sail,
  It maks a unco lee-way.

See Social Life and Glee sit down,
  All joyous and unthinking,
Till, quite transmugrified, they're grown
  Debauchery and Drinking:
O would they stay to calculate
  Th' eternal consequences;
Or your more dreaded hell to state,
  Damnation of expenses!

Ye high, exalted, virtuous dames,
  Tied up in godly laces,
Before ye gie poor Frailty names,
  Suppose a change o' cases;
A dear-lov'd lad, convenience snug,
  A treach'rous inclination—
But let me whisper i' your lug,
  Ye're aiblins nae temptation.

Then gently scan your brother man,
  Still gentler sister woman ;
Tho' they may gang a kennin wrang,
  To step aside is human ;
One point must still be greatly dark,—
  The moving *Why* they do it ;
And just as lamely can ye mark,
  How far perhaps they rue it.

Who made the heart, 'tis He alone
  Decidedly can try us ;
He knows each chord, its various tone,
  Each spring, its various bias :
Then at the balance let's be mute,
  We never can adjust it ;
What's done we partly may compute,
  But know not what's resisted.

NATURE'S LAW—A POEM

HUMBLY INSCRIBED TO GAVIN HAMILTON, ESQ.

"Great Nature spoke : observant man obey'd."—POPE

LET other heroes boast their scars,
  The marks of sturt and strife :
And other poets sing of wars,
  The plagues of human life ;
Shame fa' the fun, wi' sword and gun
  To slap mankind like lumber !
I sing his name, and nobler fame,
  Wha multiplies our number.

Great Nature spoke, with air benign,
  " Go on, ye human race ;
This lower world I you resign ;
  Be fruitful and increase.

F*

The liquid fire of strong desire
 I've pour'd it in each bosom;
Here, on this hand, does Mankind stand,
 And there is Beauty's blossom."

The Hero of these artless strains,
 A lowly bard was he,
Who sung his rhymes in Coila's plains,
 With meikle mirth an' glee;
Kind Nature's care had given his share
 Large, of the flaming current;
And, all devout, he never sought
 To stem the sacred torrent.

He felt the powerful, high behest,
 Thrill, vital, thro' and thro';
And sought a correspondent breast,
 To give obedience due:
Propitious Powers screen'd the young flow'rs
 From mildews of abortion;
And lo! the bard—a great reward—
 Has got a double portion!

Auld cantie Coil may count the day,
 As annual it returns,
The third of Libra's equal sway,
 That gave another Burns,
With future rhymes, an' other times,
 To emulate his sire:
To sing auld Coil in nobler style,
 With more poetic fire.

Ye Powers of peace and peaceful song,
 Look down with gracious eyes;
And bless auld Coila, large and long,
 With multiplying joys;

Lang may she stand to prop the land,
The flow'r of ancient nations;
And Burnses spring, her fame to sing,
To endless generations!

REPLY TO A TRIMMING EPISTLE
RECEIVED FROM A TAILOR

WHAT ails ye now, ye lousie bitch,
To thresh my back at sic a pitch?
Losh, man! hae mercy wi' your natch,
Your bodkin's bauld,
I didna suffer half sae much
Frae Daddie Auld.

What tho' at times, when I grow crouse,
I gie their wames a random pouse,
Is that enough for you to souse
Your servant sae?
Gae mind your seam, ye prick-the-louse
An' jag-the-flea!

King David, o' poetic brief,
Wrocht 'mang the lasses sic mischief
As filled his after-life wi' grief,
An' bluidy rants,
An' yet he's rank'd among the chief
O' lang-syne saunts.

And maybe, Tam, for a' my cants,
My wicked rhymes, an' drucken rants,
I'll gie auld cloven Clootie's haunts
An unco slip yet,
An' snugly sit amang the saunts,
At Davie's hip yet!

But, fegs ! the session says I maun
Gae fa' upo' anither plan
Than garrin lasses coup the cran,
   Clean heels ower body,
An' sairly thole their mother's ban
   Afore the howdy.

This leads me on to tell for sport,
How I did wi' the Session sort ;
Auld Clinkum, at the inner port,
   Cried three times, " Robin !
Come hither lad, and answer for't,
   Ye're blam'd for jobbin ! "

Wi' pinch I put a Sunday's face on,
An' snoov'd awa before the Session :
I made an open, fair confession—
   I scorn'd to lee,
An' syne Mess John beyond expression,
   Fell foul o' me.

A fornicator-loun he call'd me,
An' said my faut frae bliss expell'd me ;
I own'd the tale was true he tell'd me,
   " But, what the matter ?
(Quo' I) I fear unless ye geld me,
   I'll ne'er be better ! "

" Geld you ! (quo' he) an' what for no ?
If that your right hand, leg, or toe
Should ever prove your sp'ritual foe,
   You should remember
To cut it aff—an' what for no
   Your dearest member ? "

The Brigs of Ayr

From an engraving after David Octavius Hill

" Na, na, (quo' I,) I'm no' for that,
Gelding's nae better than 'tis ca't ;
I'd rather suffer for my faut
            A hearty flewit,
As sair owre hip as ye can draw't,
            Tho' I should rue it.

" Or, gin ye like to end the bother,
To please us a'—I've just ae ither—
When next wi' yon lass I forgather,
            Whate'er betide it,
I'll frankly gie her't a' thegither,
            An' let *her* guide it."

But, sir, this pleas'd them warst of a',
An' therefore, Tam, when that I saw,
I said " Gude night," an' cam' awa',
            An' left the Session ;·
I saw they were resolvèd a'
            On my oppression.

THE BRIGS OF AYR

A POEM

Inscribed to JOHN BALLANTINE, Esq., Ayr

THE simple Bard, rough at the rustic plough,
Learning his tuneful trade from ev'ry bough ;
The chanting linnet, or the mellow thrush,
Hailing the setting sun, sweet, in the green thorn
      bush ;
The soaring lark, the perching red-breast shrill,
Or deep-ton'd plovers grey, wild whistling o'er
      the hill ;
Shall he—nurst in the peasant's lowly shed,
To hardy independence bravely bred,

By early poverty to hardship steel'd,
And train'd to arms in stern Misfortune's field—
Shall he be guilty of their hireling crimes,
The servile, mercenary Swiss of rhymes?
Or labour hard the panegyric close,
With all the venal soul of dedicating prose?
No! though his artless strains he rudely sings,
And throws his hand uncouthly o'er the strings,
He glows with all the spirit of the Bard,
Fame, honest fame, his great, his dear reward.
Still, if some patron's gen'rous care he trace,
Skill'd in the secret to bestow with grace;
When Ballantine befriends his humble name,
And hands the rustic stranger up to fame,
With heartfelt throes his grateful bosom swells,
The godlike bliss, to give, alone excels.

'Twas when the stacks get on their winter hap,
And thack and rape secure the toil-won crap;
Potatoe-bings are snuggèd up frae skaith
O' coming Winter's biting, frosty breath;
The bees, rejoicing o'er their summer toils,
Unnumber'd buds' an' flow'rs' delicious spoils,
Seal'd up with frugal care in massive waxen piles,
Are doom'd by Man, that tyrant o'er the weak,
The death o' devils, smoor'd wi' brimstone reek.
The thundering guns are heard on ev'ry side,
The wounded coveys, reeling, scatter wide;
The feather'd field-mates, bound by Nature's tie,
Sires, mothers, children, in one carnage lie:
(What warm, poetic heart but inly bleeds,
And execrates man's savage, ruthless deeds!)
Nae mair the flow'r in field or meadow springs,
Nae mair the grove with airy concert rings,

Except perhaps the Robin's whistling glee,
Proud o' the height o' some bit half-lang tree :
The hoary morns precede the sunny days,
Mild, calm, serene, wide spreads the noontide
　　blaze,
While thick the gossamour waves wanton in the
　　rays.

'Twas in that season, when a simple Bard,
Unknown and poor—simplicity's reward!—
Ae night, within the ancient brugh of Ayr,
By whim inspir'd, or haply prest wi' care,
He left his bed, and took his wayward route,
And down by *Simpson's* wheel'd the left about :
(Whether impell'd by all-directing Fate,
To witness what I after shall narrate ;
Or whether, rapt in meditation high,
He wander'd out, he knew not where or why :)
The drowsy Dungeon-clock had number'd two,
And Wallace Tower had sworn the fact was
　　true :
The tide-swoln firth, with sullen-sounding roar,
Through the still night dash'd hoarse along the
　　shore ;
All else was hush'd as Nature's closèd e'e ;
The silent moon shone high o'er tower and tree ;
The chilly frost, beneath the silver beam,
Crept, gently-crusting, o'er the glittering stream—

When, lo ! on either hand the list'ning Bard,
The clanging sugh of whistling wings is heard ;
Two dusky forms dart through the midnight air,
Swift as the gos drives on the wheeling hare ;
Ane on th' Auld Brig his airy shape uprears,
The other flutters o'er the rising piers :

Our warlock Rhymer instantly descried
The Sprites that owre the Brigs of Ayr preside.
(That Bards are second-sighted is nae joke,
And ken the lingo of the sp'ritual folk;
Fays, Spunkies, Kelpies, a', they can explain
    them,
And even the very diels they brawly ken them).
'Auld Brig' appear'd of ancient Pictish race,
The very wrinkles Gothic in his face;
He seem'd as he wi' Time had warstl'd lang,
Yet, teughly doure, he bade an unco bang.
'New Brig' was buskit in a braw new coat,
That he, at Lon'on, frae ane Adams got;
In 's hand five taper staves as smooth 's a bead,
Wi' virls and whirlygigums at the head.
The Goth was stalking round with anxious search,
Spying the time-worn flaws in every arch;
It chanc'd his new-come neibor took his e'e,
And e'en a vexed and angry heart had he!
Wi' thieveless sneer to see his modish mien,
He, down the water, gies him this guid-e'en :—

AULD BRIG.

'I doubt na, frien', ye'll think ye're nae sheep-
    shank,
Ance ye were streekit owre frae bank to bank!
But gin ye be a brig as auld as me—
Tho' faith, that date, I doubt, ye'll never see—
There'll be, if that day come, I'll wad a boddle,
Some fewer whigmaleeries in your noddle.'

NEW BRIG.

'Auld Vandal! ye but show your little mense,
Just much about it wi' your scanty sense:

Will your poor, narrow foot-path of a street,
Where twa wheel-barrows tremble when they meet,
Your ruin'd, formless bulk o' stane and lime,
Compare wi' bonie brigs o' modern time ?
There's men of taste wou'd tak the Ducat stream,
Tho' they should cast the very sark and swim,
E'er they would grate their feelings wi' the view
O' sic an ugly, Gothic hulk as you.'

AULD BRIG.

'Conceited gowk ! puff'd up wi' windy pride !
This mony a year I've stood the flood an' tide ;
And tho' wi' crazy eild I'm sair forfairn,
I'll be a brig when ye're a shapeless cairn !
As yet ye little ken about the matter,
But twa-three winters will inform ye better.
When heavy, dark, continued, a'-day rains,
Wi' deepening deluges o'erflow the plains ;
When from the hills where springs the brawling
    Coil,
Or stately Lugar's mossy fountains boil ;
Or where the Greenock winds his moorland
    course,
Or haunted Garpal draws his feeble source,
Aroused by blustering winds an' spotting thowes,
In mony a torrent down the snaw-broo rowes ;
While crashing ice, borne on the rolling spate,
Sweeps dams, an' mills, an' brigs, a' to the gate ;
And from Glenbuck, down to the Ratton-key,
Auld Ayr is just one lengthen'd, tumbling sea—
Then down ye'll hurl, (deil nor ye never rise !)
And dash the gumlie jaups up to the pouring skies !
A lesson sadly teaching, to your cost,
That Architecture's noble art is lost ! '

NEW BRIG.

'Fine architecture, trowth, I needs must say't o't,
The Lord be thankit that we've tint the gate o't!
Gaunt, ghastly, ghaist-alluring edifices,
Hanging with threat'ning jut like precipices;
O'er-arching, mouldy, gloom-inspiring coves,
Supporting roofs, fantastic, stony groves;
Windows and doors in nameless sculptures drest,
With order, symmetry, or taste unblest;
Forms like some bedlam Statuary's dream,
The craz'd creations of misguided whim;
Forms might be worshipp'd on the bended knee,
And still the second dread command be free;
Their likeness is not found on earth, in air, or sea!
Mansions that would disgrace the building taste
Of any mason reptile, bird, or beast:
Fit only for a doited monkish race,
Or frosty maids forsworn the dear embrace,
Or cuifs of later times, wha held the notion,
That sullen gloom was sterling true devotion:
Fancies that our guid Brugh denies protection,
And soon may they expire, unblest wi' resurrec-
    tion!'

AULD BRIG.

'O ye, my dear-remember'd, ancient yealings,
Were ye but here to share my wounded feelings!
Ye worthy Proveses, an' mony a Bailie,
Wha in the paths o' righteousness did toil aye;
Ye dainty Deacons, and ye douce Conveners,
To whom our moderns are but causey-cleaners;
Ye godly Councils, wha hae blest this town;
Ye godly Brethren o' the sacred gown,

Wha meekly gie your hurdies to the smiters;
And (what would now be strange), ye godly
    Writers;
A' ye douce folk I've borne aboon the broo,
Were ye but here, what would ye say or do?
How would your spirits groan in deep vexation,
To see each melancholy alteration;
And, agonising, curse the time and place
When ye begat the base degenerate race!
Nae langer rev'rend men, their country's glory,
In plain braid Scots hold forth a plain braid
    story;
Nae langer thrifty citizens, an' douce,
Meet owre a pint, or in the Council-house;
But staumrel, corky-headed, graceless *Gentry*,
The herryment and ruin of the country;
Men, three-parts made by tailors and by barbers,
Wha waste your weel-hain'd gear on d—'d new
    brigs and harbours!'

NEW BRIG.

'Now haud you there! for faith ye've said
    enough,
And muckle mair than ye can mak to through.
As for your Priesthood, I shall say but little,
Corbies and *Clergy* are a shot right kittle:
But, under favour o' your langer beard,
Abuse o' Magistrates might weel be spar'd;
To liken them to your auld-warld squad,
I must needs say, comparisons are odd.
In Ayr, wag-wits nae mair can hae a handle
To mouth " a Citizen," a term o' scandal;
Nae mair the Council waddles down the street,
In all the pomp of ignorant conceit;

Men wha grew wise priggin owre hops and raisins,
Or gather'd lib'ral views in Bonds and Seisins :
If haply Knowledge, on a random tramp,
Had shor'd them with a glimmer of his lamp,
And would to Common-sense for once betray'd
      them,
Plain, dull Stupidity stept kindly in to aid them.'

What farther clish-ma-claver might been said,
What bloody wars, if Sprites had blood to shed,
No man can tell ; but, all before their sight,
A fairy train appear'd in order bright ;
Adown the glittering stream they featly danc'd ;
Bright to the moon their various dresses glanc'd :
They footed o'er the wat'ry glass so neat,
The infant ice scarce bent beneath their feet :
While arts of Minstrelsy among them rung,
And soul-ennobling Bards heroic ditties sung.

O had M'Lauchlan, thairm-inspiring sage,
Been there to hear this heavenly band engage,
When thro' his dear strathspeys they bore with
      Highland rage ;
Or when they struck old Scotia's melting airs,
The lover's raptured joys or bleeding cares ;
How would his Highland lug been nobler fir'd,
And ev'n his matchless hand with finer touch
      inspir'd !
No guess could tell what instrument appear'd,
But all the soul of Music's self was heard ;
Harmonious concert rung in every part,
While simple melody pour'd moving on the heart.

The Genius of the Stream in front appears,
A venerable Chief advanc'd in years ;

Address to the Toothache

Address to the Toothache

"My curse upon your venom'd stang,
That shoots my tortur'd gooms alang . . . "

His hoary head with water-lilies crown'd,
His manly leg with garter-tangle bound.
Next came the loveliest pair in all the ring,
Sweet female Beauty hand in hand with Spring;
Then, crown'd with flow'ry hay, came Rural
    Joy,
And Summer, with his fervid-beaming eye;
All-cheering Plenty, with her flowing horn,
Led yellow Autumn wreath'd with nodding
    corn;
Then Winter's time-bleach'd locks did hoary
    show,
By Hospitality with cloudless brow:
Next followed Courage with his martial stride,
From where the Feal wild-woody coverts hide;
Benevolence, with mild, benignant air,
A female form, came from the tow'rs of Stair;
Learning and Worth in equal measures trode,
From simple Catrine, their long-lov'd abode:
Last, white-rob'd Peace, crown'd with a hazel
    wreath,
To rustic Agriculture did bequeath
The broken, iron instruments of death:
At sight of whom our Sprites forgat their kind-
    ling wrath.

ADDRESS TO THE TOOTHACHE

My curse upon your venom'd stang,
That shoots my tortur'd gooms alang,
An' thro' my lug gies monie a twang,
        Wi' gnawing vengeance,
Tearing my nerves wi' bitter pang,
          Like racking engines!

A' down my beard the slavers trickle,
I throw the wee stools o'er the mickle,
While round the fire the giglets keckle,
    To see me loup,
An', raving mad, I wish a heckle
    Were i' their doup!

When fevers burn, or agues freeze us,
Rheumatics gnaw, or colics squeeze us,
Our neibor's sympathy may ease us,
    Wi' pitying moan;
But thee!—thou hell o' a' diseases—
    They mock our groan.

Of a' the numerous human dools,
Ill hairsts, daft bargains, cutty stools,
Or worthy frien's rak'd i' the mools—
    Sad sight to see!
The tricks o' knaves, or fash o' fools,
    Thou bear'st the gree!

Where'er that place be priests ca' hell,
Where a' the tones o' misery yell,
An' rankèd plagues their numbers tell,
    In dreadfu' raw,
Thou, TOOTHACHE, surely bear'st the bell,
    Amang them a'!

O thou grim, mischief-making chiel,
That gars the notes o' discord squeel,
Till daft mankind aft dance a reel
    In gore, a shoe-thick,
Gie a' the faes o' SCOTLAND's weal
    A towmond's toothache!

LINES ON MEETING WITH
LORD DAER

THIS wot ye all whom it concerns,
I, Rhymer Rab, alias Burns,
        October twenty-third,
A ne'er-to-be-forgotten day,
Sae far I sprachl'd up the brae,
        I dinner'd wi' a Lord.

I've been at drucken Writers' feasts,
Nay, been bitch-fou 'mang godly Priests—
        Wi' rev'rence be it spoken!—
I've even join'd the honour'd jorum,
When mighty Squireships of the quorum,
        Their hydra drouth did sloken.

But wi' a Lord!—stand out my shin!
A Lord—a Peer—an Earl's son!
        Up higher yet, my bonnet!
An' sic a Lord! lang Scotch ell twa,
Our Peerage he looks o'er them a',
        As I look o'er my sonnet.

But O for Hogarth's magic pow'r!
To show Sir Bardie's willyart glow'r,
        An' how he star'd and stammer'd,
When, goavin, 's he'd been led wi' branks,
An' stumpin on his ploughman shanks.
        He in the parlour hammer'd,

To meet good Stewart little pain is,
Or Scotia's sacred Demosthenes:
        Thinks I: 'They are but men!'

But 'Burns!'—'My Lord!'—Good God! I
  doited;
My knees on ane anither knoited
            As faultering I gaed ben.

I sidling shelter'd in a neuk,
An' at his Lordship staw a leuk,
            Like some portentous omen;
Except good sense and social glee,
An' (what surpris'd me) modesty,
            I markèd nought uncommon.

I watch'd the symptoms o' the Great,
The gentle pride, the lordly state,
            The arrogant assuming;
The fient a pride, nae pride had he,
Nor sauce, nor state, that I could see,
            Mair than an honest ploughman.

Then from his Lordship I shall learn,
Henceforth to meet with unconcern
            One rank as well's another;
Nae honest, worthy man need care
To meet with noble youthfu' Daer,
            For he but meets a brother.

TAM SAMSON'S ELEGY

"An honest man's the noblest work of God."—POPE.

HAS auld Kilmarnock seen the deil?
Or great Mackinlay thrawn his heel?
Or Robertson again grown weel,
            To preach an' read?
"Na, waur than a'!" cries ilka chiel,
            "Tam Samson's dead!"

Kilmarnock lang may grunt an' grane,
An' sigh, an' sab, an' greet her lane,
An' cleed her bairns, man, wife, an' wean,
          In mourning weed;
To Death she's dearly pay'd the kane—
          Tam Samson's dead!

The Brethren, o' the mystic 'level'
May hing their head in woefu' bevel,
While by their nose the tears will revel,
          Like ony bead;
Death's gien the Lodge an unco devel;
          Tam Samson's dead!

When Winter muffles up his cloak,
And binds the mire like a rock;
When to the loughs the curlers flock,
          Wi' gleesome speed,
Wha will they station at the 'cock'?
          Tam Samson's dead!

He was the king o' a' the core,
To guard, or draw, or wick a bore,
Or up the rink like Jehu roar,
          In time o' need;
But now he lags on Death's 'hog-score'—
          Tam Samson's dead!

Now safe the stately sawmont sail,
And trouts bedropp'd wi' crimson hail,
And eels, weel-ken'd for souple tail,
          And geds for greed,
Since, dark in Death's fish-creel, we wail
          Tam Samson dead!

Rejoice, ye birring paitricks a' ;
Ye cootie muircocks, crousely craw ;
Ye maukins, cock your fud fu' braw
            Withouten dread ;
Your mortal fae is now awa ;
            Tam Samson's dead !

That woefu' morn be ever mourn'd,
Saw him in shooting graith adorn'd,
While pointers round impatient burn'd,
            Frae couples free'd ;
But och ! he gaed and ne'er return'd !
            Tam Samson's dead !

In vain auld age his body batters,
In vain the gout his ancles fetters,
In vain the burns cam down like waters,
            An acre braid !
Now ev'ry auld wife, greetin, clatters
            " Tam Samson's dead ! "

Owre mony a weary hag he limpit,
An' aye the tither shot he thumpit,
Till coward Death behind him jumpit,
            Wi' deadly feid ;
Now he proclaims wi' tout o' trumpet,
            " Tam Samson's dead ! "

When at his heart he felt the dagger,
He reel'd his wonted bottle-swagger,
But yet he drew the mortal trigger,
            Wi' weel-aimed heed ;
"Lord, five ! " he cry'd, an' owre did stagger—
            Tam Samson's dead !

Tam Samson's Elegy

Tam Samson's Elegy

"Heav'n rest his saul whare'er he be!
Is the wish of mony mae than me . . . "

Ilk hoary hunter mourn'd a brither ;
Ilk sportsman youth bemoan'd a father ;
Yon auld gray stane, amang the heather,
          Marks out his head ;
Whare Burns has wrote, in rhyming blether,
          " Tam Samson's Dead ! "

There, low he lies in lasting rest ;
Perhaps upon his mould'ring breast
Some spitefu' muirfowl bigs her nest
          To hatch an' breed :
Alas ! nae mair he'll them molest !
          Tam Samson's dead !

When August winds the heather wave,
And sportsmen wander by yon grave,
Three volleys let his memory crave,
          O' pouther an' lead,
Till Echo answer frae her cave,
          " Tam Samson's dead ! "

Heav'n rest his saul whare'er he be !
Is th' wish o' mony mae than me :
He had twa fauts, or maybe three,
          Yet what remead ?
Ae social, honest man want we :
          Tam Samson's dead !

THE EPITAPH.

Tam Samson's weel-worn clay here lies
Ye canting zealots, spare him !
If honest worth in Heaven rise,
Ye'll mend or ye win near him.

PER CONTRA.

Go, Fame, an' canter like a filly
Thro' a' the streets an' neuks o' Killie ;

Tell ev'ry social honest billie
　　　　To cease his grievin ;
For, yet unskaithed by Death's gleg gullie,
　　　　Tam Samson's leevin !

EPISTLE TO MAJOR LOGAN

Hail, thairm-inspirin, rattlin Willie !
Tho' fortune's road be rough an' hilly
To every fiddling, rhyming billie,
　　　　　　We never heed,
But take it like the unbrack'd filly,
　　　　　　Proud o' her speed.

When, idly goavin, whiles we saunter,
Yirr ! fancy barks, awa we canter,
Up hill, down brae, till some mischanter,
　　　　　　Some black bog-hole,
Arrests us ; then the scathe an' banter
　　　　　　We're forced to thole.

Hale be your heart ; hale be your fiddle !
Lang may your elbuck jink and diddle,
To cheer you through the weary widdle
　　　　　　O' this vile warl'.
Until you on a crummock driddle,
　　　　　　A grey-hair'd carl.

Come wealth, come poortith late or soon,
Heaven send your heart-strings aye in tune,
And screw your temper-pins aboon
　　　　　　(A fifth or mair)
The melancholious, sairie croon
　　　　　　O' cankrie care.

May still your life from day to day,
Nae *lente largo* in the play,
But *allegretto forte* gay,
                    Harmonious flow,
A sweeping, kindling, bauld strathspey—
                    Encore ! Bravo !

A' blessings on the cheery gang
Wha dearly like a jig or sang,
An' never think o' right an' wrang
                    By square an' rule,
But, as the clegs o' feeling stang,
                    Are wise or fool.

My hand-waled curse keep hard in chase
The harpy, hoodock, purse-proud race,
Wha count on poortith as disgrace ;
                    Their tuneless hearts,
May fireside discords jar a base
                    To a' their parts !

But come, your hand, my careless brither,
I' th' ither warl', if there's anither,
(An' that there is, I've little swither
                    About the matter)
We, cheek for chow, shall jog thegither ;
                    I'se ne'er bid better.

We've faults and failings—granted clearly,
We're frail backsliding mortals merely,
Eve's bonie squad, priests wyte them sheerly
                    For our grand fa' ;
But still, but still—I like them dearly ;
                    God bless them a' !

Ochon for poor Castalian drinkers,
When they fa' foul o' earthly jinkers!
The witching, curs'd, delicious blinkers
         Hae put me hyte,
And gart me weet my waukrife winkers,
         Wi' girnin spite.

But by yon moon!—and that's high swearin—
An' every star within my hearin!
An' by her een wha was a dear ane!
         I'll ne'er forget;
I hope to gie the jads a clearin
         In fair play yet.

My loss I mourn, but not repent it;
I'll seek my pursie whare I tint it;
Ance to the Indies I were wonted,
         Some cantrip hour
By some sweet elf I'll yet be dinted;
         Then *vive l'amour!*

Faites mes baissemains respectueusè
To sentimental sister Susie,
And honest Lucky; no to roose you,
         Ye may be proud,
That sic a couple fate allows ye,
         To grace your blood.

Nae mair at present can I measure,
An' trowth! my rhymin ware's nae treasure;
But when in Ayr, some half-hour's leisure,
         Be't light, be't dark,
Sir Bard will do himself the pleasure
         To call at Park.

                 ROBERT BURNS.

Mossgiel, 30th October 1786.

A WINTER NIGHT

"Poor naked wretches, wheresoe'er you are,
That bide the pelting of this pitiless storm!
How shall your houseless heads, and unfed sides,
Your loop'd and window'd raggedness, defend you
From seasons such as these?"—SHAKESPEARE.

WHEN biting Boreas, fell and dour,
Sharp shivers thro' the leafless bow'r;
When Phœbus gies a short-liv'd glow'r,
          Far south the lift,
Dim-dark'ning thro' the flaky show'r,
          Or whirling drift:

Ae night the storm the steeples rocked,
Poor Labour sweet in sleep was locked,
While burns, wi' snawy wreaths up-choked,
          Wild-eddying swirl;
Or, thro' the mining outlet bocked,
          Down headlong hurl:

List'ning the doors an' winnocks rattle,
I thought me on the ourie cattle,
Or silly sheep, wha bide this brattle
          O' winter war,
And thro' the drift, deep-lairing, sprattle
          Beneath a scar.

Ilk happing bird,—wee, helpless thing!
That, in the merry months o' spring,
Delighted me to hear thee sing,
          What comes o' thee?
Whare wilt thou cow'r thy chittering wing,
          An' close thy e'e?

Ev'n you, on murdering errands toil'd,
Lone from your savage homes exil'd,

The blood-stain'd roost, and sheep-cote spoil'd
My heart forgets,
While pitiless the tempest wild
Sore on you beats!

Now Phœbe in her midnight reign,
Dark-muffl'd, view'd the dreary plain;
Still crowding thoughts, a pensive train,
Rose in my soul,
When on my ear this plaintive strain,
Slow, solemn, stole—

" Blow, blow, ye winds, with heavier gust!
And freeze, thou bitter-biting frost!
Descend, ye chilly, smothering snows!
Not all your rage, as now united, shows
More hard unkindness unrelenting,
Vengeful malice, unrepenting,
Than heaven-illumin'd Man on brother Man
bestows!

" See stern Oppression's iron grip,
Or mad Ambition's gory hand,
Sending, like blood-hounds from the slip,
Woe, Want, and Murder o'er the land!
Ev'n in the peaceful rural vale,
Truth, weeping, tells the mournful tale,
How pamper'd Luxury, Flatt'ry by her side,
The parasite empoisoning her ear,
With all the servile wretches in the rear,
Looks o'er proud Property, extended wide;
And eyes the simple, rustic hind,
Whose toil upholds the glitt'ring show—
A creature of another kind,
Some coarser substance, unrefin'd—
Plac'd for her lordly use, thus far, thus vile, below!

" Where, where is Love's fond, tender throe,
With lordly Honour's lofty brow,
    The pow'rs you proudly own?
Is there, beneath Love's noble name,
Can harbour dark, the selfish aim,
    To bless himself alone!
Mark maiden-innocence a prey
    To love-pretending snares :
This boasted Honour turns away,
Shunning soft Pity's rising sway,
Regardless of the tears and unavailing pray'rs!
Perhaps this hour, in Misery's squalid nest,
She strains your infant to her joyless breast,
And with a mother's fears shrinks at the rocking
        blast!

" Oh ye! who, sunk in beds of down,
Feel not a want but what yourselves create,
    Think, for a moment, on his wretched fate,
Whom friends and fortune quite disown!
Ill-satisfy'd keen nature's clamorous call,
    Stretch'd on his straw, he lays himself to
        sleep;
While through the ragged roof and chinky wall,
    Chill, o'er his slumbers, piles the drifty
        heap!
Think on the dungeon's grim confine,
Where Guilt and poor Misfortune pine!
Guilt, erring man, relenting view!
But shall thy legal rage pursue
The wretch, already crushèd low
By cruel Fortune's undeservèd blow?
Affliction's sons are brothers in distress;
A brother to relieve, how exquisite the bliss!"

G

I heard nae mair, for Chanticleer
  Shook off the pouthery snaw,
And hail'd the morning with a cheer,
  A cottage-rousing craw.
But deep this truth impress'd my mind—
  Thro' all His works abroad,
The heart benevolent and kind
  The most resembles God.

ADDRESS TO EDINBURGH

EDINA! Scotia's darling seat!
  All hail thy palaces and tow'rs,
Where once, beneath a Monarch's feet,
  Sat Legislation's sovereign pow'rs:
  From marking wildly scatt'red flow'rs,
As on the banks of Ayr I stray'd,
  And singing, lone, the lingering hours,
I shelter in thy honour'd shade.

Here Wealth still swells the golden tide,
  As busy Trade his labours plies;
There Architecture's noble pride
  Bids elegance and splendour rise:
  Here Justice, from her native skies,
High wields her balance and her rod;
  There Learning, with his eagle eyes,
Seeks Science in her coy abode.

Thy sons, Edina, social, kind,
  With open arms the stranger hail;
Their views enlarg'd, their liberal mind,
  Above the narrow, rural vale:

Address to Edinburgh

Address to Edinburgh

"Edina! Scotia's darling seat!
All hail thy palaces and tow'rs . . . "

Attentive still to Sorrow's wail,
Or modest Merit's silent claim ;
   And never may their sources fail !
And never Envy blot their name !

Thy daughters bright thy walks adorn,
   Gay as the gilded summer sky,
Sweet as the dewy, milk-white thorn,
   Dear as the raptur'd thrill of joy !
   Fair Burnet strikes th' adoring eye,
Heaven's beauties on my fancy shine ;
   I see the Sire of Love on high,
And own His work indeed divine !

There, watching high the least alarms,
   Thy rough, rude fortress gleams afar ;
Like some bold veteran, grey in arms,
   And mark'd with many a seamy scar :
   The pond'rous wall and massy bar,
Grim-rising o'er the rugged rock,
   Have oft withstood assailing war,
And oft repell'd th' invader's shock.

With awe-struck thought, and pitying tears,
   I view that noble, stately Dome,
Where Scotia's kings of other years,
   Fam'd heroes ! had their royal home :
   Alas, how chang'd the times to come !
Their royal name low in the dust !
   Their hapless race wild-wand'ring roam !
Tho' rigid Law cries out " 'twas just ! "

Wild beats my heart to trace your steps,
   Whose ancestors, in days of yore,
Thro' hostile ranks and ruin'd gaps
   Old Scotia's bloody lion bore :

Ev'n I who sing in rustic lore,
Haply my sires have left their shed,
  And fac'd grim Danger's loudest roar,
Bold-following where your fathers led.

Edina! Scotia's darling seat!
  All hail thy palaces and tow'rs;
Where once, beneath a Monarch's feet,
  Sat Legislation's sovereign pow'rs:
  From marking wildly-scatt'red flow'rs,
As on the banks of Ayr I stray'd,
  And singing, lone, the lingering hours,
I shelter in thy honour'd shade.

ADDRESS TO A HAGGIS

Fair fa' your honest, sonsie face,
Great chieftain o' the pudding-race!
Aboon them a' ye tak your place,
                    Painch, tripe, or thairm:
Weel are ye wordy o' a grace
                    As lang's my arm.

The groaning trencher there ye fill,
Your hurdies like a distant hill,
Your pin wad help to mend a mill
                    In time o' need,
While thro' your pores the dews distil
                    Like amber bead.

His knife see rustic Labour dight,
An' cut you up wi' ready sleight,
Trenching your gushing entrails bright,
                    Like ony ditch;
And then, O what a glorious sight,
                    Warm-reekin, rich!

Then, horn for horn, they stretch an' strive :
Deil tak the hindmost ! on they drive,
Till a' their weel-swall'd kytes belyve,
    Are bent lyke drums ;
Then auld Guidman, maist like to rive,
    ' Bethankit ! ' hums.

Is there that owre his French *ragout*
Or *olio* that wad staw a sow,
Or *fricassee* wad mak her spew
    Wi' perfect sconner,
Looks down wi' sneering, scornfu' view
    On sic a dinner ?

Poor devil ! see him owre his trash,
As feckless as a wither'd rash,
His spindle shank, a guid whip-lash,
    His nieve a nit ;
Thro' bloody flood or field to dash,
    O how unfit !

But mark the Rustic, haggis fed,
The trembling earth resounds his tread.
Clap in his walie nieve a blade,
    He'll mak it whissle ;
An' legs an' arms, an' heads will sned,
    Like taps o' thrissle.

Ye Pow'rs wha mak mankind your care,
And dish them out their bill o' fare,
Auld Scotland wants nae skinking ware
    That jaups in luggies ;
But, if ye wish her gratefu' prayer,
    Gie her a haggis !

EPISTLE TO MRS SCOTT

GUDEWIFE OF WAUCHOPE-HOUSE, ROXBURGHSHIRE

I MIND it weel in early date,
When I was beardless, young, and blate
  An' first could thresh the barn,
Or haud a yokin at the pleugh ;
An' tho' forfoughten sair eneugh,
  Yet unco proud to learn :
When first amang the yellow corn
  A man I reckon'd was,
An' wi' the lave ilk merry morn
  Could rank my rig and lass,
    Still shearing, and clearing
      The tither stookèd raw,
    Wi' claivers, an' haivers,
      Wearing the day awa.

E'en then, a wish, (I mind its pow'r,)
A wish that to my latest hour
  Shall strongly heave my breast,
That I for poor auld Scotland's sake
Some usefu' plan or book could make,
  Or sing a sang at least.
The rough burr-thistle, spreading wide
  Amang the bearded bear,
I turn'd the weeder-clips aside,
  An' spar'd the symbol dear :
    No nation, no station,
      My envy e'er could raise ;
    A Scot still, but blot still,
      I knew nae higher praise.

But still the elements o' sang,
In formless jumble, right an' wrang,

Wild floated in my brain;
'Till on that har'st I said before,
My partner in the merry core,
　　She rous'd the forming strain;
I see her yet, the sonsie quean,
　　That lighted up my jingle,
Her witching smile, her pawky een
　　That gart my heart-strings tingle;
　　　　I firèd, inspirèd,
　　　　　　At every kindling keek,
　　　　But bashing, and dashing,
　　　　　　I fearèd aye to speak.

Health to the sex! ilk guid chiel says:
Wi' merry dance in winter days,
　　An' we to share in common;
The gust o' joy, the balm of woe,
The saul o' life, the heaven below,
　　Is rapture-giving woman.
Ye surly sumphs, who hate the name,
　　Be mindfu' o' your mither;
She, honest woman, may think shame
　　That ye're connected with her:
　　　　Ye're wae men, ye're nae men
　　　　　　That slight the lovely dears
　　　　To shame ye, disclaim ye,
　　　　　　Ilk honest birkie swears.

For you, no bred to barn and byre,
Wha sweetly tune the Scottish lyre,
　　Thanks to you for your line:
The marled plaid ye kindly spare.
By me should gratefully be ware;
　　'Twad please me to the nine.

I'd be mair vauntie o' my hap,
　　Douce hinging owre my curple,
Than ony ermine ever lap,
　　Or proud imperial purple.
　　　Farewell then, lang hale then,
　　　　An' plenty be your fa';
　　　May losses and crosses
　　　　Ne'er at your hallan ca'!

R. Burns.

March 1787.

ADDRESS TO WM. TYTLER, ESQ., OF WOODHOUSELEE

WITH AN IMPRESSION OF THE AUTHOR'S PORTRAIT

Revered defender of beauteous Stuart,
　　Of Stuart, a name once respected;
A name, which to love was the mark of a true
　　　heart,
　　But now 'tis despis'd and neglected.

Tho' something like moisture conglobes in my eye,
　　Let no one misdeem me disloyal;
A poor friendless wand'rer may well claim a sigh,
　　Still more if that wand'rer were royal.

My fathers that name have rever'd on a throne:
　　My fathers have dièd to right it:
Those fathers would spurn their degenerate son,
　　That name should he scoffingly slight it.

Still in prayers for King George I most heartily
　　　join,
　　The Queen, and the rest of the gentry:
Be they wise, be they foolish, is nothing of mine;
　　Their title's avow'd by my country.

But why of that epocha make such a fuss,
  That gave us th' Electoral stem?
If bringing them over was lucky for us,
  I'm sure 'twas as lucky for them.

But loyalty truce! we're on dangerous ground;
  Who knows how the fashions may alter?
The doctrine, to-day, that is loyalty sound,
  To-morrow may bring us a halter!

I send you a trifle, a head of a bard,
  A trifle scarce worthy your care;
But accept it, good Sir, as a mark of regard,
  Sincere as a saint's dying prayer.

Now life's chilly evening dim shades on your
    eye,
  And ushers the long dreary night:
But you, like the star that athwart gilds the sky,
  Your course to the latest is bright.

BURLESQUE LAMENT FOR THE ABSENCE OF WILLIAM CREECH, PUBLISHER.

Auld chuckie Reekie's sair distrest,
Down droops her ance weel burnish'd crest,
Nae joy her bonie buskit nest
        Can yield ava,
Her darling bird that she lo'es best—
        Willie, 's awa.

O Willie was a witty wight,
And had o' things an unco' sleight,

G*

Auld Reekie aye he keepit tight,
     And trig an' braw:
But now they'll busk her like a fright,—
     Willie's awa!

The stiffest o' them a' he bow'd,
The bauldest o' them a' he cow'd;
They durst nae mair than he allow'd,
     That was a law:
We've lost a birkie weel worth gowd,
     Willie's awa!

Now gawkies, tawpies, gowks and fools,
Frae colleges and boarding schools,
May sprout like simmer puddock-stools
     In glen or shaw;
He wha could brush them down to mools—
     Willie, 's awa!

The brethren o' the Commerce-chaumer
May mourn their loss wi' doolfu' clamour;
He was a dictionar and grammar
     Among them a';
I fear they'll now mak mony a stammer;
     Willie's awa!

Nae mair we see his levee door
Philosophers and poets pour,
And toothy critics by the score,
     In bloody raw!
The adjutant o' a' the core—
     Willie, 's awa!

Now worthy Gregory's Latin face,
Tytler's and Greenfield's modest grace;

M'Kenzie, Stewart, such a brace
   As Rome ne'er saw ;
They a' maun meet some ither place,
   Willie's awa !

Poor Burns ev'n Scotch Drink canna quicken,
He cheeps like some bewilder'd chicken
Scar'd frae its minnie and the cleckin,
   By hoodie-craw ;
Grief's gien his heart an unco kickin,
   Willie's awa !

Now ev'ry sour-mou'd girnin blellum,
And Calvin's folk, are fit to fell him ;
Ilk self-conceited critic skellum
   His quill may draw ;
He wha could brawlie ward their bellum—
   Willie,'s awa !

Up wimpling stately Tweed I've sped,
And Eden scenes on crystal Jed,
And Ettrick banks, now roaring red,
   While tempests blaw ;
But every joy and pleasure's fled,
   Willie's awa !

May I be Slander's common speech ;
A text for Infamy to preach ;
And lastly, streekit out to bleach
   In winter snaw ;
When I forget thee, WILLIE CREECH,
   Tho' far awa !

May never wicked Fortune touzle him !
May never wicked men bamboozle him !

Until a pow as auld's Methusalem
    He canty claw!
Then to the blessed new Jerusalem
    Fleet wing awa!

ELEGY ON THE DEATH OF SIR JAMES HUNTER BLAIR

THE lamp of day with ill-presaging glare,
    Dim, cloudy, sank beneath the western wave;
Th' inconstant blast howl'd thro' the darkening air,
    And hollow whistled in the rocky cave.

Lone as I wander'd by each cliff and dell,
    Once the lov'd haunts of Scotia's royal train;
Or mus'd where limpid streams, once hallow'd, well,
    Or mould'ring ruins mark the sacred fane.

Th' increasing blast roar'd round the beetling rocks,
    The clouds, swift-wing'd, flew o'er the starry
        sky,
The groaning trees untimely shed their locks,
    And shooting meteors caught the startled eye.

The paly moon rose in the livid east,
    And 'mong the cliffs disclos'd a stately form
In weeds of woe, that frantic beat her breast,
    And mix'd her wailings with the raving storm.

Wild to my heart the filial pulses glow;
    'Twas Caledonia's trophied shield I view'd:
Her form majestic droop'd in pensive woe,
    The lightning of her eye in tears imbued.

Revers'd that spear, redoubtable in war,
    Reclined that banner, erst in fields unfurl'd,
That like a deathful meteor gleam'd afar,
    And brav'd the mighty monarchs of the world.

Petition to Bruar Water

Petition to Bruar Water

"Here, foaming down the skelvy rocks,
In twisting strength I rin . . . "

"My patriot son fills an untimely grave!"
    With accents wild and lifted arms she cried;
"Low lies the hand that oft was stretch'd to save,
    Low lies the heart that swell'd with honest
        pride.

"A weeping country joins a widow's tear;
    The helpless poor mix with the orphan's cry;
The drooping arts surround their patron's bier;
    And grateful science heaves the heart-felt sigh!

"I saw my sons resume their ancient fire;
    I saw fair Freedom's blossoms richly blow:
But ah! how hope is born but to expire!
    Relentless fate has laid their guardian low.

"My patriot falls, but shall he lie unsung,
    While empty greatness saves a worthless name?
No; every muse shall join her tuneful tongue,
    And future ages hear his growing fame.

"And I will join a mother's tender cares,
    Thro' future times to make his virtues last;
That distant years may boast of other Blairs!".....
    She said, and vanish'd with the sweeping blast.

THE HUMBLE PETITION OF
BRUAR WATER

TO THE NOBLE DUKE OF ATHOLE

My lord, I know, your noble ear
    Woe ne'er assails in vain;
Embolden'd thus, I beg you'll hear
    Your humble slave complain,

How saucy Phœbus' scorching beams,
  In flaming summer-pride,
Dry-withering, waste my foamy streams,
  And drink my crystal tide.

The lightly-jumpin, glowrin trouts,
  That thro' my waters play,
If, in their random, wanton spouts,
  They near the margin stray ;
If, hapless chance ! they linger lang,
  I'm scorching up so shallow,
They're left the whitening stanes amang,
  In gasping death to wallow.

Last day I grat wi' spite and teen,
  As poet Burns came by,
That, to a bard, I should be seen
  Wi' half my channel dry ;
A panegyric rhyme, I ween,
  Ev'n as I was, he shor'd me ;
But had I in my glory been,
  He, kneeling, wad ador'd me.

Here, foaming down the skelvy rocks,
  In twisting strength I rin ;
There, high my boiling torrent smokes,
  Wild-roaring o'er a linn :
Enjoying each large spring and well,
  As Nature gave them me,
I am, altho' I say't mysel',
  Worth gaun a mile to see.

Would then my noble master please
  To grant my highest wishes,
He'll shade my banks wi' tow'ring trees,
  And bonie spreading bushes.

Delighted doubly then, my lord,
  You'll wander on my banks,
And listen mony a grateful bird
  Return you tuneful thanks.

The sober lav'rock, warbling wild,
  Shall to the skies aspire;
The gowdspink, Music's gayest child,
  Shall sweetly join the choir;
The blackbird strong, the lintwhite clear,
  The mavis mild and mellow;
The robin pensive Autumn cheer,
  In all her locks of yellow.

This too, a covert shall ensure,
  To shield them from the storm
And coward maukin sleep secure,
  Low in her grassy form:
Here shall the shepherd make his seat,
  To weave his crown of flow'rs;
Or find a shelt'ring, safe retreat,
  From prone-descending show'rs.

And here, by sweet, endearing stealth,
  Shall meet the loving pair,
Despising worlds, with all their wealth,
  As empty idle care;
The flow'rs shall vie in all their charms,
  The hour of heav'n to grace;
And birks extend their fragrant arms
  To screen the dear embrace.

Here haply too, at vernal dawn,
  Some musing bard may stray,
And eye the smoking, dewy lawn,
  And misty mountain grey;

208 Poems and Songs

Or, by the reaper's nightly beam,
    Mild-chequering thro' the trees,
Rave to my darkly dashing stream,
    Hoarse-swelling on the breeze.

Let lofty firs, and ashes cool,
    My lowly banks o'erspread,
And view, deep-bending in the pool,
    Their shadows' wat'ry bed:
Let fragrant birks, in woodbines drest,
    My craggy cliffs adorn;
And, for the little songster's nest,
    The close embow'ring thorn.

So may old Scotia's darling hope,
    Your little angel band
Spring, like their fathers, up to prop
    Their honour'd native land!
So may, thro' Albion's farthest ken,
    To social-flowing glasses,
The grace be—"Athole's honest men,
    And Athole's bonie lasses!"

ON SCARING SOME WATER-FOWL IN LOCH TURIT

A WILD SCENE AMONG THE HILLS OF OUGHTERTYRE

Why, ye tenants of the lake,
For me your wat'ry haunt forsake?
Tell me, fellow-creatures, why
At my presence thus you fly?
Why disturb your social joys,
Parent, filial, kindred ties?—
Common friend to you and me,
Nature's gifts to all are free:

On Scaring some Water-fowl in Loch Turit

On Scaring some Water-fowl in Loch Turit

"Why, ye tenants of the lake,
For me you wat'ry haunt forsake?
Tell me, fellow creatures, why
At my presence thus you fly?"

Peaceful keep your dimpling wave,
Busy feed, or wanton lave ;
Or, beneath the sheltering rock,
Bide the surging billow's shock.

Conscious, blushing for our race,
Soon, too soon, your fears I trace.
Man, your proud usurping foe,
Would be lord of all below :
Plumes himself in freedom's pride,
Tyrant stern to all beside.

The eagle, from the cliffy brow,
Marking you his prey below,
In his breast no pity dwells,
Strong necessity compels :
But Man, to whom alone is giv'n
A ray direct from pitying Heav'n,
Glories in his heart humane—
And creatures for his pleasure slain !

In these savage, liquid plains,
Only known to wand'ring swains,
Where the mossy riv'let strays,
Far from human haunts and ways ;
All on Nature you depend,
And life's poor season peaceful spend.

Or, if man's superior might
Dare invade your native right,
On the lofty ether borne,
Man with all his pow'rs you scorn ;
Swiftly seek, on clanging wings,
Other lakes and other springs ;
And the foe you cannot brave,
Scorn at least to be his slave.

BIRTHDAY ODE
FOR 31st DECEMBER 1787

AFAR the illustrious Exile roams,
  Whom kingdoms on this day should hail;
An inmate in the casual shed,
On transient pity's bounty fed,
  Haunted by busy memory's bitter tale!
Beasts of the forest have their savage homes,
  But He, who should imperial purple wear,
Owns not the lap of earth where rests his royal
    head!
His wretched refuge, dark despair,
While ravening wrongs and woes pursue,
And distant far the faithful few
  Who would his sorrows share.

False flatterer, Hope, away!
  Nor think to lure us as in days of yore:
We solemnize this sorrowing natal day,
  To prove our loyal truth—we can no more,
And owning Heaven's mysterious sway,
  Submissive, low adore.
Ye honored, mighty Dead,
  Who nobly perished in the glorious cause,
  Your KING, your Country, and her laws,
From great DUNDEE, who smiling Victory led,
And fell a Martyr in her arms,
(What breast of northern ice but warms!)
To bold BALMERINO's undying name,
Whose soul of fire, lighted at Heaven's high
    flame,
Deserves the proudest wreath departed heroes
    claim:

Not unrevenged your fate shall lie,
  It only lags, the fatal hour,
Your blood shall, with incessant cry,
  Awake at last, th' unsparing Power ;
As from the cliff, with thundering course,
  The snowy ruin smokes along
With doubling speed and gathering force,
Till deep it, crushing, whelms the cottage in the vale;
  So Vengeance' arm, ensanguin'd, strong,
Shall with resistless might assail,
Usurping Brunswick's pride shall lay,
And STEWART's wrongs and yours, with tenfold
    weight repay.

PERDITION, baleful child of night !
Rise and revenge the injured right
  Of STEWART's royal race :
Lead on the unmuzzled hounds of hell,
Till all the frighted echoes tell
  The blood-notes of the chase !
Full on the quarry point their view,
Full on the base usurping crew,
The tools of faction, and the nation's curse !
Hark how the cry grows on the wind ;
They leave the lagging gale behind,
Their savage fury, pitiless, they pour ;
With murdering eyes already they devour ;
See Brunswick spent, a wretched prey,
His life one poor despairing day,
Where each avenging hour still ushers in a worse !
  Such havock, howling all abroad,
    Their utter ruin bring,
  The base apostates to their GOD,
    Or rebels to their KING.

ON THE
DEATH OF ROBERT DUNDAS, Esq.,
OF ARNISTON

LATE LORD PRESIDENT OF THE COURT OF SESSION

Lone on the bleaky hills the straying flocks
Shun the fierce storms among the sheltering
    rocks;
Down from the rivulets, red with dashing rains,
The gathering floods burst o'er the distant plains;
Beneath the blast the leafless forests groan;
The hollow caves return a hollow moan.

Ye hills, ye plains, ye forests, and ye caves,
Ye howling winds, and wintry swelling waves!
Unheard, unseen, by human ear or eye,
Sad to your sympathetic glooms I fly;
Where, to the whistling blast and water's roar,
Pale Scotia's recent wound I may deplore.

O heavy loss, thy country ill could bear!
A loss these evil days can ne'er repair!
Justice, the high vicegerent of her God,
Her doubtful balance eyed, and sway'd her rod:
Hearing the tidings of the fatal blow,
She sank, abandon'd to the wildest woe.

Wrongs, injuries, from many a darksome den,
Now, gay in hope, explore the paths of men:
See from his cavern grim Oppression rise,
And throw on Poverty his cruel eyes;
Keen on the helpless victim see him fly,
And stifle, dark, the feebly-bursting cry:
Mark Ruffian Violence, distained with crimes,
Rousing elate in these degenerate times,

View unsuspecting Innocence a prey,
As guileful Fraud points out the erring way :
While subtle Litigation's pliant tongue
The life-blood equal sucks of Right and Wrong :
Hark, injur'd Want recounts th' unlisten'd tale,
And much-wrong'd Mis'ry pours the unpitied
    wail !

Ye dark waste hills, ye brown unsightly plains,
Congenial scenes, ye soothe my mournful strains :
Ye tempests, rage ! ye turbid torrents, roll !
Ye suit the joyless tenor of my soul.
Life's social haunts and pleasures I resign ;
Be nameless wilds and lonely wanderings mine,
To mourn the woes my country must endure—
That wound degenerate ages cannot cure.

EPISTLE TO HUGH PARKER

In this strange land, this uncouth clime,
A land unknown to prose or rhyme ;
Where words ne'er cross't the Muse's heckles,
Nor limpit in poetic shackles :
A land that Prose did never view it,
Except when drunk he stacher't thro' it ;
Here, ambush'd by the chimla cheek,
Hid in an atmosphere of reek,
I hear a wheel thrum i' the neuk,
I hear it—for in vain I leuk.
The red peat gleams, a fiery kernel,
Enhuskèd by a fog infernal.
Here, for my wonted rhyming raptures,
I sit and count my sins by chapters ;
For life and spunk like ither Christians,
I'm dwindled down to mere existence,
Wi' nae converse but Gallowa bodies,

Wi' nae kenn'd face but Jenny Geddes.
Jenny, my Pegasean pride!
Dowie she saunters down Nithside,
And aye a westlin leuk she throws,
While tears hap o'er her auld brown nose!
Was it for this, wi' cannie care,
Thou bure the Bard through many a shire?
At howes, or hillocks never stumbled,
And late or early never grumbled?—
O had I power like inclination,
I'd heeze thee up a constellation,
To canter with the Sagitarre,
Or loup the ecliptic like a bar;
Or turn the pole like any arrow;
Or, when auld Phœbus bids good-morrow,
Down the zodiac urge the race,
And cast dirt on his godship's face;
For I could lay my bread and kail
He'd ne'er cast saut upo' thy tail.—
Wi' a' this care and a' this grief,
And sma', sma' prospect of relief,
And nought but peat-reek i' my head,
How can I write what ye can read?—
Tarbolton, twenty-fourth o' June,
Ye'll find me in a better tune;
But till we meet and weet our whistle,
Tak this excuse for nae epistle.

ROBERT BURNS.

EPISTLE TO
ROBERT GRAHAM, Esq., OF FINTRY

REQUESTING A FAVOUR

When Nature her great master-piece design'd,
And fram'd her last, best work, the human mind,

Her eye intent on all the mazy plan,
She form'd of various parts the various Man.

Then first she calls the useful many forth;
Plain plodding Industry, and sober Worth:
Thence peasants, farmers, native sons of earth,
And merchandise' whole genus take their birth:
Each prudent cit a warm existence finds,
And all mechanics' many-apron'd kinds.
Some other rarer sorts are wanted yet,
The lead and buoy are needful to the net:
The *caput mortuum* of gross desires
Makes a material for mere knights and squires;
The martial phosphorus is taught to flow,
She kneads the lumpish philosophic dough,
Then marks th' unyielding mass with grave
    designs,
Law, physic, politics, and deep divines;
Last, she sublimes th' Aurora of the poles,
The flashing elements of female souls.

The order'd system fair before her stood,
Nature, well pleas'd, pronounc'd it very good;
But ere she gave creating labour o'er,
Half-jest, she tried one curious labour more.
Some spumy, fiery, *ignis fatuus* matter.
Such as the slightest breath of air might scatter;
With arch-alacrity and conscious glee,
(Nature may have her whim as well as we,
Her Hogarth-art perhaps she meant to show it),
She forms the thing and christens it—a Poet:
Creature, tho' oft the prey of care and sorrow,
When blest to-day, unmindful of to-morrow;
A being form'd t' amuse his graver friends,
Admir'd and prais'd—and there the wages ends;

A mortal quite unfit for Fortune's strife,
Yet oft the sport of all the ills of life;
Prone to enjoy each pleasure riches give,
Yet haply wanting wherewithal to live;
Longing to wipe each tear, to heal each groan,
Yet frequent all unheeded in his own.

But honest Nature is not quite a Turk,
She laugh'd at first, then felt for her poor work:
Pitying the propless climber of mankind,
She cast about a standard tree to find;
And, to support his helpless woodbine state,
Attach'd him to the generous, truly great:
A title, and the only one I claim,
To lay strong hold for help on bounteous Graham.

Pity the tuneful Muses' hapless train,
Weak, timid landsmen on life's stormy main!
Their hearts no selfish stern absorbent stuff,
That never gives—tho' humbly takes enough;
The little fate allows, they share as soon,
Unlike sage proverb'd Wisdom's hard-wrung
    boon:
The world were blest did bliss on them depend;
Ah, that "the friendly e'er should want a friend!"
Let Prudence number o'er each sturdy son,
Who life and wisdom at one race begun,
Who feel by reason and who give by rule,
(Instinct's a brute, and sentiment a fool!)
Who make poor "will do" wait upon "I
    should"—
We own they're prudent, but who owns they're
    good?
Ye wise ones hence! ye hurt the social eye!
God's image rudely etch'd on base alloy!

But come ye who the god-like pleasure know,
Heaven's attribute distinguished—to bestow!
Whose arms of love would grasp all human race:
Come *thou* who giv'st with all a courtier's grace;
FRIEND OF MY LIFE, true patron of my rhymes!
Prop of my dearest hopes for future times.
Why shrinks my soul half blushing, half afraid,
Backward, abash'd to ask thy friendly aid?
I know my need, I know thy giving hand,
I crave thy friendship at thy kind command;
But there are such who court the tuneful Nine—
Heavens! should the branded character be mine!
Whose *verse* in manhood's pride sublimely flows,
Yet vilest reptiles in their begging *prose.*
Mark, how their lofty independent spirit
Soars on the spurning wing of injured merit!
Seek you the proofs in private life to find?
Pity the best of words should be but wind!
So, to heaven's gates the lark's shrill song ascends,
But grovelling on the earth the carol ends.
In all the clam'rous cry of starving want,
They dun Benevolence with shameless front;
Oblige them, patronise their tinsel lays—
They persecute you all your future days!
Ere my poor soul such deep damnation stain,
My horny fist assume the plough again,
The pie-bald jacket let me patch once more,
On eighteenpence a week I've liv'd before.
Tho', thanks to Heaven, I dare even that last shift,
I trust, meantime, my boon is in thy gift:
That, plac'd by thee upon the wish'd-for height,
Where, man and nature fairer in her sight,
My Muse may imp her wing for some sublimer
    flight.

WRITTEN IN FRIARS CARSE HERMITAGE ON NITHSIDE

Thou whom chance may hither lead,
Be thou clad in russet weed,
Be thou deckt in silken stole,
Grave these counsels on thy soul.

Life is but a day at most,
Sprung from night,—in darkness lost;
Hope not sunshine ev'ry hour,
Fear not clouds will always lour.

As Youth and Love with sprightly dance,
Beneath thy morning star advance,
Pleasure with her siren air
May delude the thoughtless pair;
Let Prudence bless Enjoyment's cup,
Then raptur'd sip, and sip it up.

As thy day grows warm and high,
Life's meridian flaming nigh,
Dost thou spurn the humble vale?
Life's proud summits would'st thou scale?
Check thy climbing step, elate,
Evils lurk in felon wait:
Dangers, eagle-pinioned, bold,
Soar around each cliffy hold!
While cheerful Peace, with linnet song,
Chants the lowly dells among.

As the shades of ev'ning close,
Beck'ning thee to long repose;
As life itself becomes disease,
Seek the chimney-nook of ease;

Friars Carse

From an engraving after David Octavius Hill

There ruminate with sober thought,
On all thou'st seen, and heard, and wrought,
And teach the sportive younkers round,
Saws of experience, sage and sound :
Say, man's true, genuine estimate,
The grand criterion of his fate,
Is not, art thou high or low ?
Did thy fortune ebb or flow ?
Did many talents gild thy span ?
Or frugal Nature grudge thee one ?
Tell them, and press it on their mind,
As thou thyself must shortly find,
The smile or frown of awful Heav'n,
To Virtue or to Vice is giv'n,
Say, to be just, and kind, and wise—
There solid self-enjoyment lies ;
That foolish, selfish, faithless ways
Lead to be wretched, vile, and base.

Thus resign'd and quiet, creep
To the bed of lasting sleep,—
Sleep, whence thou shalt ne'er awake,
Night, where dawn shall never break,
Till future life, future no more,
To light and joy the good restore,
To light and joy unknown before.
Stranger, go ! Heav'n be thy guide !
Quod the Beadsman of Nithside.

ELEGY ON THE YEAR 1788

For lords or kings I dinna mourn,
E'en let them die—for that they're born :
But oh ! prodigious to reflec' !
A Towmont, sirs, is gane to wreck !

O Eighty-eight, in thy sma' space,
What dire events hae taken place!
Of what enjoyments thou hast reft us!
In what a pickle thou hast left us!

The Spanish Empire's tint a head,
And my auld teethless Bawtie's dead :
The tulyie's teugh 'tween Pitt and Fox,
And our guidwife's wee birdie cocks;
The tane is game, a bluidy devil,
But to the hen-birds unco civil;
The tither's dour—has nae sic breedin,
But better stuff ne'er claw'd a middin.

Ye ministers, come mount the poupit,
An' cry till ye be hearse an' roupit,
For Eighty-eight, he wished you weel,
An' gied ye a' baith gear an' meal;
E'en mony a plack, and mony a peck,
Ye ken yoursels, for little feck!

Ye bonie lassies, dight your e'en,
For some o' you hae tint a frien';
In Eighty-eight, ye ken, was taen,
What ye'll ne'er ha'e to gie again.

Observe the very nowt an' sheep,
How dowff an' dowie now they creep;
Nay, even the yirth itsel' does cry,
For E'nburgh wells are grutten dry.

O Eighty-nine, thou's but a bairn,
An' no owre auld, I hope, to learn!
Thou beardless boy, I pray tak care,
Thou now hast got thy Daddy's chair;

Nae handcuff'd, mizzl'd, half-shackl'd Regent,
But, like himsel, a full free agent,
Be sure ye follow out the plan
Nae waur than he did, honest man!
As muckle better as you can.

January 1, 1789.

ODE, SACRED TO THE MEMORY OF MRS OSWALD OF AUCHEN-CRUIVE

Dweller in yon dungeon dark,
Hangman of creation! mark,
Who in widow-weeds appears,
Laden with unhonour'd years,
Noosing with care a bursting purse,
Baited with many a deadly curse?

STROPHE.

View the wither'd Beldam's face;
Can thy keen inspection trace
Aught of Humanity's sweet, melting grace?
Note that eye, 'tis rheum o'erflows;
Pity's flood *there* never rose,
See these hands ne'er stretched to save
Hands that took, but never gave:
Keeper of Mammon's iron chest,
Lo, there she goes, unpitied and unblest,
She goes, but not to realms of everlasting rest!

ANTISTROPHE.

Plunderer of Armies! lift thine eyes,
(A while forbear, ye torturing fiends;)
Seest thou whose step, unwilling, hither bends?
No fallen angel, hurl'd from upper skies;

'Tis thy trusty quondam Mate,
Doom'd to share thy fiery fate;
She, tardy, hell-ward plies.

EPODE.

And are they of no more avail,
Ten thousand glittering pounds a-year?
In other worlds can Mammon fail,
Omnipotent as he is here!
O, bitter mockery of the pompous bier,
While down the wretched Vital Part is
driven!
The cave-lodged Beggar, with a conscience
clear,
Expires in rags, unknown, and goes to Heaven.

ODE ON THE DEPARTED
REGENCY BILL

DAUGHTER of Chaos' doting years,
Nurse of ten thousand hopes and fears,
Whether thy airy, unsubstantial shade
(The rights of sepulture now duly paid)
Spread abroad its hideous form
On the roaring civil storm,
Deafening din and warring rage
Factions wild with factions wage;
Or under-ground,
Deep-sunk, profound,
Among the demons of the earth,
With groans that make
The mountains shake,
Thou mourn thy ill-starred, blighted birth;
Or in the uncreated Void,

Where seeds of future being fight,
With lessen'd step thou wander wide,
  To greet thy Mother—Ancient Night.
And as each jarring, monster-mass is past,
Fond recollect what once thou wast:
In manner due, beneath this sacred oak,
Hear, Spirit, hear! thy presence I invoke!
    By a Monarch's heaven-struck fate,
    By a disunited State,
    By a generous Prince's wrongs,
    By a Senate's strife of tongues,
    By a Premier's sullen pride,
    Louring on the changing tide;
    By dread Thurlow's powers to awe
    Rhetoric, blasphemy and law;
    By the turbulent ocean—
    A Nation's commotion,
    By the harlot-caresses
    Of borough addresses,
    By days few and evil,
    (Thy portion, poor devil!)
By Power, Wealth, and Show,
    (The Gods by men adored,)
By nameless Poverty,
    (Their hell abhorred,)
    By all they hope, by all they fear,
    Hear! and Appear!

Stare not on me, thou ghastly Power!
Nor, grim with chained defiance lour:
No Babel-structure would I build
    Where, order exil'd from his native sway,
Confusion may the regent-sceptre wield,
    While all would rule and none obey.

Go, to the world of man relate
The story of thy sad, eventful fate ;
And call presumptuous Hope to hear
And bid him check his blind career ;
And tell the sore-prest sons of Care,
 Never, never to despair !
Paint Charles's speed on wings of fire,
The object of his fond desire,
Beyond his boldest hopes, at hand :
Paint all the triumph of the Portland Band ;
Mark how they lift the joy-exulting voice,
And how their num'rous creditors rejoice ;
But just as hopes to warm enjoyment rise,
Cry CONVALESCENCE ! and the vision flies.

Then next pourtray a dark'ning twilight gloom,
 Eclipsing sad a gay, rejoicing morn,
While proud Ambition to th' untimely tomb
 By gnashing, grim, despairing fiends is
 borne :
Paint ruin, in the shape of high D[undas]
 Gaping with giddy terror o'er the brow ;
In vain he struggles, the fates behind him press,
 And clam'rous hell yawns for her prey below:
How fallen *That*, whose pride late scaled the
 skies !
And *This*, like Lucifer, no more to rise !
 Again pronounce the powerful word ;
See Day, triumphant from the night, restored.

 Then know this truth, ye Sons of Men !
 (Thus ends thy moral tale,)
 Your darkest terrors may be vain,
 Your brightest hopes may fail.

EPISTLE TO JAMES TENNANT OF GLENCONNER

AULD comrade dear, and brither sinner,
How's a' the folk about Glenconner?
How do you this blae eastlin wind,
That's like to blaw a body blind?
For me, my faculties are frozen,
My dearest member nearly dozen'd.
I've sent you here, by Johnie Simson,
Twa sage philosophers to glimpse on;
Smith, wi' his sympathetic feeling,
An' Reid, to common sense appealing.
Philosophers have fought and wrangled,
An' meikle Greek an' Latin mangled,
Till wi' their logic-jargon tir'd,
And in the depth of science mir'd,
To common sense they now appeal,
What wives and wabsters see and feel.
But, hark ye, friend! I charge you strictly,
Peruse them, an' return them quickly:
For now I'm grown sae cursed douce
I pray and ponder butt the house;
My shins, my lane, I there sit roastin,
Perusing Bunyan, Brown an' Boston,
Till by an' by, if I haud on,
I'll grunt a real gospel groan:
Already I begin to try it,
To cast my e'en up like a pyet,
When by the gun she tumbles o'er
Flutt'ring an' gasping in her gore:
Sae shortly you shall see me bright,
A burning an' a shining light.

H

My heart-warm love to guid auld Glen,
The ace an' wale of honest men :
When bending down wi' auld grey hairs
Beneath the load of years and cares,
May He who made him still support him,
An' views beyond the grave comfort him ;
His worthy fam'ly far and near,
God bless them a' wi' grace and gear !

My auld schoolfellow, preacher Willie,
The manly tar, my mason-billie,
And Auchenbay, I wish him joy ;
If he's a parent, lass or boy,
May he be dad, and Meg the mither,
Just five-and-forty years thegither !
And no forgetting wabster Charlie,
I'm tauld he offers very fairly.
An' Lord, remember singing Sannock,
Wi' hale breeks, saxpence, an' a bannock !
And next, my auld acquaintance, Nancy,
Since she is fitted to her fancy,
An' her kind stars hae airted till her
A guid chiel wi' a pickle siller.
My kindest, best respects, I sen' it,
To cousin Kate, an' sister Janet :
Tell them, frae me, wi' chiels be cautious,
For, faith, they'll aiblins fin' them fashious ;
To grant a heart is fairly civil,
But to grant a maidenhead's the devil.
An' lastly, Jamie, for yoursel,
May guardian angels tak a spell,
An' steer you seven miles south o' hell :
But first, before you see heaven's glory,
May ye get mony a merry story,

Mony a laugh, and mony a drink,
And aye eneugh o' needfu' clink.

Now fare ye weel, an' joy be wi' you:
For my sake, this I beg it o' you,
Assist poor Simson a' ye can,
Ye'll fin' him just an honest man;
Sae I conclude, and quat my chanter,
Your's, saint or sinner,

ROB THE RANTER.

SKETCH IN VERSE

INSCRIBED TO THE RIGHT HON. C. J. FOX

How Wisdom and Folly meet, mix, and unite,
How Virtue and Vice blend their black and their
    white,
How Genius, th' illustrious father of fiction,
Confounds rule and law, reconciles contradiction,
I sing. If these mortals, the critics, should bustle,
I care not, not I—let the critics go whistle.

But now for a Patron whose name and whose
    glory,
At once may illustrate and honour my story.

Thou first of our orators, first of our wits;
Yet whose parts and acquirements seem just
    lucky hits;
With knowledge so vast, and with judgment so
    strong,
No man with the half of 'em e'er could go wrong;
With passions so potent, and fancies so bright,
No man with the half of 'em e'er could go right;
A sorry, poor, misbegot son of the Muses,
For using thy name, offers fifty excuses.

Good Lord, what is Man! for as simple he looks,
Do but try to develop his hooks and his crooks;
With his depths and his shallows, his good and
    his evil,
All in all he's a problem must puzzle the devil.

On his one ruling passion Sir Pope hugely
    labours,
That, like th' old Hebrew walking-switch, eats
    up its neighbours:
Mankind are his show-box—a friend, would you
    know him?
Pull the string, Ruling Passion—the picture will
    show him,
What pity, in rearing so beauteous a system,
One trifling particular, *Truth*, should have miss'd
    him;
For, spite of his fine theoretic positions,
Mankind is a science defies definitions.

Some sort all our qualities each to its tribe,
And think human nature they truly describe;
Have you found this, or t'other?   There's more
    in the wind;
As by one drunken fellow his comrades you'll find.
But such is the flaw, or the depth of the plan,
In the make of that wonderful creature called Man,
No two virtues, whatever relation they claim.
Nor even two different shades of the same,
Though like as was ever twin brother to brother,
Possessing the one shall imply you've the other.

But truce with abstraction, and truce with a
    Muse
Whose rhymes you'll perhaps, Sir, ne'er deign
    to peruse ·

The Wounded Hare

The Wounded Hare

"Go live, poor wand'rer of the wood and field!"

Will you leave your justings, your jars, and your
     quarrels,
Contending with Billy for proud-nodding laurels ?
My much-honour'd Patron, believe your poor
     poet,
Your courage, much more than your prudence,
     you show it :
In vain with Squire Billy for laurels you struggle;
He'll have them by fair trade, if not, he will
     smuggle :
Not cabinets even of kings would conceal 'em,
He'd up the back stairs, and by God he would
     steal 'em !
Then feats like Squire Billy's you ne'er can
     achieve 'em ;
It is not, out-do him—the task is, out-thieve him !

THE WOUNDED HARE

Inhuman man! curse on thy barb'rous art,
   And blasted be thy murder-aiming eye ;
   May never pity soothe thee with a sigh,
Nor ever pleasure glad thy cruel heart !

Go live, poor wand'rer of the wood and field !
   The bitter little that of life remains :
   No more the thickening brakes and verdant
     plains
To thee shall home, or food, or pastime yield.

Seek, mangled wretch, some place of wonted
     rest,
   No more of rest, but now thy dying bed !
   The sheltering rushes whistling o'er thy head,
The cold earth with thy bloody bosom prest.

Oft as by winding Nith I, musing, wait
  The sober eve, or hail the cheerful dawn,
  I'll miss thee sporting o'er the dewy lawn,
And curse the ruffian's aim, and mourn thy hap-
    less fate.

ON THE LATE CAPTAIN GROSE'S

PEREGRINATIONS THRO' SCOTLAND, COLLECTING THE ANTIQUITIES OF THAT KINGDOM

Hear, land o' Cakes, and brither Scots,
Frae Maidenkirk to Johnie Groat's ;—
If there's a hole in a' your coats,
        I rede you tent it :
A chield's amang you takin notes,
        And faith he'll prent it :

If in your bounds you chance to light
Upon a fine, fat, fodgel wight,
O' stature short, but genius bright,
        That's he, mark weel ;
And wow ! he has an unco sleight
        O' cauk and keel.

By some auld, houlet-haunted biggin,
Or kirk deserted by its riggin,
It's ten to ane ye'll find him snug in
        Some eldritch part,
Wi' deils, they say, Lord save's ! colleaguin
        At some black art.

Ilk ghaist that haunts auld ha' or chaumer,
Ye gipsy-gang that deal in glamour,
And you, deep-read in hell's black grammar,
        Warlocks and witches,
Ye'll quake at his conjuring hammer,
        Ye midnight bitches.

On the late Captain Grose's Peregrinations

On the late Captain Grose's Peregrinations

"A chield's amang you takin notes"

It's tauld he was a sodger bred,
And ane wad rather fa'n than fled;
But now he's quat the spurtle-blade,
      And dog-skin wallet,
And taen the—Antiquarian trade,
      I think they call it.

He has a fouth o' auld nick-nackets:
Rusty airn caps and jinglin jackets,
Wad haud the Lothians three in tackets,
      A towmont gude;
And parritch-pats and auld saut-backets,
      Before the flood.

Of Eve's first fire he has a cinder;
Auld Tubalcain's fire-shool and fender;
That which distinguishèd the gender
      O' Balaam's ass:
A broomstick o' the witch of Endor,
      Weel shod wi' brass.

Forbye, he'll shape you aff fu' gleg
The cut of Adam's philibeg;
The knife that nickit Abel's craig
      He'll prove you fully,
It was a fauldjng jocteleg,
      Or lang-kail gullie.

But wad ye see him in his glee,
For meikle glee and fun has he,
Then set him down, and twa or three
      Gude fellows wi' him:
And port, O port! shine thou a wee,
      And THEN ye'll see him!

Now, by the Pow'rs o' verse and prose!
Thou art a dainty chield, O Grose!—
Whae'er o' thee shall ill suppose,
    They sair misca' thee;
I'd take the rascal by the nose,
    Wad say, "Shame fa' thee."

TO MARY IN HEAVEN

Thou ling'ring star, with less'ning ray,
  That lov'st to greet the early morn,
Again thou usher'st in the day
  My Mary from my soul was torn.
O Mary! dear departed shade!
  Where is thy place of blissful rest?
See'st thou thy lover lowly laid?
  Hear'st thou the groans that rend his breast?

That sacred hour can I forget,
  Can I forget the hallow'd grove,
Where, by the winding Ayr, we met,
  To live one day of parting love!
Eternity can not efface
  Those records dear of transports past,
Thy image at our last embrace,
  Ah! little thought we 'twas our last!

Ayr, gurgling, kiss'd his pebbled shore,
  O'erhung with wild-woods, thickening green;
The fragrant birch and hawthorn hoar,
  'Twin'd amorous round the raptur'd scene:
The flowers sprang wanton to be prest,
  The birds sang love on every spray;
Till too, too soon, the glowing west,
  Proclaim'd the speed of wingèd day.

To Mary in Heaven

To Mary in Heaven

"That sacred hour can I forget
Can I forget the hallow'd grove,
Where, by the winding Ayr, we met,
To live one day of parting love."

Still o'er these scenes my mem'ry wakes,
    And fondly broods with miser-care ;
Time but th' impression stronger makes,
    As streams their channels deeper wear,
My Mary ! dear departed shade !
    Where is thy place of blissful rest ?
See'st thou thy lover lowly laid ?
    Hear'st thou the groans that rend his breast ?

EPISTLE TO DR BLACKLOCK

ELLISLAND, 21*st Oct.* 1789.

Wow, but your letter made me vauntie !
And are ye hale, and weel and cantie ?
I ken'd it still, your wee bit jauntie
            Wad bring ye to :
Lord send you aye as weel's I want ye !
            And then ye'll do.

The ill-thief blaw the Heron south !
And never drink be near his drouth !
He tauld myself by word o' mouth,
            He'd tak my letter ;
I lippen'd to the chiel in trouth,
            And bade nae better.

But aiblins, honest Master Heron
Had, at the time, some dainty fair one
To ware his theologic care on,
            And holy study ;
And tired o' sauls to waste his lear on,
            E'en tried the body

But what d'ye think, my trusty fere,
I'm turn'd a gauger—Peace be here !
                H*

Parnassian queans, I fear, I fear,
          Ye'll now disdain me!
And then my fifty pounds a year
          Will little gain me.

Ye glaikit, gleesome, dainty damies,
Wha, by Castalia's wimplin streamies,
Lowp, sing, and lave your pretty limbies,
          Ye ken, ye ken,
That strang necessity supreme is
          'Mang sons o' men.

I hae a wife and twa wee laddies;
They maun hae brose and brats o' duddies;
Ye ken yoursels my heart right proud is—
          I need na vaunt—
But I'll sned besoms, thraw saugh-woodies,
          Before they want.

Lord help me thro' this warld o' care!
I'm weary sick o't late and air!
Not but I hae a richer share
          Than mony ithers;
But why should ae man better fare,
          And a' men brithers?

Come, Firm Resolve, take thou the van,
Thou stalk o' carl-hemp in man!
And let us mind, faint heart ne'er wan
          A lady fair:
Wha does the utmost that he can,
          Will whiles do mair.

But to conclude my sillie rhyme
(I'm scant o' verse and scant o' time),

To make a happy fireside clime
      To weans and wife,
That's the true pathos and sublime
      Of human life.

My compliments to sister Beckie,
And eke the same to honest Luckie;
I wat she is a daintie chuckie,
      As e'er tread clay;
And gratefully, my gude auld cockie,
      I'm yours for aye.
              ROBERT BURNS.

LAMENT OF MARY, QUEEN OF SCOTS,

ON THE APPROACH OF SPRING

Now Nature hangs her mantle green
    On every blooming tree,
And spreads her sheets o' daisies white
    Out o'er the grassy lea
Now Phœbus cheers the crystal streams,
    And glads the azure skies;
But nought can glad the weary wight
    That fast in durance lies.

Now laverocks wake the merry morn
    Aloft on dewy wing;
The merle, in his noontide bow'r,
    Makes woodland echoes ring;
The mavis wild wi' mony a note,
    Sings drowsy day to rest
In love and freedom they rejoice,
    Wi' care nor thrall opprest.

Now blooms the lily by the bank,
  The primrose down the brae;
The hawthorn's budding in the glen,
  And milk-white is the slae:
The meanest hind in fair Scotland
  May rove their sweets amang;
But I, the Queen of a' Scotland,
  Maun lie in prison strang.

I was the Queen o' bonie France,
  Where happy I hae been;
Fu' lightly raise I in the morn,
  As blythe lay down at e'en:
And I'm the sov'reign of Scotland,
  And mony a traitor there;
Yet here I lie in foreign bands,
  And never-ending care.

But as for thee, thou false woman,
  My sister and my fae,
Grim Vengeance yet shall whet a sword
  That thro' thy soul shall gae;
The weeping blood in woman's breast
  Was never known to thee;
Nor th' balm that draps on wounds of woe
  Frae woman's pitying e'e.

My son! my son! may kinder stars
  Upon thy fortune shine;
And may those pleasures gild thy reign,
  That ne'er wad blink on mine!
God keep thee frae thy mother's faes,
  Or turn their hearts to thee:
And where thou meet'st thy mother's friend,
  Remember him for me!

Lament of Mary, Queen of Scots

Lament of Mary, Queen of Scots

"And in the narrow house of death,
Let winter round me rave;
And the next flow'rs that deck the Spring,
Bloom on my peaceful grave."

O ! soon, to me, may Summer suns
  Nae mair light up the morn !
Nae mair to me the Autumn winds
  Wave o'er the yellow corn ?
And, in the narrow house of death,
  Let Winter round me rave ;
And the next flow'rs that deck the Spring,
  Bloom on my peaceful grave !

ELEGY ON
CAPTAIN MATTHEW HENDERSON

A GENTLEMAN WHO HELD THE PATENT FOR HIS
HONOURS IMMEDIATELY FROM ALMIGHTY GOD !

But now his radiant course is run,
  For Matthew's course was bright :
His soul was like the glorious sun,
  A matchless, Heavenly light.

O DEATH ! thou tyrant fell and bloody !
The meikle devil wi' a woodie
Haurl thee hame to his black smiddie,
      O'er hurcheon hides,
And like stock-fish come o'er his studdie
      Wi' thy auld sides !

He's gane, he's gane ! he's frae us torn,
The ae best fellow e'er was born !
Thee, Matthew, Nature's sel' shall mourn,
      By wood and wild,
Where haply, Pity strays forlorn,
      Frae man exil'd.

Ye hills, near neighbours o' the starns,
That proudly cock your cresting cairns !

Ye cliffs, the haunts of sailing earns,
  Where Echo slumbers!
Come join, ye Nature's sturdiest bairns,
  My wailing numbers!

Mourn, ilka grove the cushat kens!
Ye haz'ly shaws and briery dens!
Ye burnies, wimplin down your glens,
  Wi' toddlin din,
Or foaming, strang, wi' hasty stens,
  Frae lin to lin.

Mourn, little harebells o'er the lea;
Ye stately foxgloves, fair to see;
Ye woodbines hanging bonilie,
  In scented bow'rs;
Ye roses on your thorny tree,
  The first o' flow'rs.

At dawn, when ev'ry grassy blade
Droops with a diamond at his head,
At ev'n, when beans their fragrance shed,
  I' th' rustling gale,
Ye maukins, whiddin thro' the glade,
  Come join my wail.

Mourn, ye wee songsters o' the wood;
Ye grouse that crap the heather bud;
Ye curlews, calling thro' a clud;
  Ye whistling plover;
And mourn, ye whirring paitrick brood;
  He's gane for ever!

Mourn, sooty coots, and speckled teals;
Ye fisher herons, watching eels;

Ye duck and drake, wi' airy wheels
    Circling the lake;
Ye bitterns, till the quagmire reels,
    Rair for his sake.

Mourn, clam'ring craiks at close o' day;
'Mang fields o' flow'ring clover gay;
And when ye wing your annual way
    Frae our cauld shore,
Tell thae far warlds wha lies in clay,
    Wham we deplore.

Ye houlets, frae your ivy bow'r
In some auld tree, or eldritch tow'r,
What time the moon, wi' silent glow'r,
    Sets up her horn,
Wail thro' the dreary midnight hour,
    Till waukrife morn.

O rivers, forests, hills, and plains!
Oft have ye heard my canty strains:
But now, what else for me remains
    But tales of woe;
And frae my een the drapping rains
    Maun ever flow.

Mourn, Spring, thou darling of the year!
Ilk cowslip cup shall kep a tear:
Thou, Simmer, while each corny spear
    Shoots up its head,
Thy gay, green, flow'ry tresses shear,
    For him that's dead?

Thou, Autumn, wi' thy yellow hair,
In grief thy sallow mantle tear!

Thou, Winter, hurling thro' the air
    The roaring blast,
Wide o'er the naked world declare
    The worth we've lost!

Mourn him, thou Sun, great source of light!
Mourn, Empress of the silent night!
And you, ye twinkling starnies bright,
    My Matthew mourn!
For through your orbs he's ta'en his flight,
    Ne'er to return.

O Henderson! the man! the brother!
And art thou gone, and gone for ever!
And hast thou crost that unknown river,
    Life's dreary bound!
Like thee, where shall I find another,
    The world around!

Go to your sculptur'd tombs, ye Great,
In a' the tinsel trash o' state!
But by thy honest turf I'll wait,
    Thou man of worth!
And weep the ae best fellow's fate
    E'er lay in earth.

THE EPITAPH.

Stop, passenger! my story's brief,
    And truth I shall relate, man;
I tell nae common tale o' grief,
    For Matthew was a great man.

If thou uncommon merit hast,
    Yet spurn'd at Fortune's door, man;
A look of pity hither cast,
    For Matthew was a poor man.

If thou a noble sodger art,
  That passest by this grave, man ;
There moulders here a gallant heart,
  For Matthew was a brave man.

If thou on men, their works and ways,
  Canst throw uncommon light, man ;
Here lies wha weel had won thy praise,
  For Matthew was a bright man.

If thou, at Friendship's sacred ca',
  Wad life itself resign, man :
Thy sympathetic tear maun fa',
  For Matthew was a kind man.

If thou art staunch, without a stain,
  Like the unchanging blue, man ;
This was a kinsman o' thy ain,
  For Matthew was a true man.

If thou hast wit, and fun, and fire,
  And ne'er guid wine did fear, man ;
This was thy billie, dam, and sire,
  For Matthew was a queer man.

If ony whiggish, whingin sot,
  To blame poor Matthew dare, man ;
May dool and sorrow be his lot,
  For Matthew was a rare man.

TAM O' SHANTER

A TALE

" Of Brownyis and of Bogillis full is this Buke."
                              GAWIN DOUGLAS.

WHEN chapman billies leave the street,
And drouthy neibors neibors meet ;

As market days are wearing late,
And folk begin to tak the gate,
While we sit bousing at the nappy,
An' getting fou and unco happy,
We think na on the lang Scots miles,
The mosses, waters, slaps and stiles,
That lie between us and our hame,
Where sits our sulky, sullen dame,
Gathering her brows like gathering storm,
Nursing her wrath to keep it warm.

This truth fand honest Tam o' Shanter,
As he frae Ayr ae night did canter:
(Auld Ayr, wham ne'er a town surpasses,
For honest men and bonie lasses).

O Tam! had'st thou but been sae wise,
As taen thy ain wife Kate's advice!
She tauld thee weel thou was a skellum,
A blethering, blustering, drunken blellum;
That frae November till October,
Ae market-day thou was na sober;
That ilka melder wi' the Miller,
Thou sat as lang as thou had siller;
That ev'ry naig was ca'd a shoe on
The Smith and thee gat roarin fou on;
That at the Lord's house, ev'n on Sunday,
Thou drank wi' Kirkton Jean till Monday;
She prophesied that late or soon,
Thou wad be found, deep drown'd in Doon,
Or catch'd wi' warlocks in the mirk,
By Alloway's auld, haunted kirk.

Ah, gentle dames! it gars me greet,
To think how mony counsels sweet,

Tam o' Shanter

Tam o' Shanter

"The Piper loud and louder blew
The dancers quick and quicker flew."

How mony lengthen'd, sage advices,
The husband frae the wife despises!

But to our tale :—Ae market night,
Tam had got planted unco right,
Fast by an ingle, bleezing finely,
Wi' reaming swats that drank divinely;
And at his elbow, Souter Johnie,
His ancient, trusty, drouthy crony:
Tam lo'ed him like a very brither;
They had been fou for weeks thegither.
The night drave on wi' sangs an' clatter;
And aye the ale was growing better:
The Landlady and Tam grew gracious,
Wi' favours secret, sweet and precious:
The Souter tauld his queerest stories;
The Landlord's laugh was ready chorus:
The storm without might rair and rustle,
Tam did na mind the storm a whistle.

Care, mad to see a man sae happy,
E'en drown'd himsel amang the nappy.
As bees flee hame wi' lades o' treasure,
The minutes wing'd their way wi' pleasure:
Kings may be blest, but Tam was glorious,
O'er a' the ills o' life victorious!

But pleasures are like poppies spread,
You seize the flow'r, its bloom is shed;
Or like the snow falls in the river,
A moment white—then melts for ever;
Or like the Borealis race,
That flit ere you can point their place;
Or like the Rainbow's lovely form
Evanishing amid the storm.——

Nae man can tether Time nor Tide.
The hour approaches Tam maun ride ;
That hour, o' night's black arch the key-stane,
That dreary hour he mounts his beast in ;
And sic a night he taks the road in,
As ne'er poor sinner was abroad in.

The wind blew as 'twad blawn its last ;
The rattling showers rose on the blast ;
The speedy gleams the darkness swallow'd ;
Loud, deep, and lang the thunder bellow'd :
That night, a child might understand,
The deil had business on his hand.

Weel-mounted on his grey mare Meg,
A better never lifted leg,
Tam skelpit on thro' dub and mire,
Despising wind, and rain, and fire ;
Whiles holding fast his gude blue bonnet,
Whiles crooning o'er some auld Scots sonnet,
Whiles glow'rin round wi' prudent cares,
Lest bogles catch him unawares ;
Kirk-Alloway was drawing nigh,
Where ghaists and houlets nightly cry.

By this time he was cross the ford,
Where in the snaw the chapman smoor'd ;
And past the birks and meikle stane,
Where drunken Charlie brak's neck-bane ;
And thro' the whins, and by the cairn,
Where hunters fand the murder'd bairn ;
And near the thorn, aboon the well,
Where Mungo's mither hang'd hersel'.
Before him Doon pours all his floods,
The doubling storm roars thro' the woods,

The lightnings flash from pole to pole,
Near and more near the thunders roll,
When, glimmering thro' the groaning trees,
Kirk-Alloway seem'd in a bleeze,
Thro' ilka bore the beams were glancing,
And loud resounded mirth and dancing.

Inspiring bold John Barleycorn!
What dangers thou canst make us scorn!
Wi' tippenny, we fear nae evil;
Wi' usquabae, we'll face thé devil!
The swats sae ream'd in Tammie's noddle,
Fair play, he car'd na deils a boddle,
But Maggie stood, right sair astonish'd,
Till, by the heel and hand admonish d,
She ventur'd forward on the light;
And, wow! Tam saw an unco sight!

Warlocks and witches in a dance:
Nae cotillon, brent new frae France,
But hornpipes, jigs, strathspeys, and reels,
Put life and mettle in their heels.
A winnock-bunker in the east,
There sat auld Nick, in shape o' beast;
A tousie tyke, black, grim, and large,
To gie them music was his charge.
He screw'd the pipes and gart them skirl,
Till roof and rafters a' did dirl.—
Coffins stood round, like open presses,
That shaw'd the Dead in their last dresses;
And (by some devilish cantraip sleight)
Each in its cauld hand held a light.
By which heroic Tam was able
To note upon the haly table,

A murderer's banes, in gibbet-airns ;
Twa span-lang, wee, unchristened bairns ;
A thief, new-cutted frae a rape,
Wi' his last gasp his gab did gape ;
Five tomahawks, wi' blude red-rusted :
Five scimitars, wi' murder crusted ;
A garter which a babe had strangled :
A knife, a father's throat had mangled,
Whom his ain son of life bereft,
The grey hairs yet stack to the heft ;
Wi' mair of horrible and awfu',
Which even to name wad be unlawfu'.

　　As Tammie glowr'd, amaz'd, and curious,
The mirth and fun grew fast and furious ;
The Piper loud and louder blew,
The dancers quick and quicker flew,
They reel'd, they set, they cross'd, they cleekit,
Till ilka carlin swat and reekit,
And coost her duddies to the wark,
And linkit at it in her sark !

　　Now Tam, O Tam ! had they been queans,
A' plump and strapping in their teens !
Their sarks, instead o' creeshie flainen,
Been snaw-white seventeen-hunder linen !—
Thir breeks o' mine, my only pair,
That aince were plush, o' guid blue hair,
I wad hae gien them off my hurdies,
For ae blink o' the bonie burdies !
But wither'd beldams, auld and droll,
Rigwoodie hags wad spean a foal,
Louping an' flinging on a crummock,
I wonder did na turn thy stomach.

But Tam kent what was what fu' brawlie :
There was ae winsome wench and waulie
That night enlisted in the core,
Lang after ken'd on Carrick shore
(For mony a beast to dead she shot,
And perish'd mony a bonie boat,
And shook baith meikle corn and bear,
And kept the country-side in fear) ;
Her cutty sark, o' Paisley harn,
That while a lassie she had worn,
In longitude tho' sorely scanty,
It was her best, and she was vauntie.
Ah! little ken'd thy reverend grannie,
That sark she coft for her wee Nannie,
Wi' twa pund Scots ('twas a' her riches),
Wad ever grac'd a dance of witches !

But here my Muse her wing maun cour,
Sic flights are far beyond her power ;
To sing how Nannie lap and flang
(A souple jade she was and strang),
And how Tam stood, like ane bewitch'd,
And thought his very een enrich'd :
Even Satan glowr'd, and fidg'd fu' fain,
And hotch'd and blew wi' might and main :
Till first ae caper, syne anither,
Tam tint his reason a' thegither,
And roars out, " Weel done, Cutty-sark ! "
And in an instant all was dark :
And scarcely had he Maggie rallied,
When out the hellish legion sallied.

As bees bizz out wi' angry fyke,
When plundering herds assail their byke ;

As open pussie's mortal foes,
When, pop! she starts before their nose;
As eager runs the market-crowd,
When "Catch the thief!" resounds aloud;
So Maggie runs, the witches follow,
Wi' mony an eldritch skreich and hollo.

Ah, Tam! Ah, Tam! thou'll get thy
        fairin!
In hell they'll roast thee like a herrin!
In vain thy Kate awaits thy comin!
Kate soon will be a woefu' woman!
Now, do thy speedy utmost, Meg,
And win the key-stane o' the brig;
There, at them thou thy tail may toss,
A running stream they dare na cross.
But ere the key-stane she could make,
The fient a tail she had to shake!
For Nannie, far before the rest,
Hard upon noble Maggie prest,
And flew at Tam wi' furious ettle;
But little wist she Maggie's mettle!
Ae spring brought off her master hale,
But left behind her ain grey tail:
The carlin claught her by the rump,
And left poor Maggie scarce a stump.

Now, wha this tale o' truth shall read,
Ilk man, and mother's son, take heed:
Whene'er to Drink you are inclin'd,
Or Cutty-sarks rin in your mind,
Think ye may buy the joys o'er dear;
Remember Tam o' Shanter's mare.

Kirkoswald and Tam o' Shanter's Grave

From an engraving after David Octavius Hill

LAMENT FOR JAMES, EARL OF GLENCAIRN

THE wind blew hollow frae the hills,
   By fits the sun's departing beam
Look'd on the fading yellow woods,
   That wav'd o'er Lugar's winding stream :
Beneath a craigy steep, a Bard,
   Laden with years and meikle pain,
In loud lament bewail'd his lord,
   Whom Death had all untimely ta'en.

He lean'd him to an ancient aik,
   Whose trunk was mould'ring down with years ;
His locks were bleachèd white with time,
   His hoary cheek was wet wi' tears !
And as he touch'd his trembling harp,
   And as he tun'd his doleful sang,
The winds, lamenting thro' their caves,
   To Echo bore the notes alang.

" Ye scatter'd birds that faintly sing,
   The reliques o' the vernal queir !
Ye woods that shed on a' the winds
   The honours of the aged year !
A few short months, and glad and gay,
   Again ye'll charm the ear and e'e ;
But nocht in all revolving time
   Can gladness bring again to me.

" I am a bending aged tree,
   That long has stood the wind and rain ;
But now has come a cruel blast,
   And my last hald of earth is gane ;

Nae leaf o' mine shall greet the spring,
  Nae simmer sun exalt my bloom;
But I maun lie before the storm,
  And ithers plant them in my room.

" I've seen sae mony changefu' years,
  On earth I am a stranger grown :
I wander in the ways of men,
  Alike unknowing, and unknown :
Unheard, unpitied, unreliev'd,
  I bear alane my lade o' care,
For silent, low, on beds of dust,
  Lie a' that would my sorrows share.

" And last, (the sum of a' my griefs!)
  My noble master lies in clay ;
The flow'r amang our barons bold,
  His country's pride, his country's stay :
In weary being now I pine,
  For a' the life of life is dead,
And hope has left my aged ken,
  On forward wing for ever fled.

" Awake thy last sad voice, my harp !
  The voice of woe and wild despair !
Awake, resound thy latest lay,
  Then sleep in silence evermair !
And thou, my last, best, only friend,
  That fillest an untimely tomb,
Accept this tribute from the Bard
  Thou brought from Fortune's mirkest gloom.

" In Poverty's low barren vale,
  Thick mists obscure involv'd me round ;
Though oft I turn'd the wistful eye,
  Nae ray of fame was to be found :

Thou found'st me, like the morning sun
  That melts the fogs in limpid air,
The friendless bard and rustic song
  Became alike thy fostering care.

" O ! why has worth so short a date,
  While villains ripen grey with time ?
Must thou, the noble, gen'rous, great,
  Fall in bold manhood's hardy prime !
Why did I live to see that day—
  A day to me so full of woe ?
O ! had I met the mortal shaft
  That laid my benefactor low !

" The bridegroom may forget the bride
  Was made his wedded wife yestreen ;
The monarch may forget the crown
  That on his head an hour has been ;
The mother may forget the child
  That smiles sae sweetly on her knee ;
But I'll remember thee, Glencairn,
  And a' that thou hast done for me ! '

SECOND EPISTLE
TO ROBERT GRAHAM, ESQ.,
OF FINTRY

5TH OCTOBER 1791

LATE crippl'd of an arm, and now a leg,
About to beg a pass for leave to beg ;
Dull, listless, teas'd, dejected, and deprest
(Nature is adverse to a cripple's rest) ;
Will generous Graham list to his Poet's wail ?
(It soothes poor Misery, hearkening to her tale)
And hear him curse the light he first survey'd,
And doubly curse the luckless rhyming trade ?

Thou, Nature! partial Nature! I arraign;
Of thy caprice maternal I complain;
The lion and the bull thy care have found,
One shakes the forests, and one spurns the
    ground;
Thou giv'st the ass his hide, the snail his shell;
Th' envenom'd wasp, victorious, guards his cell;
Thy minions kings defend, control, devour,
In all th' omnipotence of rule and power;
Foxes and statesmen subtile wiles ensure;
The cit and polecat stink, and are secure;
Toads with their poison, doctors with their drug,
The priest and hedgehog in their robes, are snug;
Ev'n silly woman has her warlike arts
Her tongue and eyes—her dreaded spear and darts.

But O thou bitter step-mother and hard,
To thy poor, fenceless, naked child—the Bard!
A thing unteachable in world's skill,
And half an idiot too, more helpless still:
No heels to bear him from the op'ning dun;
No claws to dig, his hated sight to shun;
No horns, but those by luckless Hymen worn,
And those, alas! not, Amalthea's horn:
No nerves olfact'ry, Mammon's trusty cur,
Clad in rich Dulness' comfortable fur;
In naked feeling, and in aching pride,
He bears th' unbroken blast from ev'ry side:
Vampyre booksellers drain him to the heart,
And scorpion critics cureless venom dart.

Critics—appall'd, I venture on the name;
Those cut-throat bandits in the paths of fame
Bloody dissectors, worse than ten Munroes;
He hacks to teach, they mangle to expose.

His heart by causeless wanton malice wrung,
By blockheads' daring into madness stung ;
His well-won bays, than life itself more dear,
By miscreants torn, who ne'er one sprig must
    wear ;
Foil'd, bleeding, tortur'd in th' unequal strife,
The hapless Poet flounders on thro' life :
Till, fled each hope that once his bosom fir'd,
And fled each muse that glorious once inspir'd,
Low sunk in squalid, unprotected age,
Dead even resentment for his injur'd page,
He heeds or feels no more the ruthless critic's
    rage !
So, by some hedge, the gen'rous steed deceas'd,
For half-starv'd snarling curs a dainty feast,
By toil and famine wore to skin and bone,
Lies, senseless of each tugging bitch's son.

O Dulness ! portion of the truly blest !
Calm shelter'd haven of eternal rest !
Thy sons ne'er madden in the fierce extremes
Of Fortune's polar frost, or torrid beams.
If mantling high she fills the golden cup,
With sober selfish ease they sip it up ;
Conscious the bounteous meed they well deserve,
They only wonder "some folks" do not starve.
The grave sage hern thus easy picks his frog,
And thinks the mallard a sad worthless dog.
When disappointment snaps the clue of hope,
And thro' disastrous night they darkling grope,
With deaf endurance sluggishly they bear,
And just conclude "that fools are fortune's care."
So heavy, passive to the tempest's shocks,
Strong on the sign-post stands the stupid ox.

Not so the idle Muses' mad-cap train,
Not such the workings of their moon-struck
    brain;
In equanimity they never dwell,
By turns in soaring heav'n, or vaulted hell.

I dread thee, Fate, relentless and severe,
With all a poet's, husband's, father's fear!
Already one strong hold of hope is lost—
Glencairn, the truly noble, lies in dust
(Fled, like the sun-eclips'd as noon appears,
And left us darkling in a world of tears);
O! hear my ardent, grateful, selfish prayer!
Fintry, my other stay, long bless and spare!
Thro' a long life his hopes and wishes crown,
And bright in cloudless skies his sun go down!
May bliss domestic smooth his private path;
Give energy to life; and soothe his latest breath,
With many a filial tear circling the bed of death!

EPISTLE FROM ESOPUS TO MARIA

FROM those drear solitudes and frowsy cells,
Where Infamy with sad Repentance dwells;
Where turnkeys make the jealous portal fast,
And deal from iron hands the spare repast;
Where truant 'prentices, yet young in sin,
Blush at the curious stranger peeping in;
Where strumpets, relics of the drunken roar,
Resolve to drink, nay half—to whore no more;
Where tiny thieves, not destin'd yet to swing,
Beat hemp for others, riper for the string:
From these dire scenes my wretched lines I date,
To tell Maria her Esopus' fate.

" Alas ! I feel I am no actor here ! "
'Tis real hangmen real scourges bear !
Prepare, Maria, for a horrid tale
Will turn thy very rouge to deadly pale ;
Will make thy hair, tho' erst from gipsy poll'd,
By barber woven, and by barber sold,
Though twisted smooth with Harry's nicest care,
Like hoary bristles to erect and stare.
The hero of the mimic scene, no more
I start in Hamlet, in Othello roar ;
Or, haughty Chieftain, 'mid the din of arms
In Highland bonnet woo Malvina's charms ;
While sans-culottes stoop up the mountain high,
And steal from me Maria's prying eye.
Blest Highland bonnet ! once my proudest dress,
Now prouder still, Maria's temples press ;
I see her wave thy towering plumes afar,
And call each coxcomb to the wordy war :
I see her face the first of Ireland's sons,
And even out-Irish his Hibernian bronze ;
The crafty Colonel leaves the tartan'd lines,
For other wars, where he a hero shines :
The hopeful youth, in Scottish senate bred,
Who owns a Bushby's heart without the head,
Comes 'mid a string of coxcombs, to display
That *veni, vidi, vici,* is his way :
The shrinking Bard adown the alley skulks,
And dreads a meeting worse than Woolwich hulks :
Though there his heresies in Church and State
Might well award him Muir and Palmer's fate :
Still she undaunted reels and rattles on,
And dares the public like a noontide sun.
What scandal called Maria's jaunty stagger
The ricket reeling of a crooked swagger ?

Whose spleen (e'en worse than Burns's venom,
    when
He dips in gall unmix'd his eager pen,
And pours his vengeance in the burning line,)—
Who christen'd thus Maria's lyre divine
The idiot strum of Vanity bemus'd,
And even the abuse of Poesy abus'd?—
Who called her verse a Parish Workhouse, made
For motley foundling Fancies, stolen or strayed?

A Workhouse! ah, that sound awakes my woes,
And pillows on the thorn my rack'd repose!
In durance vile here must I wake and weep,
And all my frowsy couch in sorrow steep;
That straw, where many a rogue has lain of yore,
And vermin'd gipsies litter'd heretofore.

Why, Lonsdale, thus thy wrath on vagrants pour?
Must earth no rascal save thyself endure?
Must thou alone in guilt immortal swell,
And make a vast monopoly of hell?
Thou know'st the Virtues cannot hate thee worse;
The Vices also, must they club their curse?
Or must no tiny sin to others fall,
Because thy guilt's supreme enough for all?

Maria, send me too thy griefs and cares;
In all of thee sure thy Esopus shares,
As thou at all mankind the flag unfurls,
Who on my fair one Satire's vengeance hurls—
Who calls thee, pert, affected, vain coquette,
A wit in folly, and a fool in wit!
Who says that fool alone is not thy due,
And quotes thy treacheries to prove it true!
Our force united on thy foes we'll turn,
And dare the war with all of woman born:

For who can write and speak as thou and I ?
My periods that deciphering defy,
And thy still matchless tongue that conquers all
    reply !

ODE FOR
GENERAL WASHINGTON'S
BIRTHDAY

No Spartan tube, no Attic shell,
    No lyre Æolian I awake ;
'Tis Liberty's bold note I swell,
    Thy harp, Columbia, let me take !
See gathering thousands, while I sing,
A broken chain exulting bring,
    And dash it in a tyrant's face,
And dare him to his very beard,
And tell him he no more is feared—
    No more the despot of Columbia's race !
A tyrant's proudest insults brav'd,
They shout—a People freed ! They hail an
    Empire saved.

Where is man's godlike form ?
    Where is that brow erect and bold—
    That eye that can unmov'd behold
The wildest rage, the loudest storm
That e'er created Fury dared to raise ?
Avaunt ! thou caitiff, servile, base,
That tremblest at a despot's nod,
Yet, crouching under the iron rod,
    Canst laud the arm that struck th' insult-
    ing blow !
Art thou of man's Imperial line ?
Dost boast that countenance divine
    Each skulking feature answers, No !

But come, ye sons of Liberty,
Columbia's offspring, brave as free,
In danger's hour still flaming in the van,
Ye know, and dare maintain, the Royalty of Man!

Alfred! on thy starry throne,
   Surrounded by the tuneful choir,
   The bards that erst have struck the patriot lyre,
   And rous'd the freeborn Briton's soul of fire,
No more thy England own!
Dare injured nations form the great design,
   To make detested tyrants bleed?
   Thy England execrates the glorious deed!
   Beneath her hostile banners waving,
   Every pang of honour braving,
England in thunder calls, "The tyrant's cause is
      mine!"
That hour accurst how did the fiends rejoice
And hell, thro' all her confines, raise the exulting
      voice,
That hour which saw the generous English name
Linkt with such damnèd deeds of everlasting
      shame!

Thee, Caledonia! thy wild heaths among,
Fam'd for the martial deed, the heaven-taught song,
   To thee I turn with swimming eyes;
Where is that soul of Freedom fled?
Immingled with the mighty dead,
   Beneath that hallow'd turf where Wallace lies.
Hear it not, WALLACE! in thy bed of death.
   Ye babbling winds! in silence sweep,
   Disturb not ye the hero's sleep,
Nor give the coward secret breath!

Is this the ancient Caledonian form,
Firm as her rock, resistless as her storm?
Show me that eye which shot immortal hate,
    Blasting the despot's proudest bearing;
Show me that arm which, nerv'd with thundering
        fate,
    Crush'd Usurpation's boldest daring!—
Dark-quench'd as yonder sinking star,
No more that glance lightens afar;
That palsied arm no more whirls on the waste of
    war.

VERSES TO
COLLECTOR MITCHELL

FRIEND of the Poet, tried and leal,
Wha, wanting thee, might beg or steal;
Alake, alake, the meikle deil
        Wi' a' his witches
Are at it skelpin jig and reel
        In my poor pouches!

I modestly fu' fain wad hint it,
That *One-pound-one*, I sairly want it;
If wi' the hizzie down ye sent it,
        It would be kind;
And while my heart wi' life-blood dunted,
        I'd bear't in mind.

So may the Auld year gang out moanin
To see the New come laden, groanin,
Wi' double plenty o'er the loanin,
        To thee and thine:
Domestic peace and comforts crownin
        The hale design.

Ye've heard this while how I've been lickit,
And by fell Death was nearly nickit;
Grim loon! he got me by the fecket,
    And sair me sheuk;
But by gude luck I lap a wicket,
    And turn'd a neuk.

But by that health, I've got a share o't,
And by that life, I'm promis'd mair o't,
My hale and weel, I'll tak a care o't,
    A tentier way;
Then farewell folly, hide and hair o't,
    For ance and aye!

EPISTLE TO
COLONEL DE PEYSTER

My honor'd Colonel, deep I feel
Your interest in the Poet's weal;
Ah! now sma' heart hae I to speel
    The steep Parnassus,
Surrounded thus by bolus pill,
    And potion glasses.

O what a canty world were it,
Would pain and care and sickness spare it;
And Fortune favour worth and merit
    As they deserve;
And aye rowth o' roast-beef and claret,
    Syne, wha wad starve?

Dame Life, tho' fiction out may trick her,
And in paste gems and frippery deck her;
Oh! flickering, feeble, and unsicker
     I've found her still,
Aye wavering like the willow-wicker,
     'Tween good and ill.

Then that curst carmagnole, auld Satan,
Watches like baudrons by a ratton
Our sinfu' saul to get a claut on
     Wi' felon ire;
Syne, whip! his tail ye'll ne'er cast saut on,
     He's aff like fire.

Ah Nick! ah Nick! it is na fair,
First showing us the tempting ware,
Bright wines, and bonie lasses rare,
     To put us daft;
Syne weave, unseen, thy spider snare
     O hell's damned waft.

Poor Man, the flie, aft bizzes by,
And aft, as chance he comes thee nigh,
Thy damn'd auld elbow yeuks wi' joy
     And hellish pleasure!
Already in thy fancy's eye,
     Thy sicker treasure.

Soon, heels o'er gowdie, in he gangs,
And, like a sheep-head on a tangs,
Thy girning laugh enjoys his pangs,
     And murdering wrestle,
As, dangling in the wind, he hangs,
     A gibbet's tassel.

But lest you think I am uncivil
To plague you with this draunting drivel,
Abjuring a' intentions evil,
   I quat my pen.
The Lord preserve us frae the devil!
   Amen! Amen!

From a wood engraving by Thomas Bewick

BALLADS

—◦◦◦—

JOHN BARLEYCORN: A BALLAD

THERE was three kings into the east,
    Three kings both great and high,
And they hae sworn a solemn oath
    John Barleycorn should die.

They took a plough and plough'd him down,
    Put clods upon his head,
And they hae sworn a solemn oath
    John Barleycorn was dead.

But the cheerful Spring came kindly on,
    And show'rs began to fall;
John Barleycorn got up again,
    And sore surpris'd them all.

The sultry suns of Summer came,
    And he grew thick and strong;
His head weel arm'd wi' pointed spears,
    That no one should him wrong.

The sober Autumn enter'd mild,
    When he grew wan and pale;
His bending joints and drooping head
    Show'd he began to fail.

His colour sicken'd more and more,
    He faded into age;
And then his enemies began
    To show their deadly rage.

263

They've taen a weapon, long and sharp,
   And cut him by the knee ;
Then tied him fast upon a cart,
   Like a rogue for forgerie.

They laid him down upon his back,
   And cudgell'd him full sore ;
They hung him up before the storm,
   And turn'd him o'er and o'er.

They fillèd up a darksome pit
   With water to the brim ;
They heavèd in John Barleycorn,
   There let him sink or swim.

They laid him out upon the floor,
   To work him further woe ;
And still, as signs of life appear'd,
   They toss'd him to and fro.

They wasted, o'er a scorching flame,
   The marrow of his bones ;
But a miller us'd him worst of all,
   For he crush'd him between two stones.

And they hae taen his very heart's blood,
   And drank it round and round ;
And still the more and more they drank,
   Their joy did more abound.

John Barleycorn was a hero bold,
   Of noble enterprise ;
For if you do but taste his blood,
   'Twill make your courage rise.

'Twill make a man forget his woe ;
   'Twill heighten all his joy ;
'Twill make the widow's heart to sing,
   Tho' the tear were in her eye.

Then let us toast John Barleycorn,
Each man a glass in hand;
And may his great posterity
Ne'er fail in old Scotland!

BALLAD ON THE AMERICAN WAR

Tune—"Killiecrankie."

WHEN Guilford good our pilot stood,
An' did our hellim thraw, man,
Ae night, at tea, began a plea,
Within America, man:
Then up they gat the maskin-pat,
And in the sea did jaw, man;
An' did nae less, in full congress,
Than quite refuse our law, man.

Then thro' the lakes Montgomery takes,
I wat he was na slaw, man;
Down Lowrie's Burn he took a turn,
And Carleton did ca', man:
But yet, whatreck, he, at Quebec,
Montgomery-like did fa', man,
Wi' sword in hand, before his band,
Amang his en'mies a', man.

Poor Tammy Gage within a cage
Was kept at Boston-ha', man;
Till Willie Howe took o'er the knowe
For Philadelphia, man;
Wi' sword an' gun he thought a sin
Guid christian bluid to draw, man;
But at New-York, wi' knife an' fork,
Sir-Loin he hackèd sma', man.

1*

Burgoyne gaed up, like spur an' whip,
    Till Fraser brave did fa', man;
Then lost his way, ae misty day,
    In Saratoga shaw, man.
Cornwallis fought as lang's he dought,
    An' did the Buckskins claw, man;
But Clinton's glaive frae rust to save,
    He hung it to the wa', man.

Then Montague, an' Guilford too,
    Began to fear a fa', man;
And Sackville dour, wha stood the stour,
    The German chief to thraw, man:
For Paddy Burke, like ony Turk,
    Nae mercy had at a', man;
An' Charlie Fox threw by the box,
    An' lows'd his tinkler jaw, man.

Then Rockingham took up the game,
    Till death did on him ca', man;
When Shelburne meek held up his cheek,
    Conform to gospel law, man:
Saint Stephen's boys, wi' jarring noise,
    They did his measures thraw, man;
For North an' Fox united stocks,
    An' bore him to the wa', man.

Then clubs an' hearts were Charlie's cartes,
    He swept the stakes awa', man,
Till the diamond's ace, of Indian race,
    Led him a sair *faux pas*, man:
The Saxon lads, wi' loud placads,
    On Chatham's boy did ca', man;
An' Scotland drew her pipe an' blew,
    "Up, Willie, waur them a', man!"

Ballad on the American War

Ballad on the American War

"Then Montague, and Guilford too,
Began to fa', man . . . "

Behind the throne then Granville's gone,
  A secret word or twa, man ;
While slee Dundas arous'd the class
  Be-north the Roman wa', man :
An' Chatham's wraith, in heav'nly graith,
  (Inspirèd bardies saw, man),
Wi' kindling eyes, cry'd, " Willie, rise !
  Would I hae fear'd them a', man ? "

But, word an' blow, North, Fox, and Co.
  Gowff'd Willie like a ba', man ;
Till Suthron raise, an' coost their claise
  Behind him in a raw, man :
An' Caledon threw by the drone,
  An' did her whittle draw, man ;
An' swoor fu' rude, thro' dirt an' bluid,
  To mak it guid in law, man.

THE FÊTE CHAMPÊTRE

Tune—" Killiecrankie."

O wha will to St Stephen's House,
  To do our errands there, man ?
O wha will to St Stephen's House
  O' th' merry lads of Ayr, man ?
Or will we send a man o' law ?
  Or will we send a sodger ?
Or him wha led o'er Scotland a',
  The meikle Ursa-Major ?

Come, will ye court a noble lord,
  Or buy a score o' lairds, man ?
For worth and honour pawn their word,
  Their vote shall be Glencaird's, man.

Ane gies them coin, ane gies them wine,
   Anither gies them clatter :
Annbank, wha guessed the ladies' taste,
   He gies a Fête Champêtre.

When Love and Beauty heard the news,
   The gay green woods amang, man :
Where, gathering flowers, and busking bowers,
   They heard the blackbird's sang, man :
A vow they sealed it with a kiss,
   Sir Politics to fetter ;
As their's alone, the patent bliss,
   To hold a Fête Champêtre.

Then mounted Mirth on gleesome wing,
   O'er hill and dale she flew, man ;
Ilk wimpling burn, ilk crystal spring,
   Ilk glen and shaw she knew, man :
She summon'd every social sprite,
   That sports by wood or water,
On th' bonie banks of Ayr to meet,
   And keep this Fête Champêtre.

Cauld Boreas, wi' his boisterous crew,
   Were bound to stakes like kye, man,
And Cynthia's car, o' silver fu',
   Clamb up the starry sky, man :
Reflected beams dwell in the streams,
   Or down the current shatter ;
The western breeze steals thro' the trees,
   To view this Fête Champêtre.

How many a robe sae gaily floats !
   What sparkling jewels glance, man !
To Harmony's enchanting notes,
   As moves the mazy dance, man.

The echoing wood, the winding flood,
  Like Paradise did glitter,
When angels met, at Adam's yett,
  To hold their Fête Champêtre.

When Politics came there to mix
  And make his ether-stane, man !
He circled round the magic ground,
  But entrance found he nane, man :
He blush'd for shame, he quat his name,
  Forswore it, every letter,
Wi' humble prayer to join and share
  This festive Fête Champêtre.

CALEDONIA : A BALLAD

Tune—"Caledonian Hunts' Delight " of Mr Gow.

THERE was once a time, but old Time was then
    young,
  That brave Caledonia, the chief of her line,
From some of your northern deities sprung,
  (Who knows not that brave Caledonia's
    divine ?)
From Tweed to the Orcades was her domain,
  To hunt, or to pasture, or do what she would :
Her heav'nly relations there fixèd her reign,
  And pledg'd her their godheads to warrant it
    good.

A lambkin in peace, but a lion in war,
  The pride of her kindred, the heroine grew :
Her grandsire, old Odin, triumphantly swore,—
  "Whoe'er shall provoke thee, th' encounter
    shall rue ! "

With tillage or pasture at times she would sport,
  To feed her fair flocks by her green rustling
    corn ;
But chiefly the woods were her fav'rite resort,
  Her darling amusement, the hounds and the
    horn.

Long quiet she reigned ; till thitherward steers
  A flight of bold eagles from Adria's strand :
Repeated, successive, for many long years,
  They darken'd the air, and they plunder'd the
    land :
Their pounces were murder, and terror their cry,
  They'd conquer'd and ruin'd a world beside ;
She took to her hills, and her arrows let fly,
  The daring invaders they fled or they died.

The Cameleon-Savage disturb'd her repose,
  With tumult, disquiet, rebellion, and strife ;
Provok'd beyond bearing, at last she arose,
  And robb'd him at once of his hopes and his life:
The Anglian lion, the terror of France,
  Oft prowling, ensanguin'd the Tweed's silver
    flood ;
But, taught by the bright Caledonian lance,
  He learnèd to fear in his own native wood.

The fell Harpy-raven took wing from the north,
  The scourge of the seas, and the dread of the
    shore ;
The wild Scandinavian boar issued forth
  To wanton in carnage and wallow in gore :
O'er countries and kingdoms their fury prevail'd,
  No arts could appease them, no arms could repel;
But brave Caledonia in vain they assail'd,
  As Largs well can witness, and Loncartie tell.

Thus bold, independent, unconquer'd, and free,
  Her bright course of glory for ever shall run :
For brave Caledonia immortal must be ;
  I'll prove it from Euclid as clear as the sun :
Rectangle-triangle, the figure we'll chuse :
    The upright is Chance, and old Time is the
      base ;
But brave Caledonia's the hypothenuse ;
    Then, ergo, she'll match them, and match
    them always.

THE KIRK OF SCOTLAND'S ALARM

A BALLAD

Tune—" Come rouse, Brother Sportsman ! "

ORTHODOX! orthodox, wha believe in John Knox,
  Let me sound an alarm to your conscience :
A heretic blast has been blawn in the West,
  That what is not sense must be nonsense,
Orthodox ! That what is not sense must be
  nonsense.

Doctor Mac ! Doctor Mac, you should streek
  on a rack,
  To strike evil-doers wi' terror :
To join Faith and Sense, upon ony pretence,
  Was heretic, damnable error,
Doctor Mac ! 'Twas heretic, damnable error.

Town of Ayr ! town of Ayr, it was rash, I declare,
  To meddle wi' mischief a-brewing,
Provost John is still deaf to the Church's relief,
  And Orator Bob is its ruin,
Town of Ayr ! Yes, Orator Bob is its ruin.

D'rymple mild ! D'rymple mild, tho' your heart's
 like a child,
 And your life like the new-driven snaw,
Yet that winna save you, auld Satan must have you,
 For preaching that three's ane an' twa,
D'rymple mild !   For preaching that three's ane
 an' twa.

Calvin's sons ! Calvin's sons, seize your spiritual
 guns,
 Ammunition you never can need ;
Your hearts are the stuff will be powder enough,
 And your skulls are a storehouse o' lead,
Calvin's sons !   Your skulls are a storehouse o'
 lead.

Rumble John ! rumble John, mount the steps
 with a groan,
 Cry, " The Book is with heresy cramm'd " ;
Then out wi' your ladle, deal brimstone like aidle,
 And roar ev'ry note of the damn'd,
Rumble John !   And roar ev'ry note of the damn'd.

Simper James ! simper James, leave your fair
 Killie dames,
 There's a holier chase in your view :
I'll lay on your head, that the pack you'll soon lead,
 For puppies like you there's but few,
Simper James !   For puppies like you there's
 but few.

Singet Sawnie ! singet Sawnie, are ye huirdin
 the penny,
 Unconscious what danger awaits?
With a jump, yell, and howl, alarm ev'ry soul,
 For Hannibal's just at your gates,
Singet Sawnie ! For Hannibal's just at your gates.

Poet Willie! poet Willie, gie the Doctor a volley,
  Wi' your " Liberty's Chain " and your wit;
O'er Pegasus' side ye ne'er laid a stride,
  Ye but smelt, man, the place where he sh-t,
Poet Willie! Ye but smelt, man, the place
    where he sh-t.

Barr Steenie ! Barr Steenie, what mean ye, what
  mean ye ?
If ye meddle nae mair wi' the matter,
Ye may hae some pretence, man, to havins and
  sense, man,
  Wi' people that ken ye nae better,
Barr Steenie! Wi' people that ken ye nae better.

Jamie Goose! Jamie Goose, ye made but toom
  roose,
  In hunting the wicked Lieutenant;
But the Doctor's your mark, for the Lord's holy
  ark,
  He has cooper'd an' ca'd a wrang pin in't,
Jamie Goose! He has cooper'd an' ca'd a
  wrang pin in't.

Davie Bluster ! Davie Bluster, for a saint if ye
  muster,
  The core is no nice o' recruits ;
Yet to worth let's be just, royal blood ye might
  boast,
  If the Ass were the king o' the brutes,
Davie Bluster ! If the Ass were the king o' the
  brutes.

Cessnock-side ! Cessnock-side, wi' your turkey-
  cock pride,
  Of manhood but sma' is your share :

Ye've the figure, 'tis true, ev'n your foes maun
　　allow,
　　And your friends dare na say ye hae mair,
Cessnock-side!　And your friends dare na say
　　ye hae mair.

Muirland Jock! muirland Jock, when the Lord
　　makes a rock,
　　To crush common-sense for her sins;
If ill-manners were wit, there's no mortal so fit
　　To confound the poor Doctor at ance,
Muirland Jock! To confound the poor Doctor
　　at ance.

Andro Gowk! Andro Gowk, ye may slander
　　the Book,
　　An' the Book nought the waur, let me tell ye;
Tho' ye're rich, an' look big, yet, lay by hat an'
　　wig,
　　An' ye'll hae a calf's-head o' sma' value,
Andro Gowk! Ye'll hae a calf's head o' sma'
　　value.

Daddy Auld! daddy Auld, there's a tod in the
　　fauld,
　　A tod meikle waur than the clerk;
Tho' ye do little skaith, ye'll be in at the death,
　　For gif ye canna bite, ye may bark,
Daddy Auld! Gif ye canna bite, ye may bark.

Holy Will! holy Will, there was wit in your
　　skull,
　　When ye pilfer'd the alms o' the poor;
The timmer is scant when ye're taen for a saunt,
　　Wha should swing in a rape for an hour,
Holy Will!　Ye should swing in a rape for an
　　hour.

Poet Burns! poet Burns, wi' your priest-skelpin
turns,
  Why desert ye your auld native shire?
Your muse is a gipsy, yet were she e'en tipsy,
  She could ca' us nae waur than we are,
Poet Burns! She could ca' us nae waur than we are.

PRESENTATION STANZAS TO CORRESPONDENTS.

Factor John! Factor John, whom the Lord
  made alone,
  And ne'er made anither, thy peer,
Thy poor servant, the Bard, in respectful regard,
  He presents thee this token sincere,
Factor John! He presents thee this token sincere.

Afton's Laird! Afton's Laird, when your pen
  can be spared,
  A copy of this I bequeath,
On the same sicker score as I mention'd before,
  To that trusty auld worthy, Clackleith,
Afton's Laird! To that trusty auld worthy,
  Clackleith.

THE WHISTLE: A BALLAD

I SING of a Whistle, a Whistle of worth,
I sing of a Whistle, the pride of the North,
Was brought to the court of our good Scottish
  King,
And long with this Whistle all Scotland shall ring.

Old Loda, still rueing the arm of Fingal,
The god of the bottle sends down from his hall—
"This Whistle's your challenge, to Scotland
  get o'er,
And drink them to hell, Sir! or ne'er see me more!"

Old poets have sung, and old chronicles tell,
What champions ventur'd, what champions fell :
The son of great Loda was conqueror still,
And blew on the Whistle their requiem shrill.

Till Robert, the lord of the Cairn and the Scaur,
Unmatch'd at the bottle, unconquer'd in war,
He drank his poor god-ship as deep as the sea ;
No tide of the Baltic e'er drunker than he.

Thus Robert, victorious, the trophy has gain'd ;
Which now in his house has for ages remain'd ;
Till three noble chieftains, and all of his blood,
The jovial contest again have renew'd.

Three joyous good fellows, with hearts clear of
   flaw
Craigdarroch, so famous for wit, worth, and law ;
And trusty Glenriddel, so skill'd in old coins ;
And gallant Sir Robert, deep-read in old wines.

Craigdarroch began, with a tongue smooth as oil,
Desiring Glenriddel to yield up the spoil ;
Or else he would muster the heads of the clan,
And once more, in claret, try which was the man.

" By the gods of the ancients ! " Glenriddel
   replies,
" Before I surrender so glorious a prize,
I'll conjure the ghost of the great Rorie More,
And bumper his horn with him twenty times o'er."

Sir Robert, a soldier, no speech would pretend,
But he ne'er turn'd his back on his foe, or his
   friend ;
Said, " Toss down the Whistle, the prize of the
   field,"
And knee-deep in claret, he'd die ere he'd yield.

The Whistle

After an illustration by A.W. Huffan

The Whistle

"Six bottles a-piece had well wore out the night . . ."

To the board of Glenriddel our heroes repair,
So noted for drowning of sorrow and care ;
But, for wine and for welcome, not more known
 to fame,
Than the sense, wit, and taste, of a sweet lovely
 dame.

A bard was selected to witness the fray,
And tell future ages the feats of the day ;
A bard who detested all sadness and spleen,
And wish'd that Parnassus a vineyard had been.

The dinner being over, the claret they ply,
And ev'ry new cork is a new spring of joy ;
In the bands of old friendship and kindred so set,
And the bands grew the tighter the more they
 were wet.

Gay Pleasures ran riot as bumpers ran o'er :
Bright Phœbus ne'er witness'd so joyous a core,
And vow'd that to leave them he was quite forlorn,
Till Cynthia hinted he'd see them next morn.

Six bottles a-piece had well wore out the night.
When gallant Sir Robert, to finish the fight,
Turn'd o'er in one bumper a bottle of red,
And swore 'twas the way that their ancestor did.

Then worthy Glenriddel, so cautious and sage,
No longer the warfare ungodly would wage ;
A high Ruling Elder to wallow in wine ;
He left the foul business to folks less divine.

The gallant Sir Robert fought hard to the end ;
But who can with Fate and quart bumpers
 contend !

Though Fate said, a hero should perish in light;
So uprose bright Phœbus—and down fell the
 knight.

Next uprose our Bard, like a prophet in drink:—
" Craigdarroch, thou'lt soar when creation shall
 sink !
But if thou would flourish immortal in rhyme,
 me—one bottle more—and have at the sublime!

" Thy line, that have struggled for freedom with
 Bruce,
Shall heroes and patriots ever produce:
So thine be the laurel, and mine be the bay ;
The field thou hast won, by yon bright god of
 day ! "

THE FIVE CARLINS

AN ELECTION BALLAD

Tune—" Chevy Chase."

There was five Carlins in the South,
 They fell upon a scheme,
To send a lad to London town,
 To bring them tidings hame.

Nor only bring them tidings hame,
 But do their errands there,
And aiblins gowd and honor baith
 Might be that laddie's share.

There was Maggy by the banks o' Nith,
 A dame wi' pride eneugh ;
And Marjory o' the mony Lochs,
 A Carlin auld and teugh.

And blinkin Bess of Annandale,
    That dwelt near Solway-side;
And whisky Jean, that took her gill,
    In Galloway sae wide.

And black Joan, frae Crichton Peel,
    O' gipsy kith an' kin;
Five wighter Carlins were na found
    The South countrie within.

To send a lad to London town,
    They met upon a day;
And mony a knight, and mony a laird,
    This errand fain wad gae.

O mony a knight, and mony a laird,
    This errand fain wad gae;
But nae ane could their fancy please,
    O ne'er a ane but twae.

The first ane was a belted Knight,
    Bred of a Border band;
And he wad gae to London town,
    Might nae man him withstand.

And he wad do their errands weel,
    And meikle he wad say;
And ilka ane about the court
    Wad bid to him gude-day.

The neist cam in, a Soger youth,
    Wha spak wi' modest grace,
And he wad gae to London town,
    If sae their pleasure was.

He wad na hecht them courtly gifts,
    Nor meikle speech pretend;
But he wad hecht an honest heart,
    Wad ne'er desert his friend.

Then, wham to chuse, and wham refuse,
  At strife thir Carlins fell;
For some had Gentlefolks to please,
  And some wad please themsel'.

Then out spak mim-mou'd Meg o' Nith,
  And she spak up wi' pride,
And she wad send the Sodger youth,
  Whatever might betide.

For the auld Gudeman o' London court
  She didna care a pin;
But she wad send the Soger youth,
  To greet his eldest son.

Then up sprang Bess o' Annandale,
  And a deadly aith she's taen,
That she wad vote the Border Knight,
  Though she should vote her lane.

" For far-off fowls hae feathers fair,
  And fools o' change are fain;
But I hae tried the Border Knight,
  And I'll try him yet again."

Says black Joan frae Crichton Peel,
  A Carlin stoor and grim,
" The auld Gudeman, and the young
    Gudeman,
  For me may sink or swim;

" For fools will prate o' right or wrang,
  While knaves laugh them to scorn;
But the Soger's friends hae blawn the best,
  So he shall bear the horn."

Then whisky Jean spak owre her drink,
  " Ye weel ken, kimmers a',

The auld gudeman o' London court,
    His back's been at the wa';

" And mony a friend that kiss'd his caup,
    Is now a fremit wight;
But it's ne'er be said o' whisky Jean—
    We'll send the Border Knight."

Then slow raise Marjory o' the Lochs,
    And wrinkled was her brow,
Her ancient weed was russet gray,
    Her auld Scots bluid was true;

" There's some great folk set light by me,
    I set as light by them;
But I will send to London town
    Wham I like best at hame."

Sae how this weighty plea may end,
    Nae mortal wight can tell;
God grant the King and ilka man
    May look weel to himsel'.

ELECTION BALLAD FOR WESTERHA'

Tune—" Up and waur them a', Willie."

The Laddies by the banks o' Nith
    Wad trust his grace wi' a', Jamie;
But he'll sair them as he sair'd the King—
    Turn tail and rin awa', Jamie.

Chorus—Up and waur them a', Jamie,
    Up and waur them a';
        The Johnstones hae the guidin o't,
        Ye turncoat Whigs awa'!

The day he stude his country's friend,
  Or gied her faes a claw, Jamie,
Or frae puir man a blessin wan,
  That day the Duke ne'er saw, Jamie.
    Up and waur them, &c.

But wha is he, his country's boast?
  Like him there is na twa, Jamie;
There's no a callant tents the kye,
  But kens o' Westerha', Jamie.
    Up and waur them, &c.

To end the wark, here's Whistlebirk,
  Lang may his whistle blaw, Jamie;
And Maxwell true, o' sterling blue;
  And we'll be Johnstones a', Jamie.
    Up and waur them, &c.

ELECTION BALLAD

AT CLOSE OF THE CONTEST FOR REPRESENTING DUMFRIES BURGHS, 1790

Addressed to R. GRAHAM, Esq. of Fintry.

FINTRY, my stay in worldly strife,
Friend o' my muse, friend o' my life,
    Are ye as idle's I am?
Come then, wi' uncouth kintra fleg,
O'er Pegasus I'll fling my leg,
    And ye shall see me try him.

But where shall I gae rin or ride,
That I may splatter nane beside?
    I wad na be uncivil:
In mankind's various paths and ways
There's aye some doytin body strays,
    And *I* ride like a devil.

Thus I break aff wi' a' my birr,
And down yon dark, deep alley spur,
  Where Theologics daunder:
Alas! curst wi' eternal fogs,
And damn'd in everlasting bogs,
  As sure's the creed I'll blunder!

I'll stain a band, or jaup a gown,
Or rin my reckless, guilty crown
  Against the haly door:
Sair do I rue my luckless fate,
When, as the Muse an' Deil wad hae't,
  I rade that road before.

Suppose I take a spurt, and mix
Amang the wilds o' Politics—
  Electors and elected,
Where dogs at Court (sad sons of bitches!)
Septennially a madness touches,
  Till all the land's infected.

All hail! Drumlanrig's haughty Grace,
Discarded remnant of a race
  Once godlike—great in story;
Thy forbears' virtues all contrasted,
The very name of Douglas blasted,
  Thine that inverted glory!

Hate, envy, oft the Douglas bore,
But thou hast superadded more,
  And sunk them in contempt;
Follies and crimes have stain'd the name,
But, Queensberry, thine the virgin claim,
  From aught that's good exempt!

I'll sing the zeal Drumlanrig bears,
Who left the all-important cares
    Of princes, and their darlings:
And bent on winning borough touns,
Came shaking hands wi' wabster-loons,
    And kissing barefit carlins.

Combustion thro' our boroughs rode,
Whistling his roaring pack abroad
    Of mad unmuzzled lions;
As Queensberry blue and buff unfurl'd,
And Westerha' and Hopetoun hurled
    To every Whig defiance.

But cautious Queensberry left the war,
Th' unmanner'd dust might soil his star,
    Besides, he hated *bleeding*:
But left behind him heroes bright,
Heroes in Cæsarean fight,
    Or Ciceronian pleading.

O for a throat like huge Mons-Meg,
To muster o'er each ardent Whig
    Beneath Drumlanrig's banners;
Heroes and heroines commix,
All in the field of politics,
    To win immortal honours.

M'Murdo and his lovely spouse,
(Th' enamour'd laurels kiss her brows!)
    Led on the Loves and Graces:
She won each gaping burgess' heart,
While he, *sub rosa*, played his part,
    Amang their wives and lasses.

Craigdarroch led a light-arm'd core,
Tropes, metaphors, and figures pour,
   Like Hecla streaming thunder:
Glenriddel, skill'd in rusty coins,
Blew up each Tory's dark designs,
   And bared the treason under.

In either wing two champions fought;
Redoubted Staig, who set at nought
   The wildest savage Tory;
And Welsh who ne'er yet flinch'd his ground,
High-wav'd his magnum-bonum round
   With Cyclopeian fury.

Miller brought up th' artillery ranks,
The many-pounders of the Banks,
   Resistless desolation!
While Maxwelton, that baron bold,
'Mid Lawson's port entrench'd his hold,
   And threaten'd worse damnation.

To these what Tory hosts oppos'd,
With these what Tory warriors clos'd,
   Surpasses my descriving;
Squadrons, extended long and large,
With furious speed rush to the charge,
   Like furious devils driving.

What verse can sing, what prose narrate,
The butcher deeds of bloody Fate,
   Amid this mighty tulyie!
Grim Horror girn'd, pale Terror roar'd,
As Murder at his thrapple shor'd,
   And Hell mix'd in the brulyie.

As Highland craigs by thunder cleft,
When lightnings fire the stormy lift,
　　　Hurl down with crashing rattle;
As flames among a hundred woods,
As headlong foam a hundred floods,
　　　Such is the rage of Battle.

The stubborn Tories dare to die;
As soon the rooted oaks would fly
　　　Before th' approaching fellers;
The Whigs come on like Ocean's roar,
When all his wintry billows pour
　　　Against the Buchan Bullers.

Lo, from the shades of Death's deep night,
Departed Whigs enjoy the fight,
　　　And think on former daring:
The muffled murtherer of Charles
The Magna Charta flag unfurls,
　　　All deadly gules its bearing.

Nor wanting ghosts of Tory fame;
Bold Scrimgeour follows gallant Graham;
　　　Auld Covenanters shiver—
Forgive! forgive! much-wrong'd Montrose!
Now Death and Hell engulph thy foes,
　　　Thou liv'st on high for ever.

Still o'er the field the combat burns,
The Tories, Whigs, give way by turns;
　　　But Fate the word has spoken:
For woman's wit and strength o' man,
Alas! can do but what they can;
　　　The Tory ranks are broken.

O that my een were flowing burns!
My voice, a lioness that mourns
    Her darling cubs' undoing!
That I might greet, that I might cry,
While Tories fall, while Tories fly,
    And furious Whigs pursuing!

What Whig but melts for good Sir James,
Dear to his country, by the names,
    Friend, Patron, Benefactor!
Not Pulteney's wealth can Pulteney save;
And Hopetoun falls, the generous, brave;
    And Stewart, bold as Hector.

Thou, Pitt, shall rue this overthrow,
And Thurlow growl a curse of woe,
    And Melville melt in wailing:
Now Fox and Sheridan rejoice,
And Burke shall sing, "O Prince, arise!
    Thy power is all prevailing!"

For your poor friend, the Bard, afar
He only hears and sees the war,
    A cool spectator purely!
So, when the storm the forest rends,
The robin in the hedge descends,
    And sober chirps securely.

Now, for my friends' and brethren's sakes,
And for my dear-lov'd Land o' Cakes,
    I pray with holy fire:
Lord, send a rough-shod troop o' Hell,
O'er a' wad Scotland buy or sell,
    To grind them in the mire!

BALLADS ON MR HERON'S
ELECTION, 1795
BALLAD FIRST

Whom will you send to London town,
To Parliament and a' that?
Or wha in a' the country round
The best deserves to fa' that?
For a' that, and a' that,
Thro' Galloway and a' that,
Where is the Laird or belted Knight
The best deserves to fa' that?

Wha sees Kerroughtree's open yett,
(And wha is't never saw that?)
Wha ever wi' Kerroughtree met,
And has a doubt of a' that?
For a' that, and a' that,
Here's Heron yet for a' that!
The independent patriot,
The honest man, and a' that.

Tho' wit and worth, in either sex,
Saint Mary's Isle can shaw that,
Wi' Dukes and Lords let Selkirk mix.
And weel does Selkirk fa' that.
For a' that, and a' that,
Here's Heron yet for a' that!
The independent commoner
Shall be the man for a' that.

But why should we to Nobles jouk,
And is't against the law, that?
For why, a Lord may be a gowk,
Wi' ribband, star and a' that.

For a' that, and a' that,
  Here's Heron yet for a' that!
A Lord may be a lousy loun,
  Wi' ribband, star and a' that.

A beardless boy comes o'er the hills,
  Wi' uncle's purse and a' that;
But we'll hae ane frae mang oursels,
  A man we ken, and a' that.
    For a' that, and a' that,
    Here's Heron yet for a' that!
  For we're not to be bought and sold,
    Like naigs, and nowt, and a' that.

Then let us drink—The Stewartry,
  Kerroughtree's laird, and a' that,
Our representative to be,
  For weel he's worthy a' that.
    For a' that, and a' that,
    Here's Heron yet for a' that!
  A House of Commons such as he,
    They wad be blest that saw that

BALLAD SECOND—ELECTION DAY

Tune—" Fy, let us a' to the Bridal."

Fy, let us a' to Kirkcudbright,
  For there will be bickerin there;
For Murray's light horse are to muster,
  And O how the heroes will swear!
And there will be Murray, Commander,
  And Gordon, the battle to win;
Like brothers they'll stand by each other,
  Sae knit in alliance and kin.

K

And there will be black-nebbit Johnie,
  The tongue o' the trump to them a' ;
And he get na Hell for his haddin,
  The Deil gets na justice ava.
And there will be Kempleton's birkie,
  A boy no sae black at the bane ;
But as to his fine Nabob fortune,
  We'll e'en let the subject alane.

And there will be Wigton's new Sheriff ;
  Dame Justice fu' brawly has sped,
She's gotten the heart of a Bushby,
  But, Lord ! what's become o' the head ?
And there will be Cardoness, Esquire,
  Sae mighty in Cardoness' eyes ;
A wight that will weather damnation,
  The Devil the prey will despise.

And there will be Douglasses doughty,
  New christening towns far and near ;
Abjuring their democrat doings,
  By kissin' the arse o' a Peer :
And there will be Kenmure sae gen'rous,
  Whose honour is proof to the storm,
To save them from stark reprobation,
  He lent them his name in the Firm.

But we winna mention Redcastle,
  The body, e'en let him escape !
He'd venture the gallows for siller,
  An 'twere na the cost o' the rape.
And where is our King's Lord Lieutenant,
  Sae fam'd for his gratefu' return ?
The birkie is gettin' his Questions
  To say in Saint Stephen's the morn.

And there will be lads o' the gospel,
  Muirhead wha's as gude as he's true;
And there will be Buittle's Apostle,
  Wha's mair o' the black than the blue.
And there will be folk frae Saint Mary's
  A house o' great merit and note;
The deil ane but honours them highly—
  The deil ane will gie them his vote!

And there'll be wealthy young Richard;
  Dame Fortune should hing by the neck
For prodigal, thriftless bestowing—
  His merit had won him respect.
And there will be rich brother Nabobs,
  (Tho' Nabobs, yet men o' the first,)
And there will be Collieston's whiskers,
  And Quintin—o' lads not the worst.

And there'll be Stamp Office Johnie,
  (Tak tent how ye purchase a dram!)
And there will be gay Cassencarry,
  And there'll be gleg Colonel Tam.
[But where is the Doggerbank hero,
  That made "Hogan Mogan" to skulk?
Poor Keith's gane to hell to be fuel,
  The auld rotten wreck of a Hulk.]

But mark ye! there's trusty Kerroughtree,
  Whose honor was ever his law;
If the Virtues were pack'd in a parcel,
  His worth might be sample for a';
[And strang an' respectfu's his backing,
  The maist o' the lairds wi' him stand;
Nae gipsy-like nominal barons,
  Wha's property's paper—not land.]

And there will be Heron, the Major,
  Wha'll ne'er be forgot in the Greys;
Our flatt'ry we'll keep for some other,
  Him, only it's justice to praise.
And there will be maiden Kilkerran,
  And also Barskimming's gude Knight,
And there will be roaring Birtwhistle,
  Yet luckily roars i' the right.

And there, frae the Niddisdale border,
  The Maxwells will gather in droves,
Teugh Johnie, staunch Geordie, an' Wellwood,
  That griens for the fishes and loaves;
And there will be Logan M'Dowall,
  Sculdudd'ry an' he will be there,
And also the Wild Scot o' Galloway,
  Sogering, gunpowder Blair.

Then hey! the chaste Interest o' Broughton,
  And hey! for the blessin's 'twill bring;
It may send Balmaghie to the Commons,
  In Sodom 'twould make him a king;
And hey! for the sanctified Murray,
  Our land wha wi' chapels has stor'd;
He founder'd his horse among harlots,
  But gied the auld naig to the·Lord.

BALLAD THIRD

JOHN BUSHBY'S LAMENTATION

Tune—"Babes in the Wood."

'Twas in the seventeen hunder year
  O' grace, and ninety-five,
That year I was the wae'est man
  Of ony man alive.

In March the three-an'-twentieth morn,
 The sun raise clear an' bright;
But oh! I was a waefu' man,
 Ere to-fa' o' the night.

Yerl Galloway lang did rule this land,
 Wi' equal right and fame,
And thereto was his kinsmen join'd,
 The Murray's noble name.

Yerl Galloway's man o' men was I,
 And chief o' Broughton's host;
So twa blind beggars, on a string,
 The faithfu' tyke will trust.

But now Yerl Galloway's sceptre's broke,
 And Broughton's wi' the slain,
And I my ancient craft may try,
 Sin' honesty is gane.

'Twas by the banks o' bonie Dee,
 Beside Kirkcudbright's towers,
The Stewart and the Murray there,
 Did muster a' their powers.

Then Murray on the auld grey yaud,
 Wi' wingèd spurs did ride,
That auld grey yaud a' Nidsdale rade,
 He staw upon Nidside.

And there had na been the Yerl himsel,
 O there had been nae play;
But Garlies was to London gane,
 And sae the kye might stray.

And there was Balmaghie, I ween,
  In front rank he wad shine;
But Balmaghie had better been
  Drinkin' Madeira wine.

And frae Glenkens cam to our aid
  A chief o' doughty deed;
In case that worth should wanted be,
  O' Kenmure we had need.

And by our banners march'd Muirhead,
  And Buittle was na slack;
Whase haly priesthood nane could stain,
  For wha could dye the black?

And there was grave squire Cardoness,
  Look'd on till a' was done;
Sae in the tower o' Cardoness
  A howlet sits at noon.

And there led I the Bushby clan,
  My gamesome billie, Will,
And my son Maitland, wise as brave,
  My footsteps follow'd still.

The Douglas and the Heron's name,
  We set nought to their score;
The Douglas and the Heron's name,
  Had felt our weight before.

But Douglasses o' weight had we,
  The pair o' lusty lairds,
For building cot-houses sae fam'd,
  And christenin' kail-yards.

And then Redcastle drew his sword,
    That ne'er was stain'd wi' gore,
Save on a wand'rer lame and blind,
    To drive him frae his door.

And last cam creepin Collieston,
    Was mair in fear than wrath;
Ae knave was constant in his mind—
    To keep that knave frae scaith.

BALLAD FOURTH

THE TROGGER

Tune—" Buy Broom Besoms."

WHA will buy my troggin, fine election ware,
Broken trade o' Broughton, a' in high repair?

  Chorus—Buy braw troggin frae the banks o'
          Dee;
          Wha wants troggin let him come to
          me.

There's a noble Earl's fame and high renown,
For an auld sang—it's thought the gudes were
    stown—
        Buy braw troggin, &c.

Here's the worth o' Broughton in a needle's e'e;
Here's a reputation tint by Balmaghie.
        Buy braw troggin, &c.

Here's its stuff and lining, Cardoness's head,
Fine for a soger, a' the wale o' lead.
        Buy braw troggin, &c.

Here's a little wadset, Buittle's scrap o' truth,
Pawn'd in a gin-shop, quenching holy drouth.
          Buy braw troggin, &c.

Here's an honest conscience might a prince
          adorn ;
Frae the downs o' Tinwald, so was never worn.
          Buy braw troggin, &c.

Here's armorial bearings frae the manse o' Urr ;
The crest, a sour-crab apple, rotten at the core.
          Buy braw troggin, &c.

Here is Satan's picture, like a bizzard gled,
Pouncing poor Redcastle, sprawlin like a taed.
          Buy braw troggin, &c.

Here's the font where Douglas stane and mortar
          names ;
Lately used at Caily christening Murray's crimes.
          Buy braw troggin, &c.

Here's the worth and wisdom Collieston can
          boast ;
By a thievish midge they had been nearly lost.
          Buy braw troggin, &c.

Here is Murray's fragments o' the ten commands ;
Gifted by black Jock to get them aff his hands.
          Buy braw troggin, &c.

Saw ye e'er sic troggin ? if to buy ye're slack,
Hornie's turnin chapman—he'll buy a' the pack.
          Buy braw troggin, &c.

THE DEAN OF FACULTY

A NEW BALLAD

Tune—"The Dragon of Wantley."

DIRE was the hate at old Harlaw,
  That Scot to Scot did carry;
And dire the discord Langside saw
  For beauteous, hapless Mary:
But Scot to Scot ne'er met so hot,
  Or were more in fury seen, Sir,
Than 'twixt Hal and Bob for the famous job,
  Who should be the Faculty's Dean, Sir.

This Hal for genius, wit and lore,
  Among the first was number'd;
But pious Bob, 'mid learning's store,
  Commandment the tenth remember'd:
Yet simple Bob the victory got,
  And wan his heart's desire,
Which shews that heaven can boil the pot,
  Tho' the devil piss in the fire.

Squire Hal, besides, had in this case
  Pretensions rather brassy;
For talents, to deserve a place,
  Are qualifications saucy.
So their worships of the Faculty,
  Quite sick of merit's rudeness,
Chose one who should owe it all, d'ye see,
  To their gratis grace and goodness.

As once on Pisgah purg'd was the sight
  Of a son of Circumcision,
So may be, on this Pisgah height,
  Bob's purblind mental vision—

K*

Nay, Bobby's mouth may be opened yet,
   Till for eloquence you hail him,
And swear that he has the angel met
   That met the ass of Balaam.

In your heretic sins may you live and die,
   Ye heretic Eight-and-Thirty!
But accept, ye sublime Majority,
   My congratulations hearty.
With your honours, as with a certain king,
   In your servants this is striking,
The more incapacity they bring,
   The more they're to your liking.

From a wood engraving by Thomas Bewick

SONGS OF

ROBERT BURNS

—ᴧᴧᴧ—

HANDSOME NELL

Tune—"I am a man unmarried."

O ONCE I lov'd a bonie lass,
  Ay, and I love her still;
And whilst that virtue warms my breast,
  I'll love my handsome Nell.

As bonie lasses I hae seen,
  And mony full as braw:
But for a modest gracefu' mien
  The like I never saw.

A bonie lass, I will confess,
  Is pleasant to the e'e;
But without some better qualities
  She's no a lass for me.

But Nelly's looks are blythe and sweet,
  And what is best of a',
Her reputation is complete,
  And fair without a flaw.

She dresses aye sae clean and neat,
　　Both decent and genteel ;
And then there's something in her gait
　　Gars ony dress look weel.

A gaudy dress and gentle air
　　May slightly touch the heart ;
But it's innocence and modesty
　　That polishes the dart.

'Tis this in Nelly pleases me,
　　'Tis this enchants my soul ;
For absolutely in my breast
　　She reigns without control.

O TIBBIE, I HAE SEEN THE DAY

Tune—" Invercauld's Reel or Strathspey."

Chor.—O Tibbie, I hae seen the day,
　　Ye wadna been sae shy ;
　　For laik o' gear ye lightly me,
　　　But, trowth, I care na by.

Yestreen I met you on the moor,
Ye spak na, but gaed by like stour ;
Ye geck at me because I'm poor,
　　But fient a hair care I.
　　　　O Tibbie, I hae seen the day, &c.

When coming hame on Sunday last,
Upon the road as I cam past,
Ye snufft and ga'e your head a cast—
　　But, trowth, I care't na by.
　　　　O Tibbie, I hae seen the day, &c.

O Tibbie, I hae seen the Day

O Tibbie, I hae seen the Day

"When coming hame on Sunday last,
Upon the road as I cam past,
Ye snufft and ga'e your head a cast . . ."

I doubt na, lass, but ye may think,
Because ye hae the name o' clink,
That ye can please me at a wink,
　　Whene'er ye like to try.
　　　　O Tibbie, I hae seen the day, &c.

But sorrow tak' him that's sae mean,
Altho' his pouch o' coin were clean,
Wha follows ony saucy quean,
　　That looks sae proud and high.
　　　　O Tibbie, I hae seen the day, &c.

Altho' a lad were e'er sae smart,
If that he want the yellow dirt,
Ye'll cast your head anither airt,
　　And answer him fu' dry.
　　　　O Tibbie, I hae seen the day, &c.

But if he hae the name o' gear,
Ye'll fasten to him like a brier,
Tho' hardly he, for sense or lear,
　　Be better than the kye.
　　　　O Tibbie, I hae seen the day, &c.

But, Tibbie, lass, tak my advice :
Your daddie's gear maks you sae nice ;
The deil a ane wad speir your price,
　　Were ye as poor as I.
　　　　O Tibbie, I hae seen the day, &c.

There lives a lass beside yon park,
I'd rather hae her in her sark,
Than you wi' a' your thousand mark ;
　　That gars you look sae high.
　　　　O Tibbie, I hae seen the day, &c.

I DREAM'D I LAY.

I DREAM'D I lay where flowers were springing
  Gaily in the sunny beam;
List'ning to the wild birds singing,
  By a falling crystal stream:
Straight the sky grew black and daring;
  Thro' the woods the whirlwinds rave;
Trees with aged arms were warring,
  O'er the swelling drumlie wave.

Such was my life's deceitful morning,
  Such the pleasures I enjoyed:
But lang or noon, loud tempests storming
  A' my flowery bliss destroy'd.
Tho' fickle fortune has deceiv'd me—
  She promis'd fair, and perform'd but ill,
Of mony a joy and hope bereav'd me—
  I bear a heart shall support me still.

IN THE CHARACTER OF A RUINED FARMER

Tune—"Go from my window, Love, do."

THE sun he is sunk in the west,
All creatures retirèd to rest,
While here I sit, all sore beset
      With sorrow, grief, and woe:
And it's O, fickle Fortune, O!

The prosperous man is asleep,
Nor hears how the whirlwinds sweep;
But Misery and I must watch
      The surly tempests blow:
And it's O, fickle Fortune, O!

There lies the dear partner of my breast;
Her cares for a moment at rest:
Must I see thee, my youthful pride,
      Thus brought so very low?
And it's O, fickle Fortune, O!

There lie my sweet babies in her arms;
No anxious fear their little hearts alarms;
But for their sake my heart does ache,
      With many a bitter throe:
And it's O, fickle Fortune, O!

I once was by Fortune carest:
I once could relieve the distrest:
Now life's poor support, hardly earn'd,
      My fate will scarce bestow:
And it's O, fickle Fortune, O!

No comfort, no comfort I have!
How welcome to me were the grave!
But then my wife and children dear—
      O, whither would they go?
And it's O, fickle Fortune, O!

O whither, O whither shall I turn,
All friendless, forsaken, forlorn?
For, in this world, Rest or Peace
      I never more shall know:
And it's O, fickle Fortune, O!

MONTGOMERIE'S PEGGY

ALTHO' my bed were in yon muir,
  Amang the heather, in my plaidie;
Yet happy, happy would I be,
  Had I my dear Montgomerie's Peggy.

When o'er the hill beat surly storms,
    And winter nights were dark and rainy;
I'd seek some dell, and in my arms
    I'd shelter dear Montgomerie's Peggy.

Were I a baron proud and high,
    And horse and servants waiting ready;
Then a' 'twad gie o' joy to me,—
    The sharin't with Montgomerie's Peggy.

HERE'S TO THY HEALTH

HERE's to thy health, my bonie lass,
    Gude nicht and joy be wi' thee;
I'll come nae mair to thy bower-door,
    To tell thee that I lo'e thee.
O dinna think, my pretty pink,
    But I can live without thee:
I vow and swear I dinna care
    How lang ye look about ye.

Thou'rt aye sae free informing me,
    Thou hast nae mind to marry;
I'll be as free informing thee,
    Nae time hae I to tarry:
I ken thy friens try ilka means
    Frae wedlock to delay thee,
Depending on some higher chance,
    But fortune may betray thee.

I ken they scorn my low estate,
    But that does never grieve me;
For I'm as free as any he;
    Sma' siller will relieve me.

Montgomerie's Peggy

Montgomerie's Peggy

"When o'er the hill beat surly storms,
*   And winter's nights were dark and rainy;*
I'd seek some dell, and in my arms
*   I'd shelter dear Montgomerie's Peggy."*

I'll count my health my greatest wealth,
  Sae lang as I'll enjoy it;
I'll fear nae scant, I'll bode nae want,
  As lang's I get employment.

But far-off fowls hae feathers fair,
  And, aye until ye try them,
Tho' they seem fair, still have a care:
  They may prove as bad as I am.
But at twal' at night, when the moon shines bright,
  My dear, I'll come and see thee;
For the man that loves his mistress weel,
  Nae travel makes him weary.

THE LASS OF CESSNOCK BANKS

A SONG OF SIMILES

Tune—" If he be a Butcher neat and trim."

On Cessnock banks a lassie dwells;
  Could I describe her shape and mien;
Our lasses a' she far excels,
  An' she has twa sparkling roguish een.

She's sweeter than the morning dawn,
  When rising Phœbus first is seen,
And dew-drops twinkle o'er the lawn;
  An' she has twa sparkling roguish een.

She's stately like yon youthful ash,
  That grows the cowslip braes between,
And drinks the stream with vigour fresh;
  An' she has twa sparkling roguish een.

She's spotless like the flow'ring thorn,
  With flow'rs so white and leaves so **green,**
When purest in the dewy morn ;
  An' she has twa sparkling roguish een.

Her looks are like the vernal May,
  When ev'ning Phœbus shines serene,
While birds rejoice on every spray ;
  An' she has twa sparkling roguish een.

Her hair is like the curling mist,
  That climbs the mountain-sides at e'en,
When flow'r-reviving rains are past ;
  An' she has twa sparkling roguish een.

Her forehead's like the show'ry bow,
  When gleaming sunbeams intervene
And gild the distant mountain's brow ;
  An' she has twa sparkling roguish een.

Her cheeks are like yon crimson gem,
  The pride of all the flowery scene,
Just opening on its thorny stem ;
  An' she has twa sparkling roguish een.

Her teeth are like the nightly snow,
  When pale the morning rises keen,
While hid the murm'ring streamlets flow ;
  An' she has twa sparkling roguish een.

Her lips are like yon cherries ripe,
  That sunny walls from Boreas screen ;
They tempt the taste and charm the sight ;
  An' she has twa sparkling roguish een.

Her teeth are like a flock of sheep,
  With fleeces newly washen clean,
That slowly mount the rising steep ;
  An' she has twa sparkling roguish een.

Her breath is like the fragrant breeze,
  That gently stirs the blossom'd bean,
When Phœbus sinks behind the seas ;
  An' she has twa sparkling roguish een.

Her voice is like the ev'ning thrush,
  That sings on Cessnock banks unseen,
While his mate sits nestling in the bush ;
  An' she has twa sparkling roguish een.

But it's not her air, her form, her face,
  Tho' matching beauty's fabled queen ;
'Tis the mind that shines in ev'ry grace,
  An' chiefly in her roguish een.

BONIE PEGGY ALISON

Tune—"The Braes o' Balquhidder."

Chor.—And I'll kiss thee yet, yet,
      And I'll kiss thee o'er again :
    And I'll kiss thee yet, yet,
      My bonie Peggy Alison.

Ilk care and fear, when thou art near
  I evermair defy them, O !
Young kings upon their hansel throne
  Are no sae blest as I am, O !
        And I'll kiss thee yet, yet, &c.

When in my arms, wi' a' thy charms,
  I clasp my countless treasure, O !

I seek nae mair o' Heaven to share
  Than sic a moment's pleasure, O!
      And I'll kiss thee yet, yet, &c.

And by thy een sae bonie blue,
  I swear I'm thine for ever, O!
And on thy lips I seal my vow,
  And break it shall I never, O!
      And I'll kiss thee yet, yet, &c.

MARY MORISON

O Mary, at thy window be,
  It is the wish'd, the trysted hour!
Those smiles and glances let me see,
  That make the miser's treasure poor:
How blythely wad I bide the stour,
  A weary slave frae sun to sun,
Could I the rich reward secure,
  The lovely Mary Morison.

Yestreen, when to the trembling string
  The dance gaed thro' the lighted ha',
To thee my fancy took its wing,
  I sat, but neither heard nor saw:
Tho' this was fair, and that was braw,
  And yon the toast of a' the town,
I sigh'd, and said amang them a',
  " Ye are na Mary Morison."

Oh, Mary, canst thou wreck his peace,
  Wha for thy sake wad gladly die?
Or canst thou break that heart of his,
  Whase only faut is loving thee?

If love for love thou wilt na gie,
   At least be pity to me shown ;
A thought ungentle canna be
   The thought o' Mary Morison.

FICKLE FORTUNE

THOUGH fickle Fortune has deceived me
   (She promis'd fair and perform'd but ill),
Of mistress, friends, and wealth bereav'd me,
   Yet I bear a heart shall support me still.

I'll act with prudence as far's I'm able,
   But if success I must never find,
Then come misfortune, I bid thee welcome,
   I'll meet thee with an undaunted mind.

RAGING FORTUNE

O RAGING Fortune's withering blast
   Has laid my leaf full low, O !
O raging Fortune's withering blast
   Has laid my leaf full low, O !

My stem was fair, my bud was green,
   My blossom sweet did blow, O !
The dew fell fresh, the sun rose mild,
   And made my branches grow, O !

But luckless Fortune's northern storms
   Laid a' my blossoms low, O !
But luckless Fortune's northern storms
   Laid a' my blossoms low, O !

NO CHURCHMAN AM I

Tune—"Prepare, my dear Brethren, to the tavern
let's fly."

No churchman am I for to rail and to write,
No statesmen nor soldier to plot or to fight,
No sly man of business contriving a snare,
For a big-belly'd bottle's the whole of my care.

The peer I don't envy, I give him his bow;
I scorn not the peasant, though ever so low;
But a club of good fellows, like those that are here,
And a bottle like this, are my glory and care.

Here passes the squire on his brother—his horse;
There centum per centum, the cit with his purse;
But see you the *Crown* how it waves in the air?
There a big-belly'd bottle still eases my care.

The wife of my bosom, alas! she did die;
For sweet consolation to church I did fly;
I found that old Solomon provèd it fair,
That a big-belly'd bottle's a cure for all care.

I once was persuaded a venture to make;
A letter inform'd me that all was to wreck;
But the pursy old landlord just waddl'd upstairs,
With a glorious bottle that ended my cares.

" Life's cares they are comforts "—a maxim laid
    down
By the Bard, what d'ye call him, that wore the
    black gown;
And faith I agree with th' old prig to a hair,
For a big-belly'd bottle's a heav'n of a care.

A STANZA ADDED IN A MASON LODGE

Then fill up a bumper and make it o'erflow,
And honours masonic prepare for to throw ;
May ev'ry true Brother of the Compass and Square
Have a big-belly'd bottle when harass'd with care.

MY FATHER WAS A FARMER

Tune—" The weaver and his shuttle, O."

My father was a farmer upon the Carrick
    border, O,
And carefully he bred me in decency and order, O ;
He bade me act a manly part, though I had ne'er
    a farthing, O ;
For without an honest manly heart, no man was
    worth regarding, O.

Then out into the world my course I did
    determine, O ;
Tho' to be rich was not my wish, yet to be
    great was charming, O ;
My talents they were not the worst, nor yet my
    education, O :
Resolv'd was I at least to try to mend my situa-
    tion, O.

In many a way, and vain essay, I courted Fortune's
    favour, O ;
Some cause unseen still stept between, to frustrate
    each endeavour, O ;
Sometimes by foes I was o'erpower'd, sometimes
    by friends forsaken, O ;
And when my hope was at the top, I still was
    worst mistaken, O.

Then sore harass'd, and tir'd at last, with
    Fortune's vain delusion, O,
I dropt my schemes, like idle dreams, and came
    to this conclusion, O :
The past was bad, and the future hid, its good
    or ill untrièd, O ;
But the present hour was in my pow'r, and so I
    would enjoy it, O.

No help, nor hope, nor view had I, nor person
    to befriend me, O ;
So I must toil, and sweat, and moil, and labour
    to sustain me, O ;
To plough and sow, to reap and mow, my father
    bred me early, O ;
For one, he said, to labour bred, was a match
    for Fortune fairly, O.

Thus all obscure, unknown, and poor, thro' life
    I'm doom'd to wander, O,
Till down my weary bones I lay in everlasting
    slumber, O :
No view nor care, but shun whate'er might breed
    me pain or sorrow, O ;
I live to-day as well's I may, regardless of to-
    morrow, O.

But cheerful still, I am as well as a monarch in
    his palace, O,
Tho' Fortune's frown still hunts me down, with
    all her wonted malice, O :
I make indeed my daily bread, but ne'er can
    make it farther, O :
But as daily bread is all I need, I do not much
    regard her, O.

When sometimes by my labour, I earn a little
    money, O,
Some unforeseen misfortune comes gen'rally upon
    me, O ;
Mischance, mistake, or by neglect, or my good-
    natur'd folly, O :
But come what will, I've sworn it still, I'll ne'er
    be melancholy, O.

All you who follow wealth and power with un-
    remitting ardour, O,
The more in this you look for bliss, you leave
    your view the farther, O :
Had you the wealth Potosi boasts, or nations to
    adore you, O,
A cheerful honest-hearted clown I will prefer
    before you, O.

THE RIGS O' BARLEY

Tune—" Corn Rigs are bonie."

It was upon a Lammas night,
    When corn rigs are bonie,
Beneath the moon's unclouded light,
    I held awa to Annie ;
The time flew by, wi' tentless heed,
    Till, 'tween the late and early,
Wi' sma' persuasion she agreed
    To see me thro' the barley.

        Corn rigs, an' barley rigs,
            An' corn rigs are bonie :
        I'll ne'er forget that happy night,
            Amang the rigs wi' Annie.

The sky was blue, the wind was still,
    The moon was shining clearly;
I set her down, wi' right good will,
    Amang the rigs o' barley:
I ken't her heart was a' my ain;
    I lov'd her most sincerely;
I kiss'd her owre and owre again,
    Amang the rigs o' barley.
        Corn rigs, an' barley rigs, &c.

I lock'd her in my fond embrace;
    Her heart was beating rarely:
My blessings on that happy place,
    Amang the rigs o' barley!
But by the moon and stars so bright,
    That shone that hour so clearly!
She aye shall bless that happy night
    Amang the rigs o' barley.
        Corn rigs, an' barley rigs, &c.

I hae been blythe wi' comrades dear;
    I hae been merry drinking;
I hae been joyfu' gath'rin gear;
    I hae been happy thinking:
But a' the pleasures e'er I saw,
    Tho' three times doubl'd fairly,
That happy night was worth them a'
    Amang the rigs o' barley.
        Corn rigs, an' barley rigs, &c.

COMPOSED IN AUGUST

Tune—" I had a horse, I had nae mair."

Now westlin winds and slaught'ring guns
Bring Autumn's pleasant weather;

The moorcock springs on whirring wings
  Among the blooming heather :
Now waving grain, wide o'er the plain,
  Delights the weary farmer ;
And the moon shines bright, when I rove at night,
  To muse upon my charmer.

The partridge loves the fruitful fells,
  The plover loves the mountains ;
The woodcock haunts the lonely dells,
  The soaring hern the fountains :
Thro' lofty groves the cushat roves,
  The path of man to shun it ;
The hazel bush o'erhangs the thrush,
  The spreading thorn the linnet.

Thus ev'ry kind their pleasure find,
  The savage and the tender ;
Some social join, and leagues combine,
  Some solitary wander :
Avaunt, away ! the cruel sway,
  Tyrannic man's dominion ;
The sportsman's joy, the murd'ring cry,
  The flutt'ring, gory pinion !

But, Peggy dear, the ev'ning's clear,
  Thick flies the skimming swallow,
The sky is blue, the fields in view,
  All fading-green and yellow :
Come let us stray our gladsome way,
  And view the charms of Nature ;
The rustling corn, the fruited thorn,
  And ev'ry happy creature.

We'll gently walk, and sweetly talk,
  Till the silent moon shine clearly;
I'll grasp thy waist, and, fondly prest,
  Swear how I love thee dearly:
Not vernal show'rs to budding flow'rs
  Not Autumn to the farmer,
So dear can be as thou to me,
  My fair, my lovely charmer!

MY NANIE, O

Tune—" My Nanie, O."

BEHIND yon hills where Lugar flows,
  'Mang moors an' mosses many, O,
The wintry sun the day has clos'd,
  And I'll awa to Nanie, O.

The westlin wind blaws loud an' shill;
  The night's baith mirk and rainy, O;
But I'll get my plaid an' out I'll steal,
  An' owre the hill to Nanie, O.

My Nanie's charming, sweet, an' young;
  Nae artful wiles to win ye, O:
May ill befa' the flattering tongue
  That wad beguile my Nanie, O.

Her face is fair, her heart is true;
  As spotless as she's bonie, O:
The op'ning gowan, wat wi' dew,
  Nae purer is than Nanie, O.

A country lad is my degree,
  An' few there be that ken me, O;
But what care I how few they be,
  I'm welcome aye to Nanie, O.

My Nanie, O

My Nanie, O

"My Nanie's charming, sweet and young . . ."

My riches a's my penny-fee,
    An' I maun guide it cannie, O ;
But warl's gear ne'er troubles me,
    My thoughts are a' my Nanie, O.

Our auld guidman delights to view
    His sheep an' kye thrive bonie, O ;
But I'm as blythe that hauds his pleugh,
    An' has nae care but Nanie, O.

Come weel, come woe, I care na by ;
    I'll tak what Heav'n will sen' me, O ;
Nae ither care in life have I,
    But live, an' love my Nanie, O.

GREEN GROW THE RASHES

A FRAGMENT

Chor.—Green grow the rashes, O ;
    Green grow the rashes, O ;
    The sweetest hours that e'er I spend,
    Are spent amang the lasses, O.

THERE's nought but care on ev'ry han',
    In ev'ry hour that passes, O :
What signifies the life o' man,
    An 'twere na for the lasses, O.
                Green grow, &c.

The war'ly race may riches chase,
    An' riches still may fly them, O ;
An' tho' at last they catch them fast,
    Their hearts can ne'er enjoy them, O.
                Green grow, &c.

But gie me a cannie hour at e'en,
  My arms about my dearie, O ;
An' war'ly cares, an' war'ly men,
  May a' gae tapsalteerie, O !
                    Green grow, &c.

For you sae douce, ye sneer at this ;
  Ye're nought but senseless asses, O :
The wisest man the warl' e'er saw,
  He dearly lov'd the lasses, O.
                    Green grow, &c.

Auld Nature swears, the lovely dears
  Her noblest work she classes, O :
Her prentice han' she try'd on man,
  An' then she made the lasses, O.
                    Green grow, &c.

O LEAVE NOVELS

Tune—" Donald Blue."

O LEAVE novéls, ye Mauchline belles,
  Ye're safer at your spinning-wheel ;
Such witching books are baited hooks
  For rakish rooks like Rob Mossgiel ;

Your fine Tom Jones and Grandisons,
  They make your youthful fancies reel ;
They heat your brains, and fire your veins,
  And then you're prey for Rob Mossgiel.

Beware a tongue that's smoothly hung,
  A heart that warmly seems to feel ;
That feeling heart but acts a part—
  'Tis rakish art in Rob Mossgiel.

Green Grow the Rashes

Green Grow the Rashes

"But gie me a cannie hour at e'en,
My arms about my dearie, O . . . "

The frank address, the soft caress,
  Are worse than poisoned darts of steel;
The frank address, and politesse,
  Are all finesse in Rob Mossgiel.

THE MAUCHLINE LADY

Tune—"I had a horse, I had nae mair."

WHEN first I came to Stewart Kyle,
  My mind it was na steady;
Where'er I gaed, where'er I rade,
  A mistress still I had aye.

But when I came roun' by Mauchline toun,
  Not dreadin anybody,
My heart was caught, before I thought,
  And by a Mauchline lady.

ONE NIGHT AS I DID WANDER

Tune—"John Anderson, my jo."

ONE night as I did wander,
  When corn begins to shoot,
I sat me down to ponder,
  Upon an auld tree root;
Auld Ayr ran by before me,
  And bicker'd to the seas;
A cushat crooded o'er me,
  That echoed through the trees.

RANTIN, ROVIN ROBIN

Tune—"Dainty Davie."

THERE was a lad was born in Kyle,
But whatna day o' whatna style,
I doubt it's hardly worth the while
  To be sae nice wi' Robin.

Chor —Robin was a rovin boy,
   Rantin, rovin, rantin, rovin,
  Robin was a rovin boy,
   Rantin, rovin Robin!

Our monarch's hindmost year but ane
Was five-and-twenty days begun,
'Twas then a blast o' Janwar' win'
 Blew hansel in on Robin.
      Robin was, &c.

The gossip keekit in his loof,
Quo' scho, " Wha lives will see the proof,
This waly boy will be nae coof:
 I think we'll ca' him Robin."
      Robin was, &c.

" He'll hae misfortunes great an' sma',
But aye a heart aboon them a'.
He'll be a credit till us a' :
 We'll a' be proud o' Robin."
      Robin was, &c.

" But sure as three times three mak nine,
I see by ilka score and line,
This chap will dearly like our kin',
 So leeze me on thee! Robin."
      Robin was, &c.

"Guid faith," quo' scho, " I doubt you, sir,
Ye gar the lasses lie aspar ;
But twenty fauts ye may hae waur,
 So blessins on thee, Robin! "
      Robin was, &c.

YOUNG PEGGY BLOOMS

Tune—" Loch Eroch-side."

YOUNG Peggy blooms our boniest lass,
  Her blush is like the morning,
The rosy dawn, the springing grass,
  With early gems adorning.
Her eyes outshine the radiant beams
  That gild the passing shower,
And glitter o'er the crystal streams,
  And cheer each fresh'ning flower.

Her lips, more than the cherries bright,
  A richer dye has graced them ;
They charm th' admiring gazer's sight,
  And sweetly tempt to taste them ;
Her smile is as the evening mild,
  When feather'd pairs are courting,
And little lambkins wanton wild,
  In playful bands disporting.

Were Fortune lovely Peggy's foe,
  Such sweetness would relent her ;
As blooming Spring unbends the brow
  Of surly savage Winter.
Detraction's eye no aim can gain,
  Her winning pow'rs to lessen ;
And fretful Envy grins in vain
  The poison'd tooth to fasten.

Ye Pow'rs of Honour, Love, and Truth,
  From ev'ry ill defend her !
Inspire the highly-favour'd youth
  The destinies intend her !

L

Still fan the sweet connubial flame
Responsive in each bosom;
And bless the dear parental name
With many a filial blossom.

FAREWELL TO BALLOCHMYLE

THE Catrine woods were yellow seen,
The flowers decay'd on Catrine lee,
Nae lav'rock sang on hillock green,
But nature sicken'd on the e'e.
Thro' faded groves Maria sang,
Hersel' in beauty's bloom the while;
And aye the wild-wood echoes rang:—
"Fareweel the braes o' Ballochmyle!"

"Low in your wintry beds, ye flowers,
Again ye'll flourish fresh and fair;
Ye birdies dumb, in with'ring bowers,
Again ye'll charm the vocal air.
But here, alas! for me nae mair
Shall birdie charm, or floweret smile;
Fareweel the bonie banks of Ayr,
Fareweel, fareweel! sweet Ballochmyle!"

HER FLOWING LOCKS

HER flowing locks, the raven's wing,
Adown her neck and bosom hing;
How sweet unto that breast to cling,
And round that neck entwine her!

Her lips are roses wat wi' dew,
O, what a feast her bonie mou'!
Her cheeks a mair celestial hue,
A crimson still diviner!

Farewell to Ballochmyle

From an engraving after David Octavius Hill

Farewell to Ballochmyle

"The Catrine woods were yellow seen,
The flowers decay'd on Catrine lee . . . "

FOR A' THAT

Tho' women's minds, like winter winds,
  May shift, and turn, an' a' that,
The noblest breast adores them maist—
  A consequence I draw that.

    Chor.—For a' that, an' a' that,
      And twice as meikle's a' that;
      The bonie lass that I lo'e best
      She'll be my ain for a' that.

Great love I bear to a' the fair,
  Their humble slave, an' a' that;
But lordly will, I hold it still
  A mortal sin to thraw that.
      For a' that, &c.

But there is ane aboon the lave,
  Has wit, and sense, an' a' that;
A bonie lass, I like her best,
  And wha a crime dare ca' that?
      For a' that, &c.

In rapture sweet this hour we meet,
  Wi' mutual love an' a' that,
But for how lang the flie may stang,
  Let inclination law that.
      For a' that, &c.

Their tricks an' craft hae put me daft.
  They've taen me in, an' a' that;
But clear your decks, and here's—'The Sex!'
  I like the jads for a' that.
      For a' that, &c.

THE RANTIN DOG, THE DADDIE O'T

Tune—" Whare'll our guidman lie."

O WHA my babie-clouts will buy?
O wha will tent me when I cry?
Wha will kiss me where I lie?
    The rantin dog, the daddie o't.

O wha will own he did the faut;
O wha will buy the groanin maut?
O wha will tell me how to ca't?
    The rantin dog, the daddie o't.

When I mount the creepie-chair,
Wha will sit beside me there?
Gie me Rob, I'll seek nae mair,
    The rantin dog, the daddie o't.

Wha will crack to me my lane?
Wha will mak me fidgin fain?
Wha will kiss me o'er again?
    The rantin dog, the daddie o't.

HERE'S HIS HEALTH IN WATER

Tune—The Job of Journey-work."

ALTHO' my back be at the wa',
    And tho' he be the fauter;
Altho' my back be at the wa',
    Yet, here's his health in water.
O wae gae by his wanton sides,
    Sae brawlie's he could flatter;

Till for his sake I'm slighted sair,
And dree the kintra clatter:
But tho' my back be at the wa',
Yet here's his health in water!

COMPOSED IN SPRING

Tune—" Jockey's Grey Breeks."

AGAIN rejoicing Nature sees
Her robe assume its vernal hues:
Her leafy locks wave in the breeze,
All freshly steep'd in morning dews.

  Chorus.—And maun I still on Menie doat,
   And bear the scorn that's in her e'e?
  For it's jet, jet black, an' it's like a hawk,
   An' it winna let a body be.

In vain to me the cowslips blaw,
 In vain to me the vi'lets spring;
In vain to me in glen or shaw,
 The mavis and the lintwhite sing.
     And maun I still, &c.

The merry ploughboy cheers his team,
 Wi' joy the tentie seedsman stalks;
But life's to me a weary dream,
 A dream of ane that never wauks.
     And maun I still, &c.

The wanton coot the water skims,
 Amang the reeds the ducklings cry,
The stately swan majestic swims,
 And ev'ry thing is blest but I.
     And maun I still, &c.

The sheep-herd steeks his faulding slap,
  And o'er the moorlands whistles shill:
Wi' wild, unequal, wand'ring step,
  I meet him on the dewy hill.
                    And maun I still, &c.

And when the lark, 'tween light and dark,
  Blythe waukens by the daisy's side,
And mounts and sings on flittering wings,
  A woe-worn ghaist I hameward glide.
                    And maun I still, &c.

Come winter, with thine angry howl,
  And raging, bend the naked tree;
Thy gloom will soothe my cheerless soul,
  When nature all is sad like me!
                    And maun I still, &c.

WILL YE GO TO THE INDIES, MY MARY?

Tune—"Will ye go to the Ewe-Bughts, Marion."

WILL ye go to the Indies, my Mary,
  And leave auld Scotia's shore?
Will ye go to the Indies, my Mary,
  Across th' Atlantic's roar?

O sweet grows the lime and the orange,
  And the apple on the pine;
But a' the charms o' the Indies
  Can never equal thine.

I hae sworn by the Heavens to my Mary,
  I hae sworn by the Heavens to be true;
And sae may the Heavens forget me,
  When I forget my vow!

O plight me your faith, my Mary,
  And plight me your lily-white hand ;
O plight me your faith, my Mary,
  Before I leave Scotia's strand.

We hae plighted our troth, my Mary,
  In mutual affection to join ;
And curst be the cause that shall part us !
  The hour and the moment o' time !

MY HIGHLAND LASSIE, O

NAE gentle dames, tho' ne'er sae fair,
Shall ever be my muse's care :
Their titles a' are empty show ;
Gie me my Highland lassie, O.

  Chorus.—Within the glen sae bushy, O,
    Aboon the plain sae rashy, O,
  I set me down wi' right guid will,
    To sing my Highland lassie, O.

O were yon hills and vallies mine,
Yon palace and yon gardens fine,
The world then the love should know
I bear my Highland lassie, O.

But fickle Fortune frowns on me,
And I maun cross the raging sea !
But while my crimson currents flow,
I'll love my Highland lassie, O.

Altho' thro' foreign climes I range,
I know her heart will never change,
For her bosom burns with honour's glow,
My faithful Highland lassie, O.

For her I'll dare the billow's roar,
For her I'll trace a distant shore,
That Indian wealth may lustre throw
Around my Highland lassie, O.

She has my heart, she has my hand,
By secret troth and honour's band!
Till the mortal stroke shall lay me low,
I'm thine, my Highland lassie, O,

Farewell the glen sae bushy, O!
Farewell the plain sae rashy, O!
To other lands I now must go,
To sing my Highland lassie, O.

THE FAREWELL

TO THE BRETHREN OF ST JAMES'S LODGE, TARBOLTON

Tune—" Goodnight, and joy be wi' you a' "

ADIEU! a heart-warm fond adieu;
Dear brothers of the *mystic tie!*
Ye favourèd, *enlighten'd* few,
Companions of my social joy;
Tho' I to foreign lands must hie,
Pursuing Fortune's slidd'ry ba';
With melting heart, and brimful eye,
I'll mind you still, tho' far awa.

Oft have I met your social band,
And spent the cheerful, festive night;
Oft, honour'd with supreme command,
Presided o'er the *sons of light* :

And by that *hieroglyphic* bright,
  Which none but *Craftsmen* ever saw !
Strong Mem'ry on my heart shall write
  Those happy scenes, when far awa.

May Freedom, Harmony, and Love,
  Unite you in the *grand Design*,
Beneath th' Omniscient Eye above,
  The glorious *Architect* Divine,
That you may keep th' *unerring line*,
  Still rising by the *plummet's law*,
Till *Order* bright completely shine,
  Shall be my pray'r when far awa.

And *you*, farewell ! whose merits claim
  Justly that *highest badge* to wear :
Heav'n bless your honour'd, noble name,
  To *Masonry* and *Scotia* dear !
A last request permit me here,—
  When yearly ye assemble a',
One *round*, I ask it with a *tear*,
  To him, *the Bard that's far awa.*

FAREWELL TO ELIZA

Tune—"Gilderoy."

FROM thee, Eliza, I must go,
  And from my native shore ;
The cruel fates between us throw
  A boundless ocean's roar :
But boundless oceans, roaring wide,
  Between my love and me,
They never, never can divide
  My heart and soul from thee.

L*

Farewell, farewell, Eliza dear,
  The maid that I adore!
A boding voice is in mine ear,
  We part to meet no more!
But the latest throb that leaves my heart,
  While Death stands victor by,—
That throb, Eliza, is thy part,
  And thine that latest sigh!

THE LASS O' BALLOCHMYLE

Tune—"Ettrick Banks."

'Twas even; the dewy fields were green,
  On every blade the pearls hang;
The zephyr wanton'd round the bean,
  And bore its fragrant sweets alang:
  In ev'ry glen the mavis sang,
All nature list'ning seem'd the while,
  Except where greenwood echoes rang,
Amang the braes o' Ballochmyle.

With careless step I onward stray'd,
  My heart rejoic'd in Nature's joy,
When, musing in a lonely glade,
  A maiden fair I chanc'd to spy:
  Her look was like the morning's eye,
Her hair like Nature's vernal smile:
  Perfection whisper'd, passing by,
" Behold the lass o' Ballochmyle ! "

Fair is the morn in flowery May,
  And sweet is night is autumn mild;
When roving thro' the garden gay,
  Or wand'ring in the lonely wild:

The Lass o' Ballochmyle

The Lass o' Ballochmyle

"Perfection whisper'd, passing by,
'Behold the lass o' Ballochmyle!'"

But woman, Nature's darling child !
There all her charms she does compile ;
   Even there her other works are foil'd
By the bonie lass o' Ballochmyle.

O had she been a country maid,
   And I the happy country swain,
Tho' shelter'd in the lowest shed
   That ever rose on Scotia's plain !
   Thro' weary winter's wind and rain,
With joy, with rapture, I would toil ;
   And nightly to my bosom strain
The bonie lass o' Ballochmyle.

Then pride might climb the slipp'ry steep,
   Where fame and honours lofty shine ;
And thirst of gold might tempt the deep,
   Or downward seek the Indian mine :
   Give me the cot below the pine,
To tend the flocks or till the soil ;
   And ev'ry day have joys divine
With the bonie lass o' Ballochmyle.

THE NIGHT WAS STILL

THE night was still, and o'er the hill
   The moon shone on the castle wa' ;
The mavis sang, while dew-drops hang
   Around her on the castle wa' ;
Sae merrily they danced the ring
   Frae e'enin' till the cock did craw ;
And aye the o'erword o' the spring
   Was ' Irvine's bairns are bonie a'.'

FAREWELL SONG TO THE BANKS OF AYR

Tune—"Roslin Castle."

THE gloomy night is gath'ring fast,
Loud roars the wild, inconstant blast;
Yon murky cloud is foul with rain,
I see it driving o'er the plain;
The hunter now has left the moor,
The scatt'red coveys meet secure;
While here I wander, prest with care,
Along the lonely banks of Ayr.

The Autumn mourns her rip'ning corn
By early Winter's ravage torn;
Across her placid, azure sky,
She sees the scowling tempest fly:
Chill runs my blood to hear it rave;
I think upon the stormy wave,
Where many a danger I must dare,
Far from the bonie banks of Ayr.

'Tis not the surging billow's roar,
'Tis not that fatal, deadly shore;
Tho' death in ev'ry shape appear,
The wretched have no more to fear:
But round my heart the ties are bound,
That heart transpierc'd with many a wound;
These bleed afresh, those ties I tear,
To leave the bonie banks of Ayr.

Farewell, old Coila's hills and dales,
Her heathy moors and winding vales;
The scenes where wretched Fancy roves,
Pursuing past, unhappy loves!

Farewell, my friends! farewell, my foes!
My peace with these, my love with those:
The bursting tears my heart declare—
Farewell, the bonie banks of Ayr!

MASONIC SONG

Tune—" Shawn-boy," or " Over the water to Charlie."

Ye sons of old Killie, assembled by Willie,
    To follow the noble vocation,
Your thrifty old mother has scarce such another
    To sit in that honourèd station.
I've little to say, but only to pray,
    As praying's the *ton* of your fashion;
A prayer from the Muse you well may excuse,
    'Tis seldom her favourite passion.

"Ye powers who preside o'er the wind and the tide,
    Who markèd each element's border;
Who formèd this frame with beneficent aim,
    Whose sovereign statute is order:—
Within this dear mansion, may wayward Con-
    tention
    Or witherèd Envy ne'er enter;
May Secrecy round be the mystical bound,
    And brotherly Love be the centre!"

YON WILD MOSSY MOUNTAINS

Yon wild mossy mountains sae lofty and wide,
That nurse in their bosom the youth o' the Clyde,
Where the grouse lead their coveys thro' the
    heather to feed,
And the shepherd tents his flock as he pipes on
    his reed.

Not Gowrie's rich valley, nor Forth's sunny
  shores,
To me hae the charms o' yon wild, mossy moors ;
For there, by a lanely, sequesterèd stream,
Resides a sweet lassie, my thought and my dream.

Amang thae wild mountains shall still be my path,
Ilk stream foaming down its ain green, narrow
  strath ;
For there, wi' my lassie, the day lang I rove,
While o'er us unheeded flie the swift hours o' love.

She is not the fairest, altho' she is fair ;
O' nice education but sma' is her share ;
Her parentage humble as humble can be ;
But I lo'e the dear lassie because she lo'es me.

To Beauty what man but maun yield him a prize,
In her armour of glances, and blushes, and sighs ?
And when wit and refinement hae polish'd her
  darts,
They dazzle our een, as they flie to our hearts.

But kindness, sweet kindness, in the fond-spark-
  ling e'e,
Has lustre outshining the diamond to me ;
And the heart beating love as I'm clasp'd in her
  arms,
O, these are my lassie's all-conquering charms !

RATTLIN, ROARIN WILLIE

O, RATTLIN, roarin Willie,
  O, he held to the fair,
An' for to sell his fiddle
  And buy some other ware ;

But parting wi' his fiddle,
  The saut tear blin't his e'e—
And, rattlin, roarin Willie
  Ye're welcome hame to me !

" O Willie, come sell your fiddle,
  O, sell your fiddle sae fine !
O Willie, come sell your fiddle,
  And buy a pint o' wine ! "
" If I should sell my fiddle,
  The warld would think I was mad ;
For monie a rantin day
  My fiddle and I hae had."

As I cam by Crochallan,
  I cannilie keekit ben ;
Rattlin, roarin Willie
  Was sittin at yon boord-en' ;
Sittin at yon boord-en',
  And amang gude companie ;
Rattlin, roarin Willie,
  Ye're welcome hame to me !

BONIE DUNDEE

" O, WHAR gat ye that hauver-meal bannock ? "
  " O silly blind body, O, dinna ye see ?
I gat it frae a young brisk sodger laddie
  Between Saint Johnston and bonie Dundee.

" O, gin I saw the laddie that gae me't !
  Aft has he doudl'd me up on his knee :
May Heaven protect my bonie Scots laddie,
  And send him hame to his babie and me.

" My blessins upon thy sweet wee lippie !
 My blessins upon thy bonie e'e-brie !
Thy smiles are sae like my blythe sodger laddie,
 Thou's aye the dearer, and dearer to me !

" But I'll big a bow'r on yon bonie banks,
 Whare Tay rins wimplin by sae clear ;
An' I'll cleed thee in the tartan sae fine,
 And mak thee a man like thy daddie dear."

THE BONIE MOOR-HEN

THE heather was blooming, the meadows were
 mawn,
Our lads gaed a-hunting ae day at the dawn,
O'er moors and o'er mosses and mony a glen,
At length they discover'd a bonie moor-hen.

Chorus.—I rede you, beware at the hunting,
 young men,
 I rede you, beware at the hunting,
 young men ;
 Take some on the wing, and some as
 they spring,
 But cannily steal on a bonie moor-hen.

Sweet-brushing the dew from the brown heather
 bells
Her colours betray'd her on yon mossy fells ;
Her plumage outlustr'd the pride o' the spring
And O ! as she wanton'd sae gay on the wing.
 I rede you, &c.

Auld Phœbus himsel', as he peep'd o'er the hill,
In spite at her plumage he trièd his skill ;

He levell'd his rays where she bask'd on the brae—
His rays were outshone, and but mark'd where
    she lay.
  I rede you, &c.

They hunted the valley, they hunted the hill,
The best of our lads wi' the best o' their skill ;
But still as the fairest she sat in their sight,
Then, whirr ! she was over, a mile at a flight.
  I rede you, &c.

  *   *   *   *   *

MY LORD A-HUNTING

Chorus—My lady's gown, there's gairs upon't,
   And gowden flowers sae rare upon't ;
   But Jenny's jimps and jirkenet,
   My lord thinks meikle mair upon't.

My lord a-hunting he is gane,
But hounds or hawks wi' him are nane ;
By Colin's cottage lies his game,
If Colin's Jenny be at hame.
  My lady's gown, &c.

My lady's white, my lady's red,
And kith and kin o' Cassillis' blude ;
But her ten-pund lands o' tocher-gude ;
Were a' the charms his lordship lo'ed.
  My lady's gown, &c.

Out o'er yon muir, out o'er yon moss,
Whare gor-cocks thro' the heather pass,
There wons auld Colin's bonie lass,
A lily in a wilderness.
  My lady's gown, &c.

Sae sweetly move her genty limbs,
Like music notes o' lovers' hymns :
The diamond-dew in her een sae blue,
Where laughing love sae wanton swims.
My lady's gown, &c.

My lady's dink, my lady's drest,
The flower and fancy o' the west ;
But the lassie that a man lo'es best,
O that's the lass to mak him blest.
My lady's gown, &c.

A BOTTLE AND FRIEND

"There's nane that's blest of human kind,
But the cheerful and the gay, man,
Fal, la, la," &c.

HERE's a bottle and an honest friend !
What wad ye wish for mair, man ?
Wha kens, before his life may end,
What his share may be o' care, man ?

Then catch the moments as they fly,
And use them as ye ought, man :
Believe me, happiness is shy,
And comes not aye when sought, man.

HEY, CA' THRO'

UP wi' the carls o' Dysart,
And the lads o' Buckhaven,
And the kimmers o' Largo,
And the lasses o' Leven.

D.O. Hill. S.A.   W. Richardson

The Birks of Aberfeldy

From an engraving after David Octavius Hill

The Birks of Aberfeldy~

"Now Simmer blinks on flowery braes,
And o'er the crystal streamlets plays."

Chorus.—Hey, ca thro', ca' thro',
　　For we hae mickle ado ;
　　Hey, ca' thro', ca' thro',
　　For we hae mickle ado.

We hae tales to tell,
　　An' we hae sangs to sing ;
We hae pennies tae spend,
　　An' we hae pints to bring.
　　Hey, ca' thro', &c.

We'll live a' our days,
　　And them that comes behin',
Let them do the like,
　　An' spend the gear they win.
　　Hey, ca' thro', &c.

THE BIRKS OF ABERFELDY

Tune—" The Birks of Abergeldy."

Chorus.—Bonie lassie, will ye go,
　　Will ye go, will ye go,
　　Bonie lassie, will ye go
　　　To the birks of Aberfeldy !

Now Simmer blinks on flowery braes,
And o'er the crystal streamlets plays ;
Come let us spend the lightsome days
　In the birks of Aberfeldy.
　　Bonie lassie, &c.

The little birdies blythely sing,
While o'er their heads the hazels hing,
Or lightly flit on wanton wing
　In the birks of Aberfeldy.
　　Bonie lassie, &c.

The braes ascend like lofty wa's,
The foamy stream deep-roaring fa's,
O'erhung wi' fragrant spreading shaws—
 The birks of Aberfeldy.
  Bonie lassie, &c.

The hoary cliffs are crown'd wi' flowers,
White o'er the linns the burnie pours,
And rising, weets wi' misty showers
 The birks of Aberfeldy.
  Bonie lassie, &c.

Let Fortune's gifts at random flee,
They ne'er shall draw a wish frae me;
Supremely blest wi' love and thee,
 In the birks of Aberfeldy.
  Bonie lassie, &c.

STRATHALLAN'S LAMENT

THICKEST night, surround my dwelling!
 Howling tempests, o'er me rave !
Turbid torrents, wintry swelling,
 Roaring by my lonely cave !
Crystal streamlets gently flowing,
 Busy haunts of base mankind,
Western breezes softly blowing,
 Suit not my distracted mind.

In the cause of Right engagèd,
 Wrongs injurious to redress,
Honour's war we strongly wagèd,
 But the Heavens denied success,
Ruin's wheel has driven o'er us.
 Not a hope that dare attend,
The wide world is all before us—
 But a world without a friend.

CASTLE GORDON

STREAMS that glide in Orient plains,
Never bound by Winter's chains;
 Glowing here on golden sands,
There immixed with foulest stains
 From Tyranny's empurpled hands;
These, their richly gleaming waves,
I leave to tyrants and their slaves;
Give me the stream that sweetly laves
 The banks by Castle Gordon.

Spicy forests, ever gay,
Shading from the burning ray
 Hapless wretches sold to toil;
Or the ruthless native's way,
 Bent on slaughter, blood, and spoil:
Woods that ever verdant wave,
I leave the tyrant and the slave;
Give me the groves that lofty brave
 The storms by Castle Gordon.

Wildly here, without control,
Nature reigns and rules the whole;
 In that sober pensive mood,
Dearest to the feeling soul,
 She plants the forest, pours the flood:
Life's poor day I'll musing rave
And find at night a sheltering cave,
Where waters flow and wild woods wave
 By bonie Castle Gordon.

LADY ONLIE, HONEST LUCKY

Tune—"The Ruffian's Rant."

A' THE lads o' Thorniebank,
   When they gae to the shore o' Bucky,
They'll step in an' tak a pint
   Wi' Lady Onlie, honest lucky.

*Chorus—*Lady Onlie, honest lucky,
   Brews guid ale at shore o' Bucky;
      I wish her sale for her gude ale,
         The best on a' the shore o' Bucky.

Her house sae bien, her curch sae clean
   I wat she is a daintie chuckie;
And cheery blinks the ingle-gleed
   O' Lady Onlie, honest luckie.
      Lady Onlie, &c.

THENIEL MENZIES' BONIE MARY

Air—" The Ruffian's Rant," or *Roy's Wife.*

IN comin by the brig o' Dye,
   At Darlet we a blink did tarry;
As day was dawin in the sky,
   We drank a health to bonie Mary.

Chorus.—Theniel Menzies' bonie Mary,
      Theniel Menzies' bonie Mary,
   Charlie Grigor tint his plaidie,
      Kissin' Theniel's bonie Mary.

Her een sae bright, her brow sae white,
   Her haffet locks as brown's a berry;
And aye they dimpl't wi' a smile,
   The rosy cheeks o' bonie Mary.
      Theniel Menzies' bonie Mary, &c

We lap an' danc'd the lee-lang day,
  Till piper lads were wae and weary;
But Charlie gat the spring to pay
  For kissin' Theniel's bonie Mary.
      Theniel Menzies' bonie Mary, &c.

THE BONIE LASS OF ALBANY

Tune—" Mary's Dream."

My heart is wae, and unco wae,
  To think upon the raging sea,
That roars between her gardens green
  An' the bonie Lass of Albany.

This lovely maid's of royal blood
  That rulèd Albion's kingdoms three,
But oh, alas! for her bonie face,
  They've wrang'd the Lass of Albany.

In the rolling tide of spreading Clyde
  There sits an isle of high degree,
And a town of fame whose princely name
  Should grace the Lass of Albany.

But there is a youth, a witless youth,
  That fills the place where she should be;
We'll send him o'er to his native shore,
  And bring our ain sweet Albany.

Alas the day, and woe the day,
  A false usurper wan the gree,
Who now commands the towers and lands—
  The royal right of Albany.

We'll daily pray, we'll nightly pray,
On bended knees most fervently,
The time may come, with pipe an' drum
We'll welcome hame fair Albany.

BLYTHE WAS SHE

Tune—" Andro and his Cutty Gun."

Chorus—Blythe, blythe and merry was she,
Blythe was she but and ben ;
Blythe by the banks of Earn,
And blythe in Glenturit glen.

By Oughtertyre grows the aik,
On Yarrow banks the birken shaw ;
But Phemie was a bonier lass
Than braes o' Yarrow ever saw.
Blythe, blythe, &c.

Her looks were like a flow'r in May,
Her smile was like a simmer morn ;
She trippèd by the banks o' Earn,
As light's a bird upon a thorn.
Blythe, blythe, &c.

Her bonie face it was as meek
As ony lamb upon a lea :
The evening sun was ne'er sae sweet,
As was the blink o' Phemie's e'e.
Blythe, blythe, &c.

The Highland hills I've wander'd wide,
And o'er the Lawlands I hae been ;
But Phemie was the blythest lass
That ever trod the dewy green.
Blythe, blythe, &c.

Euphemia Murray

After a miniature by A. Stewart

Blythe was She

"... *Phemie was the blythest lass*
That ever trod the dewy green."

A ROSE-BUD BY MY EARLY WALK

A Rose-bud by my early walk,
Adown a corn-enclosed bawk,
Sae gently bent its thorny stalk,
    All on a dewy morning.
Ere twice the shades o' dawn are fled,
In a' its crimson glory spread,
And drooping rich the dewy head,
    It scents the early morning.

Within the bush her covert nest
A little linnet fondly prest;
The dew sat chilly on her breast,
    Sae early in the morning.
She soon shall see her tender brood,
The pride, the pleasure o' the wood,
Amang the fresh green leaves bedew'd,
    Awake the early morning.

So thou, dear bird, young Jeany fair,
On trembling string or vocal air,
Shall sweetly pay the tender care
    That tents thy early morning.
So thou, sweet Rose-bud, young and gay,
Shalt beauteous blaze upon the day,
And bless the parent's evening ray
    That watch'd thy early morning.

THE BANKS OF THE DEVON

Tune—" Bhanarach dhonn a' chruidh."

How pleasant the banks of the clear winding Devon,
    With green spreading bushes and flow'rs bloom-
    ing fair!

But the boniest flow'r on the banks of the Devon
　　Was once a sweet bud on the braes of the Ayr.
Mild be the sun on this sweet blushing flower,
　　In the gay rosy morn, as it bathes in the dew;
And gentle the fall of the soft vernal shower,
　　That steals on the evening each leaf to renew!

O spare the dear blossom, ye orient breezes,
　　With chill hoary wing as ye usher the dawn;
And far be thou distant, thou reptile that seizes
　　The verdure and pride of the garden or lawn!
Let Bourbon exult in his gay gilded lilies,
　　And England triumphant display her proud rose:
A fairer than either adorns the green valleys,
　　Where Devon, sweet Devon, meandering flows.

BRAVING ANGRY WINTER'S STORMS

Tune—" Neil Gow's Lament for Abercairny."

WHERE, braving angry winter's storms,
　　The lofty Ochils rise,
Far in their shade my Peggy's charms
　　First blest my wondering eyes;
As one who by some savage stream
　　A lonely gem surveys,
Astonish'd doubly, marks it beam
　　With art's most polish'd blaze.

Blest be the wild, sequester'd shade,
　　And blest the day and hour,
Where Peggy's charms I first survey'd,
　　When first I felt their pow'r!

Scene on the Devon

From an engraving after David Octavius Hill

The Banks of the Devon

"How pleasant the banks of the clear winding Devon,
With green spreading bushes and flow'rs blooming fair!"

The tyrant Death, with grim control,
　　May seize my fleeting breath ;
But tearing Peggy from my soul
　　Must be a stronger death.

MY PEGGY'S CHARMS

Tune—" Tha a' chailleach air mo dheigh."

My Peggy's face, my Peggy's form,
The frost of hermit Age might warm ;
My Peggy's worth, my Peggy's mind,
Might charm the first of human kind.

I love my Peggy's angel air,
Her face so truly heavenly fair,
Her native grace, so void of art,
But I adore my Peggy's heart.

The lily's hue, the rose's dye,
The kindling lustre of an eye ;
Who but owns their magic sway ?
Who but knows they all decay ?

The tender thrill, the pitying tear,
The generous purpose nobly dear,
The gentle look that rage disarms—
These are all immortal charms.

THE YOUNG HIGHLAND ROVER

Tune—" Morag."

Loud blaw the frosty breezes,
　　The snaws the mountains cover ;
Like winter on me seizes,
　　Since my young Highland rover
　　Far wanders nations over.

Where'er he go, where'er he stray,
  May heaven be his warden;
Return·him safe to fair Strathspey,
  And bonie Castle-Gordon!

The trees, now naked groaning,
  Shall soon wi' leaves be hinging,
The birdies, dowie moaning,
  Shall a' be blythely singing,
  And every flower be springing;
Sae I'll rejoice the lee-lang day,
  When by his mighty Warden
My youth's return'd to fair Strathspey,
  And bonie Castle-Gordon.

LOVE IN THE GUISE OF FRIENDSHIP

TALK not of love, it gives me pain,
  For love has been my foe;
He bound me in an iron chain,
  And plung'd me deep in woe.

But friendship's pure and lasting joys,
  My heart was form'd to prove;
There, welcome win and wear the prize,
  But never talk of love.

Your friendship much can make me blest,
  O why that bliss destroy?
Why urge the only, one request
  You know I will deny?

Your thought, if Love must harbour there,
  Conceal it in that thought;
Nor cause me from my bosom tear
  The very friend I sought.

The Young Highland Rover

The Young Highland Rover

"Sae I'll rejoice the lee-lang day,
When by his mighty Warden
My youth's returned to fair Strathspey,
And bonie Castle-Gordon."

GO ON, SWEET BIRD, AND SOOTHE
MY CARE

Go on, sweet bird, and soothe my care,
Thy tuneful notes will hush despair;
Thy plaintive warblings, void of art,
Thrill sweetly thro' my aching heart.
Now choose thy mate and fondly love,
And all the charming transport prove;
While I a love-lorn exile live,
Nor transport or receive or give.

For thee is laughing Nature gay,
For thee she pours the vernal day;
For me in vain is Nature drest,
While Joy's a stranger to my breast.
These sweet emotions all enjoy;
Let Love and Song thy hours employ!
Go on, sweet bird, and soothe my care,
Thy tuneful notes will hush despair.

CLARINDA, MISTRESS OF MY
SOUL

Clarinda, mistress of my soul,
The measur'd time is run!
The wretch beneath the dreary pole
So marks his latest sun.

To what dark cave of frozen night
Shall poor Sylvander hie;
Depriv'd of thee, his life and light,
The sun of all his joy.

We part—but by these precious drops,
  That fill thy lovely eyes,
No other light shall guide my steps,
  Till thy bright beams arise !

She, the fair sun of all her sex,
  Has blest my glorious day ;
And shall a glimmering planet fix
  My worship to its ray ?

I'M O'ER YOUNG TO MARRY YET

Chorus.—I'm o'er young, I'm o'er young,
    I'm o'er young to marry yet ;
    I'm o'er young, 'twad be a sin
      To tak me frae my mammy yet.

I AM my mammy's ae bairn,
  Wi' unco folk I weary, sir ;
And lying in a man's bed,
  I'm fley'd it mak me eerie, sir.
    I'm o'er young, &c.

Hallowmass is come and gane,
  The nights are lang in winter, sir,
And you an' I in ae bed,—
  In trowth, I dare na venture, sir.
    I'm o'er young, &c.

Fu' loud an' shill the frosty wind
  Blaws thro' the leafless timmer, sir ;
But if ye come this gate again,
  I'll aulder be gin simmer, sir.
    I'm o'er young, &c.

TO THE WEAVER'S GIN YE GO

My heart was ance as blythe and free
As simmer days were lang;
But a bonie, westlin weaver lad
Has gart me change my sang.

Chorus.—To the weaver's gin ye go, fair maids,
To the weaver's gin ye go;
I rede you right, gang ne'er at night,
To the weaver's gin ye go.

My mither sent me to the town,
To warp a plaiden wab;
But the weary, weary warpin o't
Has gart me sigh and sab.
To the weaver's, &c.

A bonie, westlin weaver lad
Sat working at his loom;
He took my heart as wi' a net,
In every knot and thrum.
To the weaver's, &c.

I sat beside my warpin-wheel,
And aye I ca'd it roun';
But every shot and every knock,
My heart it gae a stoun.
To the weaver's, &c.

The moon was sinking in the west,
Wi' visage pale and wan,
As my bonie, westlin weaver lad
Convoy'd me thro' the glen.
To the weaver's, &c.

But what was said, or what was done,
    Shame fa' me gin I tell ;
But Oh ! I fear the kintra soon
    Will ken as weel's mysel !
        To the weaver's, &c.

M'PHERSON'S FAREWELL

Tune—" M'Pherson's Rant."

FAREWELL, ye dungeons dark and strong,
    The wretch's destinie !
M'Pherson's time will not be long
    On yonder gallows-tree.

Chorus.—Sae rantingly, sae wantonly,
        Sae dauntingly gaed he ;
        He play'd a spring, and danc'd it round,
        Below the gallows-tree.

O what is death but parting breath ?
    On many a bloody plain
I've dared his face, and in this place
    I scorn him yet again !
        Sae rantingly, &c.

Untie these bands from off my hands,
    And bring to me my sword ;
And there's no a man in all Scotland,
    But I'll brave him at a word.
        Sae rantingly, &c.

I've liv'd a life of sturt and strife ;
    I die by treacherie :
It burns my heart I must depart,
    And not avengèd be.
        Sae rantingly, &c.

Now farewell light, thou sunshine bright,
  And all beneath the sky !
May coward shame distain his name,
  The wretch that dare not die !
     Sae rantingly, &c.

STAY MY CHARMER

Tune—" An gille dubh ciar-dhubh."

STAY my charmer, can you leave me !
Cruel, cruel to deceive me ;
Well you know how much you grieve me ;
  Cruel charmer, can you go ?
  Cruel charmer, can you go ?

By my love so ill-requited,
By the faith you fondly plighted,
By the pangs of lovers slighted,
  Do not, do not leave me so !
  Do not, do not leave me so !

MY HOGGIE

WHAT will I do gin my Hoggie die ?
  My joy, my pride, my Hoggie !
My only beast, I had nae mae,
  And vow but I was vogie !
The lee-lang night we watch'd the fauld,
  Me and my faithfu' doggie ;
We heard nocht but the roaring linn,
  Amang the braes sae scroggie.

But the houlet cry'd frae the castle wa',
  The blitter frae the boggie ;
The tod reply'd upon the hill,
  I trembled for my Hoggie.

M

When day did daw, and cocks did craw,
The morning it was foggie ;
An unco tyke lap o'er the dyke,
And maist has kill'd my Hoggie !

RAVING WINDS AROUND HER BLOWING

Tune—" M'Grigor of Roro's Lament."

RAVING winds around her blowing,
Yellow leaves the woodlands strowing,
By a river hoarsely roaring,
Isabella stray'd deploring—

" Farewell, hours that late did measure
Sunshine days of joy and pleasure ;
Hail, thou gloomy night of sorrow,
Cheerless night that knows no morrow !

" O'er the past too fondly wandering,
On the hopeless future pondering ;
Chilly grief my life-blood freezes,
Fell despair my fancy seizes.

" Life, thou soul of every blessing,
Load to misery most distressing,
Gladly how would I resign thee,
And to dark oblivion join thee ! "

UP IN THE MORNING EARLY

CAULD blaws the wind frae east to west,
The drift is driving sairly ;
Sae loud and shill's I hear the blast—
I'm sure it's winter fairly.

Chorus—Up in the morning's no for me,
    Up in the morning early ;
    When a' the hills are covered wi'
        snaw,
    I'm sure it's winter fairly.

The birds sit chittering in the thorn,
    A' day they fare but sparely ;
And lang's the night frae e'en to morn—
    I'm sure it's winter fairly.
        Up in the morning's, &c.

HOW LONG AND DREARY IS THE NIGHT

How long and dreary is the night,
    When I am frae my dearie !
I sleepless lie frae e'en to morn,
    Tho' I were ne'er so weary !

When I think on the happy days
    I spent wi' you my dearie :
And now what lands between us lie,
    How can I be but eerie !

How slow ye move, ye heavy hours,
    As ye were wae and weary !
It was na sae ye glinted by,
    When I was wi' my dearie !

HEY, THE DUSTY MILLER

Hey, the dusty Miller,
    And his dusty coat,
He will win a shilling,
    Or he spend a groat :

Dusty was the coat,
  Dusty was the colour,
Dusty was the kiss
  That I gat frae the Miller.

Hey, the dusty Miller,
  And his dusty sack;
Leeze me on the calling
  Fills the dusty peck:
Fills the dusty peck,
  Brings the dusty siller;
I wad gie my coatie
  For the dusty Miller.

DUNCAN DAVISON

There was a lass, they ca'd her Meg,
  And she held o'er the moors to spin;
There was a lad that follow'd her,
  They ca'd him Duncan Davison.
The moor was dreigh, and Meg was skeigh,
  Her favour Duncan could na win;
For wi' the rock she wad him knock,
  And aye she shook the temper-pin.

As o'er the moor they lightly foor,
  A burn was clear, a glen was green,
Upon the banks they eas'd their shanks,
  And aye she set the wheel between:
But Duncan swoor a haly aith,
  That Meg should be a bride the morn;
Then Meg took up her spinning-graith,
  And flang them a' out o'er the burn.

We will big a wee, wee house,
  And we will live like king and queen;
Sae blythe and merry's we will be,
  When ye set by the wheel at e'en.
A man may drink, and no be drunk;
  A man may fight, and no be slain;
A man may kiss a bonie lass,
  And aye be welcome back again!.

THE LAD THEY CA' JUMPIN JOHN

Her daddie forbad, her minnie forbad,
  Forbidden she wadna be:
She wadna trow't, the browst she brew'd,
  Wad taste sae bitterlie.

Chorus.—The lang lad they ca' Jumpin John
     Beguil'd the bonie lassie,
    The lang lad they ca' Jumpin John
     Beguil'd the bonie lassie.

A cow and a cauf, a yowe and a hauf,
  And thretty gude shillins and three;
A vera gude tocher, a cotter-man's dochter,
  The lass wi' the bonie black e'e.
     The lang lad, &c.

TALK OF HIM THAT'S FAR AWA

Musing on the roaring ocean,
  Which divides my love and me;
Wearying heav'n in warm devotion,
  For his weal where'er he be.

Hope and Fear's alternate billow
Yielding late to Nature's law,
Whispering spirits round my pillow,
Talk of him that's far awa.

Ye whom sorrow never wounded,
Ye who never shed a tear,
Care-untroubled, joy-surrounded,
Gaudy day to you is dear.

Gentle night, do thou befriend me,
Downy sleep, the curtain draw;
Spirits kind, again attend me,
Talk of him that's far awa!

TO DAUNTON ME

THE blude-red rose at Yule may blaw,
The simmer lilies bloom in snaw,
The frost may freeze the deepest sea;
But an auld man shall never daunton me.

Chorus.—To daunton me, to daunton me,
An auld man shall never daunton me.

To daunton me, and me sae young,
Wi' his fause heart and flatt'ring tongue,
That is the thing you ne'er shall see,
For an auld man shall never daunton me.
To daunton me, &c.

For a' his meal and a' his maut,
For a' his fresh beef and his saut,
For a his gold and white monie,
An auld man shall never daunton me.
To daunton me, &c.

The Winter it is Past

The Winter it is Past

"The winter it is past, and the summer comes at last,
And the small birds, they sing on ev'ry tree."

His gear may buy him kye and yowes,
His gear may buy him glens and knowes;
But me he shall not buy nor fee,
For an auld man shall never daunton me.
   To daunton me, &c.

He hirples twa-fauld as he dow,
Wi' his teethless gab and his auld beld pow,
And the rain rains down frae his red blear'd e'e;
That auld man shall never daunton me.
   To daunton me, &c.

THE WINTER IT IS PAST

THE winter it is past, and the summer comes at
 last,
 And the small birds, they sing on ev'ry tree;
Now ev'ry thing is glad, while I am very sad,
 Since my true love is parted from me.

The rose upon the brier, by the waters running
 clear,
 May have charms for the linnet or the bee;
Their little loves are blest, and their little hearts
 at rest,
 But my true love is parted from me.

THE BONIE LAD THAT'S FAR
AWA

O HOW can I be blythe and glad,
 Or how can I gang brisk and braw,
When the bonie lad that I lo'e best
 Is o'er the hills and far awa!

It's no the frosty winter wind,
  It's no the driving drift and snaw ;
But aye the tear comes in my e'e,
  To think on him that's far awa.

My father pat me frae his door,
  My friends they hae disown'd me a' ;
But I hae ane will tak my part,
  The bonie lad that's far awa.

A pair o' glooves he bought to me,
  And silken snoods he ga'e me twa ;
And I will wear them for his sake,
  The bonie lad that's far awa.

O weary Winter soon will pass,
  And Spring will cleed the birken shaw ;
And my young babie will be born,
  And he'll be hame that's far awa.

THE CHEVALIER'S LAMENT

Air—" Captain O'Kean."

THE small birds rejoice in the green leaves return-
    ing,
The murmuring streamlet winds clear thro' the
    vale ;
The primroses blow in the dews of the morning,
And wild scatter'd cowslips bedeck the green dale :
But what can give pleasure, or what can seem fair,
When the lingering moments are numbered by
    care ?
No birds sweetly singing, nor flow'rs gaily spring-
    ing,
Can soothe the sad bosom of joyless despair.

The deed that I dared, could it merit their
   malice?
A king and a father to place on his throne!
His right are these hills, and his right are these
   valleys,
Where the wild beasts find shelter, tho' I can
   find none!
But 'tis not my suff'rings, thus wretched, forlorn,
My brave gallant friends, 'tis your ruin I mourn;
Your faith proved so loyal in hot bloody trial,—
Alas! I can make it no better return!

THO' CRUEL FATE SHOULD BID US PART

Tune—"The Northern Lass."

Tho' cruel fate should bid us part,
   Far as the pole and line,
Her dear idea round my heart,
   Should tenderly entwine.
Tho' mountains rise, and deserts howl,
   And oceans roar between;
Yet, dearer than my deathless soul,
   I still would love my Jean.

OF A' THE AIRTS THE WIND CAN BLAW

Tune—"Miss Admiral Gordon's Strathspey."

Of a' the airts the wind can blaw,
   I dearly like the west,
For there the bonie lassie lives,
   The lassie I lo'e best ·

M*

There's wild-woods grow, and rivers row,
 And mony a hill between:
But day and night my fancy's flight
 Is ever wi' my Jean.

I see her in the dewy flowers,
 I see her sweet and fair:
I hear her in the tunefu' birds,
 I hear her charm the air:
There's not a bonie flower that springs,
 By fountain, shaw, or green;
There's not a bonie bird that sings,
 But minds me o' my Jean.

I HAE A WIFE O' MY AIN

I HAE a wife o' my ain,
 I'll partake wi' naebody;
I'll take Cuckold frae nane,
 I'll gie Cuckold to naebody.

I hae a penny to spend,
 There—thanks to naebody!
I hae naething to lend,
 I'll borrow frae naebody.

I am naebody's lord,
 I'll be slave to naebody;
I hae a gude braid sword,
 I'll tak dunts frae naebody.

I'll be merry and free,
 I'll be sad for naebody;
Naebody cares for me,
 I care for naebody.

A Mother's Lament

A Mother's Lament

"Fate gave the word, the arrow sped
And pierc'd my darling's heart;
And with him all the joys are fled
Life can to me impart."

ANNA, THY CHARMS

Anna, thy charms my bosom fire,
And waste my soul with care;
But ah! how bootless to admire,
When fated to despair!

Yet in thy presence, lovely Fair,
To hope may be forgiven;
For sure 'twere impious to despair
So much in sight of heaven.

A MOTHER'S LAMENT

FOR THE DEATH OF HER SON

Fate gave the word, the arrow sped,
And pierc'd my darling's heart;
And with him all the joys are fled
Life can to me impart.

By cruel hands the sapling drops,
In dust dishonour'd laid;
So fell the pride of all my hopes,
My age's future shade.

The mother-linnet in the brake
Bewails her ravish'd young;
So I, for my lost darling's sake,
Lament the live-day long.

Death, oft I've feared thy fatal blow.
Now, fond, I bare my breast;
O, do thou kindly lay me low
With him I love, at rest!

THE DAY RETURNS

Tune—" Seventh of November."

THE day returns, my bosom burns,
　　The blissful day we twa did meet:
Tho' winter wild in tempest toil'd,
　　Ne'er summer-sun was half sae sweet.
Than a' the pride that loads the tide,
　　And crosses o'er the sultry line ;
Than kingly robes, than crowns and globes,
　　Heav'n gave me more—it made thee mine !

While day and night can bring delight,
　　Or Nature aught of pleasure give,
While joys above my mind can move,
　　For thee, and thee alone, I live.
When that grim foe of life below
　　Comes in between to make us part,
The iron hand that breaks our band,
　　It breaks my bliss—it breaks my heart !

O WERE I ON PARNASSUS HILL

Tune—" My love is lost to me."

O WERE I on Parnassus hill,
Or had o' Helicon my fill,
That I might catch poetic skill,
　　To sing how dear I love thee !
But Nith maun be my Muse's well,
My Muse maun be thy bonie sel',
On Corsincon I'll glowr and spell,
　　And write how dear I love thee.

Then come, sweet Muse, inspire my lay!
For a' the lee-lang simmer's day
I couldna sing, I couldna say,
   How much, how dear, I love thee,
I see thee dancing o'er the green,
Thy waist sae jimp, thy limbs sae clean,
Thy tempting lips, thy roguish een—
   By Heaven and Earth I love thee!

By night, by day, a-field, at hame,
The thoughts o' thee my breast inflame:
And aye I muse and sing thy name—
   I only live to love thee.
Tho' I were doom'd to wander on,
Beyond the sea, beyond the sun,
Till my last weary sand was run;
   Till then—and then—I'd love thee!

THE FALL OF THE LEAF

The lazy mist hangs from the brow of the hill,
Concealing the course of the dark winding rill;
How languid the scenes, late so sprightly, appear,
As Autumn to Winter resigns the pale year!

The forests are leafless, the meadows are brown,
And all the gay foppery of summer is flown:
Apart let me wander, apart let me muse,
How quick Time is flying, how keen Fate
   pursues!

How long I have liv'd—but how much liv'd in
   vain,
How little of life's scanty span may remain,
What aspects old Time in his progress has worn,
What ties cruel Fate in my bosom has torn.

How foolish, or worse, till our summit is gain'd!
And downward, how weaken'd, how darken'd,
    how pain'd!
Life is not worth having with all it can give—
For something beyond it poor man sure must live.

I REIGN IN JEANIE'S BOSOM

Louis, what reck I by thee,
    Or Geordie on his ocean?
Dyvor, beggar louns to me,
    I reign in Jeanie's bosom!

Let her crown my love her law,
    And in her breast enthrone me,
Kings and nations—swith awa'!
    Reif randies, I disown ye!

IT IS NA, JEAN, THY BONIE FACE

It is na, Jean, thy bonie face,
    Nor shape that I admire;
Altho' thy beauty and thy grace
    Might weel awauk desire.

Something, in ilka part o' thee,
    To praise, to love, I find,
But dear as is thy form to me,
    Still dearer is thy mind.

Nae mair ungenerous wish I hae,
    Nor stronger in my breast,
Than, if I canna make thee sae,
    At least to see thee blest.

Auld Lang Syne

Auld Lang Syne

"We twa hae paidl'd in the burn . . ."

Content am I, if heaven shall give
But happiness to thee;
And as wi' thee I wish to live,
For thee I'd bear to die.

AULD LANG SYNE

SHOULD auld acquaintance be forgot,
And never brought to mind?
Should auld acquaintance be forgot,
And auld lang syne!

Chorus—For auld lang syne, my dear,
For auld lang syne,
We'll tak a cup o' kindness yet,
For auld lang syne.

And surely ye'll be your pint stowp!
And surely I'll be mine!
And we'll tak a cup o' kindness yet,
For auld lang syne.
For auld, &c.

We twa hae run about the braes,
And pou'd the gowans fine;
But we've wander'd mony a weary fit
Sin' auld lang syne.
For auld, &c.

We twa hae paidl'd in the burn,
Frae morning sun till dine;
But seas between us braid hae roar'd
Sin' auld lang syne.
For auld, &c

And there's a hand, my trusty fere !
And gie's a hand o' thine !
And we'll tak' a right gude-willie waught,
For auld lang syne.
For auld, &c.

MY BONIE MARY

Go, fetch to me a pint o' wine,
And fill it in a silver tassie ;
That I may drink before I go
A service to my bonie lassie.
The boat rocks at the pier o' Leith ;
Fu' loud the wind blaws frae the Ferry ;
The ship rides by the Berwick-law,
And I maun leave my bonie Mary.

The trumpets sound, the banners fly,
The glittering spears are rankèd ready :
The shouts o' war are heard afar,
The battle closes deep and bloody ;
It's not the roar o' sea or shore,
Wad mak me langer wish to tarry,
Nor shouts o' war that's heard afar—
It's leaving thee, my bonie Mary !

ROBIN SHURE IN HAIRST

Chorus—Robin shure in hairst,
I shure wi' him.
Fient a heuk had I,
Yet I stack by him.

I GAED up to Dunse,
  To warp a wab o' plaiden,
At his daddie's yett,
  Wha met me but Robin;
    Robin shure, &c.

Was na Robin bauld,
  Tho' I was a cotter,
Play'd me sic a trick,
  An' me the Eller's dochter!
    Robin shure, &c.

Robin promis'd me
  A' my winter vittle;
Fient haet he had but three
  Guse-feathers and a whittle!
    Robin shure, &c.

SWEET AFTON

Flow gently, sweet Afton! among thy green braes,
Flow gently, I'll sing thee a song in thy praise;
My Mary's asleep by thy murmuring stream,
Flow gently, sweet Afton, disturb not her dream.

Thou stock dove whose echo resounds thro' the
    glen,
Ye wild whistling blackbirds in yon thorny den,
Thou green crested lapwing, thy screaming forbear,
I charge you, disturb not my slumbering Fair.

How lofty, sweet Afton, thy neighbouring hills,
Far mark'd with the courses of clear, winding rills;
There daily I wander as noon rises high,
My flocks and my Mary's sweet cot in my eye.

How pleasant thy banks and green valleys below,
Where, wild in the woodlands, the primroses blow;
There oft, as mild Ev'ning weeps over the lea,
The sweet-scented birk shades my Mary and me.

Thy crystal stream, Afton, how lovely it glides,
And winds by the cot where my Mary resides;
How wanton thy waters her snowy feet lave,
As, gathering sweet flowerets, she stems thy clear
wave.

Flow gently, sweet Afton, amang thy green braes,
Flow gently, sweet river, the theme of my lays;
My Mary's asleep by thy murmuring stream,
Flow gently, sweet Afton, disturb not her dream.

SHE'S FAIR AND FAUSE

SHE's fair and fause that causes my smart,
    I lo'ed her meikle and lang;
She's broken her vow, she's broken my heart,
    And I may e'en gae hang.
A coof cam' in wi' routh o' gear,
And I hae tint my dearest dear;
But Woman is but warld's gear,
    Sae let the bonie lass gang

Whae'er ye be that woman love,
    To this be never blind;
Nae ferlie 'tis tho' fickle she prove,
    A woman has't by kind.
O Woman lovely, Woman fair!
An angel form's faun to thy share,
'Twad been o'er meikle to gi'en thee mair —
    I mean an angel mind.

Bonie Ann

Bonie Ann

"Ye gallants bright, I rede you right,
Beware o' bonie Ann."

BEWARE O' BONIE ANN

Ye gallants bright, I rede you right,
 Beware o' bonie Ann :
Her comely face sae fu' o' grace,
 Your heart she will trepan :
Her een sae bright, like stars by night,
 Her skin is like the swan ;
Sae jimply lac'd her genty waist,
 That sweetly ye might span.

Youth, Grace, and Love attendant move,
 And pleasure leads the van .
In a' their charms, and conquering arms,
 They wait on bonie Ann.
The captive bands may chain the hands,
 But love enslaves the man :
Ye gallants braw, I rede you a',
 Beware o' bonie Ann !

THE GARD'NER WI' HIS PAIDLE

Tune—" The Gardener's March."

When rosy May comes in wi' flowers,
To deck her gay, green-spreading bowers,
Then busy, busy are his hours,
         The Gard'ner wi' his paidle.

The crystal waters gently fa',
The merry bards are lovers a',
The scented breezes round him blaw—
         The Gard'ner wi' his paidle.

When purple morning starts the hare
To steal upon her early fare;
Then thro' the dews he maun repair—
    The Gard'ner wi' his paidle.

When day, expiring in the west,
The curtain draws o' Nature's rest,
He flies to her arms he lo'es best,
    The Gard'ner wi' his paidle.

ON A BANK OF FLOWERS

On a bank of flowers on a summer day,
    For summer lightly drest,
The youthful, blooming Nelly lay,
    With love and sleep opprest;
When Willie, wand'ring thro' the wood,
Who for her favour oft had sued;
    He gaz'd, he wish'd,
    He fear'd, he blush'd,
And trembled where he stood.

Her closèd eyes, like weapons sheath'd,
    Were seal'd in soft repose;
Her lip, still as she fragrant breath'd,
    It richer dyed the rose;
The springing lilies, sweetly prest,
Wild-wanton kissed her rival breast:
    He gaz'd, he wish'd,
    He fear'd, he blush'd,
His bosom ill at rest.

Her robes light-waving in the breeze,
    Her tender limbs embrace;
Her lovely form, her native ease,
    All harmony and grace;

Tumultuous tides his pulses roll,
A faltering, ardent kiss he stole ;
   He gaz'd, he wish'd,
   He fear'd, he blush'd,
And sigh'd his very soul.

As flies the partridge from the brake,
  On fear-inspirèd wings,
So Nelly starting, half-awake,
  Away affrighted springs ;
But Willie follow'd—as he should,
He overtook her in the wood ;
   He vow'd, he pray'd,
   He found the maid
Forgiving all and good.

YOUNG JOCKIE WAS THE BLYTHEST LAD

Young Jockie was the blythest lad,
  In a' our town or here awa ;
Fu' blythe he whistled at the gaud,
  Fu' lightly danc'd he in the ha'.

He roos'd my een sae bonie blue,
  He roos'd my waist sae genty sma' ;
An' aye my heart cam to my mou',
  When ne'er a body heard or saw.

My Jockie toils upon the plain,
  Thro' wind and weet, thro' frost and
  snaw :
And o'er the lea I leuk fu' fain,
  When Jockie's owsen hameward ca'.

An' aye the night comes round again,
  When in his arms he taks me a' ;
An' aye he vows he'll be my ain,
  As lang's he has a breath to draw.

THE BANKS OF NITH

THE Thames flows proudly to the sea,
  Where royal cities stately stand ;
But sweeter flows the Nith to me,
  Where Comyns ance had high command.
When shall I see that honour'd land,
  That winding stream I love so dear !
Must wayward Fortune's adverse hand
  For ever, ever keep me here !

How lovely, Nith, thy fruitful vales,
  Where bounding hawthorns gaily bloom ;
And sweetly spread thy sloping dales,
  Where lambkins wanton through the broom.
Tho' wandering now must be my doom,
  Far from thy bonie banks and braes,
May there my latest hours consume,
  Amang the friends of early days !

JAMIE, COME TRY ME

Chorus.—Jamie, come try me,
    Jamie, come try me,
  If thou would win my love,
    Jamie, come try me.

IF thou should ask my love,
  Could I deny thee ?
If thou would win my love,
  Jamie, come try me !
    Jamie, come try me, &c.

The Nith

D.O.HILL.S.A.

W. Richardson

From an engraving after David Octavius Hill

If thou should kiss me, love,
  Wha could espy thee ?
If thou wad be my love,
  Jamie, come try me !
    Jamie, come try me, &c.

I LOVE MY LOVE IN SECRET

My Sandy gied to me a ring,
Was a' beset wi' diamonds fine ;
But I gied him a far better thing,
I gied my heart in pledge o' his ring.

Chorus.—My Sandy O, my Sandy O,
    My bonie, bonie Sandy O ;
    Tho' the love that I owe
    To thee I dare na show,
  Yet I love my love in secret, my
    Sandy O.

My Sandy brak a piece o' gowd,
While down his cheeks the saut tears row'd ;
He took a hauf, and gied it to me,
And I'll keep it till the hour I die.
    My Sandy O, &c.

SWEET TIBBIE DUNBAR

O wilt thou go wi' me, sweet Tibbie Dunbar ?
O wilt thou go wi' me, sweet Tibbie Dunbar ?
Wilt thou ride on a horse, or be drawn in a car,
Or walk by my side, O sweet Tibbie Dunbar ?

I care na thy daddie, his lands and his money,
I care na thy kin, sae high and sae lordly ;
But say that thou'lt hae me for better or waur,
And come in thy coatie, sweet Tibbie Dunbar.

THE CAPTAIN'S LADY

Chorus.—O mount and go,
 Mount and make you ready,
O mount and go,
 And be the Captain's lady.

WHEN the drums do beat,
 And the cannons rattle,
Thou shalt sit in state,
 And see thy love in battle.
  O mount and go, &c.

When the vanquish'd foe
 Sues for peace and quiet,
To the shades we'll go,
 And in love enjoy it.
  O mount and go, &c.

JOHN ANDERSON, MY JO

JOHN ANDERSON, my jo, John,
 When we were first acquent;
Your locks were like the raven,
 Your bonie brow was brent;
But now your brow is beld, John,
 Your locks are like the snow;
But blessings on your frosty pow,
 John Anderson, my jo.

John Anderson, my jo, John,
 We clamb the hill thegither;
And mony a cantie day, John,
 We've had wi' ane anither:

John Anderson, My Jo

John Anderson, My Jo

"But now your brow is beld, John,
Your locks are like the snow;
But blessings on your frosty pow,
John Anderson, my Jo."

Now we maun totter down, John,
  And hand in hand we'll go,
And sleep thegither at the foot,
  John Anderson, my jo.

MY LOVE, SHE'S BUT A LASSIE YET

Chorus—My love, she's but a lassie yet,
  My love, she's but a lassie yet ;
We'll let her stand a year or twa,
  She'll no be half sae saucy yet.

I rue the day I sought her O !
I rue the day I sought her O !
Wha gets her needs na say he's woo'd,
  But he may say he has bought her O.

Come draw a drap o' the best o't yet,
Come draw a drap o' the best o't yet,
Gae seek for pleasure whare you will,
  But here I never miss'd it yet.

We're a' dry wi' drinkin o't,
We're a' dry wi' drinkin o't ;
The minister kiss'd the fiddler's wife ;
  He could na preach for thinkin o't.

TAM GLEN

My heart is a-breaking, dear tittie,
  Some counsel unto me come len',
To anger them a' is a pity,
  But what will I do wi' Tam Glen ?

I'm thinking, wi' sic a braw fellow,
   In poortith I might mak a fen';
What care I in riches to wallow,
   If I maunna marry Tam Glen!

There's Lowrie the Laird o' Dumeller—
   "Gude day to you, brute!" he comes ben.
He brags and he blaws o' his siller,
   But when will he dance like Tam Glen!

My minnie does constantly deave me,
   And bids me beware o' young men;
They flatter, she says, to deceive me,—
   But wha can think sae o' Tam Glen!

My daddie says, gin I'll forsake him,
   He'd gie me gude hunder marks ten;
But, if it's ordain'd I maun take him,
   O wha will I get but Tam Glen!

Yestreen at the valentines' dealing,
   My heart to my mou' gied a sten';
For thrice I drew ane without failing,
   And thrice it was written "Tam Glen"!

The last Halloween I was waukin
   My droukit sark-sleeve, as ye ken,
His likeness came up the house staukin,
   And the very grey breeks o' Tam Glen!

Come, counsel, dear tittie, don't tarry;
   I'll gie ye my bonie black hen,
Gif ye will advise me to marry
   The lad I loe dearly, Tam Glen.

Tam Glen

Tam Glen

"Come, counsel, dear Tittie, don't tarry;
I'll gie you my bonie black hen,
Gif ye will advise me to marry
The lad I loe dearly, Tam Glen."

CARLE, AN THE KING COME

Chorus.—Carle, an the King come,
  Carle, an the King come,
  Thou shalt dance and I will sing,
  Carle, an the King come.

An somebody were come again,
Then somebody maun cross the main,
And every man shall hae his ain,
  Carle, an the King come,
   Carle, an the King come, &c.

I trow we swapped for the worse,
We ga'e the boot and better horse ;
And that we'll tell them at the cross,
  Carle, an the King come.
   Carle, an the King come, &c.

Coggie, an the King come,
Coggie, an the King come,
I'se be fou, and thou'se be toom
  Coggie, an the King come.
   Coggie, an the King come, &c.

THE LADDIE'S DEAR SEL'

There's a youth in this city, it were a great pity
 That he from our lasses should wander awa' ;
For he's bonie and braw, weel-favor'd witha',
 An' his hair has a natural buckle an' a'.

His coat is the hue o' his bonnet sae blue,
 His fecket is white as the new-driven snaw ;
His hose they are blae, and his shoon like the slae,
 And his clear siller buckles, they dazzle us a'.

For beauty and fortune the laddie's been courtin;
  Weel-featur'd, weel-tocher'd, weel-mounted
    an' braw;
But chiefly the siller that gars him gang till her,
  The penny's the jewel that beautifies a'.

There's Meg wi the mailen that fain wad a haen
    him,
  And Susie, wha's daddie was laird o' the
    Ha';
There's lang-tocher'd Nancy maist fetters his
    fancy,
  But the laddie's dear sel', he loes dearest of a'

WHISTLE O'ER THE LAVE O'T

FIRST when Maggie was my care,
Heav'n, I thought, was in her air,
Now we're married—speir nae mair,
  But whistle o'er the lave o't!
Meg was meek, and Meg was mild,
Sweet and harmless as a child—
Wiser men than me's beguil'd;
  Whistle o'er the lave o't!

How we live, my Meg and me,
How we love, and how we gree,
I care na by how few may see—
  Whistle o'er the lave o't!
Wha I wish were maggot's meat,
Dish'd up in her winding-sheet,
I could write—but Meg maun see't—
  Whistle o'er the lave o't!

MY EPPIE ADAIR

Chorus.—An' O my Eppie, my jewel, my Eppie,
Wha wad na be happy wi' Eppie Adair?

By love, and by beauty, by law, and by duty,
I swear to be true to my Eppie Adair!
By love, and by beauty, by law, and by duty,
I swear to be true to my Eppie Adair!
And O my Eppie, &c.

A' pleasure exile me, dishonour defile me,
If e'er I beguile thee, my Eppie Adair!
A' pleasure exile me, dishonour defile me,
If e'er I beguile thee, my Eppie Adair!
And O my Eppie, &c.

WILLIE BREW'D A PECK O' MAUT

O WILLIE brew'd a peck o' maut,
And Rob and Allan cam to see;
Three blyther hearts, that lee-lang night,
Ye wadna found in Christendie.

Chorus.—We are na fou, we're nae that fou,
But just a drappie in our ee;
The cock may craw, the day may daw,
And aye we'll taste the barley bree.

Here are we met, three merry boys,
Three merry boys I trow are we;
And mony a night we've merry been,
And mony mae we hope to be!
We are na fou, &c.

It is the moon, I ken her horn,
That's blinkin' in the lift sae hie ;
She shines sae bright to wile us hame,
But, by my sooth, she'll wait a wee !
We are na fou, &c.

Wha first shall rise to gang awa,
A cuckold, coward loun is he !
Wha first beside his chair shall fa',
He is the King amang us three.
We are na fou, &c.

CA' THE YOWES TO THE KNOWES

Chorus—Ca' the yowes to the knowes,
Ca' them where the heather grows,
Ca' them where the burnie rowes,
My bonie dearie.

As I gaed down the water-side,
There I met my shepherd lad :
He row'd me sweetly in his plaid,
And he ca'd me his dearie.
Ca' the yowes, &c.

" Will ye gang down the water-side,
And see the waves sae sweetly glide
Beneath the hazels spreading wide,
The moon it shines fu' clearly."
Ca' the yowes, &c.

" I was bred up in nae sic school,
My shepherd lad, to play the fool,
An' a' the day to sit in dool,
An' naebody to see me."
Ca' the yowes, &c.

" Ye sall get gowns and ribbons meet,
Cauf-leather shoon upon your feet,
And in my arms ye'se lie and sleep,
  An' ye sall be my dearie."
    Ca' the yowes, &c.

" If ye'll but stand to what ye've said,
I'se gang wi' thee, my shepherd lad,
And ye may row me in your plaid,
  And I sall be your dearie."
    Ca' the yowes, &c.

" While waters wimple to the sea,
While day blinks in the lift sae hie,
Till clay-cauld death sall blin' my e'e,
  Ye sall be my dearie."
    Ca' the yowes, &c.

THE BLUE-EYED LASSIE

I GAED a waefu' gate yestreen,
  A gate I fear I'll dearly rue ;
I gat my death frae twa sweet een,
  Twa lovely een o' bonie blue.
'Twas not her golden ringlets bright,
  Her lips, like roses wat wi' dew,
Her heaving bosom, lily-white—
  It was her een sae bonie blue.

She talk'd, she smil'd, my heart she wil'd ;
  She charm'd my soul I wist na how ;
And aye the stound, the deadly wound,
  Cam frae her een sae bonie blue.

But " spare to speak, and spare to speed ; "
She'll aiblins listen to my vow :
Should she refuse, I'll lay my dead
To her twa een sae bonie blue.

HIGHLAND HARRY BACK AGAIN

My Harry was a gallant gay,
  Fu' stately strade he on the plain ;
But now he's banish'd far away,
  I'll never see him back again.

Chorus—O for him back again !
  O for him back again !
  I wad gie a' Knockhaspie's land
  For Highland Harry back again.

When a' the lave gae to their bed,
  I wander dowie up the glen ;
I set me down and greet my fill,
  And aye I wish him back again.
    O for him, &c.
O were some villains hangit high,
  And ilka body had their ain !
Then I might see the joyfu' sight,
  My Highland Harry back again.
    O for him, &c.

THE BATTLE OF SHERRAMUIR

Tune—"The Cameronian Rant."

" O CAM ye here the fight to shun,
  Or herd the sheep wi' me, man ?
Or were ye at the Sherra-moor,
  Or did the battle see, man ? "

I saw the battle, sair and teugh,
And reekin-red ran mony a sheugh ;
My heart, for fear, gaed sough for sough,
To hear the thuds, and see the cluds
O' clans frae woods, in tartan duds,
    Wha glaum'd at kingdoms three, man.
       La, la, la, la, &c.

The red-coat lads, wi' black cockauds,
    To meet them were na slaw, man ;
They rush'd and push'd, and blude outgush'd
    And mony a bouk did fa', man :
The great Argyle led on his files,
I wat they glanc'd for twenty miles ;
They hough'd the clans like nine-pin kyles,
They hack'd and hash'd, while braid-swords
    clash'd,
And thro' they dash'd, and hew'd and smash'd,
    Till fey men died awa, man.
       La, la, la, la, &c.

But had ye seen the philibegs,
    And skyrin tartan trews, man ;
When in the teeth they dar'd our Whigs,
    And covenant True-blues, man :
In lines extended lang and large,
When baiginets o'erpower'd the targe,
And thousands hasten'd to the charge ;
Wi' Highland wrath they frae the sheath
Drew blades o' death, till, out o' breath,
    They fled like frighted dows, man !
       La, la, la, la, &c.

" O how deil, Tam, can that be true ?
    The chase gaed frae the north, man ;

N

I saw mysel, they did pursue,
  The horsemen back to Forth, man;
And at Dunblane, in my ain sight,
They took the brig wi' a' their might,
And straught to Stirling wing'd their flight;
But, cursed lot! the gates were shut;
And mony a huntit poor red-coat,
  For fear amaist did swarf, man! "
    La, la, la, la, &c.

My sister Kate cam up the gate
  Wi' crowdie unto me, man;
She swoor she saw some rebels run
  To Perth and to Dundee, man;
Their left-hand general had nae skill;
The Angus lads had nae gude will
That day their neibors' blude to spill;
For fear, by foes, that they should lose
Their cogs o' brose; they scar'd at blows,
  And hameward fast did flee, man.
    La, la, la, la, &c.

They've lost some gallant gentlemen,
  Amang the Highland clans, man!
I fear my Lord Panmure is slain,
  Or in his en'mies' hands, man,
Now wad ye sing this double flight,
Some fell for wrang, and some for right,
But mony bade the world gude-night;
Say, pell and mell, wi' muskets' knell
How Tories fell, and Whigs to hell
  Flew off in frighted bands, man!
    La, la, la, la, &c.

The Braes o' Killiecrankie

The Braes o' Killiecrankie

"I faught at land, I faught at sea;
At hame I faught my auntie, O;
But I met the Devil an' Dundee,
On the braes o' Killiecrankie, O."

THE BRAES O' KILLIECRANKIE

Whare hae ye been sae braw, lad?
Whare hae ye been sae brankie, O?
Whare hae ye been sae braw, lad?
Cam ye by Killiecrankie, O?

Chorus.—An ye had been whare I hae been,
Ye wad na been sae cantie, O;
An ye had seen what I hae seen,
On the Braes o' Killiecrankie, O.

I faught at land, I faught at sea,
At hame I faught my auntie, O;
But I met the Devil an' Dundee,
On the Braes o' Killiecrankie, O.
An ye had been, &c.

The bauld Pitcur fell in a furr,
An' Clavers gat a clankie, O;
Or I had fed an Athole gled,
On the Braes o' Killiecrankie, O.
An ye had been, &c.

AWA' WHIGS, AWA'

Chorus.—Awa' Whigs, awa'!
Awa' Whigs, awa'!
Ye're but a pack o' traitor louns,
Ye'll do nae gude at a'.

Our thrissles flourish'd fresh and fair,
And bonie bloom'd our roses;
But Whigs cam' like a frost in June,
An' wither'd a' our posies.
Awa' Whigs, &c.

Our ancient crown's fa'en in the dust—
Deil blin' them wi' the stour o't !
An' write their names in his black beuk,
Wha gae the Whigs the power o't.
Awa' Whigs, &c.

Our sad decay in church and state
Surpasses my descriving :
The Whigs cam' o'er us for a curse,
An' we hae done wi' thriving.
Awa' Whigs, &c.

Grim Vengeance lang has taen a nap,
But we may see him wauken :
Gude help the day when Royal heads
Are hunted like a maukin !
Awa' Whigs, &c.

A WAUKRIFE MINNIE

WHARE are you gaun, my bonie lass,
Whare are you gaun, my hinnie ?
She answered me right saucilie,
"An errand for my minnie."

O whare live ye, my bonie lass,
O whare live ye, my hinnie ?
"By yon burnside, gin ye maun ken,
In a wee house wi' my minnie."

But I foor up the glen at e'en,
To see my bonie lassie ;
And lang before the grey morn cam,
She was na hauf sae saucie.

O weary fa' the waukrife cock,
   And the foumart lay his crawin!
He wauken'd the auld wife frae her sleep,
   A wee blink or the dawin.

An angry wife I wat she raise,
   And o'er the bed she brocht her;
And wi' a meikle hazel rung
   She made her a weel-pay'd dochter.

O fare thee weel, my bonie lass,
   O fare thee well, my hinnie!
Thou art a gay an' a bonie lass,
   But thou has a waukrife minnie.

THE CAPTIVE RIBBAND

Tune—"Robaidh dona gorach."

MYRA, the captive ribband's mine,
   'Twas all my faithful love could gain;
And would you ask me to resign
   The sole reward that crowns my pain?

Go, bid the hero who has run
   Thro' fields of death to gather fame,
Go, bid him lay his laurels down,
   And all his well-earn'd praise disclaim.

The ribband shall its freedom lose—
   Lose all the bliss it had with you,
And share the fate I would impose
   On thee, wert thou my captive too.

It shall upon my bosom live,
   Or clasp me in a close embrace;
And at its fortune if you grieve,
   Retrieve its doom, and take its place.

MY HEART'S IN THE HIGHLANDS

Tune—"Failte na Miosg."

FAREWELL to the Highlands, farewell to the North,
The birth-place of Valour, the country of Worth;
Wherever I wander, wherever I rove,
The hills of the Highlands for ever I love.

Chorus.—My heart's in the Highlands, my
heart is not here,
My heart's in the Highlands, a-
chasing the deer;
A-chasing the wild-deer, and follow-
ing the roe,
My heart's in the Highlands wher-
ever I go.

Farewell to the mountains, high-cover'd with snow,
Farewell to the straths and green valleys below;
Farewell to the forests and wild-hanging woods,
Farewell to the torrents and loud-pouring floods.
My heart's in the Highlands, &c

MERRY HAE I BEEN TEETHIN A HECKLE

Tune—"The bob o' Dumblane."

O MERRY hae I been teethin a heckle,
An' merry hae I been shapin a spoon;
O merry hae I been cloutin a kettle,
An' kissin my Katie when a' was done.
O a' the lang day I ca' at my hammer,
An' a' the lang day I whistle and sing;
O a' the lang night I cuddle my kimmer,
An' a' the lang night as happy's a king.

Bitter in dool I lickit my winnins
O' marrying Bess, to gie her a slave :
Blest be the hour she cool'd in her linens,
   And blythe be the bird that sings on her grave !
Come to my arms, my Katie, my Katie;
   O come to my arms and kiss me again !
Drucken or sober, here's to thee, Katie !
   An' blest be the day I did it again.

THE GOWDEN LOCKS OF ANNA

YESTREEN I had a pint o' wine,
   A place where body saw na ;
Yestreen lay on this breast o' mine
   The gowden locks of Anna.

The hungry Jew in wilderness,
   Rejoicing o'er his manna,
Was naething to my hinnie bliss
   Upon the lips of Anna.

Ye monarchs, take the East and West
   Frae Indus to Savannah ;
Gie me, within my straining grasp,
   The melting form of Anna.

There I'll despise Imperial charms,
   An Empress or Sultana,
While dying raptures in her arms
   I give and take wi' Anna !

Awa, thou flaunting God of Day !
   Awa, thou pale Diana !
Ilk Star, gae hide thy twinkling ray,
   When I'm to meet my Anna !

Come, in thy raven plumage, Night,
  (Sun, Moon, and Stars, withdrawn a' ;)
And bring an angel-pen to write
  My transports with my Anna !

POSTSCRIPT

The Kirk an' State may join, an' tell
  To do sic things I maunna :
The Kirk an' State may gae to hell,
  And I'll gae to my Anna.

She is the sunshine o' my e'e,
  To live but her I canna ;
Had I on earth but wishes three,
  The first should be my Anna.

GUDEWIFE, COUNT THE LAWIN

GANE is the day, and mirk's the night,
  But we'll ne'er stray for faut o' light ;
Gude ale and brandy's stars and moon,
  And blude-red wine's the risin sun.

Chorus.—Then gudewife, count the lawin,
      The lawin, the lawin,
    Then gudewife, count the lawin,
      And bring a coggie mair.

There's wealth and ease for gentlemen,
  And simple folk maun fecht and fen ;
But here we're a' in ae accord,
  For ilka man that's drunk's a lord.
    Then gudewife, &c.

Gudewife, Count the Lawin

Gudewife, Count the Lawin

"Then, gudewife, count the lawin
And bring a coggie mair."

My coggie is a haly pool
That heals the wounds o' care and dool ;
And Pleasure is a wanton trout,
And ye drink it a', ye'll find him out.
        Then gudewife, &c.

POEM ON SENSIBILITY

Sensibility, how charming,
    Thou, my friend, canst truly tell ;
But distress, with horrors arming,
    Thou alas ! hast known too well !

Fairest flower, behold the lily
    Blooming in the sunny ray ;
Let the blast sweep o er the valley,
    See it prostrate in the clav.

Hear the woodlark charm the forest,
    Telling o'er his little joys ;
But alas ! a prey the surest
    To each pirate of the skies.

Dearly bought the hidden treasure
    Finer feelings can bestow :
Chords that vibrate sweetest pleasure
    Thrill the deepest notes of woe.

THERE'LL NEVER BE PEACE TILL
JAMIE COMES HAME

By yon Castle wa', at the close of the day,
I heard a man sing, tho' his head it was grey :
And as he was singing, the tears doon came,—
There'll never be peace till Jamie comes hame.
        N*

The Church is in ruins, the State is in jars,
Delusions, oppressions, and murderous wars,
We dare na weel say't, but we ken wha's to
   blame,—
There'll never be peace till Jamie comes hame.

My seven braw sons for Jamie drew sword,
But now I greet round their green beds in the
   yerd ;
It brak the sweet heart o' my faithfu'auld dame,—
There'll never be peace till Jamie comes hame.

Now life is a burden that bows me down,
Sin' I tint my bairns, and he tint his crown ;
But till my last moments my words are the same,—
There'll never be peace till Jamie comes hame.

OUT OVER THE FORTH

Out over the Forth, I look to the north ;
   But what is the north and its Highlands to me ?
The south nor the east gie ease to my breast,
   The far foreign land, or the wide rolling sea.

But I look to the west when I gae to rest,
   That happy my dreams and my slumbers may
   be ;
For far in the west lives he I loe best,
   The man that is dear to my babie and me.

THE BANKS O' DOON

FIRST VERSION

Sweet are the banks, the banks o' Doon,
   The spreading flowers are fair,

And everything is blythe and glad,
    But I am fu' o' care.
Thou'll break my heart, thou bonie bird,
    That sings upon the bough ;
Thou minds me o' the happy days
    When my fause luve was true :
Thou'll break my heart, thou bonie bird,
    That sings beside thy mate ;
For sae I sat, and sae I sang,
    And wist na o' my fate.

Aft hae I rov'd by bonie Doon,
    To see the woodbine twine ;
And ilka bird sang o' its luve,
    And sae did I o' mine :
Wi' lightsome heart I pu'd a rose,
    Upon its thorny tree ;
But my fause luver staw my rose,
    And left the thorn wi' me :
Wi' lightsome heart I pu'd a rose,
    Upon a morn in June ;
And sae I flourished on the morn,
    And sae was pu'd or noon !

THE BANKS O' DOON

SECOND VERSION

YE flowery banks o' bonie Doon,
    How can ye blume sae fair ?
How can ye chant, ye little birds,
    And I sae fu' o' care !

Thou'll break my heart, thou bonie bird,
    That sings upon the bough !

Thou minds me o' the happy days
When my fause luve was true.

Thou'll break my heart, thou bonie bird,
That sings beside thy mate ;
For sae I sat, and sae I sang,
And wist na o' my fate.

Aft hae I rov'd by bonie Doon,
To see the woodbine twine ;
And ilka bird sang o' its luve,
And sae did I o' mine.

Wi' lightsome heart I pu'd a rose,
Upon its thorny tree ;
But my fause luver staw my rose,
And left the thorn wi' me.

THE BANKS O' DOON

THIRD VERSION

Ye banks and braes o' bonie Doon,
How can ye bloom sae fresh and fair ?
How can ye chant, ye little birds,
And I sae weary fu' o' care !
Thou'll break my heart, thou warbling bird,
That wantons thro' the flowering thorn :
Thou minds me o' departed joys,
Departed never to return.

Aft hae I rov'd by Bonie Doon,
To see the rose and woodbine twine :
And ilka bird sang o' its luve,
And fondly sae did I o' mine.

Scene on the Doon

From an engraving after David Octavius Hill

Wi' lightsome heart I pu'd a rose,
  Fu' sweet upon its thorny tree !
And my fause luver staw my rose,
  But ah ! he left the thorn wi' me.

CRAIGIEBURN WOOD

SWEET closes the ev'ning on Craigieburn Wood,
  And blythely awaukens the morrow ;
But the pride o' the spring in the Craigieburn
  Wood
Can yield me nought but sorrow.

[*Chorus.*—Beyond thee, dearie, beyond thee,
        dearie,
      And O to be lying beyond thee !
      O sweetly, soundly, weel may he sleep
      That's laid in the bed beyond thee!]

I see the spreading leaves and flowers,
  I hear the wild birds singing ;
But pleasure they hae nane for me,
  While care my heart is wringing.
      Beyond thee, &c.

I can na tell, I maun na tell,
  I daur na for your anger ;
But secret love will break my heart,
  If I conceal it langer.
      Beyond thee, &c.

I see thee gracefu', straight and tall,
  I see thee sweet and bonie ;
But oh, what will my torment be,
  If thou refuse thy Johnie !
      Beyond thee, &c.

To see thee in another's arms,
   In love to lie and languish,
'Twad be my dead, that will be seen,
   My heart wad burst wi' anguish.
      Beyond thee, &c.

But Jeanie, say thou wilt be mine,
   Say thou lo'es nane before me ;
And a' my days o' life to come
   I'll gratefully adore thee,
      Beyond thee, &c.

THE BONIE WEE THING

Chorus.—Bonie wee thing, cannie wee thing,
      Lovely wee thing, wert thou mine,
   I wad wear thee in my bosom,
      Lest my jewel it should tine.

WISHFULLY I look and languish
   In that bonie face o' thine,
And my heart it stounds wi' anguish,
   Lest my wee thing be na mine.
      Bonie wee thing, &c.

Wit and Grace, and Love, and Beauty,
   In ae constellation shine ;
To adore thee is my duty,
   Goddess o' this soul o' mine !
      Bonie wee thing, &c.

THE CHARMS OF LOVELY DAVIES

Tune—" Miss Muir."

O HOW shall I, unskilfu' try
   The poet's occupation ?

The tunefu' powers, in happy hours,
   That whisper inspiration,
Even they maun dare an effort mair
   Than aught they ever gave us,
Ere they rehearse, in equal verse,
   The charms o' lovely Davies.

Each eye it cheers, when she appears,
   Like Phœbus in the morning,
When past the shower, and every flower
   The garden is adorning:
As the wretch looks o'er Siberia's shore
   When winter-bound the wave is,
Sae droops our heart, when we maun part
   Frae charming, lovely Davies.

Her smile's a gift frae 'boon the lift,
   That maks us mair than princes;
A sceptred hand, a king's command,
   Is in her darting glances;
The man in arms 'gainst female charms
   Even he her willing slave is,
He hugs his chain, and owns the reign
   Of conquering, lovely Davies.

My Muse to dream of such a theme
   Her feeble powers surrender:
The eagle's gaze alone surveys
   The sun's meridian splendour.
I wad in vain essay the strain,
   The deed too daring brave is;
I'll drap the lyre, and mute admire
   The charms o' lovely Davies.

WHAT CAN A YOUNG LASSIE DO
WI' AN AULD MAN

WHAT can a young lassie, what shall a young
lassie,
  What can a young lassie do wi' an auld man?
Bad luck on the penny that tempted my minnie
  To sell her puir Jenny for siller an' lan'!

He's always compleenin frae mornin to eenin,
  He hoasts and he hirples the weary day lang;
He's doylt and he's dozin, his blude it is
  frozen,—
  O dreary's the night wi' a crazy auld man!

He hums and he hankers, he frets and he cankers,
  I never can please him do a' that I can;
He's peevish and jealous o' a' the young fellows,—
  O dool on the day I met wi' an auld man!

My auld auntie Katie upon me taks pity,
  I'll do my endeavour to follow her plan;
I'll cross him an' wrack him, until I heartbreak
  him
  And then his auld brass will buy me a new pan!

THE POSIE

O LUVE will venture in where it daur na weel be
  seen,
O luve will venture in where wisdom ance has
  been;
But I will doun yon river rove, amang the wood
  sae green,
    And a' to pu' a posie to my ain dear May.

What can a Young Lassie do wi' an Auld Man

What can a Young Lassie do wi' an Auld Man

"He's always complainin frae mornin to eenin,
He boasts and he hirples the weary day lang."

The primrose I will pu', the firstling o' the year,
And I will pu' the pink, the emblem o' my dear;
For she's the pink o' womankind, and blooms
without a peer,
    And a' to be a posie to my ain dear May.

I'll pu' the budding rose, when Phœbus peeps in
view,
For it's like a baumy kiss o' her sweet, bonie
mou;
The hyacinth's for constancy wi' its unchanging
blue,
    And a' to be a posie to my ain dear May.

The lily it is pure, and the lily it is fair,
And in her lovely bosom I'll place the lily
there;
The daisy's for simplicity and unaffected air,
    And a' to be a posie to my ain dear May.

The hawthorn I will pu', wi' its locks o' siller
gray,
Where, like an aged man, it stands at break o'
day;
But the songster's nest within the bush I winna
tak away
    And a' to be a posie to my ain dear May.

The woodbine I will pu', when the e'ening star
is near,
And the diamond draps o' dew shall be her een
sae clear;
The violet's for modesty, which weel she fa's to
wear,
    And a' to be a posie to my ain dear May.

I'll tie the posie round wi' the silken band o' luve,
And I'll place it in her breast, and I'll swear by
　　a' above,
That to my latest draught o' life the band shall
　　ne'er remove,
　　　　And this will be a posie to my ain dear
　　　　May.

THE GALLANT WEAVER

Where Cart rins rowin to the sea,
By mony a flower and spreading tree,
There lives a lad, the lad for me,
　　He is a gallant Weaver.
O, I had wooers aught or nine,
They gied me rings and ribbons fine;
And I was fear'd my heart wad tine,
　　And I gied it to the Weaver.

My daddie sign'd my tocher-band,
To gie the lad that has the land,
But to my heart I'll add my hand,
　　And give it to the Weaver.
While birds rejoice in leafy bowers,
While bees delight in opening flowers,
While corn grows green in summer showers,
　　I love my gallant weaver.

YOU'RE WELCOME, WILLIE STEWART

Chorus.—You're welcome, Willie Stewart,
　　　　You're welcome, Willie Stewart,
　　　There's ne'er a flower that blooms in May,
　　　That's half sae welcome's thou art!

Come, bumpers high, express your joy,
 The bowl we maun renew it;
The tappet hen, gae bring her ben,
 To welcome Willie Stewart.
  You're welcome, Willie Stewart, &c.

May foes be strang, and friends be slack,
 Ilk action, may he rue it,
'May woman on him turn her back
 That wrangs thee, Willie Stewart!
  You're welcome, Willie Stewart, &c.

LOVELY POLLY STEWART

Chorus.—O lovely Polly Stewart,
  O charming Polly Stewart,
 There's ne'er a flower that blooms in May,
  That's half so fair as thou art!

The flower it blaws, it fades, it fa's,
 And art can ne'er renew it;
But worth and truth eternal youth
 Will gie to Polly Stewart.
  O lovely Polly Stewart, &c.

May he whase arms shall fauld thy charms
 Possess a leal and true heart!
To him be given to ken the heaven
 He grasps in Polly Stewart!
  O lovely Polly Stewart, &c.

WHA IS THAT AT MY BOWER-DOOR

Tune—"Lass, an I come near thee."

" Wha is that at my bower-door?"
 'O wha is it but Findlay!'

" Then gae your gate, ye'se nae be here : "
'Indeed maun I,' quo' Findlay ;
" What mak' ye, sae like a thief ? "
'O come and see,' quo' Findlay ;
" Before the morn ye'll work mischief : "
'Indeed will I,' quo' Findlay.

" Gif I rise and let you in "—
'Let me in,' quo' Findlay ;
" Ye'll keep me waukin wi' your din : "
'Indeed will I,' quo' Findlay ;
" In my bower if ye should stay "—
'Let me stay,' quo' Findlay ;
" I fear ye'll bide till break o' day : "
'Indeed will I,' quo' Findlay.

" Here this night if ye remain "
'I'll remain,' quo' Findlay ;
" I dread ye'll learn the gate again : "
'Indeed will I,' quo' Findlay.
" What may pass within this bower "—
'Let it pass,' quo' Findlay ;
'Ye maun conceal till your last hour : "
'Indeed will I,' quo' Findlay.

JOHNIE LAD, COCK UP YOUR BEAVER

[WHEN first my brave Johnie lad came to the
town,
He had a blue bonnet that wanted the crown ;
But now he has gotten a hat and a feather,
Hey, brave Johnie lad, cock up your beaver !]

Cock up your beaver, and cock it fu' sprush,
We'll over the border, and gie them a brush;
There's somebody there we'll teach better be-
haviour,
Hey, brave Johnie lad, cock up your beaver!

MY EPPIE MACNAB

O saw ye my dearie, my Eppie Macnab?
O saw ye my dearie, my Eppie Macnab?
 She's down in the yard, she's kissin the laird,
She winna come hame to her ain Jock Rab.

O come thy ways to me, my Eppie Macnab;
O come thy ways to me, my Eppie Macnab;
 Whate'er thou hast dune, be it late, be it sune,
Thou's welcome again to thy ain Jock Rab.

What says she, my dearie, my Eppie Macnab?
What says she, my dearie, my Eppie Macnab?
 She let's thee to wit that she has thee forgot,
And for ever disowns thee, her ain Jock Rab.

O had I ne'er seen thee, my Eppie Macnab!
O had I ne'er seen thee, my Eppie Macnab!
 As light as the air, and as fause as thou's fair,
Thou's broken the heart o' thy ain Jock Rab.

ALTHO' HE HAS LEFT ME

Altho' he has left me for greed o' the siller,
 I dinna envy him the gains he can win;
I rather wad bear a' the lade o' my sorrow,
 Than ever hae acted sae faithless to him.

MY TOCHER'S THE JEWEL

O MEIKLE thinks my luve o' my beauty,
　And meikle thinks my luve o' my kin ;
But little thinks my luve I ken brawlie
　My tocher's the jewel has charms for him.
It's a' for the apple he'll nourish the tree,
　It's a' for the hinny he'll cherish the bee,
My laddie's sae meikle in luve wi' the siller,
　He canna hae luve to spare for me.

Your proffer o' luve's an airle-penny,
　My tocher's the bargain ye wad buy ;
But an ye be crafty, I am cunnin,
　Sae ye wi' anither your fortune may try.
Ye're like to the timmer o' yon rotten wood,
　Ye're like to the bark o' yon rotten tree,
Ye'll slip frae me like a knotless thread,
　And ye'll crack your credit wi' mae nor me.

O FOR ANE AN' TWENTY, TAM

Chorus.—An' O for ane an' twenty, Tam !
　　　　　And hey, sweet ane an' twenty, Tam !
　　　　　I'll learn my kin a rattlin sang,
　　　　　An I saw ane an' twenty, Tam.

THEY snool me sair, and haud me down,
　An' gar me look like bluntie, Tam ;
But three short years will soon wheel roun',
　An' then comes ane and twenty, Tam.
　　An' O for, &c.

Thou fair Eliza

Thou fair Eliza

"Turn again, thou fair Eliza!
Ae kind blink before we part."

A glieb o' lan', a claut o' gear,
  Was left me by my auntie, Tam;
At kith or kin I need na spier,
  An I saw ane an' twenty, Tam.
    An' O for, &c.

They'll hae me wed a wealthy coof,
  Tho' I mysel' hae plenty, Tam;
But hear'st thou, laddie! there's my loof,
  I'm thine at ane an' twenty, Tam.
    An' O for, &c.

THOU FAIR ELIZA

Turn again, thou fair Eliza!
  Ae kind blink before we part;
Rue on thy despairing lover,
  Can'st thou break his faithfu' heart?
Turn again, thou fair Eliza!
  If to love thy heart denies,
Oh, in pity hide the sentence
  Under friendship's kind disguise!

Thee, sweet maid, hae I offended?
  My offence is loving thee;
Can'st thou wreck his peace for ever,
  Wha for thine would gladly die?
While the life beats in my bosom,
  Thou shalt mix in ilka throe:
Turn again, thou lovely maiden,
  Ae sweet smile on me bestow.

Not the bee upon the blossom,
  In the pride o' sinny noon;
Not the little sporting fairy,
  All beneath the simmer moon;

Not the Minstrel, in the moment
    Fancy lightens in his e'e,
Kens the pleasure, feels the rapture,
    That thy presence gies to me.

MY BONIE BELL

THE smiling Spring comes in rejoicing,
    And surly Winter grimly flies ;
Now crystal clear are the falling waters,
    And bonie blue are the sunny skies.
Fresh o'er the mountains breaks forth the morning,
    The ev'ning gilds the ocean's swell ;
All creatures joy in the sun's returning,
    And I rejoice in my bonie Bell.

The flowery Spring leads sunny Summer,
    The yellow Autumn presses near ;
Then in his turn comes gloomy Winter,
    Till smiling Spring again appear :
Thus seasons dancing, life advancing,
    Old Time and Nature their changes tell ;
But never ranging, still unchanging,
    I adore my bonie Bell.

NITHSDALE'S WELCOME HAME

THE noble Maxwells and their powers
    Are coming o'er the border,
And they'll gae big Terreagles' towers,
    And set them a' in order.
And they declare Terreagles fair,
    For their abode they choose it ;
There's no a heart in a' the land
    But's lighter at the news o't.

Nithsdale

From an engraving by David Octavius Hill

Tho' stars in skies may disappear,
 And angry tempests gather;
The happy hour may soon be near
 That brings us pleasant weather:
The weary night o' care and grief
 May hae a joyfu' morrow;
So dawning day has brought relief,
 Fareweel our night o' sorrow.

FRAE THE FRIENDS AND LAND
I LOVE

Tune—" Carron Side.

FRAE the friends and land I love
 Driv'n by Fortune's felly spite,
Frae my best belov'd I rove,
 Never mair to taste delight:
Never mair maun hope to find
 Ease frae toil, relief frae care;
When Remembrance wracks the mind,
 Pleasures but unveil despair.

Brightest climes shall mirk appear,
 Desert ilka blooming shore,
Till the Fates, nae mair severe,
 Friendship, love, and peace restore.
Till Revenge, wi' laurel'd head,
 Bring our banished hame again;
And ilk loyal, bonie lad
 Cross the seas, and win his ain.

SUCH A PARCEL OF ROGUES
IN A NATION

FAREWEEL to a' our Scottish fame,
 Fareweel our ancient glory;

Fareweel ev'n to the Scottish name,
  Sae fam'd in martial story.
Now Sark rins over Solway sands,
  An' Tweed rins to the ocean,
To mark where England's province stands—
  Such a parcel of rogues in a nation !

What force or guile could not subdue,
  Thro' many warlike ages,
Is wrought now by a coward few,
  For hireling traitor's wages.
The English steel we could disdain,
  Secure in valour's station ;
But English gold has been our bane—
  Such a parcel of rogues in a nation !

O would, or I had seen the day
  That Treason thus could sell us,
My auld grey head had lien in clay
  Wi' Bruce and loyal Wallace !
But pith and power, till my last hour
  I'll mak this declaration ;
We're bought and sold for English gold—
  Such a parcel of rogues in a nation !

YE JACOBITES BY NAME

YE Jacobites by name, give an ear, give an ear,
Ye Jacobites by name, give an ear,
  Ye Jacobites by name,
  Your faults I will proclaim,
Your doctrines I maun blame, you shall hear.

What is Right, and what is Wrang, by the law,
    by the law ?
What is Right, and what is Wrang, by the law ?

What is Right, and what is Wrang?
A short sword, and a lang,
A weak arm and a strang, for to draw.

What makes heroic strife, famed afar, famed afar?
What makes heroic strife, famed afar?
What makes heroic strife?
To whet th' assassin's knife,
Or hunt a Parent's life, wi' bluidy war?

Then let your schemes alone, in the state, in the
    state,
Then let your schemes alone, in the state.
Then let your schemes alone,
Adore the rising sun,
And leave a man undone, to his fate.

I HAE BEEN AT CROOKIEDEN

I HAE been at Crookieden,
    My bonie laddie, Highland laddie,
Viewing Willie and his men,
    My bonie laddie, Highland laddie.
There our foes that burnt and slew,
    My bonie laddie, Highland laddie,
There, at last, they gat their due,
    My bonie laddie, Highland laddie.

Satan sits in his black neuk,
    My bonie laddie, Highland laddie,
Breaking sticks to roast the Duke,
    My bonie laddie, Highland laddie.
The bloody monster ga'e a yell,
    My bonie laddie, Highland laddie,
And loud the laugh gaed round a' hell,
    My bonie laddie, Highland laddie.

O KENMURE'S ON AND AWA, WILLIE

O Kenmure's on and awa, Willie,
  O Kenmure's on and awa :
An' Kenmure's lord's the bravest lord
  That ever Galloway saw.

Success to Kenmure's band, Willie !
  Success to Kenmure's band !
There's no a heart that fears a Whig,
  That rides by Kenmure's hand.

Here's Kenmure's health in wine, Willie !
  Here's Kenmure's health in wine !
There ne'er was a coward o' Kenmure's blude,
  Nor yet o' Gordon's line.

O Kenmure's lads are men, Willie,
  O Kenmure's lads are men ;
Their hearts and swords are metal true,
  And that their faes shall ken.

They'll live or die wi' fame, Willie ;
  They'll live or die wi' fame ;
But sune, wi' sounding victorie,
  May Kenmure's lord come hame !

Here's him that's far awa, Willie !
  Here's him that's far awa !
And here's the flower that I loe best,
  The rose that's like the snaw.

THE SONG OF DEATH

Tune—"Oran an aoig."

FAREWELL, thou fair day, thou green earth and
    ye skies,
  Now gay with the broad setting sun ;
Farewell, loves and friendships, ye dear tender ties,
  Our race of existence is run !
Thou grim King of Terrors ! thou Life's gloomy
    foe !
  Go, frighten the coward and slave ;
Go, teach them to tremble, fell tyrant ! but know
  No terrors hast thou to the brave !

Thou strik'st the dull peasant—he sinks in the
    dark,
  Nor saves e'en the wreck of a name ;
Thou strik'st the young hero—a glorious mark ;
  He falls in the blaze of his fame !
In the field of proud honour, our swords in our
    hands,
  Our King and our country to save ;
While victory shines on Life's last ebbing sands,—
  O who would not die with the brave ?

O MAY, THY MORN

O MAY, thy morn was ne'er so sweet
  As the mirk night o' December !
For sparkling was the rosy wine,
  And private was the chamber :
And dear was she I dare na name,
  But I will aye remember .
And dear was she I dare na name,
  But I will aye remember.

And here's to them that, like oursel,
  Can push about the jorum!
And here's to them that wish us weel,
  May a' that's guid watch o'er 'em!
And here's to them we dare na tell,
  The dearest o' the quorum!
And here's to them we dare na tell,
  The dearest o' the quorum.

AE FOND KISS, AND THEN WE SEVER

Tune—"Rory Dall's Port."

Ae fond kiss, and then we sever;
Ae fareweel, and then forever!
Deep in heart-wrung tears I'll pledge thee,
Warring sighs and groans I'll wage thee.
Who shall say that Fortune grieves him,
While the star of hope she leaves him?
Me, nae cheerful twinkle lights me;
Dark despair around benights me.

I'll ne'er blame my partial fancy,
Naething could resist my Nancy:
But to see her was to love her;
Love but her, and love for ever.
Had we never lov'd sae kindly,
Had we never lov'd sae blindly,
Never met—or never parted,
We had ne'er been broken-hearted.

Fare-thee-weel, thou first and fairest!
Fare-thee-weel, thou best and dearest!
Thine be ilka joy and treasure,
Peace, Enjoyment, Love and Pleasure!

Ae fond kiss, and then we sever!
Ae fareweel, alas, for ever!
Deep in heart-wrung tears I'll pledge thee,
Warring sighs and groans I'll wage thee.

BEHOLD THE HOUR, THE BOAT, ARRIVE

BEHOLD the hour, the boat, arrive!
  My dearest Nancy, O fareweel!
Severed frae thee, can I survive,
  Frae thee whom I hae lov'd sae weel?

Endless and deep shall be my grief;
  Nae ray of comfort shall I see,
But this most precious, dear belief,
  That thou wilt still remember me!

Alang the solitary shore
  Where flitting sea-fowl round me cry,
Across the rolling, dashing roar,
  I'll westward turn my wishful eye.

" Happy thou Indian grove," I'll say,
  " Where now my Nancy's path shall be!
While thro' your sweets she holds her way,
  O tell me, does she muse on me?"

THOU GLOOMY DECEMBER

ANCE mair I hail thee, thou gloomy December!
  Ance mair I hail thee wi' sorrow and care;
Sad was the parting thou makes me remember—
  Parting wi' Nancy, oh, ne'er to meet mair!

Fond lovers' parting is sweet, painful pleasure,
  Hope beaming mild on the soft parting hour;
But the dire feeling, O farewell for ever!
  Anguish unmingled, and agony pure!

Wild as the winter now tearing the forest,
  Till the last leaf o' the summer is flown;
Such is the tempest has shaken my bosom,
  Till my last hope and last comfort is gone.

Still as I hail thee, thou gloomy December,
  Still shall I hail thee wi' sorrow and care;
For sad was the parting thou makes me remember,
  Parting wi' Nancy, oh, ne'er to meet mair.

MY NATIVE LAND SAE FAR AWA

O SAD and heavy, should I part,
  But for her sake sae far awa;
Unknowing what my way may thwart,—
  My native land sae far awa.

Thou that of a' things Maker art,
  That formed this Fair sae far awa,
Gie body strength, then I'll ne'er start
  At this my way sae far awa.

How true is love to pure desert
  Like mine for her sae far awa
And nocht can heal my bosom's smart.
  While, oh, she is sae far awa!

Nane other love, nane other dart
  I feel but her's sae far awa;
But fairer never touch'd a heart
  Than her's, the Fair, sae far awa.

Thou Gloomy December

Thou Gloomy December

"Ance mair I hail thee, thou gloomy December!
Ance mair I hail thee wi' sorrow and care . . . "

I DO CONFESS THOU ART SAE FAIR

I DO confess thou art sae fair,
   I wad been o'er the lugs in luve,
Had I na found the slightest prayer
   That lips could speakthy heart could muve.

I do confess thee sweet, but find
   Thou art so thriftless o' thy sweets,
Thy favours are the silly wind
   That kisses ilka thing it meets.

See yonder rosebud, rich in dew,
   Amang its native briers sae coy;
How sune it tines its scent and hue,
   When pu'd and worn a common toy.

Sic fate ere lang shall thee betide,
   Tho' thou may gaily bloom awhile;
And sune thou shalt be thrown aside,
   Like ony common weed and vile.

THE WEARY PUND O' TOW

Chorus—The weary pund, the weary pund,
   The weary pund o' tow;
   I think my wife will end her life,
   Before she spin her tow.

I BOUGHT my wife a stane o' lint,
   As gude as e'er did grow,
And a' that she has made o' that
   Is ae puir pund o' tow.
   The weary pund, &c.

O

There sat a bottle in a bole,
  Beyont the ingle low;
And aye she took the tither souk,
  To drouk the stourie tow.
    The weary pund, &c.

Quoth I, " For shame, ye dirty dame,
  Gae spin your tap o' tow ! "
She took the rock, and wi' a knock,
  She brak it o'er my pow.
    The weary pund, &c.

At last her feet—I sang to see't !
  Gaed foremost o'er the knowe,
And or I wad anither jad,
  I'll wallop in a tow.
    The weary pund, &c.

WHEN SHE CAM' BEN SHE BOBBED

O when she cam' ben she bobbed fu' law,
O when she cam' ben she bobbed fu' law,
And when she cam' ben, she kiss'd Cockpen,
  And syne she denied she did it at a'

And was na Cockpen right saucy witha' ?
And was na Cockpen right saucy witha' ?
In leaving the daughter of a lord,
  And kissin a collier lassie an a' !

O never look down, my lassie, at a ,
O never look down, my lassie, at a',
Thy lips are as sweet, and thy figure complete,
  As the finest dame in castle or ha'.

Tho' thou has nae silk, and holland sae sma',
Tho' thou has nae silk, and holland sae sma',
Thy coat and thy sark are thy ain handiwark,
And Lady Jean was never sae braw.

MY COLLIER LADDIE

" O, WHARE live ye, my bonie lass ?
    And tell me what they ca' ye ? "
" My name," she says, " is mistress Jean,
    And I follow the Collier laddie."
            My name, she says, &c.

" O, see you not yon hills and dales
    The sun shines on sae brawlie ?
They a' are mine, and they shall be thine,
    Gin ye'll leave your Collier laddie.
            They a' are mine, &c.

" And ye shall gang in gay attire,
    Weel buskit up sae gaudy ;
And ane to wait on every hand,
    Gin ye'll leave your Collier laddie."
            And ane to wait, &c.

" Tho' ye had a' the sun shines on,
    And the earth conceals sae lowly,
I wad turn my back on you and it a',
    And embrace my Collier laddie.
            I wad turn my back, &c.

" I can win my five pennies in a day,
    An' spend it at night fu' brawlie :
And make my bed in the collier's neuk,
    And lie down wi' my Collier laddie.
            And make my bed, &c.

" Love for love is the bargain for me,
    Tho' the wee cot-house should haud me ;
And the world before me to win my bread,
    And fair fa' my Collier laddie ! "
                    And the warld before me, &c.

SIC A WIFE AS WILLIE HAD

Willie Wastle dwalt on Tweed,
    The spot they ca'd it Linkumdoddie ;
Willie was a wabster gude,
    Could stown a clue wi' ony body :
He had a wife was dour and din,
    O Tinkler Maidgie was her mither ;
Sic a wife as Willie had,
    I wad na gie a button for her.

She has an e'e, she has but ane,
    The cat has twa the very colour ;
Five rusty teeth forbye a stump,
    A clapper tongue wad deave a miller ;
A whiskin beard about her mou',
    Her nose and chin they threaten ither ;
Sic a wife as Willie had,
    I wad na gie a button for her.

She's bow-hough'd, she's hem-shinn'd,
    Ae limpin leg a hand-breed shorter ;
She's twisted right, she's twisted left,
    To balance fair in ilka quarter :
She has a hump upon her breast,
    The twin o' that upon her shouther ;
Sic a wife as Willie had,
    I wad na gie a button for her.

Auld Baudrons by the ingle sits,
 An' wi' her loof her face a-washin;
But Willie's wife is nae sae trig,
 She dights her grunzie wi' a hushion:
Her walie nieves like midden-creels,
 Her face wad fyle the Logan Water;
Sic a wife as Willie had,
 I wad na gie a button for her.

LADY MARY ANN

O Lady Mary Ann looks o'er the Castle wa',
She saw three bonie boys playing at the ba',
The youngest he was the flower amang them a',
 My bonie laddie's young, but he's growin'
  yet.

"O father, O father, an ye think it fit,
We'll send him a year to the college yet,
We'll sew a green ribbon round about his hat,
 And that will let them ken he's to marry
  yet."

Lady Mary Ann was a flower in the dew,
Sweet was its smell and bonie was its hue,
And the longer it blossom'd the sweeter it
  grew,
 For the lily in the bud will be bonier yet.

Young Charlie Cochran was the sprout of an
  aik,
Bonie and bloomin' and straught was its make,
The sun took delight to shine for its sake,
 And it will be the brag o' the forest yet.

The simmer is gane when the leaves they were
　　green,
And the days are awa' that we hae seen,
But far better days I trust will come again ;
　　For my bonie laddie's young, but he's
　　growin' yet.

KELLY BURN BRAES

THERE lived a carl in Kelly Burn Braes,
　　Hey, and the rue grows bonie wi' thyme ;
And he had a wife was the plague of his days,
　　And the thyme it is wither'd, and rue is in
　　prime.

Ae day as the carl gaed up the lang glen,
　　Hey, and the rue grows bonie wi' thyme ;
He met with the Devil, says, " How do you
　　fen ? "
　　And the thyme it is wither'd, and rue is in
　　prime.

" I've got a bad wife, sir, that's a' my complaint,"
　　Hey, and the rue grows bonie wi' thyme ;
" For, savin your presence, to her ye're a saint,"
　　And the thyme it is wither'd, and rue is in
　　prime.

" It's neither your stot nor your staig I shall crave,"
　　Hey, and the rue grows bonie wi' thyme ;
" But gie me your wife, man, for her I must
　　have,"
　　And the thyme it is wither'd, and rue is in
　　prime.

" O welcome most kindly ! " the blythe carl said,
  Hey, and the rue grows bonie wi' thyme ;
" But if ye can match her ye're waur than ye're
    ca'd,"
    And the thyme it is wither'd, and rue is in
    prime.

The Devil has got the auld wife on his back,
  Hey, and the rue grows bonie wi' thyme ;
And like a poor pedlar he's carried his pack,
    And the thyme it is wither'd, and rue is in
    prime.

He's carried her hame to his ain hallan door,
  Hey, and the rue grows bonie wi' thyme :
Syne bade her gae in for a bitch, and a whore,
    And the thyme it is wither'd, and rue is in
    prime.

Then straight he makes fifty, the pick o' his band,
  Hey, and the rue grows bonie wi' thyme :
Turn out on her guard in the clap o' a hand,
    And the thyme it is wither'd, and rue is in
    prime.

The carlin gaed thro' them like ony wud bear,
  Hey, and the rue grows bonie wi' thyme ;
Whae'er she gat hands on cam near her nae mair,
    And the thyme it is wither'd, and rue is in
    prime.

A reekit wee deevil looks over the wa',
  Hey, and the rue grows bonie wi' thyme ;
" O help, maister, help, or she'll ruin us a' ! '
    And the thyme it is wither'd, and rue is in
    prime ;

The Devil he swore by the edge o' his knife,
  Hey, and the rue grows bonie wi' thyme ;
He pitied the man that was tied to a wife,
  And the thyme it is wither'd, and rue is in
    prime.

The Devil he swore by the kirk and the bell,
  Hey, and the rue grows bonie wi' thyme ;
He was not in wedlock, thank Heav'n, but in
  hell,
  And the thyme it is wither'd, and rue is in
    prime.

Then Satan has travell'd again wi' his pack,
  Hey, and the rue grows bonie wi' thyme ;
And to her auld husband he's carried her back,
  And the thyme it is wither'd, and rue is in
    prime.

" I hae been a Deevil the feck o' my life,"
  Hey, and the rue grows bonie wi' thyme ;
" But ne'er was in hell till I met wi' a wife,"
  And the thyme it is wither'd, and rue is in
    prime.

THE SLAVE'S LAMENT

It was in sweet Senegal that my foes did me
    enthral,
  For the lands of Virginia,-ginia, O :
Torn from that lovely shore, and must never see
    it more ;
  And alas ! I am weary, weary O :
Torn from that lovely shore, and must never see
    it more :
  And alas ! I am weary, weary O.

All on that charming coast is no bitter snow and
    frost,
  Like the lands of Virginia,-ginia, O :
There streams for ever flow, and there flowers
    for ever blow,
  And alas ! I am weary, weary O :
There streams for ever flow, and there flowers
    for ever blow,
  And alas ! I am weary, weary O.

The burden I must bear, while the cruel scourge
    I fear,
  In the lands of Virginia,-ginia, O :
And I think on friends most dear, with the bitter,
    bitter tear,
  And alas ! I am weary, weary O :
And I think on friends most dear, with the bitter,
    bitter tear,
  And alas ! I am weary, weary O.

O CAN YE LABOUR LEA?

Chorus.—O can ye labour lea, young man,
    O can ye labour lea ?
    Gae back the gate ye came again :
    Ye'se never scorn me.

  I FEE'D a man at Michaelmas,
    Wi' airle-pennies three ;
  But a' the faut I had to him,
    He could na labour lea,
      O can ye labour lea, &c.

  O clappin's guid in Febarwar,
    An' kissin's sweet in May ;
     o*

But what signifies a young man's love,
  An 't dinna last for aye ?
      O can ye labour lea, &c.

O kissin is the key o' luve,
  And clappin is the lock ;
An' makin o's the best thing yet,
  That e'er a young thing gat.
      O can ye labour lea, &c.

THE DEUKS DANG O'ER MY DADDIE

THE bairns gat out wi' an unco shout,
  " The deuks dang o'er my daddie, O ! "
"The fien-ma-care," quo' the feirrie auld wife,
  " He was but a paidlin body, O !
He paidles out, and he paidles in,
  An' he paidles late and early, O !
This seven lang years I hae lien by his side,
  An' he is but a fusionless carlie, O."

" O haud your tongue, my feirrie auld wife,
  O haud your tongue, now Nansie, O :
I've seen the day, and sae hae ye,
  Ye wad na been sae donsie, O.
I've seen the day ye butter'd my brose,
  And cuddl'd me late and early, O ;
But downa-do's come o'er me now,
  And och, I find it sairly, O ! "

THE DEIL'S AWA WI' THE EXCISEMAN

THE deil cam fiddlin thro' the town,
  And danc'd awa wi' th' Exciseman,

And ilka wife cries, "Auld Mahoun,
  I wish you luck o' the prize, man."

Chorus.—The deil's awa, the deil's awa,
    The deil's awa wi' the Exciseman,
    He's danced awa, he's danc'd awa,
    He's danc'd awa wi' the Exciseman.

We'll mak our maut, and we'll brew our drink,
  We'll laugh, sing, and rejoice, man,
And mony braw thanks to the meikle black deil,
  That danc'd awa wi' th' Exciseman.
             The deil's awa, &c.

There's threesome reels, there's foursome reels,
  There's hornpipes and strathspeys, man,
But the ae best dance ere came to the land
  Was "The deil's awa wi' th' Exciseman."
             The deil's awa, &c.

THE COUNTRY LASS

In simmer, when the hay was mawn,
  And corn wav'd green in ilka field,
While claver blooms white o'er the lea
  And roses blaw in ilka bield !
Blythe Bessie in the milking shiel
  Says—"I'll be wed, come o't what will."
Out spake a dame in wrinkled eild ;
  "O' gude advisement comes nae ill.

"It's ye hae wooers mony ane,
  And lassie, ye're but young, ye ken ;
Then wait a wee, and cannie wale
  A routhie butt, a routhie ben ;

There's Johnie o' the Buskie-glen,
　　Fu' is his barn, fu' is his byre ;
Take this frae me, my bonie hen,
　　It's plenty beets the luver's fire."

" For Johnie o' the Buskie-glen,
　　I dinna care a single flie ;
He lo'es sae weel his craps and kye,
　　He has nae love to spare for me ;
But blythe's the blink o' Robie's e'e,
　　And weel I wat he lo'es me dear :
Ae blink o' him I wad na gie
　　For Buskie-glen and a' his gear."

" O thoughtless lassie, life's a faught ;
　　The canniest gate, the strife is sair ;
But aye fu'-han't is fechtin best ;
　　A hungry care's an unco care :
But some will spend and some will spare,
　　An' wilfu' folk maun hae their will ;
Syne as ye brew, my maiden fair,
　　Keep mind that ye maun drink the yill."

" O gear will buy me rigs o' land,
　　And gear will buy me sheep and kye ;
But the tender heart o' leesome love,
　　The gowd and siller canna buy ;
We may be poor—Robie and I—
　　Light is the burden love lays on ;
Content and love brings peace and joy—
　　What mair hae Queens upon a throne ? "

BESSY AND HER SPINNIN WHEEL

O leeze me on my spinnin-wheel,
And leeze me on my rock and reel :

Bessy and her Spinnin-Wheel

Bessy and her Spinnin-Wheel

"I'll set me down and sing and spin,
While laigh descends the simmer sun,
Blest wi' content, and milk and meal,
O leeze me on my spinnin-wheel."

Frae tap to tae that cleeds me bien,
And haps me fiel and warm at e'en ;
I'll set me down and sing and spin,
While laigh descends the simmer sun,
Blest wi' content, and milk and meal,
O leeze me on my spinnin-wheel.

On ilka hand the burnies trot,
And meet below my theekit cot ;
The scented birk and hawthorn white
Across the pool their arms unite,
Alike to screen the birdie's nest
And little fishes' caller rest ;
The sun blinks kindly in the biel',
Where blythe I turn my spinnin-wheel.

On lofty aiks the cushats wail,
And Echo cons the doolfu' tale ;
The lintwhites in the hazel braes,
Delighted, rival ither's lays ;
The craik amang the claver hay,
The paitrick whirring o'er the ley,
The swallow jinkin round my shiel,
Amuse me at my spinnin-wheel.

Wi' sma' to sell and less to buy,
Aboon distress, below envy,
O wha wad leave this humble state,
For a' the pride of a' the great ?
Amid their flairing, idle toys,
Amid their cumbrous, dinsome joys,
Can they the peace and pleasure feel
Of Bessie at her spinnin-wheel ?

NO COLD APPROACH

No cold approach, no altered mien,
  Just what would make suspicion start ;
No pause the dire extremes between,
  He made me blest—and broke my heart.

LET LOVE SPARKLE

Let love sparkle in her e'e ;
Let her lo'e nae man but me ;
That's the tocher-gude I prize,
There the lover's treasure lies.

SAW YE BONIE LESLEY

O saw ye bonie Lesley,
  As she gaed o'er the Border ?
She's gane, like Alexander,
  To spread her conquests farther.

To see her is to love her,
  And love but her for ever ;
For Nature made her what she is,
  And never made anither !

Thou art a queen, fair Lesley,
  Thy subjects, we before thee ;
Thou art divine, fair Lesley,
  The hearts o' men adore thee.

The deil he could na scaith thee,
  Or aught that wad belang thee ;
He'd look into thy bonie face,
  And say—" I canna wrang thee ! "

The Powers aboon will tent thee,
 Misfortune sha'na steer thee ;
Thou'rt like themselves sae lovely,
 That ill they'll ne'er let near thee.

Return again, fair Lesley,
 Return to Caledonie !
That we may brag we hae a lass
 There's nane again sae bonie.

I'LL MEET THEE ON THE
LEA RIG

When o'er the hill the e'ening star
 Tells bughtin time is near, my jo,
And owsen frae the furrow'd field
 Return sae dowf and weary O ;
Down by the burn, where scented birks
 Wi' dew are hangin clear, my jo,
I'll meet thee on the lea-rig,
 My ain kind dearie O.

At midnight hour, in mirkest glen,
 I'd rove, and ne'er be eerie O,
If thro' that glen I gaed to thee,
 My ain kind dearie O ;
Altho' the night were ne'er sae wild,
 And I were ne'er sae weary O,
I'll meet thee on the lea-rig,
 My ain kind dearie O.

The hunter lo'es the morning sun ;
 To rouse the mountain deer, my jo ;
At noon the fisher takes the glen
 Adown the burn to steer, my jo;

Gie me the hour o' gloamin grey,
    It maks my heart sae cheery O,
To meet thee on the lea-rig,
    My ain kind dearie O.

MY WIFE'S A WINSOME WEE THING

Air—" My Wife's a Wanton Wee Thing."

Chorus.—She is a winsome wee thing,
    She is a handsome wee thing,
    She is a lo'esome wee thing,
        This sweet wee wife o' mine.

I NEVER saw a fairer,
I never lo'ed a dearer,
And neist my heart I'll wear her,
    For fear my jewel tine,
        She is a winsome, &c.

The warld's wrack, we share o't,
The warstle and the care o't;
Wi' her I'll blythely bear it,
    And think my lot divine.
        She is a winsome, &c.

HIGHLAND MARY

Tune—" Katherine Ogie."

YE banks and braes and streams around
    The castle o' Montgomery!
Green be your woods, and fair your flowers,
    Your waters never drumlie:
There Simmer first unfald her robes,
    And there the langest tarry;

Highland Mary

Highland Mary

"There Simmer first unfald her robes,
And there the langest tarry;
For there I took the lass fareweel
O' my sweet Highland Mary."

For there I took the last fareweel
O' my sweet Highland Mary.

How sweetly bloom'd the gay, green birk,
How rich the hawthorn's blossom,
As underneath their fragrant shade,
I clasp'd her to my bosom !
The golden Hours on angel wings,
Flew o'er me and my dearie ;
For dear to me, as light and life,
Was my sweet Highland Mary.

Wi' mony a vow, and lock'd embrace,
Our parting was fu' tender ;
And, pledging aft to meet again,
We tore oursels asunder ;
But O, fell Death's untimely frost,
That nipt my flower sae early !
Now green's the sod, and cauld's the clay
That wraps my Highland Mary !

O pale, pale now, those rosy lips,
I aft hae kiss'd sae fondly !
And clos'd for aye, the sparkling glance
That dwalt on me sae kindly !
And mouldering now in silent dust,
That heart that lo'ed me dearly !
But still within my bosom's core
Shall live my Highland Mary.

AULD ROB MORRIS

There's Auld Rob Morris that wons in yon glen,
He's the King o' gude fellows, and wale o' auld
    men ;

He has gowd in his coffers, he has owsen and
    kine,
And ae bonie lass, his dautie and mine.

She's fresh as the morning, the fairest in May;
She's sweet as the ev'ning amang the new hay;
As blythe and as artless as the lambs on the lea,
And dear to my heart as the light to my e'e.

But oh! she's an heiress, auld Robin's a laird,
And my daddie has nought but a cot-house and
    yard;
A wooer like me maunna hope to come speed,
The wounds I must hide that will soon be my
    dead.

The day comes to me, but delight brings me nane;
The night comes to me, but my rest it is gane;
I wander my lane like a night-troubled ghaist,
And I sigh as my heart it wad burst in my breast.

O had she but been of a lower degree,
I then might hae hop'd she wad smil'd upon me!
O how past descriving had then been my bliss,
As now my distraction nae words can express.

DUNCAN GRAY

Duncan Gray cam' here to woo,
    Ha, ha, the wooing o't,
On blythe Yule-night when we were fou,
    Ha, ha, the wooing o't,
Maggie coost her head fu' heigh,
Look'd asklent and unco skeigh,
Gart poor Duncan stand abeigh;
    Ha, ha, the wooing o't.

Duncan Gray

Duncan Gray

"Duncan Gray cam' here to woo . . ."

Duncan fleech'd and Duncan pray'd;
　　Ha, ha, the wooing o't,
Meg was deaf as Ailsa craig,
　　Ha, ha, the wooing o't:
Duncan sigh'd baith out and in,
Grat his e'en baith blear't an' blin',
Spak o' lowpin o'er a linn;
　　Ha, ha, the wooing o't.

Time and Chance are but a tide,
　　Ha, ha, the wooing o't,
Slighted love is sair to bide,
　　Ha, ha, the wooing o't:
" Shall I like a fool," quoth he,
" For a haughty hizzie die?
She may gae to—France for me!"
　　Ha, ha, the wooing o't.

How it comes let doctors tell,
　　Ha, ha, the wooing o't;
Meg grew sick, as he grew hale,
　　Ha, ha, the wooing o't.
Something in her bosom wrings,
For relief a sigh she brings:
And O! her een they spak sic things!
　　Ha, ha, the wooing o't.

Duncan was a lad o' grace,
　　Ha, ha, the wooing o't:
Maggie's was a piteous case,
　　Ha, ha, the wooing o't:
Duncan could na be her death,
Swelling Pity smoor'd his wrath;
Now they're crouse and canty baith,
　　Ha, ha, the wooing o't.

HERE'S A HEALTH TO THEM THAT'S AWA

Here's a health to them that's awa,
　　Here's a health to them that's awa;
And wha winna wish gude luck to our cause,
　　May never gude luck be their fa'!
It's gude to be merry and wise,
　　It's gude to be honest and true;
It's gude to support Caledonia's cause,
　　And bide by the buff and the blue.

Here's a health to them that's awa,
　　Here's a health to them that's awa,
Here's a health to Charlie the chief o' the
　　　clan,
　　Altho' that his band be but sma'!
May Liberty meet wi' success!
　　May Prudence protect her frae evil!
May tyrants and Tyranny tine i' the mist,
　　And wander their way to the devil!

Here's a health to them that's awa,
　　Here's a health to them that's awa;
Here's a health to Tammie, the Norlan' laddie,
　　That lives at the lug o' the law!
Here's freedom to them that wad read,
　　Here's freedom to them that wad write,
There's nane ever fear'd that the truth should
　　　be heard,
　　But they whom the truth would indite.

Here's a health to them that's awa,
　　An' here's to them that's awa!

Here's to Maitland and Wycombe, let wha
    doesna like 'em
  Be built in a hole in the wa' ;
Here's timmer that's red at the heart,
    Here's fruit that is sound at the core ;
And may he that wad turn the buff and blue coat
  Be turn'd to the back o' the door.

Here's a health to them that's awa,
    Here's a health to them that's awa ;
Here's chieftain M'Leod, a chieftain worth gowd,
  Tho' bred amang mountains o' snaw ;
Here's friends on baith sides o' the firth,
    And friends on baith sides o' the Tweed ;
And wha wad betray old Albion's right,
  May they never eat of her bread !

POORTITH CAULD AND RESTLESS
LOVE

Tune—" Cauld Kail in Aberdeen."

O POORTITH cauld, and restless love,
  Ye wrack my peace between ye ;
Yet poortith a' I could forgive,
  An 'twere na for my Jeanie.

Chorus—O why should Fate sic pleasure have,
    Life's dearest bands untwining ?
  Or why sae sweet a flower as love
    Depend on Fortune's shining ?

The warld's wealth, when I think on,
  Its pride and a' the lave o't ;
My curse on silly coward man,
  That he should be the slave o't !
    O why, &c.

Her e'en, sae bonie blue, betray
How she repays my passion ;
But prudence is her o'erword aye,
She talks o' rank and fashion.
O why, &c.

O wha can prudence think upon,
And sic a lassie by him ?
O wha can prudence think upon,
And sae in love as I am ?
O why, &c.

How blest the wild-wood Indian's fate.
He woos his artless dearie ;
The silly bogles, wealth and state,
Can never make him eerie.
O why, &c.

BRAW LADS O' GALLA WATER

Braw, braw lads on Yarrow-braes,
They rove amang the blooming heather ;
But Yarrow braes, nor Ettrick shaws
Can match the lads o' Galla Water.

But there is ane, a secret ane,
Aboon them a' I lo'e him better ;
And I'll be his, and he'll be mine,
The bonie lad o' Galla Water.

Altho' his daddie was nae laird,
And tho' I hae nae meikle tocher,
Yet rich in kindest, truest love,
We'll tent our flocks by Galla Water.

Lord Gregory

Lord Gregory

"O mirk, mirk is this midnight hour,
And loud the tempest's roar;
O waefu' wanderer seeks they tower, —
Lord Gregory, ope thy door."

It ne'er was wealth, it ne'er was wealth,
   That coft contentment, peace, or pleasure:
The bands and bliss o' mutual love,
   O that's the chiefest warld's treasure.

LORD GREGORY

O MIRK, mirk is this midnight hour,
   And loud the tempest's roar;
A waefu' wanderer seeks thy tower,—
   Lord Gregory, ope thy door.
An exile frae her father's ha',
   And a' for sake o' thee;
At least some pity on me shaw,
   If love it may na be.

Lord Gregory, mind'st thou not the grove
   By bonie Irwine side,
Where first I own'd that virgin love
   I lang, lang had denied.
How aften didst thou pledge and vow
   Thou wad for aye be mine!
And my fond heart, itsel' sae true,
   It ne'er mistrusted thine.

Hard is thy heart, Lord Gregory,
   And flinty is thy breast:
Thou bolt of Heaven that flashest by,
   O, wilt thou bring me rest!
Ye mustering thunders from above,
   Your willing victim see;
But spare and pardon my fause Love
   His wrangs to Heaven and me.

WANDERING WILLIE

First Version

HERE awa, there awa, wandering Willie,
  Now tired with wandering, haud awa hame;
Come to my bosom, my ae only dearie,
  And tell me thou bring'st me my Willie the same.
Loud blew the cauld winter winds at our parting;
  It was na the blast brought the tear in my e'e;
Now welcome the Simmer, and welcome my
    Willie,
  The Simmer to Nature, my Willie to me.

Ye hurricanes rest in the cave o' your slumbers,
  O how your wild horrors a lover alarms!
Awaken ye breezes, row gently ye billows,
  And waft my dear laddie ance mair to my arms.
But if he's forgotten his faithfullest Nannie,
  O still flow between us, thou wide roaring main;
May I never see it, may I never trow it,
  But, dying, believe that my Willie's my ain!

WANDERING WILLIE

Revised Version

HERE awa, there awa, wandering Willie,
  Here awa, there awa, haud awa hame;
Come to my bosom, my ain only dearie,
  Tell me thou bring'st me my Willie the same.
Winter winds blew loud and cauld at our parting,
  Fears for my Willie brought tears in my e'e,
Welcome now Simmer, and welcome my Willie,
  The Simmer to Nature my Willie to me.

Rest, ye wild storms, in the cave of your slumbers,
　How your dread howling a lover alarms !
Wauken ye breezes, row gently ye billows,
　And waft my dear laddie ance mair to my
　　arms.
But oh, if he's faithless, and minds na his Nannie,
　Flow still between us, thou wide roaring
　　main !
May I never see it, may I never trow it,
　But, dying, believe that my Willie's my ain.

OPEN THE DOOR TO ME, O

O, OPEN the door, some pity to shew,
　If love it may na be, O.
Tho' thou hast been false, I'll ever prove true,
　O, open the door to me, O.

Cauld is the blast upon my pale cheek,
　But caulder thy love for me, O :
The frost that freezes the life at my heart,
　Is nought to my pains frae thee, O.

The wan Moon is setting behind the white wave,
　And Time is setting with me, O :
False friends, false love, farewell ! for mair
　I'll ne'er trouble them nor thee, O.

She has open'd the door, she has open'd it
　wide,
　She sees the pale corse on the plain, O :
" My true love ! " she cried, and sank down by
　his side,
　Never to rise again, O.

LOVELY YOUNG JESSIE

TRUE hearted was he, the sad swain o' the Yarrow,
  And fair are the maids on the banks of the
      Ayr;
But by the sweet side o' the Nith's winding
    river,
  Are lovers as faithful, and maidens as fair :
To equal young JESSIE seek Scotia all over;
  To equal young JESSIE you seek it in vain,
Grace, beauty, and elegance fetter her lover,
  And maidenly modesty fixes the chain.

Fresh is the rose in the gay, dewy morning,
  And sweet is the lily at evening close ;
But in the fair presence o' lovely young JESSIE,
  Unseen is the lily, unheeded the rose.
Love sits in her smile, a wizard ensnaring ;
  Enthron'd in her een he delivers his law :
And still to her charms she alone is a stranger ;
  Her modest demeanour's the jewel of a'.

MEG O' THE MILL

First Version

O KEN ye what Meg o' the Mill has gotten,
An' ken ye what Meg o' the Mill has gotten?
A braw new naig wi' the tail o' a rottan,
And that's what Meg o' the Mill has gotten.

O ken ye what Meg o' the Mill lo'es dearly,
An' ken ye what Meg o' the Mill lo'es dearly?
A dram o' guid strunt in the morning early,
And that's what Meg o' the Mill lo'es dearly.

O ken ye how Meg o' the Mill was married,
An' ken ye how Meg o' the Mill was married?
The priest he was oxter'd, the clark he was
carried,
And that's how Meg o' the Mill was married.

O ken ye how Meg o' the Mill was bedded,
An' ken ye how Meg o' the Mill was bedded?
The groom gat sae fou', he fell awald beside it,
And that's how Meg o' the Mill was bedded.

MEG O' THE MILL

Second Version

O ken ye what Meg o' the mill has gotten,
An' ken ye what Meg o' the mill has gotten?
She's gotten a coof wi' a claut o' siller,
And broken the heart o' the barley miller.

The miller was strappin, the miller was ruddy;
A heart like a lord, and a hue like a lady;
The laird was a widdifu', bleerit knurl;
She's left the gude fellow, and taen the churl.

The miller he hecht her a heart leal and loving;
The laird did address her wi' matter mair moving,
A fine pacing-horse wi' a clear chainèd bridle,
A whip by her side, and a bonie side-saddle.

O wae on the siller, it is sae prevailin,
And wae on the love that is fixed on a mailen!
A tocher's nae word in a true lover's parle,
But gie me my love, and a fig for the warl'!

THE SOLDIER'S RETURN

Air—" The Mill, Mill, O."

WHEN wild War's deadly blast was blawn,
  And gentle Peace returning,
Wi' mony a sweet babe fatherless,
  And mony a widow mourning;
I left the lines and tented field,
  Where lang I'd been a lodger,
My humble knapsack a' my wealth,
  A poor and honest sodger.

A leal, light heart was in my breast,
  My hand unstain'd wi' plunder;
And for fair Scotia, hame again,
  I cheery on did wander:
I thought upon the banks o' Coil,
  I thought upon my Nancy,
And ay I mind't the witching smile
  That caught my youthful fancy.

At length I reach'd the bonie glen,
  Where early life I sported;
I pass'd the mill and trysting thorn,
  Where Nancy aft I courted:
Wha spied I but my ain dear maid,
  Down by her mother's dwelling!
And turn'd me round to hide the flood
  That in my e'en was swelling.

Wi' alter'd voice, quoth I, " Sweet lass,
  Sweet as yon hawthorn's blossom,
O ! happy, happy may he be,
  That's dearest to thy bosom:

The Soldier's Return

The Soldier's Return

*"She sank within my arms and cried,
'Art thou my ain dear Willie?'"*

My purse is light, I've far to gang,
    And fain would be thy lodger ;
I've serv'd my king and country lang—
    Take pity on a sodger."

Sae wistfully she gaz'd on me,
    And lovelier was than ever ;
Quo' she, " A sodger ance I lo'ed,
    Forget him shall I never :
Our humble cot, and hamely fare,
    Ye freely shall partake it ;
That gallant badge—the dear cockade,
    Ye're welcome for the sake o't."

She gaz'd—she redden'd like a rose—
    Syne pale like ony lily ;
She sank within my arms, and cried,
    " Art thou my ain dear Willie ? "
" By him who made yon sun and sky !
    By whom true love's regarded,
I am the man ; and thus may still
    True lovers be rewarded !

" The wars are o'er, and I'm come hame,
    And find thee still true-hearted ;
Tho' poor in gear, we're rich in love,
    And mair we'se ne'er be parted."
Quo' she, " My grandsire left me gowd,
    A mailen plenish'd fairly ;
And come, my faithfu' sodger lad,
    Thou'rt welcome to it dearly ! "

For gold the merchant ploughs the main,
    The farmer ploughs the manor ;
But glory is the sodger's prize,
    The sodger's wealth is honor :

The brave poor sodger ne'er despise,
    Nor count him as a stranger ;
Remember he's his country's stay,
    In day and hour of danger.

ON GENERAL DUMOURIER'S DE-
SERTION FROM THE FRENCH
REPUBLICAN ARMY

You're welcome to Despots, Dumourier ;
You're welcome to Despots, Dumourier :
    How does Dampiere do ?
    Ay, and Bournonville too ?
Why did they not come along with you, Du-
    mourier ?

I will fight France with you, Dumourier ;
I will fight France with you, Dumourier ;
    I will fight France with you,
    I will take my chance with you,
By my soul, I'll dance with you, Dumourier.

Then let us fight about, Dumourier ;
Then let us fight about, Dumourier ;
    Then let us fight about,
    Till Freedom's spark be out,
Then we'll be damn'd, no doubt, Dumourier.

THE LAST TIME I CAME O'ER
THE MOOR

THE last time I came o'er the moor,
    And left Maria's dwelling,
What throes, what tortures passing cure,
    Were in my bosom swelling :

Condemn'd to see my rival's reign,
  While I in secret languish ;
To feel a fire in every vein,
  Yet dare not speak my anguish.

Love's veriest wretch, despairing, I
  Fain, fain, my crime would cover :
Th' unweeting groan, the bursting sigh,
  Betray the guilty lover.
I know my doom must be despair,
  Thou wilt nor canst relieve me ;
But O, Maria, hear my prayer,
  For Pity's sake, forgive me !

The music of thy tongue I heard,
  Nor wist while it enslav'd me ;
I saw thine eyes, yet nothing fear'd,
  Till fear no more had sav'd me :
The unwary sailor thus, aghast,
  The wheeling torrent viewing,
'Mid circling horrors yields at last
  To overwhelming ruin.

BLYTHE HAE I BEEN ON YON HILL

Tune—"The Quaker's Wife."

BLYTHE hae I been on yon hill,
  As the lambs before me ;
Careless ilka thought and free,
  As the breeze flew o'er me ;
Now nae langer sport and play,
  Mirth or sang can please me ;
LESLEY is sae fair and coy,
  Care and anguish seize me.

Heavy, heavy is the task,
  Hopeless love declaring ;
Trembling, I dow nocht but glow'r,
  Sighing, dumb despairing !
If she winna ease the thraws
  In my bosom swelling,
Underneath the grass-green sod
  Soon maun be my dwelling.

LOGAN BRAES

Tune—" Logan Water."

O LOGAN, sweetly didst thou glide,
That day I was my Willie's bride,
And years sin syne hae o'er us run,
Like Logan to the simmer sun :
But now thy flowery banks appear
Like drumlie Winter, dark and drear,
While my dear lad maun face his faes,
Far, far frae me and Logan braes.

Again the merry month of May
Has made our hills and valleys gay ;
The birds rejoice in leafy bowers,
The bees hum round the breathing flowers;
Blythe Morning lifts his rosy eye,
And Evening's tears are tears o' joy :
My soul, delightless a' surveys,
While Willie's far frae Logan braes.

Within yon milk-white hawthorn bush,
Amang her nestlings sits the thrush :
Her faithfu' mate will share her toil,
Or wi' his song her cares beguile ;

But I wi' my sweet nurslings here,
Nae mate to help, nae mate to cheer,
Pass widow'd nights and joyless days,
While Willie's far frae Logan braes.

O wae be to you, Men o' State,
That brethren rouse in deadly hate!
As ye make mony a fond heart mourn,
Sae may it on your heads return!
How can your flinty hearts enjoy
The widow's tear, the orphan's cry?
But soon may peace bring happy days,
And Willie hame to Logan braes!

O WERE MY LOVE YON LILAC FAIR

Air—"Hughie Graham."

O were my love yon Lilac fair,
  Wi' purple blossoms to the Spring,
And I, a bird to shelter there,
  When wearied on my little wing!
How I wad mourn when it was torn
  By Autumn wild, and Winter rude!
But I wad sing on wanton wing,
  When youthfu' May its bloom renew'd.

O gin my love were yon red rose,
  That grows upon the castle wa';
And I mysel a drap o' dew,
  Into her bonie breast to fa'!
O there, beyond expression blest,
  I'd feast on beauty a' the night;
Seal'd on her silk-saft faulds to rest,
  Till fley'd awa by Phœbus' light!

P

THERE WAS A LASS

THERE was a lass, and she was fair,
　At kirk or market to be seen;
When a' our fairest maids were met,
　The fairest maid was bonie Jean.

And aye she wrought her country wark,
　And aye she sang sae merrilie;
The blythest bird upon the bush
　Had ne'er a lighter heart than she.

But hawks will rob the tender joys
　That bless the little lintwhite's nest;
And frost will blight the fairest flowers,
　And love will break the soundest rest.

Young Robie was the brawest lad,
　The flower and pride of a' the glen;
And he had owsen, sheep, and kye,
　And wanton naigies nine or ten

He gaed wi' Jeanie to the tryste,
　He danc'd wi' Jeanie on the down;
And, lang ere witless Jeanie wist,
　Her heart was tint, her peace was stown!

As in the bosom of the stream,
　The moon-beam dwells at dewy e'en;
So trembling pure was tender love
　Within the breast of bonie Jean.

And now she works her country wark,
　And aye she sighs wi' care and pain;
Yet wist na what her ail might be,
　Or what wad make her weel again.

Phillis the Fair

Phillis the Fair

"While larks, with little wing,
Fann'd the pure air,
Viewing the breathing Spring,
Forth I did fare."

But did na Jeanie's heart loup light,
  And didna joy blink in her e'e,
As Robie tauld a tale o' love
  Ae e'ening on the lily lea?

The sun was sinking in the west,
  The birds sang sweet in ilka grove;
His cheek to hers he fondly laid,
  And whisper'd thus his tale o' love:

" O Jeanie fair, I lo'e thee dear;
  O canst thou think to fancy me,
Or wilt thou leave thy mammie's cot,
  And learn to tent the farms wi' me?

" At barn or byre thou shalt na drudge,
  Or naething else to trouble thee;
But stray amang the heather-bells,
  And tent the waving corn wi' me."

Now what could artless Jeanie do?
  She had nae will to say him na:
At length she blush'd a sweet consent,
  And love was aye between them twa.

PHILLIS THE FAIR

Tune—" Robin Adair."

WHILE larks, with little wing,
  Fann'd the pure air,
Viewing the breathing Spring,
  Forth I did fare:
Gay the sun's golden eye
Peep'd o'er the mountains high;
" Such thy bloom!" did I cry,
  " Phillis the fair."

In each bird's careless song,
  Glad I did share ;
While yon wild-flowers among,
  Chance led me there !
Sweet to the op'ning day,
Rosebuds bent the dewy spray ;
" Such thy bloom ! " did I say,
  " Phillis the fair."

Down in a shady walk,
  Doves cooing were ;
I mark'd the cruel hawk
  Caught in a snare :
So kind may Fortune be,
Such make his destiny,
He who would injure thee,
  Phillis the fair.

HAD I A CAVE

Tune—" Robin Adair."

HAD I a cave on some wild distant shore,
Where the winds howl to the wave's dashing
    roar :
  There would I weep my woes,
  There seek my lost repose,
  Till grief my eyes should close,
    Ne'er to wake more !

Falsest of womankind, can'st thou declare
All thy fond, plighted vows fleeting as air !
  To thy new lover hie,
  Laugh o'er thy perjury ;
  Then in thy bosom try
    What peace is there !

BY ALLAN STREAM

By Allan stream I chanc'd to rove,
  While Phœbus sank beyond Benledi;
The winds were whispering thro' the grove,
  The yellow corn was waving ready:
I listen'd to a lover's sang,
  An' thought on youthfu' pleasures monie;
And aye the wild-wood echoes rang—
  " O, my love Annie's very bonie!

" O, happy be the woodbine bower,
  Nae nightly bogle make it eerie;
Nor ever sorrow stain the hour,
  The place and time I met my dearie!
Her head upon my throbbing breast,
  She, sinking said, ' I'm thine for ever!'
While mony a kiss the seal imprest—
  The sacred vow we ne'er should sever."

The haunt o' Spring's the primrose-brae,
  The Summer joys the flocks to follow;
How cheery thro' her short'ning day,
  Is Autumn in her weeds o' yellow;
But can they melt the glowing heart,
  Or chain the soul in speechless pleasure?
Or thro' each nerve the rapture dart,
  Like meeting her, our bosom's treasure?

WHISTLE AN' I'LL COME TO YE, MY LAD

Chorus.—O whistle an' I'll come to ye, my
      lad,
    O whistle an I'll come to ye, my lad,

Tho' father an' mother an' a' should gae
  mad,
O whistle an' I'll come to ye, my lad.

But warily tent when ye come to court me,
And come nae unless the back-yett be a-jee;
Syne up the back-stile, and let naebody see,
And come as ye were na comin to me,
And come as ye were na comin to me.
  O whistle an' I'll come, &c.

At kirk, or at market, whene'er ye meet me,
Gang by me as tho' that ye car'd na a flie;
But steal me a blink o' your bonie black e'e,
Yet look as ye were na lookin to me,
Yet look as ye were na lookin to me.
  O whistle an' I'll come, &c.

Aye vow and protest that ye care na for me,
And whiles ye may lightly my beauty a-wee;
But court na anither, tho' jokin ye be,
For fear that she wile your fancy frae me,
For fear that she wile your fancy frae me.
  O whistle and I'll come, &c.

PHILLIS THE QUEEN O' THE FAIR

Tune—"The Muckin o' Geordie's Byre."

Adown winding Nith I did wander,
  To mark the sweet flowers as they spring;
Adown winding Nith I did wander,
  Of Phillis to muse and to sing.

Chorus.—Awa' wi' your belles and your beauties,
  They never wi' her can compare,
 Whaever has met wi' my Phillis,
  Has met wi' the queen o' the fair.

The daisy amus'd my fond fancy,
 So artless, so simple, so wild ;
"Thou emblem," said I, "o' my Phillis "—
 For she is Simplicity's child.
  Awa' wi' your belles, &c.

The rose-bud's the blush o' my charmer,
 Her sweet balmy lip when 'tis prest :
How fair and how pure is the lily !
 But fairer and purer her breast.
  Awa' wi' your belles, &c.

Yon knot of gay flowers in the arbour,
 They ne'er wi' my Phillis can vie :
Her breath is the breath of the woodbine,
 Its dew-drop o' diamond her eye.
  Awa' wi' your belles, &c.

Her voice is the song o' the morning,
 That wakes thro' the green-spreading grove,
When Phœbus peeps over the mountains,
 On music, and pleasure, and love.
  Awa' wi' your belles, &c.

But beauty, how frail and how fleeting !
 The bloom of a fine summer's day !
While worth in the mind o' my Phillis,
 Will flourish without a decay.
  Awa' wi' your belles, &c.

COME, LET ME TAKE THEE TO MY BREAST

COME, let me take thee to my breast,
 And pledge we ne'er shall sunder,
And I shall spurn as vilest dust
 The world's wealth and grandeur.
And do I hear my Jeanie own
 That equal transports move her?
I ask for dearest life alone,
 That I may live to love her.

Thus, in my arms, wi' a' her charms,
 I clasp my countless treasure;
I'll seek nae mair o' Heav'n to share,
 Than sic a moment's pleasure
And by thy e'en sae bonie blue,
 I swear I'm thine for ever!
And on thy lips I seal my vow,
 And break it shall I never.

DAINTY DAVIE

Now rosy May comes in wi' flowers,
To deck her gay, green-spreading bowers;
And now comes in the happy hours,
 To wander wi' my Davie.

Chorus.—Meet me on the warlock knowe,
 Dainty Davie, Dainty Davie;
 There I'll spend the day wi' you,
 My ain dear Dainty Davie.

The crystal waters round us fa',
The merry birds are lovers a',

The scented breezes round us blaw,
A wandering wi' my Davie.
Meet me on, &c.

As purple morning starts the hare,
To steal upon her early fare,
Then thro' the dews I will repair,
To meet my faithfu' Davie.
Meet me on, &c.

When day, expiring in the west,
The curtain draws o' Nature's rest,
I flee to his arms I lo'e the best,
And that's my ain dear Davie.
Meet me on, &c.

ROBERT BRUCE'S MARCH TO BANNOCKBURN

Scots, wha hae wi' Wallace bled,
Scots, wham Bruce has aften led,
Welcome to your gory bed,
Or to victorie !

Now's the day, and now's the hour ;
See the front o' battle lour ;
See approach proud Edward's power—
Chains and slaverie !

Wha will be a traitor knave ?
Wha can fill a coward's grave ?
Wha sae base as be a slave ?
Let him turn and flee !

P*

Wha, for Scotland's King and Law,
Freedom's sword will strongly draw,
Free-man stand, or Free-man fa',
                    Let him on wi' me!

By Oppression's woes and pains!
By your sons in servile chains!
We will drain our dearest veins,
                    But they shall be free!

Lay the proud Usurpers low!
Tyrants fall in every foe!
Liberty's in every blow!—
                    Let us do or die!

BEHOLD THE HOUR, THE BOAT
ARRIVE

BEHOLD the hour, the boat arrive;
    Thou goest, the darling of my heart;
Sever'd from thee, can I survive?
    But Fate has will'd and we must part.
I'll often greet the surging swell,
    Yon distant Isle will often hail:
" E'en here I took the last farewell;
    There, latest mark'd her vanish'd sail."

Along the solitary shore,
    While flitting sea-fowl round me cry,
Across the rolling, dashing roar,
    I'll westward turn my wistful eye:
" Happy, thou Indian grove," I'll say,
    " Where now my Nancy's path may be!
While thro' thy sweets she loves to stray,
    O tell me, does she muse on me! "

DOWN THE BURN, DAVIE

As down the burn they took their way,
  And thro' the flowery dale ;
His cheek to hers he aft did lay,
  And love was aye the tale :
With " Mary, when shall we return,
  Sic pleasure to renew ? "
Quoth Mary—" Love, I like the burn,
  And aye shall follow you."

THOU HAST LEFT ME EVER, JAMIE

Tune—" Fee him, father, fee him."

Thou hast left me ever, Jamie,
  Thou hast left me ever ;
Thou hast left me ever, Jamie,
  Thou hast left me ever :
Aften hast thou vow'd that Death
  Only should us sever ;
Now thou'st left thy lass for aye—
  I maun see thee never, Jamie,
  I'll see thee never.

Thou hast me forsaken, Jamie,
  Thou hast me forsaken ;
Thou hast me forsaken, Jamie,
  Thou hast me forsaken ;
Thou canst love another jo,
  While my heart is breaking ;
Soon my weary een I'll close,
  Never mair to waken, Jamie,
  Never mair to waken !

WHERE ARE THE JOYS I HAVE MET

Tune—"Saw ye my father."

WHERE are the joys I have met in the morning,
That danc'd to the lark's early song?
Where is the peace that awaited my wand'ring,
At evening the wild-woods among?

No more a winding the course of yon river,
And marking sweet flowerets so fair,
No more I trace the light footsteps of Pleasure,
But Sorrow and sad-sighing Care.

Is it that Summer's forsaken our valleys,
And grim, surly Winter is near?
No, no, the bees humming round the gay roses
Proclaim it the pride of the year.

Fain would I hide what I fear to discover,
Yet long, long, too well have I known;
All that has caus`ed this wreck in my bosom,
Is Jenny, fair Jenny alone.

Time cannot aid me, and griefs are immortal,
Nor Hope dare a comfort bestow:
Come then, enamour'd and fond of my anguish,
Enjoyment I'll seek in my woe.

DELUDED SWAIN, THE PLEASURE

Tune—"The Collier's Dochter."

DELUDED swain, the pleasure
    The fickle Fair can give thee,
Is but a fairy treasure;
    Thy hopes will soon deceive thee:

The billows on the ocean,
  The breezes idly roaming,
The cloud's uncertain motion,
  They are but types of Woman

O art thou not ashamèd
  To doat upon a feature?
If Man thou wouldst be namèd,
  Despise the silly creature.
Go, find an honest fellow,
  Good claret set before thee,
Hold on till thou art mellow,
  And then to bed in glory!

THINE AM I, MY FAITHFUL FAIR

Tune—"The Quaker's Wife."

THINE am I, my faithful Fair,
  Thine, my lovely Nancy;
Ev'ry pulse along my veins,
  Ev'ry roving fancy.
To thy bosom lay my heart,
  There to throb and languish;
Tho' despair had wrung its core,
  That would heal its anguish.

Take away those rosy lips,
  Rich with balmy treasure;
Turn away thine eyes of love,
  Lest I die with pleasure!
What is life when wanting Love?
  Night without a morning:
Love's the cloudless summer sun,
  Nature gay adorning.

MY SPOUSE NANCY

Tune—"My Jo Janet."

"Husband, husband, cease your strife,
  Nor longer idly rave, Sir;
Tho' I am your wedded wife
  Yet I am not your slave, Sir."
"One of two must still obey,
  Nancy, Nancy;
Is it Man or Woman, say,
  My spouse Nancy?"

"If 'tis still the lordly word,
  Service and obedience,
I'll desert my sov'reign lord,
  And so, good-bye, allegiance!"
"Sad will I be, so bereft,
  Nancy, Nancy;
Yet I'll try to make a shift,
  My spouse Nancy."

"My poor heart, then break it must,
  My last hour I am near it:
When you lay me in the dust,
  Think how you will bear it."
"I will hope and trust in Heaven,
  Nancy, Nancy;
Strength to bear it will be given,
  My spouse Nancy."

"Well, Sir, from the silent dead,
  Still I'll try to daunt you;
Ever round your midnight bed
  Horrid sprites shall haunt you!"

"I'll wed another like my dear
    Nancy, Nancy;
Then all hell will fly for fear,
    My spouse Nancy."

WILT THOU BE MY DEARIE

Tune—"The Suitor's Dochter."

WILT thou be my dearie?
When Sorrow wrings thy gentle heart,
    O wilt thou let me cheer thee?
By the treasure of my soul—
    That's the love I bear thee—
I swear and vow that only thou
    Shall ever be my dearie!
Only thou, I swear and vow,
    Shall ever be my dearie!

Lassie, say thou lo'es me;
Or, if thou wilt na be my ain,
    Say na thou'lt refuse me!
If it winna, canna be,
    Thou for thine may choose me,
Let me, lassie, quickly die,
    Trusting that thou lo'es me!
Lassie, let me quickly die,
    Trusting that thou lo'es me!

A FIDDLER IN THE NORTH

Tune—"The King o' France he rade a race."

AMANG the trees, where humming bees,
    At buds and flowers were hinging, O,
Auld Caledon drew out her drone,
    And to her pipe was singing, O:

'Twas Pibroch, Sang, Strathspeys, and Reels,
  She dirl'd them aff fu' clearly, O :
When there cam' a yell o' foreign squeels,
  That dang her tapsalteerie, O.

Their capon craws an' queer "ha, ha's,"
  They made our lugs grow eerie, O ;
The hungry bike did scrape and fyke,
  Till we were wae and weary, O ;
But a royal ghaist, wha ance was cas'd
  A prisoner, aughteen year awa',
He fir'd a Fiddler in the North,
  That dang them tapsalteerie, O.

THE MINSTREL AT LINCLUDEN

Tune—" Cumnock Psalms."

As I stood by yon roofless tower,
  Where the wa'flow'r scents the dewy air,
Where the howlet mourns in her ivy bower,
  And tells the midnight moon her care.

Chorus.—A lassie all alone, was making her moan,
      Lamenting our lads beyond the sea ;
    In the bluidy wars they fa', and our
      honour's gane an' a',
    And broken-hearted we maun die.

The winds were laid, the air was still,
  The stars they shot along the sky ;
The tod was howling on the hill,
  And the distant-echoing glens reply.
    A lassie all alone, &c.

The Minstrel at Lincluden

The Minstrel at Lincluden

"And frae his harp sic strains did flow
Might rous'd the slumbering dead to hear."

The burn, adown its hazelly path,
  Was rushing by the ruin'd wa',
Hasting to join the sweeping Nith,
  Whase roarings seem'd to rise and fa'.
    A lassie all alone, &c.

The cauld blae North was streaming forth
  Her lights, wi' hissing, eerie din,
Athort the lift they start and shift,
  Like Fortune's favours, tint as win.
    A lassie all alone, &c.

Now, looking over frith and fauld,
  Her horn the pale-faced Cynthia rear'd,
When lo! in form of Minstrel auld,
  A stern and stalwart ghaist appear'd.
    A lassie all alone, &c.

And frae his harp sic strains did flow,
  Might rous'd the slumbering Dead to hear;
But O, it was a tale of woe,
  As ever met a Briton's ear!
    A lassie all alone, &c.

He sang wi' joy his former day,
  He, weeping, wail'd his latter times;
But what he said—it was nae play,
  I winna ventur't in my rhymes.
    A lassie all alone, &c.

A RED, RED ROSE

O my luve is like a red, red rose,
  That's newly sprung in June:
O my luve is like the melodie,
  That's sweetly play'd in tune.

As fair art thou, my bonie lass,
　So deep in luve am I;
And I will luve thee still, my dear,
　Till a the seas gang dry.

Till a' the seas gang dry, my dear,
　And the rocks melt wi' the sun;
And I will luve thee still, my dear,
　While the sands o' life shall run.

And fare-thee-weel, my only luve!
　And fare-thee-weel a while!
And I will come again, my luve,
　Tho' it were ten thousand mile

YOUNG JAMIE, PRIDE OF A' THE PLAIN

Tune—" The Carlin of the Glen.

YOUNG JAMIE, pride of a the plain,
Sae gallant and sae gay a swain,
Thro' a' our lasses he did rove,
And reign'd resistless King of Love.

But now, wi' sighs and starting tears,
He strays amang the woods and breirs;
Or in the glens and rocky caves,
His sad complaining dowie raves :—

" I wha sae late did range and rove,
And chang'd with every moon my love,
I little thought the time was near,
Repentance I should buy sae dear.

"The slighted maids my torments see,
And laugh at a' the pangs I dree;
While she, my cruel, scornful Fair,
Forbids me e'er to see her mair."

THE FLOWERY BANKS OF CREE

HERE is the glen, and here the bower
  All underneath the birchen shade;
The village-bell has tolled the hour;
  O what can stay my lovely maid?

'Tis not Maria's whispering call;
  'Tis but the balmy breathing gale,
Mixt with some warbler's dying fall
  The dewy star of eve to hail.

It is Maria's voice I hear;
  So calls the woodlark in the grove,
His little, faithful mate to cheer;
  At once tis music and tis love.

And art thou come? and art thou true?
  O welcome dear to love and me!
And let us all our vows renew,
  Along the flowery banks of Cree.

THE LOVELY LASS O' INVERNESS

THE lovely lass o Inverness,
  Nae joy nor pleasure can she see;
For e'en to morn she cries "alas!"
  And aye the saut tear blin's her e'e.

"Drumossie moor, Drumossie day—
  A waefu' day it was to me

For there I lost my father dear,
  My father dear, and brethren three.

" Their winding-sheet the bluidy clay,
  Their graves are growin green to see ;
And by them lies the dearest lad
  That ever blest a woman's e'e !

" Now wae to thee, thou cruel lord,
  A bluidy man I trow thou be ;
For mony a heart thou has made sair,
  That ne'er did wrang to thine or thee ! "

CHARLIE, HE'S MY DARLING

'Twas on a Monday morning,
  Right early in the year,
That Charlie came to our town,
  The young Chevalier.

Chorus—An' Charlie, he's my darling,
  My darling, my darling,
  Charlie, he's my darling,
  The young Chevalier.

As he was walking up the street,
  The city for to view,
O there he spied a bonie lass
  The window looking through.
    An' Charlie, &c.

Sae light's he jumped up the stair,
  And tirl'd at the pin ;
And wha sae ready as hersel'
  To let the laddie in.
    An' Charlie, &c.

He sets his Jenny on his knee,
　All in his Highland dress;
For brawlie weel he ken'd the way
To please a bonie lass,
　　　An' Charlie, &c.

It's up yon heathery mountain,
　An' down yon scroggie glen,
We daur na gang a milking,
For Charlie and his men,
　　　An' Charlie, &c.

BANNOCKS O' BEAR MEAL

Chorus—Bannocks o' bear meal,
　　　Bannocks o' barley,
　　Here's to the Highlandman's
　　　Bannocks o' barley!

Wha, in a brulyie, will
　First cry a parley?
Never the lads wi' the
　Bannocks o' barley,
　　　Bannocks o' bear meal, &c.

Wha, in his wae days,
　Were loyal to Charlie?
Wha but the lads wi' the
　Bannocks o' barley!
　　　Bannocks o' bear meal, &c.

THE HIGHLAND BALOU

Hee balou, my sweet wee Donald,
Picture o' the great Clanronald;
Brawlie kens our wanton Chief
Wha gat my young Highland thief.

Leeze me on thy bonie craigie,
An' thou live, thou'll steal a naigie,
Travel the country thro' and thro',
And bring hame a Carlisle cow.

Thro' the Lawlands, o'er the Border,
Weel, my babie, may thou furder!
Harry the louns o' the laigh Countrie,
Syne to the Highlands hame to me.

THE HIGHLAND WIDOW'S LAMENT

O, I am come to the Low Countrie,
 Ochon, Ochon, Ochrie!
Without a penny in my purse,
 To buy a meal to me.

It was na sae in the Highland hills,
 Ochon, Ochon, Ochrie!
Nae woman in the country wide,
 Sae happy was as me.

For then I had a score o' kye,
 Ochon, Ochon, Ochrie!
Feeding on yon hill sae high,
 And giving milk to me.

And there I had three score o' yowes,
 Ochon, Ochon, Ochrie!
Skipping on yon bonie knowes,
 And casting woo to me.

I was the happiest of a' the Clan,
 Sair, sair, may I repine;
For Donald was the brawest man,
 And Donald he was mine.

Till Charlie Stewart cam at last,
  Sae far to set us free ;
My Donald's arm was wanted then,
  For Scotland and for me.

Their waefu' fate what need I tell,
  Right to the wrang did yield ;
My Donald and his country fell,
  Upon Culloden field.

Ochon ! O Donald, oh !
  Ochon, Ochon, Ochrie !
Nae woman in the warld wide,
  Sae wretched now as me.

IT WAS A' FOR OUR RIGHTFU' KING

It was a' for our rightfu' King
  We left fair Scotland's strand ;
It was a' for our rightfu' King
  We e'er saw Irish land, my dear,
  We e'er saw Irish land.

Now a' is done that men can do,
  And a' is done in vain ;
My Love and Native Land fareweel,
  For I maun cross the main, my dear,
  For I maun cross the main.

He turn'd him right and round about,
  Upon the Irish shore ;
And gae his bridle reins a shake,
  With adieu for evermore, my dear,
  And adieu for evermore.

The soger frae the wars returns,
    The sailor frae the main;
But I hae parted frae my love,
    Never to meet again, my dear,
    Never to meet again.

When day is gane, and night is come,
    And a' folk bound to sleep;
I think on him that's far awa,
    The lee-lang night and weep, my dear,
    The lee-lang night and weep.

ON THE SEAS AND FAR AWAY

Tune—" O'er the hills and far away."

How can my poor heart be glad,
When absent from my sailor lad;
How can I the thought forego—
He's on the seas to meet the foe?
Let me wander, let me rove,
Still my heart is with my love;
Nightly dreams, and thoughts by day,
Are with him that's far away.

Chorus.—On the seas and far away,
        On stormy seas and far away;
        Nightly dreams and thoughts by day,
        Are aye with him that's far away.

When in summer noon I faint,
As weary flocks around me pant,
Haply in this scorching sun,
My sailor's thund'ring at his gun;

S. Mc Kenzie. S.A.   W. Holl.

Mrs Burns and one of her Grandchildren

After the portrait by S. M'Enzie

Bullets, spare my only joy !
Bullets, spare my darling boy !
Fate, do with me what you may,
Spare but him that's far away.
    On the seas and far away,
    On stormy seas and far away;
    Fate, do with me what you may
    Spare but him that's far away.

At the starless, midnight hour
When Winter rules with boundless power,
As the storms the forests tear,
And thunders rend the howling air,
Listening to the doubling roar,
Surging on the rocky shore,
All I can—I weep and pray
For his weal that's far away
    On the seas and far away,
    On stormy seas and far away ;
    All I can—I weep and pray,
    For his weal that's far away.

Peace, thy olive wand extend,
And bid wild War his ravage end,
Man with brother Man to meet,
And as brother kindly greet ;
Then may heav'n with prosperous gales
Fill my sailor s welcome sails ;
To my arms their charge convey,
My dear lad that's far away.
    On the seas and far away,
    On stormy seas and far away ;
    To my arms their charge convey,
    My dear lad that's far away.

CA' THE YOWES TO THE KNOWES

Second Version

Chorus.—Ca' the yowes to the knowes,
    Ca' them where the heather grows,
    Ca' them where the burnie rowes,
      My bonie dearie.

HARK the mavis' e'ening sang,
Sounding Clouden's woods amang;
Then a-faulding let us gang,
    My bonie dearie.
      Ca' the yowes, &c.

We'll gae down by Clouden side,
Thro' the hazels, spreading wide,
O'er the waves that sweetly glide,
    To the moon sae clearly.
      Ca' the yowes, &c.

Yonder Clouden's silent towers,
Where, at moonshine's midnight hours,
O'er the dewy bending flowers,
    Fairies dance sae cheery.
      Ca' the yowes, &c.

Ghaist nor bogle shalt thou fear,
Thou'rt to love and Heav'n sae dear,
Nocht of ill may come thee near;
    My bonie dearie.
      Ca' the yowes, &c.

Fair and lovely as thou art,
Thou hast stown my very heart;
I can die—but canna part,
    My bonie dearie.
      Ca' the yowes, &c.

SAE FLAXEN WERE HER RINGLETS

Tune—" Oonagh's Waterfall."

SAE flaxen were her ringlets,
  Her eyebrows of a darker hue,
Bewitchingly o'er-arching
  Twa laughing e'en o' lovely blue;
Her smiling, sae wiling,
  Wad make a wretch forget his woe;
What pleasure, what treasure,
  Unto these rosy lips to grow!
Such was my Chloris' bonie face,
  When first that bonie face I saw;
And aye my Chloris' dearest charm—
  She says, she lo'es me best of a'.

Like harmony her motion,
  Her pretty ankle is a spy,
Betraying fair proportion,
  Wad make a saint forget the sky:
Sae warming, sae charming,
  Her fautless form and gracefu' air;
Ilk feature—auld Nature
  Declar'd that she could do nae mair:
Hers are the willing chains o' love,
  By conquering Beauty's sovereign law;
And still my Chloris' dearest charm—
  She says, she lo'es me best of a'.

Let others love the city,
  And gaudy show, at sunny noon;
Gie me the lonely valley,
  The dewy eve and rising moon,

Fair beaming, and streaming
  Her silver light the boughs amang;
While falling, recalling,
  The amorous thrush concludes his sang;
There, dearest Chloris, wilt thou rove
  By wimpling burn and leafy shaw,
And hear my vows o' truth and love,
  And say thou lo'es me best of a' ?

PRETTY PEG

As I gaed up by yon gate-end,
  When day was waxin weary,
Wha did I meet come down the street,
  But pretty Peg, my dearie !

Her air sae sweet, an' shape complete,
  Wi' nae proportion wanting,
The Queen of Love did never move
  Wi' motion mair enchanting.

Wi' linkèd hands we took the sands,
  Adown yon winding river;
And O, that hour and shady bower,
  Can I forget it ? Never !

ESTEEM FOR CHLORIS

Ah, Chloris, since it may not be,
  That thou of love wilt hear;
If from the lover thou maun flee,
  Yet let the friend be dear.

Altho' I love my Chloris mair
  Than ever tongue could tell;
My passion I will ne'er declare—
  I'll say, I wish thee well.

Tho' a' my daily care thou art.
And a' my nightly dream,
I'll hide the struggle in my heart,
And say it is esteem.

SAW YE MY DEAR, MY PHILLY

Tune—" When she cam ben she bobbit."

O SAW ye my dear, my Philly?
O saw ye my dear, my Philly,
She's down i' the grove, she's wi' a new Love,
She winna come hame to her Willy.

What says she my dear, my Philly?
What says she my dear, my Philly?
She lets thee to wit she has thee forgot,
And forever disowns thee, her Willy.

O had I ne'er seen thee, my Philly!
O had I ne'er seen thee, my Philly!
As light as the air, and fause as thou's fair,
Thou's broken the heart o' thy Willy.

HOW LANG AND DREARY IS
THE NIGHT

How lang and dreary is the night
When I am frae my dearie;
I restless lie frae e'en to morn
Though I were ne'er sae weary.

Chorus.—For O, her lanely nights are lang!
And O, her dreams are eerie;
And O, her widow'd heart is sair,
That's absent frae her dearie!

When I think on the lightsome days
I spent wi' thee, my dearie ;
And now what seas between us roar,
How can I be but eerie ?
For oh, &c.

How slow ye move, ye heavy hours ;
The joyless day how dreary :
It was na sae ye glinted by,
When I was wi' my dearie !
For oh, &c.

INCONSTANCY IN LOVE

Tune—" Duncan Gray "

LET not women e'er complain
Of inconstancy in love ;
Let not women e'er complain
Fickle man is apt to rove :
Look abroad thro' Nature's range,
Nature's mighty Law is change,
Ladies, would it not seem strange
Man should then a monster prove !

Mark the winds, and mark the skies,
Ocean's ebb and ocean's flow ;
Sun and moon but set to rise ;
Round and round the seasons go.
Why then ask of silly man
To oppose great Nature's plan ?
We'll be constant while we can—
You can be no more you know.

THE LOVER'S MORNING SALUTE
TO HIS MISTRESS

Tune—" Deil tak the wars."

Sleep'st thou, or wak'st thou, fairest creature?
  Rosy morn now lifts his eye,
Numbering ilka bud which Nature
  Waters wi' the tears o' joy.
  Now to the streaming fountain,
  Or up the heathy mountain,
The hart, hind, and roe, freely, wildly-wanton
    stray;
  In twining hazel bowers
  Its lay the linnet pours;
  The laverock to the sky
  Ascends, wi' sangs o joy,
While the sun and thou arise to bless the day.

Phœbus, gilding the brow of morning,
  Banishes ilk darksome shade,
Nature gladdening and adorning;
  Such to me my lovely maid.
  When frae my Chloris parted,
  Sad, cheerless, broken-hearted,
The night's gloomy shades, cloudy, dark, o'er-
    cast my sky.
  But when she charms my sight,
  In pride of Beauty's light—
  When thro' my very heart
  Her beaming glories dart;
'Tis then—'tis then I wake to life and joy!

THE WINTER OF LIFE

But lately seen in gladsome green,
    The woods rejoic'd the day;
Thro' gentle showers, the laughing flowers
    In double pride were gay:
But now our joys are fled
    On winter blasts awa;
Yet maiden May, in rich array,
    Again shall bring them a'.

But my white pow, nae kindly thowe
    Shall melt the snaws of Age;
My trunk of eild, but buss or beild,
    Sinks in Time's wintry rage.
Oh, Age has weary days,
    And nights o' sleepless pain:
Thou golden time o' youthfu' prime,
    Why comes thou not again!

MY CHLORIS, MARK HOW GREEN THE GROVES

Tune—"My lodging is on the cold ground."

My Chloris, mark how green the groves,
    The primrose banks how fair;
The balmy gales awake the flowers,
    And wave thy flaxen hair.

The lav'rock shuns the palace gay,
    And o'er the cottage sings:
For Nature smiles as sweet, I ween,
    To shepherds as to kings.

Let minstrels sweep the skilfu' string,
　　In lordly lighted ha' :
The shepherd stops his simple reed,
　　Blythe in the birken shaw.

The princely revel may survey
　　Our rustic dance wi' scorn ;
But are their hearts as light as ours,
　　Beneath the milk-white thorn ?

The shepherd in the flowery glen
　　In shepherd's phrase will woo :
The courtier tells a finer tale,
　　But is his heart as true ?

These wild-wood flowers I've pu'd, to deck
　　That spotless breast o' thine :
The courtiers' gems may witness love,
　　But 'tis na love like mine.

THE CHARMING MONTH OF MAY

Tune—" Daintie Davie."

It was the charming month of May,
When all the flow'rs were fresh and gay,
One morning, by the break of day,
　　The youthful, charming Chloe,
From peaceful slumber she arose,
Girt on her mantle and her hose,
And o'er the flow'ry mead she goes—
　　The youthful, charming Chloe.

Chorus.—Lovely was she by the dawn,
　　　　Youthful Chloe, charming Chloe,
　　　Tripping o'er the pearly lawn,
　　　　The youthful, charming Chloe.

Q

The feather'd people you might see
Perch'd all around on every tree,
In notes of sweetest melody
   They hail the charming Chloe;
Till, painting gay the eastern skies,
The glorious sun began to rise,
Outrival'd by the radiant eyes
   Of youthful, charming Chloe.
      Lovely was she, &c.

LASSIE WI' THE LINT-WHITE LOCKS

Tune—"Rothiemurchie's Rant."

Chorus—Lassie wi' the lint-white locks,
         Bonie lassie, artless lassie,
         Wilt thou wi' me tent the flocks,
            Wilt thou be my dearie, O?

Now Nature cleeds the flowery lea,
And a' is young and sweet like thee,
O wilt thou share its joys wi' me,
   And say thou'lt be my dearie, O?
      Lassie wi' the, &c.

The primrose bank, the wimpling burn,
The cuckoo on the milk-white thorn,
The wanton lambs at early morn,
   Shall welcome thee, my dearie, O.
      Lassie wi' the, &c.

And when the welcome simmer shower
Has cheer'd ilk drooping little flower,
We'll to the breathing wood-bine bower,
   At sultry noon, my dearie, O.
      Lassie wi' the, &c.

When Cynthia lights, wi' silver ray,
The weary shearer's hameward way,
Thro' yellow waving fields we'll stray,
　　And talk o' love, my dearie, O.
　　Lassie wi' the, &c.

And when the howling wintry blast
Disturbs my lassie's midnight rest,
Enclaspèd to my faithfu' breast,
　　I'll comfort thee, my dearie, O.
　　Lassie wi' the, &c.

PHILLY AND WILLY

Tune—" The Sow's tail to Geordie."

He.　O PHILLY, happy be that day,
　　When roving thro' the gather'd hay,
　　My youthfu' heart was stown away,
　　　　And by thy charms, my Philly.
She.　O Willy, aye I bless the grove
　　Where first I own'd my maiden love,
　　Whilst thou did pledge the Powers above
　　　　To be my ain dear Willy.
Both.　For a' the joys that gowd can gie,
　　I dinna care a single flie;
　　The $\left\{{lad \atop lass}\right\}$ I love's the $\left\{{lad \atop lass}\right\}$ for me,
　　　And that's my ain dear $\left\{{Willy. \atop Philly.}\right\}$

He.　As songsters of the early year,
　　Are ilka day mair sweet to hear,
　　So ilka day to me mair dear
　　　　And charming is my Philly.

She. As on the brier the budding rose,
Still richer breathes and fairer blows,
So in my tender bosom grows
    The love I bear my Willy.
Both. For a' the joys, &c.

He. The milder sun and bluer sky
That crown my harvest cares wi' joy,
Were ne'er sae welcome to my eye
    As is a sight o' Philly.
She. The little swallow's wanton wing,
Tho' wafting o'er the flowery Spring,
Did ne'er to me sic tidings bring
    As meeting o' my Willy,
Both. For a' the joys, &c.

He. The bee that thro' the sunny hour
Sips nectar in the op'ning flower,
Compar'd wi' my delight is poor
    Upon the lips o' Philly.
She. The woodbine in the dewy weet,
When ev'ning shades in silence meet,
Is nocht sae fragrant or sae sweet
    As is a kiss o' Willy.
Both. For a' the joys, &c.

He. Let fortune's wheel at random rin,
And fools may tine, and knaves may win;
My thoughts are a' bound up in ane,
    And that's my ain dear Philly.
She. What's a' the joys that gowd can gie?
I dinna care a single flie;
The lad I love's the lad for me,
    And that's my ain dear Willy.
Both. For a' the joys, &c.

CONTENTED WI' LITTLE AND CANTIE WI' MAIR

Tune—"Lumps o' Puddin'."

CONTENTED wi' little, and cantie wi' mair,
Whene'er I forgather wi' Sorrow and Care,
I gie them a skelp as they're creeping alang,
Wi' a cog o' gude swats and an auld Scottish sang.
　　　　Chorus—Contented wi' little, &c.

I whiles claw the elbow o' troublesome thought;
But Man is a soger, and Life is a faught;
My mirth and gude humour are coin in my pouch,
And my Freedom's my lairdship nae monarch
　　dare touch.
　　　　　　　Contented wi' little, &c.

A towmond o' trouble, should that be my fa',
A night o' gude fellowship sowthers it a':
When at the blythe end o' our journey at last,
Wha the deil ever thinks o' the road he has past ?
　　　　　　　Contented wi' little, &c.

Blind Chance, let her snapper and stoyte on her
　　way ;
Be't to me, be't frae me, e'en let the jade gae :
Come Ease, or come Travail, come Pleasure or
　　Pain,
My warst word is : "Welcome, and welcome
　　again ! "
　　　　　　　Contented wi' little, &c.

FAREWELL THOU STREAM

Air—Nansie's to the greenwood gane."

FAREWELL, thou stream that winding flows
　　Around Eliza's dwelling ;

O mem'ry ! spare the cruel throes
  Within my bosom swelling.
Condemn d to drag a hopeless chain
  And yet in secret languish ;
To feel a fire in every vein,
  Nor dare disclose my anguish.

Love's veriest wretch, unseen, unknown,
  I fain my griefs would cover ;
The bursting sigh, th' unweeting groan,
  Betray the hapless lover.
I know thou doom'st me to despair,
  Nor wilt, nor can'st relieve me ;
But, O Eliza, hear one prayer—
  For pity's sake forgive me !

The music of thy voice I heard,
  Nor wist while it enslav'd me ;
I saw thine eyes, yet nothing fear'd,
  Till fears no more had sav'd me.
Th' unwary sailor thus, aghast
  The wheeling torrent viewing,
'Mid circling horrors sinks at last,
  In overwhelming ruin.

CANST THOU LEAVE ME THUS,
MY KATIE

Tune—" Roy's Wife."

Chorus—Canst thou leave me thus, my Katie ?
        Canst thou leave me thus, my Katie ?
        Well thou know'st my aching heart,
        And canst thou leave me thus, for pity ?

Is this thy plighted, fond regard,
   Thus cruelly to part, my Katie?
Is this thy faithful swain's reward—
   An aching, broken heart, my Katie!
      Canst thou leave me, &c.

Farewell! and ne'er such sorrows tear
   That fickle heart of thine, my Katie!
Thou mayst find those will love thee dear,
   But not a love like mine, my Katie,
      Canst thou leave me, &c.

MY NANIE'S AWA

Tune—"There'll never be peace till Jamie comes hame."

Now in her green mantle blythe Nature arrays,
And listens the lambkins that bleat o'er the braes;
While birds warble welcomes in ilka green shaw,
But to me it's delightless—my Nanie's awa.

The snawdrap and primrose our woodlands adorn,
And violets bathe in the weet o' the morn;
They pain my sad bosom, sae sweetly they blaw,
They mind me o' Nanie—and Nanie's awa.

Thou lav'rock that springs frae the dews of the
      lawn,
The shepherd to warn o' the grey-breaking dawn,
And thou mellow mavis that hails the night-fa',
Give over for pity—my Nanie's awa.

Come Autumn, sae pensive, in yellow and grey,
And soothe me wi' tidings o' Nature's decay:
The dark, dreary Winter, and wild-driving snaw
Alane can delight me—now Nanie's awa.

THE TEAR-DROP

Wae is my heart, and the tear's in my e'e;
Lang, lang Joy's been a stranger to me :
Forsaken and friendless, my burden I bear,
And the sweet voice o' Pity ne'er sounds in my
    ear.

Love thou hast pleasures, and deep hae I lov'd;
Love, thou hast sorrows, and sair hae I prov'd;
But this bruisèd heart that now bleeds in my breast,
I can feel by its throbbings, will soon be at rest.

Of, if I were—where happy I hae been—
Down by yon stream, and yon bonie castle-green;
For there he is wand'ring and musing on me,
Wha wad soon dry the tear frae his Phillis' e'e.

FOR THE SAKE O' SOMEBODY

My heart is sair—I dare na tell,
    My heart is sair for Somebody;
I could wake a winter night
    For the sake o' Somebody.
        O-hon! for Somebody!
        O-hey! for Somebody!
I could range the world around,
    For the sake o' Somebody.

Ye Powers that smile on virtuous love,
    O, sweetly smile on Somebody!
Frae ilka danger keep him free,
    And send me safe my Somebody!
        O-hon! for Somebody!
        O-hey! for Somebody!
I wad do—what wad I not!
    For the sake o' Somebody

A MAN'S A MAN FOR A' THAT

Tune—" For a' that."

Is there for honesty poverty
  That hings his head, an' a' that;
The coward slave—we pass him by,
  We dare be poor for a' that!
For a' that, an' a' that,
  Our toils obscure an' a' that,
The rank is but the guinea's stamp,
  The man's the gowd for a' that.

What though on hamely fare we dine,
  Wear hoddin grey, an' a' that?
Gie fools their silks, and knaves their wine,
  A man's a man for a' that.
For a' that, an' a' that,
  Their tinsel show, an' a' that,
The honest man, tho' e'er sae poor,
  Is king o' men for a' that.

Ye see yon birkie ca'd a lord,
  Wha struts, an' stares, an' a' that;
Tho' hundreds worship at his word,
  He's but a coof for a' that.
For a' that, an' a' that,
  His ribband, star, an' a' that,
The man o' independent mind
  He looks an' laughs at a' that.

A prince can mak a belted knight,
  A marquis, duke, an' a' that;
But an honest man's aboon his might,
  Gude faith, he maunna fa' that!

Q*

For a' that, an' a' that,
  Their dignities an' a' that,
The pith o' sense, an' pride o' worth,
  Are higher rank than a' that.

Then let us pray that come it may,
  (As come it will for a' that,)
That Sense and Worth, o'er a' the earth,
  Shall bear the gree, an' a' that.
For a' that, an' a' that,
  It's coming yet for a' that,
That man to man, the world o'er,
  Shall brithers be for a' that.

CRAIGIEBURN WOOD

Sweet fa's the eve on Craigieburn,
  And blythe awakes the morrow;
But a' the pride o' Spring's return
  Can yield me nocht but sorrow.

I see the flowers and spreading trees,
  I hear the wild birds singing;
But what a weary wight can please,
  And Care his bosom wringing!

Fain, fain would I my griefs impart,
  Yet dare na for your anger;
But secret love will break my heart,
  If I conceal it langer.

If thou refuse to pity me,
  If thou shalt love another,
When yon green leaves fade frae the tree,
  Around my grave they'll wither.

Craigieburn Wood

Craigieburn Wood

"Sweet fa's the eve on Craigieburn
And blythe awakes the morrow . . . "

BONIE PEG-A-RAMSAY

CAULD is the e'enin blast,
   O' Boreas o'er the pool,
An' dawin it is dreary,
   When birks are bare at Yule.

Cauld blaws the e'enin blast,
   When bitter bites the frost,
And, in the mirk and dreary drift,
   The hills and glens are lost :

Ne'er sae murky blew the night
   That drifted o'er the hill,
But bonie Peg-a-Ramsay
   Gat grist to her mill.

THERE WAS A BONIE LASS

THERE was a bonie lass, and a bonie, bonie lass,
   And she lo'ed her bonie laddie dear ;
Till War's loud alarms tore her laddie frae her
   arms,
   Wi' mony a sigh, and a tear.

Over sea, over shore, where the cannons loudly
   roar,
   He still was a stranger to fear ;
And nocht could him quail, or his bosom assail,
   But the bonie lass he lo'ed sae dear.

WEE WILLIE GRAY

Tune—" Wee Totum Fogg."

WEE Willie Gray, an' his leather wallet,
Peel a willow wand to be him boots and jacket ;

The rose upon the breir will be him trews an'
    doublet,
The rose upon the breir will be him trews an'
    doublet.

Wee Willie Gray, and his leather wallet,
Twice a lily-flower will be him sark and gravat;
Feathers of a flee wad feather up his bonnet,
Feathers of a flee wad feather up his bonnet.

O AYE MY WIFE SHE DANG ME

Chorus—O aye my wife she dang me,
        An' aft my wife she bang'd me,
    If ye gie a woman a' her will,
        Gude faith ! she'll soon o'er-gang ye.

On peace an' rest my mind was bent,
    And, fool I was ! I married ;
But never honest man's intent
    Sae cursedly miscarried.
        O aye my wife, &c.

Some sairie comfort at the last,
    When a' thir days are done, man,
My pains o' hell on earth is past,
    I'm sure o' bliss aboon, man.
        O aye my wife, &c.

SCROGGAM, MY DEARIE

There was a wife wonn'd in Cockpen, Scroggam ;
She brew'd gude ale for gentlemen ;
    Sing auld Cowl lay ye down by me,
    Scroggam, my dearie, ruffum.

The gudewife's dochter fell in a fever, Scroggam;
The priest o' the parish he fell in anither;
　　Sing auld Cowl lay ye down by me,
　　　　Scroggam, my dearie, ruffum.

They laid the twa i' the bed thegither, Scroggam;
That the heat o' the tane might cool the tither;
　　Sing auld Cowl, lay ye down by me,
　　　　Scroggam, my dearie, ruffum.

GUDE ALE KEEPS THE HEART ABOON

Chorus—O gude ale comes and gude ale goes;
　　　　Gude ale gars me sell my hose,
　　　　Sell my hose, and pawn my shoon—
　　　　Gude ale keeps my heart aboon!

I HAD sax owsen in a pleugh,
And they drew a' weel eneugh:
I sell'd them a' just ane by ane—
Gude ale keeps the heart aboon!
　　O gude ale comes, &c.

Gude ale hauds me bare and busy,
Gars me moop wi' the servant hizzie,
Stand i' the stool when I hae done—
Gude ale keeps the heart aboon!
　　O gude ale comes, &c.

O STEER HER UP AN' HAUD HER GAUN

O STEER her up, an' haud her gaun,
　　Her mither's at the mill, jo;
An' gin she winna tak a man,
　　E'en let her tak her will, jo.

First shore her wi' a gentle kiss,
 And ca' anither gill, jo;
An' gin she tak the thing amiss,
 E'en let her flyte her fill, jo.

O steer her up, an' be na blate,
 An' gin she tak it ill, jo,
Then leave the lassie till her fate,
 And time nae langer spill, jo:
Ne'er break your heart for ae rebute,
 But think upon it still, jo:
That gin the lassie winna do't,
 Ye'll find anither will, jo.

O LET ME IN THIS AE NIGHT

O LASSIE, are ye sleepin yet,
Or are ye waukin, I wad wit?
For Love has bound me hand an' fit,
 And I would fain be in, jo.

 Chorus—O let me in this ae night,
   This ae, ae, ae night;
   O let me in this ae night,
   And rise, and let me in!

Thou hear'st the winter wind an' weet;
Nae star blinks thro' the driving sleet;
Tak pity on my weary feet,
 And shield me frae the rain, jo.
   O let me in, &c.

The bitter blast that round me blaws,
Unheeded howls, unheeded fa's;
The cauldness o' thy heart's the cause
 Of a' my care and pine, jo.
   O let me in, &c.

O let me in this ae night

O let me in this ae Night

"O let me in this ae night
This ae, ae, ae night."

HER ANSWER

O tell na me o' wind an' rain,
Upbraid na me wi' cauld disdain,
Gae back the gate ye cam again,
   I winna let ye in, jo.

    Chorus—I tell you now this ae night,
          This ae, ae, ae night ;
          And ance for a' this ae night,
          I winna let ye in, jo.

The snellest blast, at mirkest hours,
That round the pathless wand'rer pours
Is nocht to what poor she endures,
   That's trusted faithless man, jo.
         I tell you now, &c.

The sweetest flower that deck'd the mead,
Now trodden like the vilest weed—
Let simple maid the lesson read
   The weird may be her ain, jo.
         I tell you now, &c.

The bird that charm'd his summer day,
And now the cruel fowler's prey ;
Let that to witless woman say
   The gratefu' heart of man, jo !
         I tell you now, &c.

I'LL AYE CA' IN BY YON TOWN

Air—" I'll gang nae mair to yon toun."

Chorus—I'll aye ca' in by yon town,
        And by yon garden green again ;
    I'll aye ca' in by yon town,
        And see my bonie Jean again.

THERE's nane sall ken, there's nane can guess
　　What brings me back the gate again,
But she, my fairest faithfu' lass,
　　And stownlins we sall meet again.
　　　　　　I'll aye ca' in, &c.

She'll wander by the aiken tree,
　　When trystin time draws near again ;
And when her lovely form I see,
　　O haith ! she's doubly dear again.
　　　　　　I'll aye ca' in, &c.

O WAT YE WHA'S IN YON TOWN

Tune—" I'll gang nae mair to yon toun."

Chorus.—O wat ye wha's in yon town,
　　　　Ye see the e'enin sun upon,
　　　　　　The dearest maid's in yon town,
　　　　　　　That e'ening sun is shining on.

Now haply down yon gay green shaw,
　　She wanders by yon spreading tree ;
How blest ye flowers that round her blaw,
　　Ye catch the glances o' her e'e !
　　　　　　O wat ye wha's, &c.

How blest ye birds that round her sing,
　　And welcome in the blooming year ;
And doubly welcome be the Spring,
　　The season to my Jeanie dear.
　　　　　　O wat ye wha's, &c.

The sun blinks blythe in yon town,
　　Among the broomy braes sae green ;
But my delight in yon town,
　　And dearest pleasure, is my Jean.
　　　　　　O wat ye wha's, &c.

Without my Fair, not a' the charms
O' Paradise could yield me joy ;
But give me Jeanie in my arms
And welcome Lapland's dreary sky !
O wat ye wha's, &c.

My cave wad be a lover's bower,
Tho' raging Winter rent the air ;
And she a lovely little flower,
That I wad tent and shelter there.
O wat ye wha's, &c.

O sweet is she in yon town,
The sinkin sun's gane down upon ;
A fairer than's in yon town,
His setting beam ne'er shone upon.
O wat ye wha's, &c.

If angry Fate is sworn my foe,
And suff'ring I am doom'd to bear,
I careless quit aught else below,
But spare, O spare me Jeanie dear.
O wat ye wha's, &c.

For while life's dearest blood is warm,
Ae thought frae her shall ne'er depart,
And she, as fairest is her form,
She has the truest, kindest heart.
O wat ye wha's, &c.

THE CARDIN O'T, THE SPINNIN O'T

I coft a stane o' haslock woo,
To mak a wab to Johnie o't ;
For Johnie is my only jo,
I lo'e him best of onie yet.

Chorus—The cardin o't, the spinnin o't,
     The warpin o't, the winnin o't;
   When ilka ell cost me a groat,
     The tailor staw the lynin o't.

For tho' his locks be lyart grey,
   And tho' his brow be beld aboon,
Yet I hae seen him on a day,
   The pride of a' the parishen.
                    The cardin o't, &c.

THE LASS O' ECCLEFECHAN

Tune—"Jack o' Latin."

Gat ye me, O gat ye me,
   O gat ye me wi' naething?
Rock and reel, and spinning wheel,
   A mickle quarter basin:
Bye attour my gutcher has
   A heich house and a laich ane,
A' forbye my bonie sel,
   The toss o' Ecclefechan.

O haud your tongue now, Lucky Lang,
   O haud your tongue and jauner;
I held the gate till you I met,
   Syne I began to wander:
I tint my whistle and my sang,
   I tint my peace and pleasure;
But your green graff, now Lucky Lang,
   Wad airt me to my treasure.

THE COOPER O' CUDDY

Tune—" Bab at the Bowster."

Chorus—We'll hide the Cooper behint the door,
    Behint the door, behint the door,
    We'll hide the Cooper behint the door,
      And cover him under a mawn, O.

THE Cooper o' Cuddy came here awa,
He ca'd the girrs out o'er us a' ;
An' our gudewife has gotten a ca',
    That's anger'd the silly gudeman O.
      We'll hide the Cooper, &c.

He sought them out, he sought them in,
Wi' deil hae her ! an' deil hae him !
But the body he was sae doited and blin',
    He wist na where he was gaun O.
      We'll hide the Cooper, &c.

They cooper'd at e'en, they cooper'd at morn,
Till our gudeman has gotten the scorn ;
On ilka brow she's planted a horn,
    And swears that there they sall stan' O.
      We'll hide the Cooper, &c.

THE LASS THAT MADE THE BED TO ME

WHEN Januar' wind was blawing cauld,
    As to the north I took my way,
The mirksome night did me enfauld,
    I knew na whare to lodge till day :

By my gude luck a maid I met,
  Just in the middle o' my care,
And kindly she did me invite
  To walk into a chamber fair.

I bow'd fu' low unto this maid,
  And thank'd her for her courtesie;
I bow'd fu' low unto this maid,
  An' bade her make a bed to me;
She made the bed baith large and wide,
  Wi' twa white hands she spread it doun;
She put the cup to her rosy lips,
  And drank—"Young man, now sleep ye
  soun'."

  Chorus—The bonie lass made the bed to me,
        The braw lass made the bed to me,
        I'll ne'er forget till the day I die,
        The lass that made the bed to me.

She snatch'd the candle in her hand,
  And frae my chamber went wi' speed;
But I call'd her quickly back again,
  To lay some mair below my head:
A cod she laid below my head,
  And servèd me with due respect,
And, to salute her wi' a kiss,
  I put my arms about her neck.
        The bonie lass, &c.

"Haud aff your hands, young man!" she said,
  "And dinna sae uncivil be;
Gif ye hae ony luve for me,
  O wrang na my virginitie."

Her hair was like the links o' **gowd,**
  Her teeth were like the ivorie,
Her cheeks like lilies dipt in wine,
  The lass that made the bed to me :
      The bonie lass, &c.

Her bosom was the driven snaw,
  Twa drifted heaps sae fair to see ;
Her limbs the polish'd marble stane,
  The lass that made the bed to me.
I kiss'd her o'er and o'er again,
  And aye she wist na what to say :
I laid her 'tween me and the wa' ;
  The lassie thocht na lang till day.
      The bonie lass, &c.

Upon the morrow when we raise,
  I thank'd her for her courtesie ;
But aye she blush'd and aye she sigh'd,
  And said, " Alas, ye've ruin'd me."
I clasp'd her waist, and kiss'd her syne,
  While the tear stood twinklin' in her e'e ;
I said, " My lassie, dinna cry,
  For ye aye shall make the bed to me."
      The bonie lass, &c.

She took her mither's holland sheets,
  An' made them a' in sarks to me ;
Blythe and merry may she be,
  The lass that made the bed to me.

Chorus—The bonie lass made the bed to me,
     The braw lass made the bed to me ;
    I'll ne'er forget till the day I die.
     The lass that made the bed to me.

HAD I THE WYTE? SHE BADE ME

Had I the wyte, had I the wyte,
    Had I the wyte? she bade me;
She watch'd me by the hie-gate side,
    And up the loan she shaw'd me.
And when I wadna venture in,
    A coward loon she ca'd me:
Had Kirk an' State been in the gate,
    I'd lighted when she bade me.

Sae craftilie she took me ben,
    And bade me mak nae clatter;
" For our ramgunshoch, glum gudeman
    Is o'er ayont the water."
Whae'er shall say I wanted grace,
    When I did kiss and dawt her,
Let him be planted in my place,
    Syne say, I was the fautor.

Could I for shame, could I for shame,
    Could I for shame refus'd her?
And wadna manhood been to blame,
    Had I unkindly used her?
He claw'd her wi' the ripplin-kame,
    And blae and bluidy bruis'd her;
When sic a husband was frae hame,
    What wife but wad excus'd her!

I dighted aye her e'en sae blue,
    An' bann'd the cruel randy,
And weel I wat, her willing mou
    Was sweet as sugar-candie.

At gloamin-shot, it was I wot,
  I lighted on the Monday ;
But I cam thro' the Tyseday's dew,
  To wanton Willie's brandy.

DOES HAUGHTY GAUL INVASION THREAT

Tune—" Push about the Jorum."

Does haughty Gaul invasion threat ?
  Then let the louns beware, Sir ;
There's wooden walls upon our seas,
  And volunteers on shore, Sir :
The Nith shall run to Corsincon,
  And Criffel sink in Solway,
Ere we permit a Foreign Foe
  On British ground to rally !
We'll ne'er permit a Foreign Foe
  On British ground to rally !

O let us not, like snarling curs,
  In wrangling be divided,
Till, slap ! come in an unco loun,
  And wi' a rung decide it !
Be Britain still to Britain true,
  Among ourselves united ;
For never but by British hands
  Maun British wrangs be righted
No ! never but by British hands
  Shall British wrangs be righted !

The kettle o' the Kirk and State,
  Perhaps a clout may fail in't ;
But deil a foreign tinkler loun
  Shall ever ca' a nail in't.

Our fathers' blude the kettle bought,
　And wha wad dare to spoil it,
By Heav'ns! the sacrilegious dog
　Shall fuel be to boil it!
By Heav'ns! the sacrilegious dog
　Shall fuel be to boil it!

The wretch that would a tyrant own,
　And the wretch, his true-sworn brother,
Who would set the Mob above the Throne,
　May they be damn'd together!
Who will not sing "God save the King,"
　Shall hang as high's the steeple;
But while we sing "God save the King,"
　We'll ne'er forget THE PEOPLE!
But while we sing "God save the King,"
　We'll ne'er forget THE PEOPLE!

ADDRESS TO THE WOODLARK

Tune—" Loch Erroch Side."

O STAY, sweet warbling woodlark, stay,
Nor quit for me the trembling spray!
A hapless lover courts thy lay,
　Thy soothing, fond complaining.
Again, again that tender part,
That I may catch thy melting art;
For surely that wad touch her heart
　Wha kills me wi' disdaining.

Say, was thy little mate unkind,
And heard thee as the careless wind?
Oh, nocht but love and sorrow join'd,
　Sic notes o' woe could wauken!

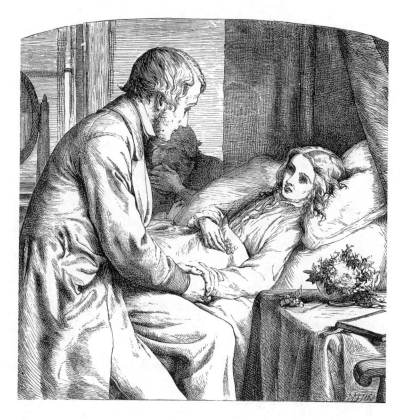

On Chloris being Ill

On Chloris being Ill

"Long, long the night
Heavy comes the morrow
While my soul's delight
Is on her bed of sorrow."

Thou tells o' never-ending care;
O' speechless grief, and dark despair:
For pity's sake, sweet bird, nae mair!
Or my poor heart is broken.

ON CHLORIS BEING ILL

Tune—" Aye wauken O."

Chorus—Long, long the night,
　　　Heavy comes the morrow
　　While my soul's delight
　　　Is on her bed of sorrow.

Can I cease to care?
　　Can I cease to languish,
While my darling Fair
　　Is on the couch of anguish?
　　　Long, long, &c.

Ev'ry hope is fled,
　　Ev'ry fear is terror;
Slumber ev'n I dread,
　　Ev'ry dream is horror.
　　　Long, long, &c.

Hear me, Powers Divine!
　　O, in pity, hear me!
Take aught else of mine,
　　But my Chloris spare me!
　　　Long, long, &c.

HOW CRUEL ARE THE PARENTS

Tune—" John Anderson, my jo."

How cruel are the parents
　　Who riches only prize,

And to the wealthy booby
  Poor Woman sacrifice !
Meanwhile, the hapless daughter
  Has but a choice of strife ;
To shun a tyrant father's hate—
  Become a wretched wife.

The ravening hawk pursuing,
  The trembling dove thus flies,
To shun impelling ruin,
  Awhile her pinions tries ;
Till, of escape despairing,
  No shelter or retreat,
She trusts the ruthless falconer,
  And drops beneath his feet.

MARK YONDER POMP OF COSTLY FASHION

Air—"Deil tak the wars."

MARK yonder pomp of costly fashion
  Round the wealthy, titled bride :
But when compar'd with real passion,
  Poor is all that princely pride.

  What are the showy treasures,
  What are the noisy pleasures ?
The gay, gaudy glare of vanity and art :
  The polish'd jewels blaze
  May draw the wond'ring gaze ;
  And courtly grandeur bright
  The fancy may delight,
But never, never can come near the heart.

But did you see my dearest Chloris,
  In simplicity's array ;

Lovely as yonder sweet opening flower is,
Shrinking from the gaze of day.

O then, the heart alarming,
And all resistless charming,
In Love's delightful fetters she chains the willing
    soul !
Ambition would disown
The world's imperial crown,
Ev'n Avarice would deny
His worshipp'd deity,
And feel thro' every vein Love's raptures roll.

'TWAS NA HER BONIE BLUE E'E

Tune—" Laddie, lie near me."

'Twas na her bonie blue e'e was my ruin,
Fair tho' she be, that was ne'er my undoin' ;
'Twas the dear smile when nae body did mind us,
'Twas the bewitching, sweet, stown glance o'
    kindness :
'Twas the bewitching, sweet, stown glance o'
    kindness.

Sair do I fear that to hope is denied me,
Sair do I fear that despair maun abide me,
But tho' fell fortune should fate us to sever,
Queen shall she be in my bosom for ever :
Queen shall she be in my bosom for ever.

Chloris, I'm thine wi' a passion sincerest,
And thou hast plighted me love o' the dearest,
And thou'rt the angel that never can alter—
Sooner the sun in his motion would falter :
Sooner the sun in his motion would falter.

THEIR GROVES O' SWEET MYRTLE

Tune—" Humours of Glen."

THEIR groves o' sweet myrtle let foreign lands
  reckon,
  Where bright-beaming summers exalt the per-
  fume ;
Far dearer to me yon lone glen o' green breckan,
  Wi' the burn stealing under the lang, yellow
  broom.
Far dearer to me are yon humble broom bowèrs
  Where the blue-bell and gowan lurk, lowly,
  unseen ;
For there, lightly tripping among the wild flowèrs,
  A-list'ning the linnet, aft wanders my Jean.

Tho' rich is the breeze in their gay, sunny valleys,
  And cauld Caledonia's blast on the wave ;
Their sweet-scented woodlands that skirt the
  proud palace,
  What are they ?—the haunt of the Tyrant and
  Slave.
The Slave's spicy forests, and gold-bubbling
  fountains,
  The brave Caledonian views wi' disdain ;
He wanders as free as the winds of his mountains,
  Save Love's willing fetters—the chains of his
  Jean.

FORLORN, MY LOVE, NO COM-FORT NEAR

Air—" Let me in this ae night."

FORLORN, my Love, no comfort near,
Far, far from thee, I wander here :

Far, far from thee, the fate severe,
  At which I most repine, Love.

Chorus—O wert thou, Love, but near me !
  But near, near, near me,
  How kindly thou wouldst cheer me,
    And mingle sighs with mine, Love.

Around me scowls a wintry sky,
Blasting each bud of hope and joy ;
And shelter, shade, nor home have I
  Save in these arms of thine, Love.
      O wert thou, &c.

Cold, alter'd friendship's cruel part,
To poison Fortune's ruthless dart—
Let me not break thy faithful heart,
  And say that fate is mine, Love.
      O wert thou, &c.

But, dreary tho' the moments fleet,
O let me think we yet shall meet ;
That only ray of solace sweet,
  Can on thy Chloris shine, Love !
      O wert thou, &c.

WHY, WHY TELL THY LOVER

Tune—"Caledonian Hunt's delight."

Why, why tell thy lover
  Bliss he never must enjoy ?
Why, why undeceive him,
  And give all his hopes the lie ?

O why, while fancy raptur'd slumbers,
 "Chloris, Chloris," all the theme,
Why, why would'st thou, cruel,
 Wake thy lover from his dream.

THE BRAW WOOER

Tune—" The Lothian Lassie."

LAST May, a braw wooer cam doun the lang
 glen,
 And sair wi' his love he did deave me;
I said, there was naething I hated like men—
 The deuce gae wi'm to believe me, believe
 me;
 The deuce gae wi'm to believe me.

He spak o' the darts in my bonie black e'en,
 And vow'd for my love he was diein,
I said, he might die when he likèd for Jean—
 The Lord forgie me for liein, for liein;
 The Lord forgie me for liein!

A weel-stockèd mailen, himsel' for the laird,
 And marriage aff-hand, were his proffers;
I never loot on that I kenn'd it, or car'd;
 But thought I might hae waur offers, waur
 offers;
 But thought I might hae waur offers.

But what wad ye think?—in a fortnight or less
 (The deil tak his taste to gae near her!)
He up the Gate-slack to my black cousin, Bess—
 Guess ye how, the jad! I could bear her,
 could bear her;
 Guess ye how, the jad! I could bear her.

The Braw Wooer

The Braw Wooer

"He beggèd for gudesake, I wad be his wife,
Or else I wad kill him wi' sorrow . . . "

But a' the niest week, as I petted wi' care,
  I gaed to the tryst o' Dalgarnock;
But wha but my fine fickle wooer was there,
  I glowr'd as I'd seen a warlock, a warlock,
  I glowr'd as I'd seen a warlock.

But owre my left shouther I gae him a blink,
  Lest neibours might say I was saucy;
My wooer he caper'd as he'd been in drink,
  And vow'd I was his dear lassie, dear lassie,
  And vow'd I was his dear lassie.

I spier'd for my cousin fu' couthy and sweet,
  Gin she had recover'd her hearin,
And how her new shoon fit her auld schachl't
    feet;
  But heavens! how he fell a swearing, a
    swearing,
  But heavens! how he fell a swearin.

He begged for gudesake, I wad be his wife,
  Or else I wad kill him wi' sorrow;
So e'en to preserve the poor body in life,
  I think I maun wed him to-morrow, to-
    morrow;
  I think I maun wed him to-morrow.

THIS IS NO MY AIN LASSIE

Tune—"This is no my house."

Chorus—This is no my ain lassie,
        Fair tho' the lassie be;
      Weel ken I my ain lassie,
        Kind love is in her e'e.

I SEE a form, I see a face,
Ye weel may wi' the fairest place ;
It wants, to me, the witching grace,
    The kind love that's in her e'e.
            This is no my ain, &c.

She's bonie, blooming, straight, and tall,
And lang has had my heart in thrall ;
And aye it charms my very saul,
    The kind love that's in her e'e.
            This is no my ain, &c.

A thief sae pawkie is my Jean,
To steal a blink, by a' unseen ;
But gleg as light are lover's een,
    When kind love is in the e'e.
            This is no my ain, &c.

It may escape the courtly sparks,
It may escape the learned clerks ;
But well the watching lover marks
    The kind love that's in her e'e.
            This is no my ain, &c.

O BONIE WAS YON ROSY BRIER

O BONIE was yon rosy brier,
    That blooms sae far frae haunt o' man ;
And bonie she, and ah, how dear !
    It shaded frae the e'ening sun.

Yon rosebuds in the morning dew,
    How pure, amang the leaves sae green ;
But purer was the lover's vow
    They witnessed in their shade yestreen.

Now Spring has Clad

Now Spring has Clad

"Now spring has clad the grove in green,
And strew'd the lea wi' flowers . . . "

All in its rude and prickly bower,
  That crimson rose, how sweet and fair ;
But love is far a sweeter flower,
  Amid life's thorny path o' care.

The pathless wild, and wimpling burn,
  Wi' Chloris in my arms, be mine ;
And I the warld nor wish nor scorn,
  Its joys and griefs alike resign.

NOW SPRING HAS CLAD

Now spring has clad the grove in green,
  And strew'd the lea wi' flowers ;
The furrow'd, waving corn is seen
  Rejoice in fostering showers.
While ilka thing in nature join
  Their sorrows to forego,
O why thus all alone are mine
  The weary steps o' woe !

The trout in yonder wimpling burn
  That glides, a silver dart,
And, safe beneath the shady thorn,
  Defies the angler's art—
My life was ance that careless stream,
  That wanton trout was I ;
But Love, wi' unrelenting beam,
  Has scorch'd my fountains dry.

That little floweret's peaceful lot,
  In yonder cliff that grows,
Which, save the linnet's flight, I wot,
  Nae ruder visit knows,
Was mine, till Love has o'er me past,
  And blighted a' my bloom ;

R

And now, beneath the withering blast,
My youth and joy consume.

The waken'd lav'rock warbling springs,
And climbs the early sky,
Winnowing blythe his dewy wings
In morning's rosy eye;
As little reck'd I sorrow's power,
Until the flowery snare
O' witching Love, in luckless hour,
Made me the thrall o' care.

O had my fate been Greenland snows,
Or Afric's burning zone,
Wi' man and nature leagued my foes,
So Peggy ne'er I'd known !
The wretch whose doom is "hope nae mair"
What tongue his woes can tell ;
Within whose bosom, save Despair,
Nae kinder spirits dwell.

O THAT'S THE LASSIE O' MY HEART

Tune—" Morag."

O WAT ye wha that lo'es me
And has my heart a-keeping?
O sweet is she that lo'es me,
As dews o' summer weeping,
In tears the rosebuds steeping !

Chorus—O that's the lassie o' my heart,
My lassie ever dearer ;
O she's the queen o' womankind,
And ne'er a ane to peer her

If thou shalt meet a lassie,
 In grace and beauty charming,
That e'en thy chosen lassie,
 Erewhile thy breast sae warming,
 Had ne'er sic powers alarming ;
  O that's the lassie, &c.

If thou hadst heard her talking,
 And thy attention's plighted,
That ilka body talking,
 But her, by thee is slighted,
 And thou art all-delighted ;
  O that's the lassie, &c.

If thou hast met this Fair One,
 When frae her thou hast parted,
If every other Fair One
 But her thou hast deserted,
 And thou art broken-hearted ;
  O that's the lassie o' my heart,
  My lassie ever dearer ;
  O that's the queen o' womankind,
  And ne'er a ane to peer her.

NEWS, LASSES, NEWS

There's news, lasses, news,
 Gude news I've to tell !
There's a boatfu' o' lads
 Come to our town to sell.

Chorus—The wean wants a cradle,
   And the cradle wants a cod :
  I'll no gang to my bed,
   Until I get a nod.

Father, quo' she, Mither, quo' she,
 Do what you can,
I'll no gang to my bed,
 Until I get a man.
             The wean, &c.

I hae as gude a craft-rig
 As made o' yird and stane ;
And waly fa' the ley-crap,
 For I maun till'd again.
             The wean, &c.

CROWDIE EVER MAIR

O THAT I had ne'er been married,
 I wad never had nae care,
Now I've gotten wife an' weans,
 An' they cry "Crowdie" ever mair.

Chorus—Ance crowdie, twice crowdie,
       Three times crowdie in a day ;
    Gin ye crowdie ony mair,
       Ye'll crowdie a' my meal away.

Waefu' Want and Hunger fley me,
 Glowrin by the hallan en' ;
Sair I fecht them at the door,
 But aye I'm eerie they come ben.
             Ance crowdie, &c.

MALLY'S MEEK, MALLY'S SWEET

Chorus.—Mally's meek, Mally sweet,
       Mally's modest and discreet ;
    Mally's rare, Mally's fair,
    Mally's every way complete.

As I was walking up the street,
　A barefit maid I chanc'd to meet;
But O the road was very hard
　For that fair maiden's tender feet.
　　　　　Mally's meek, &c.

It were mair meet that those fine feet
　Were weel laced up in silken shoon;
An' 'twere more fit that she should sit
　Within yon chariot gilt aboon.
　　　　　Mally's meek, &c.

Her yellow hair, beyond compare,
　Comes trinkling down her swan-white neck,
And her two eyes, like stars in skies,
　Would keep a sinking ship frae wreck.
　　　　　Mally's meek, &c.

JOCKEY'S TAEN THE PARTING KISS

Air—" Bonie lass tak a man."

Jockey's taen the parting kiss,
　O'er the mountains he is gane,
And with him is a' my bliss,
　Nought but griefs with me remain.
Spare my Love, ye winds that blaw,
　Plashy sleets and beating rain!
Spare my Love, thou feath'ry snaw,
　Drifting o'er the frozen plain!

When the shades of evening creep
　O'er the day's fair, gladsome e'e.
Sound and safely may he sleep,
　Sweetly blythe his waukening be.

He will think on her he loves,
  Fondly he'll repeat her name ;
For where'er he distant roves,
  Jockey's heart is still the same.

A LASS WI' A TOCHER

Tune—" Ballinamona Ora."

Awa' wi' your witchcraft o' Beauty's alarms,
The slender bit Beauty you grasp in your arms,
O, gie me the lass that has acres o' charms,
O, gie me the lass wi' the weel-stockit farms.

> *Chorus.*—Then hey, for a lass wi' a tocher,
>   Then hey, for a lass wi' a tocher ;
>   Then hey, for a lass wi' a tocher ;
>   The nice yellow guineas for me.

Your Beauty's a flower, in the morning that
    blows,
And withers the faster, the faster it grows :
But the rapturous charm o' the bonie green knowes,
Ilk spring they're new deckit wi' bonie white
    yowes.
                    Then hey, for a lass, &c.

And e'en when this Beauty your bosom hath
    blest,
The brightest o' Beauty may cloy when possess'd ;
But the sweet, yellow darlings wi' Geordie im-
    press'd,
The langer ye hae them, the mair they're carest.
                    Then hey, for a lass, &c.

O LAY THY LOOF IN MINE, LASS

Chorus.—O lay thy loof in mine, lass,
 In mine, lass, in mine, lass ;
 And swear on thy white hand, lass,
  That thou wilt be my ain.

A SLAVE to Love's unbounded sway,
 He aft has wrought me meikle wae ;
But now he is my deadly fae,
  Unless thou be my ain.
   O lay thy loof, &c.

There's mony a lass has broke my rest,
 That for a blink I hae lo'ed best ;
But thou art Queen within my breast,
  For ever to remain.
   O lay thy loof, &c.

A HEALTH TO ANE I LO'E DEAR

Chorus.—Here's a health to ane I lo'e dear,
  Here's a health to ane I lo'e dear ;
 Thou art sweet as the smile when fond
   lovers meet,
  And soft as their parting tear—Jessy.

ALTHO' thou maun never be mine,
 Altho' even hope is denied ;
'Tis sweeter for thee despairing,
 Than ought in the world beside—Jessy.
  Here's a health. &c.

I mourn thro' the gay, gaudy day,
    As hopeless I muse on thy charms;
But welcome the dream o' sweet slumber,
    For then I am lockt in thine arms—Jessy.
            Here's a health, &c.

I guess by the dear angel smile,
    I guess by the love-rolling e'e;
But why urge the tender confession,
    'Gainst Fortune's fell, cruel decree?—Jessy.
            Here's a health, &c.

O WERT THOU IN THE CAULD BLAST

O WERT thou in the cauld blast,
    On yonder lea, on yonder lea,
My plaidie to the angry airt,
    I'd shelter thee, I'd shelter thee;
Or did Misfortune s bitter storms
    Around thee blaw, around thee blaw,
Thy bield should be my bosom,
    To share it a', to share it a'

Or were I in the wildest waste,
    Sae black and bare, sae black and bare,
The desert were a Paradise,
    If thou wert there, if thou wert there;
Or were I Monarch o' the globe,
    Wi' thee to reign, wi' thee to reign,
The brightest jewel in my Crown
    Wad be my Queen, wad be my Queen.

Scene on the Devon

From an engraving after David Octavius Hill

Fairest Maid on Devon Banks

"Crystal Devon, winding Devon,
Wilt thou lay that frown aside,
And smile as thou wert wont to do?"

FAIREST MAID ON DEVON BANKS

Tune—" Rothiemurchie."

Chorus.—Fairest maid on Devon banks,
　　　Crystal Devon, winding Devon,
　　Wilt thou lay that frown aside,
　　　And smile as thou wert wont to do?

FULL well thou know'st I love thee dear,
Couldst thou to malice lend an ear !
O did not Love exclaim : " Forbear,
　Nor use a faithful lover so."
　　　Fairest maid, &c.

Then come, thou fairest of the fair,
Those wonted smiles, O, let me share ;
And by thy beauteous self I swear,
　No love but thine my heart shall know.
　　　Fairest maid, &c.

From a wood engraving by Thomas Bewick

EARLY AND MINOR PIECES
FRAGMENTS, EPIGRAMS AND EPITAPHS

TRAGIC FRAGMENT

ALL villain as I am—a damnèd wretch,
A hardened, stubborn, unrepenting sinner,—
Still my heart melts at human wretchedness;
And with sincere but unavailing sighs
I view the helpless children of distress:
With tears indignant I behold the oppressor
Rejoicing in the honest man's destruction,
Whose unsubmitting heart was all his crime.—
Ev'n you, ye hapless crew! I pity you;
Ye, whom the seeming good think sin to pity;
Ye poor, despised, abandoned vagabonds,
Whom Vice, as usual, has turn'd o'er to ruin.
Oh! but for friends and interposing Heaven,
I had been driven forth like you forlorn,
The most detested, worthless wretch among you!
O injured God! Thy goodness has endow'd me
With talents passing most of my compeers,
Which I in just proportion have abused—
As far surpassing other common villains
As Thou in natural parts has given me more.

THE TARBOLTON LASSES

IF ye gae up to yon hill-tap,
    Ye'll there see bonie Peggy;
She kens her father is a laird,
    And she forsooth's a leddy.

There Sophy tight, a lassie bright,
　　Besides a handsome fortune :
Wha canna win her in a night,
　　Has little art in courtin.

Gae down by Faile, and taste the ale,
　　And tak a look o' Mysie ;
She's dour and din, a deil within,
　　But aiblins she may please ye.

If she be shy, her sister try,
　　Ye'll maybe fancy Jenny ;
If ye'll dispense wi' want o' sense—
　　She kens hersel she's bonie.

As ye gae up by yon hillside,
　　Speir in for bonie Bessy ;
She'll gie ye a beck, and bid ye light,
　　And handsomely address ye.

There's few sae bonie, nane sae guid,
　　In a' King George' dominion ;
If ye should doubt the truth o' this—
　　It's Bessy's ain opinion !

THE RONALDS OF THE BENNALS

In Tarbolton, ye ken, there are proper young
　　men,
　　And proper young lasses and a', man ;
But ken ye the Ronalds that live in the Bennals,
　　They carry the gree frae them a', man.

Their father's a laird, and weel he can spare't,
　　Braid money to tocher them a', man ;
To proper young men, he'll clink in the hand
　　Gowd guineas a hundred or twa, man.

Tarbolton

From an engraving after David Octavius Hill

There's ane they ca' Jean, I'll warrant ye've seen
  As bonie a lass or as braw, man ;
But for sense and guid taste she'll vie wi' the
    best,
  And a conduct that beautifies a', man.

The charms o' the min', the langer they shine,
  The mair admiration they draw, man ;
While peaches and cherries, and roses and lilies,
  They fade and they wither awa, man.

If ye be for Miss Jean, tak this frae a frien',
  A hint o' a rival or twa, man ;
The Laird o' Blackbyre wad gang through the
    fire,
  If that wad entice her awa, man.

The Laird o' Braehead has been on his speed,
  For mair than a towmond or twa, man ;
The Laird o' the Ford will straught on a board,
  If he canna get her at a', man.

Then Anna comes in, the pride o' her kin,
  The boast of our bachelors a', man :
Sae sonsy and sweet, sae fully complete,
  She steals our affections awa, man.

If I should detail the pick and the wale
  O' lasses that live here awa, man,
The fau't wad be mine if they didna shine
  The sweetest and best o' them a', man.

I lo'e her mysel, but darena weel tell,
  My poverty keeps me in awe, man ;
For making o' rhymes, and working at times,
  Does little or naething at a', man.

Yet I wadna choose to let her refuse,
  Nor hae't in her power to say na, man:
For though I be poor, unnoticed, obscure,
  My stomach's as proud as them a', man.

Though I canna ride in weel-booted pride,
  And flee o'er the hills like a craw, man,
I can haud up my head wi' the best o' the breed,
  Though fluttering ever so braw, man.

My coat and my vest, they are Scotch o' the
    best,
  O' pairs o' guid breeks I hae twa, man;
And stockings and pumps to put on my stumps,
  And ne'er a wrang steek in them a', man.

My sarks they are few, but five o' them new,
  Twal' hundred, as white as the snaw, man,
A ten-shillings hat, a Holland cravat;
  There are no mony poets sae braw, man.

I never had frien's weel stockit in means,
  To leave me a hundred or twa, man;
Nae weel-tocher'd aunts, to wait on their drants,
  And wish them in hell for it a', man.

I never was cannie for hoarding o' money,
  Or claughtin 't together at a', man;
I've little to spend, and naething to lend,
  But deevil a shilling I awe, man.

WINTER: A DIRGE

The wintry west extends his blast,
  And hail and rain does blaw;
Or the stormy north sends driving forth
  The blinding sleet and snaw:

Winter: A Dirge

Winter: A Dirge

"While tumbling brown, the burn comes down,
and roars frae bank to brae . . . "

While, tumbling brown, the burn comes down,
  And roars frae bank to brae;
And bird and beast in covert rest,
  And pass the heartless day.

"The sweeping blast, the sky o'ercast,"
  The joyless winter day
Let others fear, to me more dear
  Than all the pride of May:
The tempest's howl, it soothes my soul,
  My griefs it seems to join;
The leafless trees my fancy please,
  Their fate resembles mine!

Thou Power Supreme whose mighty scheme
  These woes of mine fulfil,
Here firm I rest; they must be best,
  Because they are Thy will!
Then all I want—O do Thou grant
  This one request of mine!—
Since to enjoy Thou dost deny,
  Assist me to resign.

A PRAYER UNDER THE PRESSURE OF VIOLENT ANGUISH

O Thou Great Being! what Thou art,
  Surpasses me to know;
Yet sure I am, that known to Thee
  Are all Thy works below.

Thy creature here before Thee stands,
  All wretched and distrest;
Yet sure those ills that wring my soul
  Obey Thy high behest.

Sure Thou, Almighty, canst not act
　　From cruelty or wrath!
O, free my weary eyes from tears,
　　Or close them fast in death!

But, if I must afflicted be,
　　To suit some wise design,
Then man my soul with firm resolves,
　　To bear and not repine!

PARAPHRASE OF THE FIRST PSALM

The man, in life wherever plac'd,
　　Hath happiness in store,
Who walks not in the wicked's way,
　　Nor learns their guilty lore!

Nor from the seat of scornful pride
　　Casts forth his eyes abroad,
But with humility and awe
　　Still walks before his God.

That man shall flourish like the trees,
　　Which by the streamlets grow;
The fruitful top is spread on high,
　　And firm the root below.

But he whose blossom buds in guilt
　　Shall to the ground be cast,
And, like the rootless stubble, tost
　　Before the sweeping blast.

For why? that God the good adore,
　　Hath giv'n them peace and rest,
But hath decreed that wicked men
　　Shall ne'er be truly blest.

THE FIRST SIX VERSES OF THE NINETIETH PSALM VERSIFIED

O Thou, the first, the greatest friend
    Of all the human race !
Whose strong right hand has ever been
    Their stay and dwelling-place !

Before the mountains heav'd their heads
    Beneath Thy forming hand,
Before this ponderous globe itself,
    Arose at Thy command ;

That Pow'r which rais'd and still upholds
    This universal frame,
From countless, unbeginning time
    Was ever still the same.

Those mighty periods of years
    Which seem to us so vast,
Appear no more before Thy sight
    Than yesterday that's past.

Thou giv'st the word : Thy creature, man,
    Is to existence brought ;
Again Thou say'st, " Ye sons of men,
    Return ye into nought ! "

Thou layest them, with all their cares,
    In everlasting sleep ;
As with a flood Thou tak'st them off
    With overwhelming sweep.

They flourish like the morning flow'r,
    In beauty's pride array'd ;
But long ere night cut down it lies
    All wither'd and decay'd.

A PRAYER IN THE PROSPECT
OF DEATH

O Thou unknown, Almighty Cause
  Of all my hope and fear!
In whose dread presence, ere an hour,
  Perhaps I must appear!

If I have wander'd in those paths
  Of life I ought to shun,
As something, loudly, in my breast,
  Remonstrates I have done;

Thou know'st that Thou hast formed me
  With passions wild and strong;
And list'ning to their witching voice
  Has often led me wrong.

Where human weakness has come short,
  Or frailty stept aside,
Do Thou, All-Good—for such Thou art—
  In shades of darkness hide.

Where with intention I have err'd,
  No other plea I have,
But, Thou art good; and Goodness still
  Delighteth to forgive.

STANZAS, ON THE SAME
OCCASION

Why am I loth to leave this earthly scene?
  Have I so found it full of pleasing charms?
Some drops of joy with draughts of ill between;
  Some gleams of sunshine 'mid renewing storms.

Is it departing pangs my soul alarms?
Or death's unlovely, dreary, dark abode?
    For guilt, for guilt, my terrors are in arms;
I tremble to approach an angry God,
And justly smart beneath His sin-avenging rod.

Fain would I say, "Forgive my foul offence!"
Fain promise never more to disobey;
But, should my Author health again dispense,
    Again I might desert fair virtue's way;
    Again in folly's path might go astray;
Again exalt the brute and sink the man;
    Then how should I for heavenly mercy
        pray
Who act so counter heavenly mercy's plan?
Who sin so oft have mourn'd, yet to temptation
        ran?

O Thou, great Governor of all below!
    If I may dare a lifted eye to Thee,
Thy nod can make the tempest cease to blow,
    Or still the tumult of the raging sea:
    With that controlling pow'r assist ev'n me,
Those headlong furious passions to confine,
    For all unfit I feel my pow'rs to be,
To rule their torrent in th' allowèd line;
O, aid me with Thy help, Omnipotence Divine!

APOSTROPHE TO FERGUSON

WRITTEN ABOVE AND BELOW HIS PORTRAIT

CURSE on ungrateful man, that can be pleas'd
And yet can starve the author of the pleasure!

O thou, my elder brother in misfortune,
By far my elder brother in the Muse,
With tears I pity thy unhappy fate !
Why is the Bard unfitted for the world,
Yet has so keen a relish of its pleasures.

I'LL GO AND BE A SODGER

O why the deuce should I repine,
　And be an ill foreboder ?
I'm twenty-three, and five feet nine,
　I'll go and be a sodger !

I gat some gear wi' mickle care,
　I held it weel thegither ;
But now it's gane, and something mair—
　I'll go and be a sodger !

AH, WOE IS ME, MY MOTHER DEAR

Paraphrase of Jeremiah, xv 10.

Ah, woe is me, my Mother dear !
　A man of strife ye've born me :
For sair contention I maun bear ;
　They hate, revile, and scorn me.

I ne'er could lend on bill or band,
　That five per cent. might blest me ;
And borrowing, on the tither hand,
　The deil a ane wad trust me.

Yet I, a coin-denièd wight,
　By Fortune quite discarded ;
Ye see how I am, day and night,
　By lad and lass blackguarded !

REMORSE—A FRAGMENT

OF all the numerous ills that hurt our peace,
That press the soul, or wring the mind with
    anguish,
Beyond comparison the worst are those
By our own folly, or our guilt brought on :
In ev'ry other circumstance, the mind
Has this to say, " It was no deed of mine : "
But, when to all the evil of misfortune
This sting is added, " Blame thy foolish self ! "
Or worser far, the pangs of keen remorse,
The torturing, gnawing consciousness of guilt—
Of guilt, perhaps, when we've involvèd others,
The young, the innocent, who fondly lov'd us ;
Nay more, that very love their cause of ruin !
O burning hell ! in all thy store of torments
There's not a keener lash !
Lives there a man so firm, who, while his heart
Feels all the bitter horrors of his crime,
Can reason down its agonizing throbs ;
And, after proper purpose of amendment,
Can firmly force his jarring thoughts to peace ?
O happy, happy, enviable man !
O glorious magnanimity of soul !

EPITAPH ON WM. HOOD, SENR., IN TARBOLTON

HERE Souter Hood in death does sleep ;
    To hell if he's gane thither,
Satan, gie him thy gear to keep ;
    He'll haud it weel thegither.

EPITAPH ON JAMES GRIEVE, LAIRD OF BOGHEAD, TAR- BOLTON

HERE lies Boghead amang the dead
  In hopes to get salvation;
But if such as he in Heav'n may be,
  Then welcome, hail! damnation.

EPITAPH ON MY OWN FRIEND AND MY FATHER'S FRIEND, WM. MUIR IN TARBOLTON MILL

AN honest man here lies at rest,
As e'er God with his image blest;
The friend of man, the friend of truth,
The friend of age, and guide of youth:
Few hearts like his, with virtue warm'd,
Few heads with knowledge so inform'd:
If there's another world, he lives in bliss;
If there is none, he made the best of this.

EPITAPH ON MY EVER HONOURED FATHER

O YE whose cheek the tear of pity stains,
  Draw near with pious rev'rence, and attend!
Here lie the loving husband's dear remains,
  The tender father, and the gen'rous friend;
The pitying heart that felt for human woe,
  The dauntless heart that fear'd no human pride;
The friend of man—to vice alone a foe;
  For "ev'n his failings lean'd to virtue's side.

EPITAPH ON A NOISY POLEMIC

BELOW thir stanes lie Jamie's banes;
    O Death, it's my opinion,
Thou ne'er took such a bleth'rin bitch
    Into thy dark dominion!

EPITAPH ON A HENPECKED
COUNTRY SQUIRE

As father Adam first was fool'd,
    (A case that's still too common,)
Here lies a man a woman ruled,
    The devil ruled the woman.

EPIGRAM ON THE SAID
OCCASION

O DEATH, had'st thou but spar'd his life,
    Whom we this day lament,
We freely wad exchanged the wife,
    And a' been weel content.
Ev'n as he is, cauld in his graff,
    The swap we yet will do't;
Tak thou the carlin's carcase aff,
    Thou'se get the saul o' boot.

ANOTHER

ONE Queen Artemisia, as old stories tell,
When deprived of her husband she lovèd so well,
In respect for the love and affection he show'd her,
She reduc'd him to dust and she drank up the
    powder.

But Queen Netherplace, of a diff'rent complexion,
When called on to order the fun'ral direction,
Would have eat her dead lord, on a slender
    pretence,
Not to show her respect, but—to save the ex-
    pense !

ON TAM THE CHAPMAN

As Tam the chapman on a day,
Wi' Death forgather'd by the way,
Weel pleas'd, he greets a wight so famous,
And Death was nae less pleas'd wi' Thomas,
Wha cheerfully lays down his pack,
And there blaws up a hearty crack :
His social, friendly, honest heart
Sae tickled Death, they could na part ;
Sae, after viewing knives and garters,
Death taks him hame to gie him quarters.

EPITAPH ON JOHN RANKINE

Ae day, as Death, that gruesome carl,
Was driving to the tither warl'
A mixtie-maxtie motley squad,
And mony a guilt-bespotted lad—
Black gowns of each denomination,
And thieves of every rank and station,
From him that wears the star and garter,
To him that wintles in a halter :
Ashamed himself to see the wretches,
He mutters, glowrin at the bitches,
" By God I'll not be seen behint them,
Nor 'mang the sp'ritual core present them,

Without, at least, ae honest man,
To grace this damn'd infernal clan ! "
By Adamhill a glance he threw,
" Lord God ! " quoth he, " I have it now ;
There's just the man I want, i' faith ! "
And quickly stoppit Rankine's breath.

REPLY TO AN ANNOUNCEMENT
BY J. RANKINE

I AM a keeper of the law
In some sma' points, altho' not a' ;
Some people tell me gin I fa',
　　Ae way or ither,
The breaking of ae point, tho' sma',
　　Breaks a' thegither.

I hae been in for't ance or twice,
And winna say o'er far for thrice ;
Yet never met wi' that surprise
　　That broke my rest ;
But now a rumour's like to rise—
　　A whaup 's i' the nest !

THE BELLES OF MAUCHLINE

In Mauchline there dwells six proper young belles,
　　The pride of the place and its neighbourhood a' ;
Their carriage and dress, a stranger would guess,
　　In Lon'on or Paris, they'd gotten it a'.

Miss Miller is fine, Miss Markland's divine,
　　Miss Smith she has wit, and Miss Betty is braw :
There's beauty and fortune to get wi' Miss Morton,
　　But Armour's the jewel for me o' them a'.

EPITAPH ON JOHN DOVE, INNKEEPER

Here lies Johnie Pigeon;
What was his religion
　Whae'er desires to ken,
To some other warl'
Maun follow the carl,
　For here Johnie Pigeon had nane!

Strong ale was ablution,
Small beer persecution,
　A dram was *memento mori*;
But a full-flowing bowl
Was the saving his soul,
　And port was celestial glory.

EPITAPH FOR JAMES SMITH

Lament him, Mauchline husbands a',
　He aften did assist ye;
For had ye staid hale weeks awa,
　Your wives they ne'er had miss'd ye.

Ye Mauchline bairns, as on ye pass
　To school in bands thegither,
O tread ye lightly on his grass,—
　Perhaps he was your father!

ELEGY ON THE DEATH OF ROBERT RUISSEAUX

Now Robin lies in his last lair,
He'll gabble rhyme, nor sing nae mair;

Cauld poverty, wi' hungry stare,
> Nae mair shall fear him ;
Nor anxious fear, nor cankert care,
> E'er mair come near him.

To tell the truth, they seldom fash'd him,
Except the moment that they crush'd him ;
For sune as chance or fate had hush'd 'em
> Tho' e'er sae short,
Then wi' a rhyme or sang he lash'd 'em,
> And thought it sport.

Tho' he was bred to kintra-wark,
And counted was baith wight and stark,
Yet that was never Robin's mark
> To mak a man ;
But tell him, he was learn'd and clark,
> Ye roos'd him then !

A MAUCHLINE WEDDING

When Eighty-five was seven months auld
> And wearing thro' the aught,
When rolling rains and Boreas bauld
> Gied farmer-folks a faught ;
Ae morning quondam Mason W . . .
> Now Merchant Master Miller,
Gaed down to meet wi' Nansie B . . .
> And her Jamaica siller
> > To wed, that day.

The rising sun o'er Blacksideen
> Was just appearing fairly,
When Nell and Bess got up to dress
> Seven lang half-hours o'er early !

Now presses clink, and drawers jink
  For linens and for laces :
But modest Muses only *think*
  What ladies' underdress is
      On sic a day.

But we'll suppose the stays are lac'd,
  And bonie bosoms steekit,
Tho' thro' the lawn—but guess the rest !
  An angel scarce durst keek it.
Then stockins fine o' silken twine
  Wi' cannie care are drawn up,
An' garten'd tight whare mortal wight

   .   .   .

But now the gown wi' rustling sound
  Its silken pomp displays ;
Sure there's na sin in being vain
  O' siccan bonie claes !
Sae jimp the waist, the tail sae vast—
  Trouth, they were bonie birdies !
O Mither Eve, ye wad been grieve
  To see their ample hurdies
      Sae large that day.

Then Sandy, wi's red jacket braw,
  Comes whip-jee-woa ! about,
And in he gets the bonie twa,—
  Lord send them safely out.
And auld John Trot wi' sober phiz,
  As braid and braw's a Bailie,
His shouthers and his Sunday's jiz
  Wi' powther and wi' ulzie
      Weel smear'd that day.

   .   .   .

SUPPRESSED STANZAS OF "THE VISION"

After the 18th stanza of *Duan I.* (at "His native land"):—

WITH secret throes I marked that earth,
That cottage, witness of my birth;
And near I saw, bold issuing forth
    In youthful pride,
A Lindsay race of noble worth,
    Famed far and wide.

Where, hid behind a spreading wood,
An ancient Pict-built mansion stood,
I spied, among an angel brood,
    A female pair;
Sweet shone their high maternal blood,
    And father's air.

An ancient tower to memory brought
How Dettingen's bold hero fought;
Still, far from sinking into nought,
    It owns a lord
Who far in western climates fought,
    With trusty sword.

Among the rest I well could spy
One gallant, graceful, martial boy,
The *soldier* sparkled in his eye,
    A diamond water.
I blest that noble badge with joy,
    That owned me *frater.*

After the 20th stanza (at "Dispensing good"):—

Near by arose a mansion fine,
The seat of many a muse divine;

Not rustic muses such as mine,
  With holly crown'd,
But th' ancient, tuneful, laurell'd Nine,
  From classic ground.

I mourn'd the card that Fortune dealt,
To see where bonie Whitefoords dwelt;
But other prospects made me melt,
  That village near;
There Nature, Friendship, Love, I felt,
  Fond-mingling, dear!

Hail! Nature's pang, more strong than death!
Warm Friendship's glow, like kindling wrath!
Love, dearer than the parting breath
  Of dying friend!
Not ev'n with life's wild devious path,
  Your force shall end!

The Power that gave the soft alarms
In blooming Whitefoord's rosy charms,
Still threats the tiny, feather'd arms,
  The barbèd dart,
While lovely Wilhelmina warms
  The coldest heart.

After the 21st stanza (at " That, to adore ") :—

Where Lugar leaves his moorland plaid,
Where lately Want was idly laid,
I markèd busy, bustling Trade,
  In fervid flame,
Beneath a Patroness's aid,
  Of noble name.

Wild, countless hills I could survey,
And countless flocks as wild as they;
But other scenes did charms display,
            That better please,
Where polish'd manners dwell with Gray,
            In rural ease.

Where Cessnock pours with gurgling sound;
And Irwine, marking out the bound,
Enamour'd of the scenes around,
            Slow runs his race,
A name I doubly honour'd found,
            With knightly grace.

Brydon's brave ward, I saw him stand,
Fame humbly offering her hand,
And near, his kinsman's rustic band,
            With one accord,
Lamenting their late blessed land
            Must change its lord.

The owner of a pleasant spot,
Near sandy wilds, I last did note;
A heart too warm, a pulse too hot
            At times, o'erran:
But large in ev'ry feature wrote,
            Appear'd the Man.

INSCRIBED ON A WORK OF
HANNAH MORE'S

PRESENTED TO THE AUTHOR BY A LADY

THOU flatt'ring mark of friendship kind,
Still may thy pages call to mind

The dear, the beauteous donor ;
Tho' sweetly female ev'ry part,
Yet such a head, and more the heart
    Does both the sexes honour :
She show'd her taste refin'd and just,
    When she selected thee ;
Yet deviating, own I must,
    For sae approving me :
        But kind still I'll mind still
        The giver in the gift ;
        I'll bless her, an' wiss her
        A Friend aboon the lift.

VERSIFIED REPLY TO AN INVITATION

SIR,

Yours this moment I unseal,
    And faith I'm gay and hearty !
To tell the truth and shame the deil,
    I am as fou as Bartie :
But Foorsday, sir, my promise leal,
    Expect me o' your party,
If on a beastie I can speel,
    Or hurl in a cartie.
                        Yours,
                        ROBERT BURNS.

MAUCHLIN, *Monday night,* 10 *o'clock.*

TO JOHN KENNEDY, DUMFRIES HOUSE

Now, Kennedy, if foot or horse
E'er bring you in by Mauchlin corss,

(Lord, man, there's lasses there wad force
    A hermit's fancy;
An' down the gate in faith they're worse,
    An' mair unchancy).

But as I'm sayin, please step to Dow's,
An' taste sic gear as Johnie brews,
Till some bit callan bring me news
    That ye are there;
An' if we dinna hae a bouze,
    I'se ne'er drink mair.

It's no I like to sit an' swallow,
Then like a swine to puke an' wallow;
But gie me just a true guid fallow,
    Wi' right ingine,
And spunkie ance to mak us mellow,
    An' then we'll shine.

Now if ye're ane o' warl's folk,
Wha rate the wearer by the cloak,
An' sklent on poverty their joke,
    Wi' bitter sneer,
Wi' you nae friendship I will troke,
    Nor cheap nor dear.

But if, as I'm informèd weel,
Ye hate as ill's the very Deil
The flinty heart that canna feel—
    Come, sir, here's to you!
Hae, there's my haun', I wiss you weel,
    An' Gude be wi' you.
      ROBT. BURNESS.

MOSSGIEL, 3rd *March* 1786

TO MR M'ADAM, OF CRAIGEN-
GILLAN

IN ANSWER TO AN OBLIGING LETTER HE SENT IN THE COMMENCEMENT OF MY POETIC CAREER

Sir, o'er a gill I gat your card,
    I trow it made me proud;
" See wha taks notice o' the bard! "
    I lap and cried fu' loud.

Now deil-ma-care about their jaw,
    The senseless, gawky million;
I'll cock my nose abune them a',
    I'm roos'd by Craigen-Gillan!

'Twas noble, sir; 'twas like yoursel',
    To grant your high protection:
A great man's smile, ye ken fu'. well,
    Is aye a blest infection.

Tho', by his banes wha in a tub
    Match'd Macedonian Sandy!
On my ain legs thro' dirt and dub,
    I independent stand aye.

And when those legs to gude, warm kail,
    Wi' welcome canna bear me,
A lee dyke-side, a sybow-tail,
    An' barley-scone shall cheer me.

Heaven spare you lang to kiss the breath
    O' mony flow'ry simmers!
An' bless your bonie lasses baith,
    I'm tauld they're lo'esome kimmers!

Mauchline: Gavin Hamilton's House

From an engraving after David Octavius Hill

An' God bless young Dunaskin's laird,
  The blossom of our gentry !
An' may he wear an auld man's beard,
  A credit to his country.

TO GAVIN HAMILTON, ESQ., MAUCHLINE

RECOMMENDING A BOY

MOSSGAVILLE, *May* 3, 1786.

I HOLD it, sir, my bounden duty
To warn you how that Master Tootie,
  Alias, Laird M'Gaun,
Was here to hire yon lad away
'Bout whom ye spak the tither day,
  An' wad hae don't aff han' ;
But lest he learn the callan tricks—
  As faith I muckle doubt him—
Like scrapin out auld Crummie's nicks,
  An' tellin lies about them ;
    As lieve them, I'd have then
      Your clerkship he should sair,
    If sae be ye may be
      Not fitted otherwhere.

Altho' I say't, he's gleg enough,
An 'bout a house that's rude an' rough,
  The boy might learn to swear ;
But then wi' *you* he'll be sae taught,
An' get sic fair example straught,
  I hae na ony fear.
Ye'll catechise him, every quirk,
  An' shore him weel wi' hell ;

An' gar him follow to the kirk—
Aye when ye gang yoursel !
If ye then maun be then
Frae hame this comin Friday,
Then please sir, to lea'e, sir,
The orders wi' your lady.

My word of honour I hae gi'en,
In Paisley John's, that night at e'en,
To meet the warld's worm ;
To try to get the twa to gree,
An' name the airles an' the fee,
In legal mode an' form :
I ken he weel a snick can draw,
When simple bodies let him :
An' if a Devil be at a',
In faith he's sure to get him.
To phrase you and praise you,
Ye ken your Laureat scorns :
The pray'r still you share still
Of grateful Minstrel Burns.

EPITAPH FOR GAVIN HAMILTON, ESQ.

The poor man weeps—here Gavin sleeps,
Whom canting wretches blam'd ;
But with such as he, where'er he be,
May I be sav'd or damn'd !

EPITAPH ON WEE JOHNIE

Hic Jacet wee Johnie

Whoe'er thou art, O, reader, know
That Death has murder'd Johnie ;
An' here his *body* lies fu' low ;
For *saul* he ne'er had ony.

EPITAPH FOR ROBERT AIKEN, ESQ.

Know thou, O stranger to the fame
Of this much lov'd, much honoured name!
(For none that knew him need be told)
A warmer heart death ne'er made cold.

VERSIFIED NOTE TO DR MAC-KENZIE, MAUCHLINE

Friday first's the day appointed
By the Right Worshipful anointed,
    To hold our grand procession;
To get a blaud o' Johnie's morals,
And taste a swatch o' Manson's barrels
    I' the way of our profession.
The Master and the Brotherhood
    Would a' be glad to see you;
For me I would be mair than proud
    To share the mercies wi' you.
    If Death, then, wi' skaith then,
        Some mortal heart is hechtin,
    Inform him, and storm him,
        That Saturday you'll fecht him.
                                ROBERT BURNS.
Mossgiel, 14th June A. M. 5790.

STANZAS ON NAETHING

EXTEMPORE EPISTLE TO GAVIN HAMILTON, ESQ.

To you, sir, this summons I've sent,
    Pray, whip till the pownie is freathing;
But if you demand what I want,
    I honestly answer you—naething.

Ne'er scorn a poor Poet like me,
 For idly just living and breathing,
While people of every degree
 Are busy employed about—naething.

Poor Centum-per-centum may fast,
 And grumble his hurdies their claithing,
He'll find, when the balance is cast,
 He's gane to the devil for—naething.

The courtier cringes and bows,
 Ambition has likewise its plaything;
A coronet beams on his brows;
 And what is a coronet?—naething

Some quarrel the Presbyter gown,
 Some quarrel Episcopal graithing;
But every good fellow will own
 Their quarrel is a' about—naething.

The lover may sparkle and glow,
 Approaching his bonie bit gay thing:
But marriage will soon let him know
 He's gotten—a buskit-up naething.

The Poet may jingle and rhyme,
 In hopes of a laureate wreathing,
And when he has wasted his time,
 He's kindly rewarded wi'—naething.

The thundering bully may rage,
 And swagger and swear like a heathen;
But collar him fast, I'll engage
 You'll find that his courage is—naething.

Last night wi' a feminine whig—
 A poet she couldna put faith in;

But soon we grew lovingly big,
    I taught her, her terrors were—naething.

Her whigship was wonderful pleased,
    But charmingly tickled wi' ae thing ;
Her fingers I lovingly squeezed,
    And kissed her, and promised her—naething

The priest anathèmas may threat—
    Predicament, sir, that we're baith in ;
But when honour's reveillé is beat,
    The holy artillery's—naething.

And now I must mount on the wave—
    My voyage perhaps there is death in ;
But what is a watery grave ?
    The drowning a Poet is—naething.

And now, as grim death's in my thought,
    To you, sir, I make this bequeathing ;
My service as long as ye've ought,
    And my friendship, by God, when ye've
        naething.

THE FAREWELL

The valiant, in himself, what can he suffer ?
Or what does he regard his single woes ?
But when, alas ! he multiplies himself,
To dearer selves, to the lov'd tender fair,
To those whose bliss, whose beings hang upon him,
To helpless children,—then, Oh then, he feels
The point of misery festering in his heart,
And weakly weeps his fortunes like a coward :
Such, such am I !—undone !
                THOMSON's *Edward and Eleanora.*

FAREWELL, old Scotia's bleak domains,
    Far dearer than the torrid plains,

s*

Where rich ananas blow!
Farewell, a mother's blessing dear!
A brother's sigh! a sister's tear!
My Jean's heart-rending throe!
Farewell, my Bess! tho' thou'rt bereft
  Of my paternal care,
A faithful brother I have left,
  My part in him thou'lt share!
    Adieu, too, to you too,
      My Smith, my bosom frien';
    When kindly you mind me,
      O then befriend my Jean!

What bursting anguish tears my heart;
From thee, my Jeany, must I part!
  Thou, weeping, answ'rest—"No!"
Alas! misfortune stares my face,
And points to ruin and disgrace,
  I for thy sake must go!
Thee, Hamilton, and Aiken dear,
  A grateful, warm adieu:
I, with a much-indebted tear,
  Shall still remember you!
    All hail then, the gale then,
      Wafts me from thee, dear shore!
    It rustles, and whistles
      I'll never see thee more!

THE CALF

To the Rev. JAMES STEVEN, on his text, MALACHI, ch.
iv. vers, 2. "And ye shall go forth, and grow up, as
CALVES of the stall."

RIGHT, sir! your text I'll prove it true,
  Tho' heretics may laugh;

For instance, there's yoursel just now,
    God knows, an unco *calf*.

And should some patron be so kind,
    As bless you wi' a kirk,
I doubt na, sir, but then we'll find,
    Ye're still as great a *stirk*.

But, if the lover's raptur'd hour,
    Shall ever be your lot,
Forbid it, ev'ry heavenly Power,
    You e'er should be a *stot !*

Tho' when some kind connubial dear
    Your but-and-ben adorns,
The like has been that you may wear
    A noble head of *horns*.

And, in your lug, most reverend James,
    To hear you roar and rowt,
Few men o' sense will doubt your claims
    To rank amang the *nowt*.

And when ye're number'd wi' the dead,
    Below a grassy hillock,
With justice they may mark your head—
    " Here lies a famous *bullock !* "

MOTTO PREFIXED TO THE AUTHOR'S FIRST PUBLICATION

THE simple Bard, unbroke by rules of art,
He pours the wild effusions of the heart;
And if inspir'd, 'tis Nature's pow'rs inspire;
Her's all the melting thrill, and her's the kindling
    fire.

LINES TO MR JOHN KENNEDY

FAREWELL, dear friend ! may guid luck hit you,
And 'mang her favourites admit you :
If e'er Detraction shore to smit you,
   May nane believe him,
And ony deil that thinks to get you,
   Good Lord, deceive him !

LINES TO AN OLD SWEETHEART

ONCE fondly lov'd, and still remember'd dear,
 Sweet early object of my youthful vows,
Accept this mark of friendship, warm, sincere,
 Friendship ! 'tis all cold duty now allows.

And when you read the simple artless rhymes,
 One friendly sigh for him——he asks no more,
Who, distant, burns in flaming torrid climes,
 Or haply lies beneath th' Atlantic roar.

LINES WRITTEN ON A BANKNOTE

WAE worth thy power, thou cursed leaf,
Fell source o' a' my woe and grief ;
For lack o' thee I've lost my lass,
For lack o' thee I scrimp my glass :
I see the children of affliction
Unaided, through thy curst restriction :
I've seen the oppressor's cruel smile
Amid his hapless victim's spoil ;
And for thy potence vainly wished,
To crush the villain in the dust :
For lack o' thee, I leave this much-lov'd shore,
Never, perhaps, to greet old Scotland more.
       R. B.

KYLE.

WILLIE CHALMERS

Wi' braw new branks in mickle pride,
    And eke a braw new brechan,
My Pegasus I'm got astride,
    And up Parnassus pechin ;
Whiles owre a bush wi' downward crush
    The doited beastie stammers ;
Then up he gets, and off he sets,
    For sake o' Willie Chalmers.

I doubt na, lass, that weel-ken'd name
    May cost a pair o' blushes ;
I am nae stranger to your fame,
    Nor his warm-urgèd wishes.
Your bonie face, sae mild and sweet,
    His honest heart enamours ;
And faith ye'll no be lost a whit,
    Tho' wair'd on Willie Chalmers.

Auld Truth hersel' might swear ye're fair,
    And Honour safely back her ;
And Modesty assume your air,
    And ne'er a ane mistak her :
And sic twa love-inspiring een
    Might fire even holy palmers ;
Nae wonder then they've fatal been
    To honest Willie Chalmers.

I doubt na fortune may you shore
    Some mim-mou'd pouther'd priestie,
Fu' lifted up wi' Hebrew lore,
    And band upon his breastie :

But oh ! what signifies to you
  His lexicons and grammars ?
The feeling heart's the royal blue,
  And that's wi' Willie Chalmers.

Some gapin, glowrin countra laird
  May warsle for your favour ;
May claw his lug, and straik his beard,
  And hoast up some palaver :
My bonie maid, before ye wed
  Sic clumsy-witted hammers,
Seek Heaven for help, and barefit skelp
  Awa wi' Willie Chalmers.

Forgive the Bard ! my fond regard
  For ane that shares my bosom,
Inspires my Muse to gie 'm his dues,
  For deil a hair I roose him.
May powers aboon unite you soon,
  And fructify your amours,—
And every year come in mair dear
  To you and Willie Chalmers.

PRAYER.—O THOU DREAD POWER

O Thou dread Power, who reign'st above,
  I know thou wilt me hear,
When for this scene of peace and love
  I make this prayer sincere.

The hoary Sire—the mortal stroke,
  Long, long be pleas'd to spare ;
To bless his little filial flock,
  And show what good men are

George Lawrie D.D.

George Lawrie D.D.

*"It was in George Lawrie's house that
the Prayer was written."*

She, who her lovely offspring eyes
  With tender hopes and fears,
O bless her with a mother's joys,
  But spare a mother's tears !

Their hope, their stay, their darling youth,
  In manhood's dawning blush,
Bless him, Thou God of love and truth,
  Up to a parent's wish.

The beauteous, seraph sister-band—
  With earnest tears I pray—
Thou know'st the snares on ev'ry hand,
  Guide Thou their steps alway.

When, soon or late, they reach that coast,
  O'er Life's rough ocean driven,
May they rejoice, no wand'rer lost,
  A family in Heaven !

FRAGMENT ON SENSIBILITY

RUSTICITY's ungainly form
  May cloud the highest mind ;
But when the heart is nobly warm,
  The *good* excuse will find.

Propriety's cold, cautious rules
  Warm fervour may o'erlook :
But spare poor sensibility
  Th' ungentle, harsh rebuke.

TO MISS LOGAN

WITH BEATTIE'S POEMS FOR A NEW-YEAR'S GIFT,
JAN. 1, 1787

AGAIN the silent wheels of time
  Their annual round have driven,

And you, tho' scarce in maiden prime,
Are so much nearer Heaven.

No gifts have I from Indian coasts
The infant year to hail;
I send you more than India boasts,
In Edwin's simple tale.

Our sex with guile, and faithless love,
Is charg'd, perhaps too true;
But may, dear maid, each lover prove
An Edwin still to you.

EXTEMPORE IN THE COURT OF SESSION

Tune—"Killiecrankie."

LORD ADVOCATE

HE clenched his pamphlets in his fist,
He quoted and he hinted,
Till, in a declamation-mist,
His argument he tint it:
He gapèd for't, he grapèd for't,
He fand it was awa, man;
But what his common sense came short,
He ekèd out wi' law, man.

MR ERSKINE

Collected, Harry stood awee,
Then open'd out his arm, man;
His Lordship sat wi' ruefu' e'e,
And ey'd the gathering storm, man:
Like wind-driven hail it did assail,
Or torrents owre a lin, man:
The BENCH sae wise lift up their eyes,
Half-wauken'd wi' the din, man.

INSCRIPTION FOR THE HEAD-STONE OF FERGUSSON THE POET

No sculptured marble here, nor pompous lay,
"No storied urn nor animated bust;"
This simple stone directs pale Scotia's way,
To pour her sorrows o'er the Poet's dust.

ADDITIONAL STANZAS

She mourns, sweet tuneful youth, thy hapless fate;
Tho' all the powers of song thy fancy fired,
Yet Luxury and Wealth lay by in state,
And, thankless, starv'd what they so much
admired.

This humble tribute, with a tear, he gives,
A brother Bard—he can no more bestow:
But dear to fame thy Song immortal lives,
A nobler monument than Art can shew.

EPIGRAM AT ROSLIN INN

My blessings on ye, honest wife!
I ne'er was here before;
Ye've wealth o' gear for spoon and knife—
Heart could not wish for more.
Heav'n keep you clear o' sturt and strife,
Till far ayont fourscore,
And by the Lord o' death and life,
I'll ne'er gae by your door!

EPIGRAM ADDRESSED TO AN ARTIST

Dear———, I'll gie ye some advice,
You'll tak it no uncivil:

You shouldna paint at angels, man,
　But try and paint the devil.
To paint an Angel's kittle wark,
　Wi' Nick there's little danger :
You'll easy draw a lang-kent face,
　But no sae weel a stranger.

TO MISS ISABELLA MACLEOD

THE crimson blossom charms the bee,
　The summer sun the swallow :
So dear this tuneful gift to me
　From lovely Isabella.

Her portrait fair upon my mind
　Revolving time shall mellow,
And mem'ry's latest effort find
　The lovely Isabella.

No bard nor lover's rapture this
　In fancies vain and shallow !
She is, so come my soul to bliss,
　The lovely Isabella.

EDINBURGH, *March* 16*th,* 1787.

PASSION'S CRY

MILD zephyrs waft thee to life's farthest shore,
Nor think of me and my distresses more.—
Falsehood accurst !　No ! still I beg a place,
Still near thy heart some little, little trace :
For that dear trace the world I would resign :
O let me live, and die, and think it mine !

By all I lov'd neglected and forgot,
No friendly face e'er lights my squalid cot ;
Shunn'd, hated, wrong'd, unpitied, unredrest !
The mock'd quotation of the scorner's jest !

Ev'n the poor súpport of my wretched life,
Snatched by the violence of legal strife.
Oft grateful for my very daily bread
To those my family's once large bounty fed ;
A welcome inmate at their homely fare,
My griefs, my woes, my sighs, my tears they share :
Their vulgar souls unlike the souls refin'd,
The fashioned marble of the polished mind.

"I burn, I burn, as when thro' ripen'd corn
By driving winds the crackling flames are borne."
Now raving-wild, I curse that fatal night,
Then bless the hour that charm'd my guilty sight :
In vain the laws their feeble force oppose,
Chain'd at Love's feet, they groan, his vanquish'd
      foes ;
In vain Religion meets my shrinking eye,
I dare not combat, but I turn and fly :
Conscience in vain upbraids th' unhallow'd fire,
Love grasps her scorpions—stifled they expire !
Reason drops headlong from his sacred throne,
Your dear idea reigns, and reigns alone ;
Each thought intoxicated homage yields,
And riots wanton in forbidden fields.
By all on high adoring mortals know !
By all the conscious villain fears below !
By your dear self !—the last great oath I swear,
Not life, nor soul, were ever half so dear !

VERSES INTENDED TO BE WRITTEN BELOW A NOBLE EARL'S PICTURE

Whose is that noble, dauntless brow ?
    And whose that eye of fire ?

And whose that generous princely mien,
    Ev'n rooted foes admire?

Stranger! to justly show that brow,
    And mark that eye of fire,
Would take *His* hand, whose vernal tints
    His other works admire.

Bright as a cloudless summer sun,
    With stately port he moves;
His guardian Seraph eyes with awe
    The noble Ward he loves.

Among the illustrious Scottish sons
    That chief thou may'st discern,
Mark Scotia's fond-returning eye,—
    It dwells upon Glencairn.

PROLOGUE

SPOKEN BY MR WOODS ON HIS BENEFIT-NIGHT,
MONDAY, 16TH APRIL 1787

When, by a generous Public's kind acclaim,
That dearest meed is granted—honest fame;
When here your favour is the actor's lot,
Nor even the man in private life forgot;
What breast so dead to heavenly Virtue's glow,
But heaves impassion'd with a grateful throe?

Poor is the task to please a barb'rous throng,
It needs no Siddons' powers in Southern's song;
But here an ancient nation, fam'd afar
For genius, learning high, as great in war,—
Hail, CALEDONIA, name for ever dear!
Before whose sons I'm honour'd to appear!

Where every science, every nobler art,
That can inform the mind or mend the heart,
Is known ; as grateful nations oft have found,
Far as the rude barbarian marks the bound.
Philosophy, no idle pedant dream,
Here holds her search by heaven-taught Reason's
    beam ;
Here History paints with elegance and force
The tide of Empire's fluctuating course ;
Here Douglas forms wild Shakespeare into plan,
And Harley rouses all the God in man.
When well-form'd taste and sparkling wit unite
With manly lore, or female beauty bright,
(Beauty, where faultless symmetry and grace
Can only charm us in the second place),
Witness my heart, how oft with panting fear,
As on this night, I've met these judges here !
But still the hope Experience taught to live,
Equal to judge—you're candid to forgive.
No hundred-headed riot here we meet,
With decency and law beneath his feet ;
Nor insolence assumes fair Freedom's name :
Like CALEDONIANS, you applaud or blame.

O Thou, dread Power ! whose empire-giving hand
Has oft been stretch'd to shield the honour'd land !
Strong may she glow with all her ancient fire ;
May every son be worthy of his sire ;
Firm may she rise, with generous disdain
At Tyranny's, or direr Pleasure's chain ;
Still Self-dependent in her native shore,
Bold may she brave grim Danger's loudest roar,
Till Fate the curtain drop on worlds to be no
    more.

THE BOOK-WORMS

THROUGH and through th' inspirèd leaves,
　Ye maggots, make your windings ;
But O respect his lordship's taste,
　And spare the golden bindings.

ON ELPHINSTONE'S TRANSLA-
TION OF MARTIAL'S EPIGRAMS

O THOU whom Poesy abhors,
Whom Prose has turnèd out of doors,
Heard'st thou yon groan ?—proceed no further,
'Twas laurel'd Martial calling " murther."

ON JOHNSON'S OPINION OF
HAMPDEN

For shame !
Let Folly and Knavery Freedom oppose :
'Tis suicide, Genius, to mix with her foes.

LINES WRITTEN UNDER THE PIC-
TURE OF THE CELEBRATED
MISS BURNS

CEASE, ye prudes, your envious railing,
　Lovely Burns has charms—confess :
True it is, she had ae failing,
　Had ae woman ever less ?

EPITAPH FOR WILLIAM NICOL, OF
THE HIGH SCHOOL, EDINBURGH

YE maggots, feed on Nicol's brain,
　For few sic feasts you've gotten ;
And fix your claws in Nicol's heart,
　For deil a bit o't's rotten.

From: Ian Anderson <misa.manorgreen@virgin.net>
To: eking@easynet.co.uk <eking@easynet.co.uk>
Date: 13 October 1999 06:10
Subject: Burns Poem

The poem I was telling you about is called:-
    Epitaph on a Schoolmaster
in Cleish Parish, Kinross-shire.

    Here lie Willie Michie's banes;
    O Satan, when ye tak him,
    Gie him the schoolin' of your weans,
    For clever diels he'll mak them!

I hope Mr Michie's family were amused by it!
    Rgds, Ian

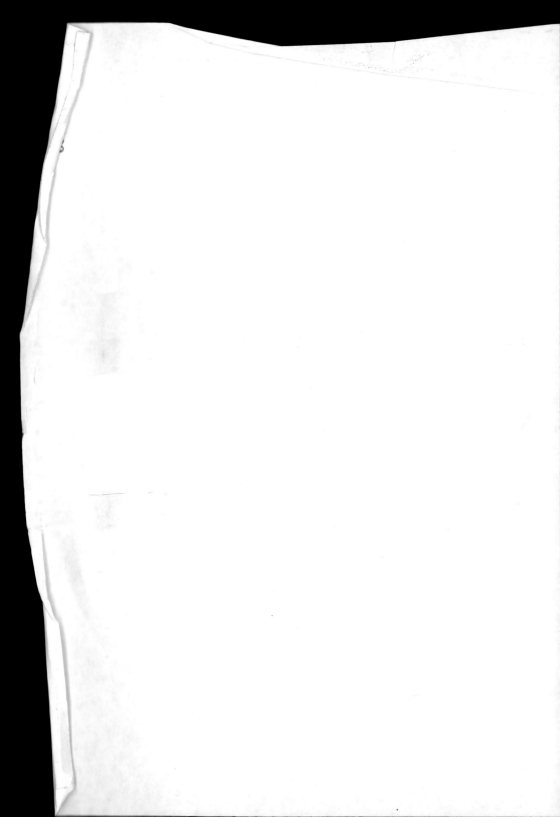

EPITAPH FOR MR WILLIAM MICHIE

SCHOOLMASTER OF CLEISH PARISH, FIFESHIRE

HERE lie Willie Michie's banes :
O Satan, when ye tak him,
Gie him the schulin o' your weans,
For clever deils he'll mak them !

EPIGRAM TO MISS AINSLIE IN CHURCH

FAIR maid, you need not take the hint,
Nor idle texts pursue :
'Twas guilty sinners that he meant,
Not Angels such as you.

NOTE TO MR RENTON OF LAMERTON

YOUR billet, Sir, I grant receipt ;
Wi' you I'll canter ony gate,
Tho' 'twere a trip to yon blue warl',
Whare birkies march on burning marl :
Then, Sir, God willing, I'll attend ye,
And to his goodness I commend ye.
                                   R. BURNS.

EPIGRAM TO MISS JEAN SCOTT

O HAD each Scot of ancient times
Been Jeanie Scott, as thou art,
The bravest heart on English ground
Had yielded like a coward.

THE BARD AT INVERARY

Whoe'er he be that sojourns here,
 I pity much his case,
Unless he come to wait upon
 The Lord their God,—His Grace.

There's naething here but Highland pride,
 And Highland scab and hunger:
If Providence has sent me here,
 'Twas surely in an anger.

ON THE DEATH OF JOHN M'LEOD, ESQ.

BROTHER TO A YOUNG LADY, A PARTICULAR FRIEND OF THE AUTHOR'S

Sad thy tale, thou idle page,
 And rueful thy alarms:
Death tears the brother of her love
 From Isabella's arms.

Sweetly deckt with pearly dew
 The morning rose may blow;
But cold successive noontide blasts
 May lay its beauties low.

Fair on Isabella's morn
 The sun propitious smil'd;
But, long ere noon, succeeding clouds
 Succeeding hopes beguil'd.

Fate oft tears the bosom chords
 That Nature finest strung;
So Isabella's heart was form'd,
 And so that heart was wrung.

Dread Omnipotence alone
 Can heal the wound he gave—
Can point the brimful grief-worn eyes
 To scenes beyond the grave.

Virtue's blossoms there shall blow,
 And fear no withering blast;
There Isabella's spotless worth
 Shall happy be at last.

TO MISS FERRIER

ENCLOSING THE ELEGY ON SIR J. H. BLAIR

Nae heathen name shall I prefix,
 Frae Pindus or Parnassus;
Auld Reekie dings them a' to sticks,
 For rhyme-inspiring lasses.

Jove's tunefu' dochters three times three
 Made Homer deep their debtor;
But, gien the body half an e'e,
 Nine Ferriers wad done better!

Last day my mind was in a bog,
 Down George's Street I stoited;
A creeping cauld prosaic fog
 My very senses doited.

Do what I dought to set her free,
 My saul lay in the mire;
Ye turned a neuk, I saw your e'e,
 She took the wing like fire!

The mournfu' sang I here enclose,
 In gratitude I send you,
And pray, in rhyme as weel as prose,
 A' gude things may attend you!

IMPROMPTU ON CARRON IRON WORKS

WE cam na here to view your warks,
    In hopes to be mair wise,
But only, lest we gang to hell,
    It may be nae surprise :

But when we tirl'd at your door
    Your porter dought na bear us ;
Sae may, shou'd we to Hell's yetts come,
    Your billy Satan sair us !

WRITTEN BY SOMEBODY ON THE WINDOW

OF AN INN AT STIRLING, ON SEEING THE ROYAL PALACE IN RUINS

HERE Stuarts once in glory reigned,
And laws for Scotland's weal ordained ;
But now unroof'd their palace stands,
Their sceptre fallen to other hands ;
Fallen indeed, and to the earth
Whence grovelling reptiles take their birth.
The injured Stuart line is gone,
A race outlandish fills their throne ;
An idiot race, to honour lost ;
Who know them best despise them most.

THE POET'S REPLY TO THE THREAT OF A CENSORIOUS CRITIC

WITH Esop's lion, Burns says, sore I feel
Each other blow, but damn that ass's heel !

THE LIBELLER'S SELF-REPROOF

Rash mortal, and slanderous poet, thy name
Shall no longer appear in the records of Fame !
Dost not know that old Mansfield, who writes
    like the Bible,
Says, the more 'tis a truth, sir, the more 'tis a
    libel !

VERSES WRITTEN WITH A PENCIL

OVER THE CHIMNEY-PIECE, IN THE PARLOUR OF
THE INN AT KENMORE, TAYMOUTH

Admiring Nature in her wildest grace,
These northern scenes with weary feet I trace ;
O'er many a winding dale and painful steep,
Th' abodes of covey'd grouse and timid sheep,
My savage journey, curious, I pursue,
Till fam'd Breadalbane opens to my view.—
The meeting cliffs each deep-sunk glen divides,
The woods wild scatter'd, clothe their ample
    sides ;
Th' outstretching lake, imbosomed 'mong the
    hills,
The eye with wonder and amazement fills ;
The Tay meand'ring sweet in infant pride,
The palace rising on his verdant side,
The lawns wood-fring'd in Nature's native taste,
The hillocks dropt in Nature's careless haste,
The arches striding o'er the new-born stream,
The village glittering in the noontide beam—
   *   *   *   *   *

Poetic ardours in my bosom swell,
Lone wand'ring by the hermit's mossy cell;
The sweeping theatre of hanging woods,
Th' incessant roar of headlong tumbling floods—
* * * * *

Here Poesy might wake her heav'n-taught lyre,
And look through Nature with creative fire;
Here, to the wrongs of Fate half reconcil'd,
Misfortune's lighten'd steps might wander wild;
And Disappointment, in these lonely bounds,
Find balm to soothe her bitter rankling wounds:
Here heart-struck Grief might heav'nward stretch
     her scan,
And injur'd Worth forget and pardon man.
* * * * *

LINES ON THE FALL OF FYERS
NEAR LOCH-NESS
WRITTEN WITH A PENCIL ON THE SPOT

AMONG the heathy hills and ragged woods
The roaring Fyers pours his mossy floods;
Till full he dashes on the rocky mounds,
Where, thro' a shapeless breach, his stream
     resounds.
As high in air the bursting torrents flow,
As deep recoiling surges foam below,
Prone down the rock the whitening sheet descends,
And viewless Echo's ear, astonished, rends.
Dim-seen, through rising mists and ceaseless·
     show'rs,
The hoary cavern, wide surrounding, lours:
Still thro' the gap the struggling river toils,
And still, below, the horrid cauldron boils—
* * * * *

The Fall of Fyers

The Fall of Fyers

"Among the heathy hills and ragged woods
The roaring Fyers pours his mossy floods."

EPIGRAM ON PARTING WITH A KIND HOST IN THE HIGHLANDS

When Death's dark stream I ferry o'er,
(A time that surely shall come),
In Heav'n itself I'll ask no more,
Than just a Highland welcome.

TO MISS CRUICKSHANK

A very Young Lady

WRITTEN ON THE BLANK LEAF OF A BOOK, PRE-
SENTED TO HER BY THE AUTHOR

Beauteous Rosebud, young and gay,
Blooming on thy early May,
Never may'st thou, lovely flower,
Chilly shrink in sleety shower!
Never Boreas' hoary path,
Never Eurus' pois'nous breath,
Never baleful stellar lights,
Taint thee with untimely blights!
Never, never reptile thief
Riot on thy virgin leaf!
Nor even Sol too fiercely view
Thy bosom blushing still with dew!

May'st thou long, sweet crimson gem,
Richly deck thy native stem;
Till some ev'ning, sober, calm,
Dropping dews, and breathing balm,
While all around the woodland rings,
And ev'ry bird thy requiem sings;

Thou, amid the dirgeful sound,
Shed thy dying honours round,
And resign to parent Earth
The loveliest form she e'er gave birth.

FOR WILLIAM CRUICKSHANK, A.M.

Now honest William's gaen to Heaven,
  I wat na gin't can mend him :
The fauts he had in Latin lay,
  For nane in English kend them.

SYLVANDER TO CLARINDA

EXTEMPORE REPLY TO VERSES ADDRESSED TO THE
AUTHOR BY A LADY, UNDER THE SIGNA-
TURE OF "CLARINDA"

WHEN dear Clarinda, matchless fair,
  First struck Sylvander's raptur'd view,
He gaz'd, he listened to despair,
  Alas ! 'twas all he dared to do.

Love, from Clarinda's heavenly eyes,
  Transfixed his bosom thro' and thro';
But still in Friendship's guarded guise,
  For more the demon fear'd to do.

That heart, already more than lost,
  The imp beleaguer'd all *perdu* ;
For frowning Honour kept his post—
  To meet that frown he shrunk to do.

His pangs the Bard refused to own,
  Tho' half he wish'd Clarinda knew ;

But Anguish wrung the unweeting groan—
  Who blames what frantic Pain must do?

That heart, where motley follies blend,
  Was sternly still to Honour true:
To prove Clarinda's fondest friend,
  Was what a lover sure might do.

The Muse his ready quill employed,
  No nearer bliss he could pursue;
That bliss Clarinda cold deny'd—
  " Send word by Charles how you do ! "

The chill behest disarm'd his muse,
  Till passion all impatient grew:
He wrote, and hinted for excuse,
  'Twas 'cause " he'd nothing else to do."

But by those hopes I have above !
  And by those faults I dearly rue !
The deed, the boldest mark of love,
  For thee that deed I dare to do !

O could the Fates but name the price
  Would bless me with your charms and
    you !
With frantic joy I'd pay it thrice,
  If human art and power could do !

Then take, Clarinda, friendship's hand,
  (Friendship, at least, I may avow;)
And lay no more your chill command,—
  I'll write, whatever I've to do.
                SYLVANDER.

VERSES TO CLARINDA

SENT WITH A PAIR OF WINE-GLASSES

Fair Empress of the poet's soul,
  And Queen of poetesses;
Clarinda, take this little boon,
  This humble pair of glasses:

And fill them up with generous juice,
  As generous as your mind;
And pledge them to the generous toast,
  " The whole of human kind! "

" To those who love us! " second fill;
  But not to those whom *we* love;
Lest we love those who love not us—
  A third—" To thee and me, love! "

TO ALEX. CUNNINGHAM

July 27th, 1788, ELLISLAND IN NITHSDALE

My godlike friend—nay, do not stare,
  You think the praise is odd-like;
But " God is love," the saints declare,
  Then surely thou art god-like.

And is thy ardour still the same?
  And kindled still in Anna?
Others may boast a partial flame,
  But thou art a volcano!

Ev'n Wedlock asks not love beyond
  Death's tie-dissolving portal;
But thou, omnipotently fond,
  May'st promise love immortal!

Verses to Clarinda

Verses to Clarinda

"Fair Empress of the poet's soul,
And Queen of poetesses . . . "

Thy wounds such healing powers defy,
  Such symptoms dire attend them,
That last great antihectic try—
  Marriage perhaps may mend them.

Sweet Anna has an air—a grace,
  Divine, magnetic, touching:
She talks, she charms—but who can trace
  The process of bewitching?.

VERSES IN FRIARS' CARSE HERMITAGE

First Version

Thou whom chance may hither lead,
Be thou clad in russet weed,
Be thou deckt in silken stole,
Grave these maxims on thy soul.

Life is but a day at most,
Sprung from night, in darkness lost:
Hope not sunshine every hour,
Fear not clouds will always lour.

Happiness is but a name,
Make content and ease thy aim,
Ambition is a meteor-gleam;
Fame a restless idle dream;

Pleasures, insects on the wing
Round peace, the tend'rest flow'r of spring;
Those that sip the dew alone—
Make the butterflies thy own;
Those that would the bloom devour—
Crush the locusts, save the flower.

T

For the future be prepar'd,
Guard wherever thou can'st guard;
But thy utmost duly done,
Welcome what thou can'st not shun.
Follies past, give thou to air,
Make their *consequence* thy care:
Keep the name of Man in mind,
And dishonour not thy kind.
Reverence with lowly heart
Him, whose wondrous work thou art;
Keep His Goodness still in view,
Thy trust, and thy example, too.

Stranger, go! Heaven be thy guide!
Quod the Beadsman of Nidside.

AT WHIGHAM'S INN, SANQUHAR

Envy, if thy jaundiced eye
Through this window chance to spy,
To thy sorrov' thou shalt find
All that's generous, all that's kind,
Friendship, virtue, every grace,
Dwelling in this happy place.

VERSICLES ON SIGN-POSTS

He looked just as your sign-post Lions do,
With aspect fierce, and quite as harmless too.

So heavy, passive to the tempest's shocks,
Dull on the sign-post stands the stupid ox.

His face with smile eternal drest,
Just like the landlord to his guest,
High as they hang with creaking din,
To index out the Country Inn.

A head, pure, sinless quite of brain and soul,
The very image of a barber's poll ;
Just shews a human face, and wears a wig,
And looks, when well friseur'd, amazing big.

PEGASUS AT WANLOCKHEAD

With Pegasus upon a day,
  Apollo weary flying
(Through frosty hills the journey lay),
  On foot the way was plying.

Poor slipshod giddy Pegasus
  Was but a sorry walker ;
To Vulcan then Apollo goes
  To get a frosty caulker.

Obliging Vulcan fell to work,
  Threw by his coat and bonnet,
And did Sol's business in a`crack ;
  Sol paid him with a sonnet.

Ye Vulcan's sons of Wanlockhead,
  Pity my sad disaster !
My Pegasus is poorly shod,
  I'll pay you like my master.

ON WILLIAM CREECH

A little, upright, pert, tart, tripping wight,
And still his precious self his dear delight ;
Who loves his own smart shadow in the streets,
Better than e'er the fairest She he meets ;
Much specious lore, but little understood,
(Veneering oft outshines the solid wood),

His solid sense, by inches you must tell,
But mete his cunning by the Scottish ell!
A man of fashion too, he made his tour,
Learn'd "vive la bagatelle et vive l'amour;"
So travell'd monkeys their grimace improve,
Polish their grin—nay, sigh for ladies' love!
His meddling vanity, a busy fiend,
Still making work his selfish craft must mend.

ON WILLIAM SMELLIE

  * * * Crochallan came,
The old cock'd hat, the brown surtout the same;
His grisly beard just bristling in its might—
'Twas four long nights and days to shaving-night;
His uncomb'd, hoary locks, wild-staring, thatch'd
A head, for thought profound and clear, un-
  match'd;
Yet, tho' his caustic wit was biting-rude,
His heart was warm, benevolent and good.

THE POET'S PROGRESS

Thou, Nature, partial Nature, I arraign;
Of thy caprice maternal I complain.
 The peopled fold thy kindly care have found,
The horned bull, tremendous, spurns the ground;
The lordly lion has enough and more,
The forest trembles at his very roar;
Thou giv'st the ass his hide, the snail his shell,
The poisonous wasp, victorious, guards his cell.
Thy minion, man, exulting in his powers
In field, court, camp, by altars base devours.
Foxes and statesmen subtle wiles ensure;
The cit and polecat stink, and are secure:

Toads with their poison, doctors with their drug,
The priest and hedgehog, in their robes, are snug :
Kings bear the civil, priests the sacred blade,
Soldiers and hangmen murder by their trade ;
Even silly women have defensive arts,
Their eyes, their tongues—and nameless other
  parts.
  But O thou cruel stepmother and hard,
To that poor fenceless, naked thing, a Bard !
A thing unteachable in worldly skill,
And half an idiot too, more helpless still :
No heels to bear him from the op'ning dun,
No claws to dig, his hated sight to shun :
No horns, but those by luckless Hymen worn,
And those, alas ! not Amalthea's horn :
His dart satyric, his unheeded sting :
And idle fancy's pinions, all his wing :
The silly sheep that wanders wild astray,
Not more unfriended, and not more a prey ;
Vampyre-booksellers drain him to the heart,
And butcher-critics cut him up by art.
  Critics ! appall'd I venture on the name,
Those bandits that infest the paths of fame,
Bloody dissectors, worse than ten Monroes,
He hacks to teach, they mangle to expose :
His heart by wanton, causeless malice wrung,
By blockhead's daring into madness stung,
Torn, bleeding, tortur'd in th' unequal strife,
The hapless Poet flounces on through life,
Extinct each ray that once his bosom fired,
Till fled each Muse that glorious once inspir'd,
Low-sunk in feeble, unprotected age,
Dead even resentment for his inspir'd page,
He feels no more the ruthless critics' rage.

So by some hedge the generous steed deceas'd,
To half-starv'd, snarling curs a dainty feast,
By toil and famine worn to skin and bone,
Lies, senseless of each tugging bitch's son.

RHYMING REPLY TO A NOTE FROM CAPTAIN RIDDELL

DEAR SIR, at ony time or tide,
I'd rather sit wi' you than ride,
   Though 'twere wi' royal Geordie;
And trowth, your kindness, soon and late,
Aft gars me to mysel' look blate—
   The Lord in Heav'n reward ye!
               R. BURNS.
ELLISLAND.

IMPROMPTU LINES TO CAPTAIN RIDDELL

ON RETURNING A NEWSPAPER

YOUR News and Review, sir,
I've read through and through, sir,
With little admiring or blaming;
   The Papers are barren
   Of home-news or foreign,
No murders or rapes worth the naming.

Our friends, the Reviewers,
Those chippers and hewers,
Are judges of mortar and stone, sir;
   But of meet or unmeet,
   In a fabric complete,
I'll boldly pronounce they are none, sir;

My goose-quill too rude is
To tell all your goodness
Bestow'd on your servant, the Poet;
Would to God I had one
Like a beam of the sun,
And then all the world, sir, should know it!

LINES TO JOHN M'MURDO, ESQ. OF DRUMLANRIG

SENT WITH SOME OF THE AUTHOR'S POEMS

O COULD I give thee India's wealth,
As I this trifle send;
Because thy joy in both would be
To share them with a friend.

But golden sands did never grace
The Heliconian stream;
Then take what gold could never buy—
An honest bard's esteem.

A NEW PSALM FOR THE CHAPEL OF KILMARNOCK

ON THE THANKSGIVING-DAY FOR HIS MAJESTY'S
RECOVERY

O SING a new song to the Lord;
Make, all and every one,
A joyful noise, even for the king
His restoration.

The sons of Belial in the land
Did set their heads together;
Come, let us sweep them off, said they,
Like an o'erflowing river.

They set their heads together, I say,
    They set their heads together;
On right, and left, and every hand,
    We saw none to deliver.

Thou madest strong two chosen ones
    To quell the Wicked's pride;
That Young Man, great in Issachar,
    The burden-bearing tribe.

And him, among the Princes, chief
    In our Jerusalem,
The judge that's mighty in thy law,
    The man that fears thy name.

Yet they, even they, with all their strength,
    Began to faint and fail:
Even as two howling, rav'ning wolves
    To dogs do turn their tail.

Th' ungodly o'er the just prevail'd,
    For so thou hadst appointed;
That thou might'st greater glory give
    Unto thine own anointed.

And now thou hast restored our State,
    Pity our Kirk also;
For she by tribulations
    Is now brought very low.

Consume that high-place, Patronage,
    From off thy holy hill;
And in thy fury burn the book—
    Even of that man M'Gill.

Now hear our prayer, accept our song,
  And fight thy chosen's battle:
We seek but little, Lord, from thee,
  Thou kens we get as little.

A GRACE BEFORE DINNER,
EXTEMPORE

O THOU who kindly dost provide
  For every creature's want!
We bless Thee, God of Nature wide,
  For all Thy goodness lent:
And, if it please Thee, heavenly Guide,
  May never worse be sent;
But, whether granted or denied,
  Lord, bless us with content. Amen!

A GRACE AFTER DINNER,
EXTEMPORE

O THOU, in whom we live and move—
  Who made the sea and shore;
Thy goodness constantly we prove,
  And grateful would adore;
And, if it please Thee, Power above!
  Still grant us, with such store,
The friend we trust, the fair we love—
  And we desire no more. Amen!

SONNET ON RECEIVING A FAVOUR

10 Aug., 1789

ADDRESSED TO ROBERT GRAHAM, ESQ. OF FINTRY

I CALL no Goddess to inspire my strains,
A fabled Muse may suit a bard that feigns:

T*

Friend of my life ! my ardent spirit burns,
And all the tribute of my heart returns,
For boons accorded, goodness ever new,
The gifts still dearer, as the giver you.
Thou orb of day ! thou other paler light !
And all ye many sparkling stars of night !
If aught that giver from my mind efface,
If I that giver's bounty e'er disgrace,
Then roll to me along your wand'ring spheres,
Only to number out a villain's years !
I lay my hand upon my swelling breast,
And grateful would, but cannot speak the rest.

EXTEMPORANEOUS EFFUSION

ON BEING APPOINTED TO AN EXCISE DIVISION

Searching auld wives' barrels,
    Ochon the day !
That clarty barm should stain my laurels :
    But what'll ye say ?
These movin' things ca'd wives an' weans,
Wad move the very hearts o' stanes !

LINES TO A GENTLEMAN

WHO HAD SENT THE POET A NEWSPAPER, AND OFFERED TO CONTINUE IT FREE OF EXPENSE

Kind Sir, I've read your paper through,
And faith, to me, 'twas really new !
How guessed ye, Sir, what maist I wanted ?
This mony a day I've grain'd and gaunted,
To ken what French mischief was brewin ;
Or what the drumlie Dutch were doin ;

That vile doup-skelper, Emperor Joseph,
If Venus yet had got his nose off;
Or how the collieshangie works
Atween the Russians and the Turks;
Or if the Swede, before he halt,
Would play anither Charles the twalt;
If Denmark, any body spak o't;
Or Poland, wha had now the tack o't:
How cut-throat Prussian blades were hingin;
How libbet Italy was singing;
If Spaniard, Portuguese, or Swiss
Were sayin or takin aught amiss;
Or how our merry lads at hame
In Britain's court kept up the game;
How royal George, the Lord leuk o'er him!
Was managing St Stephen's quorum;
If sleekit Chatham Will was livin,
Or glaikit Charlie got his nieve in;
How daddie Burke the plea was cookin;
If Warren Hastings' neck was yeukin;
How cesses, stents, and fees were rax'd,
Or if bare arses yet were tax'd;
The news o' princes, dukes, and earls,
Pimps, sharpers, bawds, and opera-girls;
If that daft buckie, Geordie Wales,
Was threshing still at hizzies' tails;
Or if he was grown oughtlins douser,
And no a perfect kintra cooser:
A' this and mair I never heard of;
And, but for you, I might despair'd of.
So, gratefu', back your news I send you,
And pray a' gude things may attend you.

ELLISLAND, *Monday Morning.*

TO PETER STUART

Dear Peter, dear Peter,
We poor sons of metre
Are often negleckit, ye ken;
For instance your sheet, man
(Tho' glad I'm to see't, man),
I get it no ae day in ten.

ON ROBERT MUIR

What man could esteem, or what woman could
love,
Was he who lies under the sod;
If such Thou refusest admission above,
Then whom wilt Thou favour, Good God.

I MURDER HATE

I murder hate by flood or field,
Tho' glory's name may screen us;
In wars at home I'll spend my blood—
Life-giving wars of Venus.
The deities that I adore
Are social Peace and Plenty;
I'm better pleas'd to make one more,
Than be the death of twenty.

I would not die like Socrates,
For all the fuss of Plato;
Nor would I with Leonidas,
Nor yet would I with Cato:
The zealots of the Church and State
Shall ne'er my mortal foes be;
But let me have bold Zimri's fate,
Within the arms of Cozbi!

THE RAPTURES OF FOLLY

THE greybeard, old Wisdom ! may boast of his
  treasures ;
  Give me with gay Folly to live ;
I grant him his calm - blooded, time-settled
  pleasures,
  But Folly has raptures to give.

POLITICS

In politics if thou would'st mix
  And mean thy fortunes be,
Bear this in mind : Be deaf and blind,
  Let great folks hear and see.

EXTEMPORE REPLY TO AN INVITATION

THE King's most humble servant, I
  Can scarcely spare a minute ;
But I'll be wi' you by an' by,
  Or else the Deil's be in it.

GRACE BEFORE MEAT

O LORD, when hunger pinches sore,
  Do thou stand us in stead,
And send us, from thy bounteous store,
  A tup- or wether-head ! Amen.

GRACE AFTER MEAT

LORD, [Thee] we thank, and Thee alone,
  For temporal gifts we little merit ;
At present we will ask no more—
  Let William Hislop bring the spirit.

O LORD, since we have feasted thus,
    Which we so little merit,
Let Meg now take the flesh away,
    And Jock bring in the spirit!   Amen.

THE HENPECKED HUSBAND

CURS'D be the man, the poorest wretch in life,
The crouching vassal to a tyrant wife!
Who has no will but by her high permission,
Who has not sixpence but in her possession,
Who must to her his dear friend's secrets tell,
Who dreads a curtain lecture worse than hell.
Were such the wife had fallen to my part,
I'd break her spirit or I'd break her heart;
I'd charm her with the magic of a switch,
I'd kiss her maids, and kick the perverse bitch.

ON MARRIAGE

THAT hackney'd judge of human life,
    The Preacher and the King,
Observes:—" The man that gets a wife,
    He gets a noble thing."
But how capricious are mankind,
    Now loathing, now desirous!
We married men, how oft we find
    The best of things will tire us!

A SONNET UPON SONNETS

FOURTEEN, a sonneteer thy praises sings;
What magic mysteries in that number lie!
Your hen hath fourteen eggs beneath her wings
That fourteen chickens to the roost may fly.

Fourteen full pounds the jockey's stone must be;
His age fourteen—a horse's prime is past.
Fourteen long hours too oft the Bard must fast;
Fourteen bright bumpers,—bliss he ne'er must
    see !
Before fourteen, a dozen yields the strife;
Before fourteen,—e'en thirteen's strength is vain.
Fourteen good years—a woman gives us life;
Fourteen good men—we lose that life again.
What lucubrations can be more upon it?
Fourteen good measur'd verses make a sonnet.

VERSES ON CAPTAIN GROSE

WRITTEN ON AN ENVELOPE, ENCLOSING A LETTER TO HIM

KEN ye ought o' Captain Grose?—*Igo and ago,*
If he's amang his friends or foes?—*Iram, coram,*
    dago.

Is he south or is he north?—*Igo and ago,*
Or drownèd in the river Forth?—*Iram, coram,*
    dago.

Is he slain by Hielan' bodies?—*Igo and ago,*
And eaten like a wether haggis?—*Iram, coram,*
    dago.

Is he to Abra'm's bosom gane?—*Igo and ago,*
Or haudin Sarah by the wame?—*Iram, coram,*
    dago.

Where'er he be, the Lord be near him!—*Igo*
    and ago,
As for the deil, he daur na steer him.—*Iram,*
    coram, dago.

But please transmit th' enclosèd letter,—*Igo and ago,*
Which will oblige your humble debtor.—*Iram, coram, dago.*

So may ye hae auld stanes in store,—*Igo and ago,*
The very stanes that Adam bore.—*Iram, coram, dago.*

So may ye get in glad possession,—*Igo and ago,*
The coins o' Satan's coronation!—*Iram, coram dago.*

EPIGRAM ON FRANCIS GROSE
THE ANTIQUARY

THE Devil got notice that Grose was a-dying,
So whip! at the summons, old Satan came flying;
But when he approached where poor Francis
        lay moaning,
And saw each bed-post with its burthen a-
        groaning,
Astonish'd, confounded, cries Satan—" By God,
I'll want him ere take such a damnable load! "

PROLOGUE SPOKEN AT THE
THEATRE OF DUMFRIES

ON NEW YEAR'S DAY EVENING, 1790

No song nor dance I bring from yon great city,
That queens it o'er our taste—the more's the pity:
Tho' by the bye, abroad why will you roam?
Good sense and taste are natives here at home:
But not for panegyric I appear,
I come to wish you all a good New Year!

Francis Grose F.S.A.

Engraved after a portrait by N. Dance R.A.

Old Father Time deputes me here before ye,
Not for to preach, but tell his simple story :
The sage, grave Ancient cough'd, and bade me
    say,
" You're one year older this important day."
If *wiser* too—he hinted some suggestion,
But 'twould be rude, you know, to ask the
    question ;
And with a would-be-roguish leer and wink,
Said—" Sutherland, in one word, bid them
    THINK ! "

Ye sprightly youths, quite flush with hope
    and spirit,
Who think to storm the world by dint of merit,
To you the dotard has a deal to say,
In his sly, dry, sententious proverb way !
He bids you mind, amid your thoughtless rattle,
That the first blow is ever half the battle ;
That tho' some by the skirt may try to snatch him,
Yet by the forelock is the hold to catch him ;
That whether doing, suffering, or forbearing,
You may do miracles by persevering.

Last, tho' not least in love, ye youthful fair,
Angelic forms, high Heaven's peculiar care !
To you old bald-pate smoothes his wrinkled
    brow,
And humbly begs you'll mind the important—
    NOW !
To crown your happiness he asks your leave,
And offers, bliss to give and to receive.

For our sincere, tho' haply weak endeavours,
With grateful pride we own your many favours ;

And howsoe'er our tongues may ill reveal it,
Believe our glowing bosoms truly feel it.

ELEGY ON WILLIE NICOL'S MARE

PEG NICHOLSON was a good bay mare,
  As ever trod on airn ;
But now she's floating down the Nith,
  And past the mouth o' Cairn.

Peg Nicholson was a good bay mare,
  An' rode thro' thick an' thin ;
But now she's floating down the Nith,
  And wanting even the skin.

Peg Nicholson was a good bay mare,
  And ance she bore a priest ;
But now she's floating down the Nith,
  For Solway fish a feast.

Peg Nicholson was a good bay mare,
  An' the priest he rode her sair ;
And much oppress'd, and bruis'd she was,
  As priest-rid cattle are.

SCOTS PROLOGUE FOR MR SUTHERLAND

ON HIS BENEFIT-NIGHT, AT THE THEATRE, DUMFRIES

WHAT needs this din about the town o' Lon'on,
How this new play an' that new sang is comin ?
Why is outlandish stuff sae meikle courted ?
Does nonsense mend, like brandy, when imported ?
Is there nae poet, burning keen for fame,
Will try to gie us sangs and plays at hame ?

For Comedy abroad he need na toil,
A fool and knave are plants of every soil;
Nor need he hunt as far as Rome or Greece,
To gather matter for a serious piece;
There's themes enow in Caledonian story,
Would shew the Tragic Muse in a' her glory.—

Is there no daring Bard will rise and tell
How glorious Wallace stood, how hapless fell?
Where are the Muses fled that could produce
A drama worthy o' the name o' Bruce?
How here, even here, he first unsheath'd the
   sword
'Gainst mighty England and her guilty Lord;
And after mony a bloody, deathless doing,
Wrench'd his dear country from the jaws of Ruin!
O for a Shakespeare, or an Otway scene,
To draw the lovely, hapless Scottish Queen!
Vain all th' omnipotence of female charms
'Gainst headlong, ruthless, mad Rebellion's arms:
She fell, but fell with spirit truly Roman,
To glut that direst foe—a vengeful woman;
A woman, (tho' the phrase may seem uncivil,)
As able and as wicked as the Devil!
One Douglas lives in Home's immortal page,
But Douglasses were heroes every age:
And tho' your fathers, prodigal of life,
A Douglas followed to the martial strife,
Perhaps, if bowls row right, and Right succeeds,
Ye yet may follow where a Douglas leads!

As ye hae generous done, if a' the land
Would take the Muses' servants by the hand;
Not only hear, but patronize, befriend them,
And where he justly can commend, commend them;

And aiblins when they winna stand the test,
Wink hard, and say " The folks hae done their
    best ! "
Would a' the land do this, then I'll be caition,
Ye'll soon hae Poets o' the Scottish nation
Will gar Fame blaw until her trumpet crack,
And warsle Time, an' lay him on his back !

For us and for our Stage, should ony spier,
" Whase aught thae chiels maks a' this bustle
    here ? "
My best leg foremost, I'll set up my brow—
We have the honour to belong to you !
We're your ain bairns, e'en guide us as ye like,
But like good mithers shore before ye strike ;
And gratefu' still, I trust ye'll ever find us,
For gen'rous patronage, and meikle kindness
We've got frae a' professions, setts and ranks :
God help us ! we're but poor—ye'se get but
    thanks.

SKETCH FOR AN ELEGY

CRAIGDARROCH, fam'd for speaking art
And every virtue of the heart,
Stops short, nor can a word impart
        To end his sentence,
When memory strikes him like a dart
        With auld acquaintance.

Black James—whase wit was never laith,
But, like a sword had tint the sheath,
Ay ready for the work o' death—
        He turns aside,

And strains wi' suffocating breath
    His grief to hide.

Even philosophic Smellie tries
To choak the stream that floods his eyes:
So Moses wi' a hazel-rice
    Came o'er the stane;
But tho' it cost him speaking twice,
    It gush'd amain.

Go to your marble graffs, ye great,
In a' the tinkler-trash of state!
But by thy honest turf I'll wait,
    Thou man o' worth,
And weep the ae best fallow's fate
    E'er laid in earth.

ON THE BIRTH OF A POSTHU-
MOUS CHILD

BORN IN PECULIAR CIRCUMSTANCES OF FAMILY
DISTRESS

SWEET flow'ret, pledge o' meikle love,
    And ward o' mony a prayer,
What heart o' stane wad thou na move,
    Sae helpless, sweet, and fair.

November hirples o'er the lea,
    Chill, on thy lovely form:
And gane, alas! the shelt'ring tree,
    Should shield thee frae the storm.

May He who gives the rain to pour,
    And wings the blast to blaw,
Protect thee frae the driving show'r,
    The bitter frost and snaw.

May He, the friend o' Woe and Want,
Who heals life's various stounds,
Protect and guard the mother plant,
And heal her cruel wounds.

But late she flourish'd, rooted fast,
Fair on the summer morn,
Now, feebly bends she, in the blast,
Unshelter'd and forlorn.

Blest be thy bloom, thou lovely gem,
Unscath'd by ruffian hand!
And from thee many a parent stem
Arise to deck our land!

LINES TO SIR JOHN WHITE-FOORD, BART.

Thou, who thy honor as thy God rever'st,
Who, save thy mind's reproach, nought earthly
fear'st,
To thee this votive offering I impart,
The tearful tribute of a broken heart.
The *Friend* thou valued'st, I, the *Patron* lov'd;
His worth, his honour, all the world approved:
We'll mourn till we too go as he has gone,
And tread the shadowy path to that dark world
unknown.

EPIGRAM ON MISS DAVIES

ON BEING ASKED WHY SHE HAD BEEN FORMED SO
LITTLE, AND MRS S—— SO BIG

Ask why God made the gem so small,
And why so huge the granite?—
Because God meant mankind should set
That higher value on it.

Elizabeth Burnet

Engraved after a drawing by M. McClea

Elegy on the Late Miss Burnet of
Monboddo

*"Life ne'er exulted in so rich a prize,
As Burnet, lovely from her native skies . . . "*

LINES ON FERGUSSON, THE POET

ILL-FATED genius!   Heaven-taught Fergusson!
  What heart that feels and will not yield a tear,
To think Life's sun did set e'er well begun
  To shed its influence on thy bright career.

O why should truest Worth and Genius pine
  Beneath the iron grasp of Want and Woe,
While titled knaves and idiot-greatness shine
  In all the splendour Fortune can bestow?

ELEGY ON THE LATE MISS BURNET OF MONBODDO

LIFE ne'er exulted in so rich a prize,
As Burnet, lovely from her native skies;
Nor envious death so triumph'd in a blow,
As that which laid th' accomplish'd Burnet low.

Thy form and mind, sweet maid, can I forget?
In richest ore the brightest jewel set!
In thee, high Heaven above was truest shown,
As by His noblest work the Godhead best is
    known.

In vain ye flaunt in summer's pride, ye groves;
  Thou crystal streamlet with thy flowery shore,
Ye woodland choir that chaunt your idle loves,
  Ye cease to charm; Eliza is no more.

Ye heathy wastes, immix'd with reedy fens;
  Ye mossy streams, with sedge and rushes
    stor'd:
Ye rugged cliffs, o'erhanging dreary glens,
  To you I fly—ye with my soul accord.

Princes, whose cumb'rous pride was all their
    worth,
  Shall venal lays their pompous exit hail,
And thou, sweet Excellence ! forsake our earth,
  And not a Muse with honest grief bewail ?

We saw thee shine in youth and beauty's pride,
  And Virtue's light, that beams beyond the
    spheres ;
But, like the sun eclips'd at morning tide,
  Thou left us darkling in a world of tears.

The parent's heart that nestled fond in thee,
  That heart how sunk, a prey to grief and
    care ;
So deckt the woodbine sweet yon aged tree ;
  So, from it ravish'd, leaves it bleak and bare.

SKETCH—NEW YEAR'S DAY [1791]

TO MRS DUNLOP

  This day, Time winds th' exhausted chain
To run the twelvemonth's length again :
I see the old bald-pated fellow,
With ardent eyes, complexion sallow,
Adjust the unimpair'd machine,
To wheel the equal, dull routine.

  The absent lover, minor heir,
In vain assail him with their prayer ;
Deaf as my friend, he sees them press,
Nor makes the hour one moment less,
Will you (the Major's with the hounds,
The happy tenants share his rounds ;
Coila's fair Rachel's care to-day,

And blooming Keith's engaged with Gray)
From housewife cares a minute borrow,
(That grandchild's cap will do to-morrow,)
And join with me a-moralising;
This day's propitious to be wise in.

First, what did yesternight deliver?
" Another year has gone for ever."
And what is this day's strong suggestion?
" The passing moment's all we rest on ! "
Rest on—for what? what do we here?
Or why regard the passing year?
Will Time, amus'd with proverb'd lore,
Add to our date one minute more?
A few days may—a few years must—
Repose us in the silent dust.
Then, is it wise to damp our bliss?
Yes—all such reasonings are amiss !
The voice of Nature loudly cries,
And many a message from the skies,
That something in us never dies:
That on this frail, uncertain state
Hang matters of eternal weight:
That future life in worlds unknown
Must take its hue from this alone ;
Whether as heavenly glory bright,
Or dark as Misery's woeful night.

Since then, my honour'd first of friends,
On this poor being all depends,
Let us th' important *now* employ,
And live as those who never die.
Tho' you, with days and honours crown'd,
Witness that filial circle round,

(A sight life's sorrows to repulse,
A sight pale Envy to convulse),
Others now claim your chief regard;
Yourself, you wait your bright reward.

ON GLENRIDDELL'S FOX BREAK-
ING HIS CHAIN

A FRAGMENT, 1791

THOU, Liberty, thou art my theme;
Not such as idle poets dream,
Who trick thee up a heathen goddess
That a fantastic cap and rod has;
Such stale conceits are poor and silly;
I paint thee out, a Highland filly,
A sturdy, stubborn, handsome dapple,
As sleek's a mouse, as round's an apple,
That when thou pleasest canst do wonders;
But when thy luckless rider blunders,
Or if thy fancy should demur there,
Wilt break thy neck ere thou go further.

These things premised, I sing a Fox,
Was caught among his native rocks,
And to a dirty kennel chained,
How he his liberty regained.

Glenriddell! a Whig without a stain,
A Whig in principle and grain,
Could'st thou enslave a free-born creature,
A native denizen of Nature?
How could'st thou, with a heart so good,
(A better ne'er was sluiced with blood)
Nail a poor devil to a tree,
That ne'er did harm to thine or thee?

Mrs Dunlop

From an engraving by H. Robinson

Mrs Dunlop

" . . . my honour'd first of friends . . . "

The staunchest Whig Glenriddell was,
Quite frantic in his country's cause;
And oft was Reynard's prison passing,
And with his brother-Whigs canvassing
The Rights of Men, the Powers of Women,
With all the dignity of Freemen.

    Sir Reynard daily heard debates
Of Princes', Kings', and Nations' fates,
With many rueful, bloody stories
Of Tyrants, Jacobites, and Tories:
From liberty how angels fell,
That now are galley-slaves in hell;
How Nimrod first the trade began
Of binding Slavery's chains on Man;
How fell Semiramis—God damn her!
Did first, with sacrilegious hammer,
(All ills till then were trivial matters)
For Man dethron'd forge hen-peck fetters;
How Xerxes, that abandoned Tory,
Thought cutting throats was reaping glory,
Until the stubborn whigs of Sparta
Taught him great Nature's Magna Charta;
How mighty Rome her fiat hurl'd
Resistless o'er a bowing world,
And, kinder than they did desire,
Polish'd mankind with sword and fire
With much, too tedious to relate,
Of ancient and of modern date,
But ending still, how Billy Pitt
(Unlucky boy!) with wicked wit
Has gagg'd old Britain, drain'd her coffer,
As butchers bind and bleed a heifer.

Thus wily Reynard by degrees,
In kennel listening at his ease,
Suck'd in a mighty stock of knowledge,
As much as some folks at a College;
Knew Britain's rights and constitution,
Her aggrandisement, diminution,
How fortune wrought us good from evil;
Let no man, then, despise the Devil,
As who should say, " I ne'er can need him,"
Since we to scoundrels owe our freedom.

ADDRESS TO THE SHADE OF
THOMSON

ON CROWNING HIS BUST AT EDNAM, ROX-
BURGHSHIRE, WITH A WREATH OF BAYS

WHILE virgin Spring by Eden's flood
Unfolds her tender mantle green,
Or pranks the sod in frolic mood,
Or tunes Eolian strains between.

While Summer, with a matron grace,
Retreats to Dryburgh's cooling shade,
Yet oft, delighted, stops to trace
The progress of the spiky blade.

While Autumn, benefactor kind,
By Tweed erects his aged head,
And sees, with self-approving mind,
Each creature on his bounty fed.

While maniac Winter rages o'er
The hills whence classic Yarrow flows,
Rousing the turbid torrent's roar,
Or sweeping, wild, a waste of snows.

So long, sweet Poet of the year!
  Shall bloom that wreath thou well hast
    won;
While Scotia, with exulting tear,
  Proclaims that THOMSON was her son.

TO WILLIAM STEWART

IN honest Bacon's ingle-neuk
  Here maun I sit and think,
Sick o' the warld and warld's folk,
  An' sick, damn'd sick, o' drink!
I see, I see there is nae help,
  But still down I maun sink,
Till some day laigh enough I yelp,
  "Wae worth that cursed drink!"
Yestreen, alas! I was sae fu'
  I could but yisk and wink;
And now, this day, sair, sair I rue
  The weary, weary drink.
Satan, I fear thy sooty claws,
  I hate thy brunstane stink,
And aye I curse the luckless cause—
  The wicked soup o' drink.
In vain I would forget my woes
  In idle rhyming clink,
For, past redemption damn'd in prose,
  I can do nought but drink.
To you my trusty well-tried friend,
  May heaven still on you blink!
And may your life flow to the end,
  Sweet as a dry man's drink.

EPIGRAM AT BROWNHILL INN

At Brownhill we always get dainty good cheer,
And plenty of bacon each day in the year;
We've a' thing that's nice, and mostly in season,
But why always Bacon—come tell me the reason?

THE TOAD-EATER

Of Lordly acquaintance you boast,
    And the Dukes that you dined wi' yestreen;
Yet an insect's an insect at most,
    Tho' it crawl on the curl of a Queen!

DIVINE SERVICE IN THE KIRK OF LAMINGTON

As cauld a wind as ever blew,
A cauld kirk, and in't but few:
As cauld a minister's ever spak;
Ye'se a' be het or I come back.

THE KEEKIN-GLASS

How daur ye ca' me "Howlet-face"?
    Ye blear-e'ed, withered spectre!
Ye only spied the keekin-glass,
    An' there ye saw your picture.

EPISTLE TO JOHN MAXWELL, ESQ., OF TERRAUGHTIE

ON HIS BIRTHDAY

Health to the Maxwell's veteran Chief!
Health, aye unsour'd by care or grief:
Inspir'd, I turn'd Fate's sibyl leaf,
            This natal morn,
I see thy life is stuff o' prief,
            Scarce quite half-worn.

This day thou metes threescore eleven,
And I can tell that bounteous Heaven
(The second-sight, ye ken, is given
    To ilka Poet)
On thee a tack o' seven times seven
    Will yet bestow it.

If envious buckies view wi' sorrow
Thy lengthen'd days on this blest morrow,
May Desolation's lang-teeth'd harrow,
    Nine miles an hour,
Rake them, like Sodom and Gomorrah,
    In brunstane stour.

But for thy friends, and they are mony,
Baith honest men, and lassies bonie,
May couthie Fortune, kind and cannie,
    In social glee,
Wi' mornings blythe, and e'enings funny,
    Bless them and thee !

Fareweel, auld birkie ! Lord be near ye,
And then the deil, he daurna steer ye :
Your friends aye love, your faes aye fear ye ;
    For me, shame fa' me,
If neist my heart I dinna wear ye,
    While Burns they ca' me.

THE RIGHTS OF WOMAN

AN OCCASIONAL ADDRESS

SPOKEN BY MISS FONTENELLE ON HER BENEFIT NIGHT,
NOVEMBER 26, 1792.

While Europe's eye is fix'd on mighty things,
The fate of empires and the fall of kings ;

While quacks of State must each produce his plan,
And even children lisp the Rights of Man;
Amid this mighty fuss just let me mention,
The Rights of Woman merit some attention.

First, in the sexes' intermix'd connection,
One sacred Right of Woman is *protection*.—
The tender flower that lifts its head, elate,
Helpless, must fall before the blasts of fate,
Sunk on the earth, defac'd its lovely form,
Unless your shelter ward th' impending storm.

Our second Right—but needless here is caution,
To keep that right inviolate's the fashion;
Each man of sense has it so full before him,
He'd die before he'd wrong it—'tis *decorum*.—
There was, indeed, in far less polish'd days,
A time, when rough rude men had naughty ways:
Would swagger, swear, get drunk, kick up a riot,
Nay even thus invade a lady's quiet.

Now, thank our stars! these Gothic times are fled;
Now, well-bred men—and you are all well-bred—
Most justly think (and we are much the gainers)
Such conduct neither spirit, wit, nor manners.

For Right the third, our last, our best, our dearest,
That right to fluttering female hearts the nearest;
Which even the Rights of Kings, in low
        prostration,
Most humbly own—'tis dear, dear *admiration !*
In that blest sphere alone we live and move;
There taste that life of life—immortal love.
Smiles, glances, sighs, tears, fits, flirtations, airs;
'Gainst such an host what flinty savage dares,

When awful Beauty joins with all her charms—
Who is so rash as rise in rebel arms ?

But truce with kings, and truce with constitutions,
With bloody armaments and revolutions ;
Let Majesty your first attention summon,
Ah ! ça ira ! THE MAJESTY OF WOMAN !

EPIGRAM ON SEEING MISS FON-
TENELLE IN A FAVOURITE
CHARACTER

SWEET naïveté of feature,
　Simple, wild, enchanting elf,
Not to thee, but thanks to Nature,
　Thou art acting but thyself.

Wert thou awkward, stiff, affected,
　Spurning Nature, torturing art,
Loves and Graces all rejected,—
　Then indeed thou'd'st act a part.

EXTEMPORE ON SOME COM-
MEMORATIONS OF THOMSON

Dost thou not rise, indignant shade,
　And smile wi' spurning scorn,
When they wha wad hae starved thy life,
　Thy senseless turf adorn ?

They wha about thee mak sic fuss
　Now thou art but a name,
Wad seen thee damn'd ere they had spar'd
　Ae plack to fill thy wame.

Helpless, alane, thou clamb the brae,
　Wi' meikle honest toil,

U

And claught th' unfading garland there—
Thy sair-won, rightful spoil.

And wear it there ! and call aloud
This axiom undoubted—
Would thou hae Nobles' patronage ?
First learn to live without it !

To whom hae much, more shall be given,
Is every great man's faith ;
But he, the helpless, needful wretch,
Shall lose the mite he hath.

ON HEARING A THRUSH SING IN A MORNING WALK, IN JANUARY

Sing on, sweet thrush, upon the leafless bough,
Sing on, sweet bird, I listen to thy strain,
See aged Winter, 'mid his surly reign,
At thy blythe carol, clears his furrowed brow.

So in lone Poverty's dominion drear,
Sits meek Content with light, unanxious
heart ;
Welcomes the rapid moments, bids them part,
Nor asks if they bring ought to hope or fear.

I thank thee, Author of this opening day !
Thou whose bright sun now gilds yon orient
skies !
Riches denied, thy boon was purer joys—
What wealth could never give nor take away !

Yet come, thou child of poverty and care,
The mite high heav'n bestow'd, that mite with
thee I'll share.

D.O.H. R.S.A

T J Kelley

Burns' Cottage

THE TRUE LOYAL NATIVES

Ye true " Loyal Natives " attend to my song,
In uproar and riot rejoice the night long ;
From Envy and Hatred your core is exempt,
But where is your shield from the darts of Con-
    tempt !

ON COMMISSARY GOLDIE'S
BRAINS

Lord, to account who dares thee call,
    Or e'er dispute thy pleasure ?
Else why, within so thick a wall,
    Enclose so poor a treasure ?

LINES INSCRIBED IN A LADY'S
POCKET ALMANAC

Grant me, indulgent Heaven, that I may live,
To see the miscreants feel the pains they give ;
Deal Freedom's sacred treasures free as air,
Till Slave and Despot be but things that were.

ON THE COMMEMORATION OF
RODNEY'S VICTORY

Instead of a song, boys, I'll give you a toast ;
Here's the memory of those on the Twelfth that
    we lost !—
We lost, did I say ?—No, by Heav'n, that we
    found ;
For their fame it shall live while the world goes
    round.

The next in succession I'll give you the King!
And who would betray him, on high may he
    swing!
And here's the grand fabric, our free Constitution,
As built on the base of the great Revolution!
And longer with Politics not to be cramm'd,
Be Anarchy curs'd, and be Tyranny damn'd!
And who would to Liberty e'er prove dis-
    loyal,
May his son be a hangman—and he his first
    trial!

KING'S ARMS, DUMFRIES, 12th April 1793.

KIRK AND STATE EXCISEMEN

YE men of wit and wealth, why all this sneering
'Gainst poor Excisemen?   Give the cause a
    hearing :
What are your Landlord's rent-rolls?—taxing
    ledgers!
What Premiers? — what ev'n Monarchs? —
    mighty Gaugers?
Nay, what are Priests? (those seeming godly
    wise-men,)
What are they, pray, but Spiritual Excisemen!

LINES ON JOHN M'MURDO, ESQ.

BLEST be M'Murdo to his latest day!
No envious cloud o'ercast his evening ray;
No wrinkle, furrow'd by the hand of care,
Nor ever sorrow add one silver hair!
O may no son the father's honour stain,
Nor ever daughter give the mother pain!

EPITAPH ON A LAP-DOG

In wood and wild, ye warbling throng,
  Your heavy loss deplore ;
Now, half extinct your powers of song,—
  Sweet Echo is no more.

Ye jarring, screeching things around,
  Scream your discordant joys ;
Now, half your din of tuneless sound
  With Echo silent lies.

EPIGRAMS AGAINST THE EARL OF GALLOWAY

What dost thou in that mansion fair ?
  Flit, Galloway, and find
Some narrow, dirty, dungeon cave,
  The picture of thy mind.

No Stewart art thou, Galloway,
  The Stewarts all were brave ;
Besides, the Stewarts were but fools,
  Not one of them a knave.

Bright ran thy line, O Galloway,
  Thro' many a far-fam'd sire !
So ran the far-famed Roman way,
  And ended in a mire.

Spare me thy vengeance, Galloway !
  In quiet let me live :
I ask no kindness at thy hand,
  For thou hast none to give.

u*

EPIGRAM ON THE LAIRD OF LAGGAN

WHEN Morine, deceas'd, to the Devil went
    down,
'Twas nothing would serve him but Satan's own
    crown.
" Thy fool's head," quoth Satan, " that crown
    shall wear never ;
I grant thou'rt as wicked, but not quite so
    clever."

ON MRS RIDDELL'S BIRTHDAY

4TH NOVEMBER 1793

OLD Winter, with his frosty beard,
Thus once to Jove his prayer preferred :
" What have I done of all the year,
To bear this hated doom severe ?
My cheerless suns no pleasure know ;
Night's horrid car drags dreary slow ;
My dismal months no joys are crowning,
But spleeny English hanging, drowning.

" Now Jove, for once be mighty civil ;
To counterbalance all this evil,
Give me, and I've no more to say,
Give me Maria's natal day !
That brilliant gift shall so enrich me,
Spring, Summer, Autumn, cannot match me."
" 'Tis done ! " says Jove ; so ends my story,
And Winter once rejoiced in glory.

ADDRESS

SPOKEN BY MISS FONTENELLE ON HER BENEFIT NIGHT,
DECEMBER 4TH, 1793, AT THE THEATRE,
DUMFRIES

STILL anxious to secure your partial favour,
And not less anxious, sure, this night than ever,
A Prologue, Epilogue, or some such matter,
'Twould vamp my bill, said I, if nothing better ;
So sought a poet, roosted near the skies,
Told him I came to feast my curious eyes ;
Said, nothing like his works was ever printed ;
And last, my prologue-business slily hinted.
" Ma'am, let me tell you," quoth my man of
    rhymes,
" I know your bent—these are no laughing times :
Can you—but, Miss, I own I have my fears—
Dissolve in pause, and sentimental tears ?
With laden sighs, and solemn-rounded sentence,
Rouse from his sluggish slumbers, fell Repentance ;
Paint Vengeance as he takes his horrid stand,
Waving on high the desolating brand,
Calling the storms to bear him o'er a guilty land ? "

I could no more—askance the creature eyeing,
" D'ye think," said I, " this face was made for
    crying ?
I'll laugh, that's poz—nay more, the world shall
    know it ;
And so, your servant ! gloomy Master Poet ! "

Firm as my creed, Sirs, 'tis my fix'd belief,
That Misery's another word for Grief :

I also think—so may I be a bride.!
That so much laughter, so much life enjoy'd.

Thou man of crazy care and ceaseless sigh,
Still under bleak Misfortune's blasting eye ;
Doom'd to that sorest task of man alive—
To make three guineas do the work of five ;
Laugh in Misfortune's face—the beldam witch !
Say, you'll be merry, tho' you can't be rich.

Thou other man of care, the wretch in love,
Who long with jiltish airs and arts hast strove ;
Who, as the boughs all temptingly project,
Measur'st in desperate thought—a rope—thy
    neck—
Or, where the beetling cliff o'erhangs the deep,
Peerest to meditate the healing leap :
Would'st thou be cur'd, thou silly, moping elf ?
Laugh at her follies—laugh e'en at thyself :
Learn to despise those frowns now so terrific,
And love a kinder—that's your grand specific.

To sum up all, be merry, I advise ;
And as we're merry, may we still be wise.

INSCRIPTION TO MISS GRAHAM
OF FINTRY

Here, where the Scottish Muse immortal lives,
    In sacred strains and tuneful numbers joined,
Accept the gift ; though humble he who gives,
    Rich is the tribute of the grateful mind.

So may no ruffian feeling in thy breast,
    Discordant, jar thy bosom-chords among ;
But Peace attune thy gentle soul to rest,
    Or Love ecstatic wake his seraph song,

Or Pity's notes, in luxury of tears,
  As modest Want the tale of woe reveals;
While conscious Virtue all the strains endears,
  And heaven-born Piety her sanction seals.
DUMFRIES, 31*st January* 1794.

COMPLIMENTARY EPIGRAM ON MARIA RIDDELL

"PRAISE Woman still," his lordship roars,
  "Deserv'd or not, no matter?"
But thee, whom all my soul adores,
  Ev'n Flattery cannot flatter:

MARIA, all my thought and dream,
  Inspires my vocal shell;
The more I praise my lovely theme,
  The more the truth I tell.

REMORSEFUL APOLOGY

THE friend whom wild from Wisdom's way
  The fumes of wine infuriate send,
(Not moony madness more astray)
  Who but deplores that hapless friend?

Mine was th' insensate frenzied part,
  Ah! why should I such scenes outlive?
Scenes so abhorrent to my heart!—
  'Tis thine to pity and forgive.

PINNED TO MRS WALTER RIDDELL'S CARRIAGE

IF you rattle along like your Mistress's tongue,
  Your speed will outrival the dart;
But a fly for your load, you'll break down on
    the road,
  If your stuff be as rotten's her heart.

EPITAPH FOR MR WALTER RIDDELL

Sic a reptile was Wat, sic a miscreant slave,
That the worms ev'n damn'd him when laid in
   his grave ;
" In his flesh there's a famine," a starved reptile
   cries,
" And his heart is rank poison ! " another replies.

MONODY

ON A LADY FAMED FOR HER CAPRICE

How cold is that bosom which folly once fired,
   How pale is that cheek where the rouge lately
     glisten'd ;
How silent that tongue which the echoes oft tired,
   How dull is that ear which to flatt'ry so
     listen'd !

If sorrow and anguish their exit await,
   From friendship and dearest affection remov'd ;
How doubly severer, Maria, thy fate,
   Thou diedst unwept, as thou livedst unlov'd.

Loves, Graces, and Virtues, I call not on you ;
   So shy, grave, and distant, ye shed not a tear:
But come, all ye offspring of Folly so true,
   And flowers let us cull for Maria's cold bier.

We'll search through the garden for each silly
   flower,
   We'll roam thro' the forest for each idle
     weed ;

These is intended to be written below a noble Earl's picture

Whose is that noble, dauntless brow?
    And whose that eye of fire?
And whose that generous, Princely mien,
    Ev'n rooted Foes admire?

Stranger, to justly show that brow,
    And mark that eye of fire,
Would take His hand, whose vernal tints,
    His other Works admire.

Bright as a cloudless Summer-sun,
    With stately front he moves;
His guardian Seraph eyes with awe
    The noble Ward he loves.

Among th' illustrious Scottish Sons
    That Chief thou may'st discern,
Mark Scotia's fond, returning eye,
    It dwells upon Glencairn

Burns' Handwriting

But chiefly the nettle, so typical, shower,
  For none e'er approach'd her but rued the
  rash deed.

We'll sculpture the marble, we'll measure the lay;
  Here Vanity strums on her idiot lyre;
There keen Indignation shall dart on his prey,
  Which spurning Contempt shall redeem from
  his ire.

THE EPITAPH

HERE lies, now a prey to insulting neglect,
  What once was a butterfly, gay in life's beam:
Want only of wisdom denied her respect,
  Want only of goodness denied her esteem.

SONNET ON THE DEATH OF ROBERT RIDDELL

OF GLENRIDDELL AND FRIARS' CARSE

No more, ye warblers of the wood! no more;
  Nor pour your descant grating on my soul;
  Thou young-eyed Spring! gay in thy verdant
  stole,
More welcome were to me grim Winter's wildest
  roar.

How can ye charm, ye flowers, with all your
  dyes?
  Ye blow upon the sod that wraps my friend!
  How can I to the tuneful strain attend?
That strain flows round the untimely tomb where
  Riddell lies.

Yes, pour, ye warblers! pour the notes of woe,
  And soothe the Virtues weeping o'er his bier:
  The man of worth (and hath not left his peer!)
Is in his "narrow house," for ever darkly low.

Thee, Spring! again with joy shall others greet;
Me, memory of my loss will only meet.

EPITAPH ON A NOTED COXCOMB

CAPT. WM. RODDICK, OF CORBISTON

Light lay the earth on Billy's breast,
  His chicken heart so tender;
But build a castle on his head,
  His scull will prop it under.

ON CAPT. LASCELLES

When Lascelles thought fit from this world to
  depart,
Some friends warmly spoke of embalming his
  heart;
A bystander whispers—"Pray don't make so
  much o't,
The subject is poison, no reptile will touch it."

ON WM. GRAHAM, ESQ. OF MOSSKNOWE

"Stop thief!" dame Nature call'd to Death,
As Willy drew his latest breath;
"How shall I make a fool again?
My choicest model thou hast ta'en."

ON JOHN BUSHBY, ESQ., TINWALD DOWNS

HERE lies John Bushby—honest man,
Cheat him, Devil—if you can!

THANKSGIVING FOR A NATIONAL VICTORY

YE hypocrites! are these your pranks?
To murder men and give God thanks!
Desist, for shame!—proceed no further;
God won't accept your thanks for MURTHER!

IN VAIN WOULD PRUDENCE

IN vain would Prudence with decorous sneer
Point out a censuring world, and bid me fear:
Above that world on wings of love I rise,
I know its worst, and can that worst despise.
"Wrong'd, injur'd, shunn'd, unpitied, unredrest,
The mock'd quotation of the scorner's jest."
Let Prudence' direst bodements on me fall,
Clarinda, rich reward! o'erpays them all.

TO DR MAXWELL

ON MISS JESSIE STAIG'S RECOVERY

MAXWELL, if here you merit crave,
    That merit I deny;
You save fair Jessie from the grave!—
    An Angel could not die.!

TO THE BEAUTIFUL MISS ELIZA
J——N
ON HER PRINCIPLES OF LIBERTY AND EQUALITY

How, Liberty! girl, can it be by thee nam'd?
Equality too! hussy, art not asham'd?
Free and Equal indeed, while mankind thou
    enchainest,
And over their hearts a proud Despot so reignest.

ON CHLORIS
REQUESTING ME TO GIVE HER A SPRIG OF
BLOSSOMED THORN

FROM the white-blossom'd sloe my dear Chloris
    requested
    A sprig, her fair breast to adorn:
"No, by Heaven!" I exclaim'd, "let me perish
    for ever,
    Ere I plant in that bosom a thorn!"

TO THE HON. WM. R. MAULE
OF PANMURE

THOU Fool, in thy phaeton towering,
    Art proud when that phaeton's prais'd?
'Tis the pride of a Thief's exhibition
    When higher his pillory's rais'd.

ON SEEING MRS KEMBLE IN
YARICO

KEMBLE, thou cur'st my unbelief
    Of Moses and his rod;
At Yarico's sweet note of grief
    The rock with tears had flow'd.

EPIGRAM ON A COUNTRY LAIRD

NOT QUITE SO WISE AS SOLOMON

BLESS Jesus Christ, O Cardoness,
  With grateful, lifted eyes,
Who taught that not the soul alone,
  But body too shall rise;
For had He said, "The soul alone
  From death I will deliver,"
Alas, alas! O Cardoness,
  Then hadst thou lain for ever.

ON BEING SHEWN A BEAUTIFUL COUNTRY SEAT

BELONGING TO THE SAME LAIRD

WE grant they're thine, those beauties all,
  So lovely in our eye;
Keep them, thou eunuch, Cardoness,
  For others to enjoy!

ON HEARING IT ASSERTED FALSEHOOD

IS EXPRESSED IN THE REV. DR BABINGTON'S VERY LOOKS

THAT there is falsehood in his looks,
  I must and will deny:
They say their Master is a knave,
  And sure they do not lie.

ON A SUICIDE

HERE lies in earth a root of Hell
  Set by the Deil's ain dibble;
This worthless body damn'd himsel',
  To save the Lord the trouble.

ON A SWEARING COXCOMB

HERE cursing, swearing Burton lies,
A buck, a beau, or " Dem my eyes ! "
Who in his life did little good,
And his last words were " Dem my blood ! "

ON AN INNKEEPER NICKNAMED
"THE MARQUIS"

HERE lies a mock Marquis, whose titles were
    shamm'd ;
If ever he rise, it will be to be damn'd.

ON ANDREW TURNER

IN se'enteen hunder 'n forty-nine,
The deil gat stuff to mak a swine,
    An' coost it in a corner ;
But wilily he chang'd his plan,
An' shap'd it something like a man,
    An' ca'd it Andrew Turner.

THE SOLEMN LEAGUE AND
COVENANT

THE Solemn League and Covenant
    Now brings a smile, now brings a tear ;
But sacred Freedom, too, was theirs :
    If thou'rt a slave, indulge thy sneer.

COMPLIMENTS TO JOHN SYME
OF RYEDALE

LINES SENT WITH A PRESENT OF A DOZEN OF PORTER

O HAD the malt thy strength of mind,
Or hops the flavour of thy wit,
'Twere drink for first of human kind,
A gift that even for Syme were fit.

JERUSALEM TAVERN, DUMFRIES.

INSCRIPTION ON A GOBLET

THERE'S Death in the cup, so beware!
Nay, more—there is danger in touching;
But who can avoid the fell snare,
The man and his wine's so bewitching!

APOLOGY FOR DECLINING AN
INVITATION TO DINE

No more of your guests, be they titled or not,
And cookery the first in the nation;
Who is proof to thy personal converse and wit,
Is proof to all other temptation.

EPITAPH FOR MR GABRIEL
RICHARDSON

HERE Brewer Gabriel's fire's extinct,
And empty all his barrels:
He's blest—if, as he brew'd, he drink,—
In upright, virtuous morals.

EPIGRAM ON MR JAMES GRACIE

GRACIE, thou art a man of worth,
  O be thou Dean for ever!
May he be damn'd to hell henceforth,
  Who fauts thy weight or measure!

INSCRIPTION AT FRIARS' CARSE HERMITAGE

TO THE MEMORY OF ROBERT RIDDELL

To RIDDELL, much lamented man,
  This ivied cot was dear;
Wand'rer, dost value matchless worth?
  This ivied cot revere.

INSCRIPTION FOR AN ALTAR OF INDEPENDENCE

AT KERROUGHTREE, THE SEAT OF MR HERON

THOU of an independent mind,
With soul resolv'd, with soul resign'd;
Prepar'd Power's proudest frown to brave,
Who wilt not be, nor have a slave;
Virtue alone who dost revere,
Thy own reproach alone dost fear—
Approach this shrine, and worship here.

INSCRIPTION

Written on the blank leaf of a copy of the last
  edition of my poems, presented to the
  Lady whom, in so many fictitious reveries
  of passion, but with the most ardent senti-
  ments of real friendship, I have so often
  sung under the name of Chloris.

'Tis Friendship's pledge, my young, fair Friend,
   Nor thou the gift refuse,
Nor with unwilling ear attend
   The moralising Muse.

Since thou, in all thy youth and charms,
   Must bid the world adieu,
(A world 'gainst Peace in constant arms)
   To join the Friendly Few;

Since, thy gay morn of life o'ercast,
   Chill came the tempest's lour
(And ne'er Misfortune's eastern blast
   Did nip a fairer flower);

Since life's gay scenes must charm no more,
   Still much is left behind,
Still nobler wealth hast thou in store—
   The comforts of the mind!

Thine is the self-approving glow,
   Of conscious Honour's part;
And (dearest gift of Heaven below)
   Thine Friendship's truest heart.

The joys refin'd of Sense and Taste,
   With every Muse to rove:
And doubly were the Poet blest,
   These joys could he improve.

COMPLIMENTARY VERSICLES TO JESSIE LEWARS

THE TOAST

Fill me with the rosy wine,
Call a toast, a toast divine;

Give the Poet's darling flame,
Lovely Jessie be her name;
Then thou mayest freely boast,
Thou hast given a peerless toast.

THE MENAGERIE

Talk not to me of savages
  From Afric's burning sun;
No savage e'er could rend my heart
  As, Jessie, thou hast done:
But Jessie's lovely hand in mine,
  A mutual faith to plight,
Not even to view the heavenly choir
  Would be so blest a sight.

JESSIE'S ILLNESS

Say, sages, what's the charm on earth
  Can turn Death's dart aside!
It is not purity and worth,
  Else Jessie had not died.

ON HER RECOVERY

But rarely seen since Nature's birth
  The natives of the sky;
Yet still one seraph's left on earth,
  For Jessie did not die.

INSCRIPTION TO MISS JESSY LEWARS

ON A COPY OF THE SCOTS MUSICAL MUSEUM, IN FOUR VOLUMES, PRESENTED TO HER BY BURNS

THINE be the volumes, Jessy fair,
And with them take the Poet's prayer,

That Fate may, in her fairest page,
With ev'ry kindliest, best presage
Of future bliss, enrol thy name :
With native worth and spotless fame,
And wakeful caution, still aware
Of ill—but chief, Man's felon snare ;
All blameless joys on earth we find,
And all the treasures of the mind—
These be thy guardian and reward ;
So prays thy faithful friend, the Bard.

DUMFRIES, *June* 26, 1796

LINES ON THE AUTHOR'S DEATH

HE who of Rankine sang, lies stiff and dead,
And a green grassy hillock hides his head ;
Alas ! alas ! a devilish change indeed.

From a wood engraving by Thomas Bewick

Glossary

A', *all.*
Aback, *behind, at the back.*
Abeigh, *at bay, aloof.*
Aboon, *above.*
Abread, *abroad.*
Abreed, *in breadth.*
Acquent, *acquainted.*
A'-day, *all day.*
Adle, *putrid water.*
Ae, *one; only.*
Aff, *off.*
Aff-hand, *at once, offhand.*
Aff-loof, *off-hand.*
Afore, *before.*
Aften, *often.*
A-gley, *off the right line; asquint..*
Aiblins, *perhaps.*
Aik, *an oak.*
Aiken, *oaken.*
Ain, *own.*
Air *or* ear', *early.*
Airl-penny, *earnest money.*
Airn, *iron.*
Airns, *irons.*
Airt, *point or quarter of the earth or sky; to direct.*
Airted, *directed.*
Aith, *an oath.*
Aiths, *oaths.*
Aits, *oats.*
Aiver, *horse no longer young.*
Aizle, *a hot cinder.*
Ajee, *to the one side.*

Alake! *alas!*
Alang, *along.*
Amaist, *almost.*
Amang, *among.*
An', *and.*
An's, *and is.*
Ance, *once.*
Ane, *one.*
Anes, *ones.*
Anither, *another.*
Arles, *earnest-money.*
Ase, *ashes.*
Asklent, *obliquely.*
Asteer, *astir.*
A'thegither, *altogether.*
Athort, *athwart.*
Atween, *between.*
Aught, *eight.*
Aughteen, *eighteen.*
Aughtlins, *anything, in the least.*
Auld, *old.*
Auldfarran, *sagacious, old-fashioned.*
Aumous, *alms.*
Ava, *at all.*
Awa, *away.*
Awe, *to owe.*
Awee, *a little time.*
Awfu', *awful.*
Awnie, *bearded* (said of barley).
Aye, *always.*
Ayont, *beyond.*

Ba', *a ball.*

Babie-clouts, *baby-clothes.*
Backets, *buckets.*
Bade, *endured, desired.*
Baggie (dim. of *bag*), *the stomach.*
Bainie, *bony, muscular.*
Bairns, *children.*
Bairntime, *all the children of one mother.*
Baith, *both.*
Bakes, *biscuits.*
Ballats, *ballads.*
Ban', *band.*
Banes, *bones.*
Bang, *a stroke.*
Bannet, *a bonnet.*
Bannock, *a cake of oatmeal bread, or a barley scon.*
Bardie, dim. of *bard.*
Barefit, *barefooted.*
Barkit, *barked.*
Barin' (of a stone-pit), *laying bare the stones by removing the turf.*
Barley-bree, *ale or whisky.*
Barm, *yeast.*
Barmie, *frothing or fermenting.*
Batch, *a party or quantity.*
Batts, *the botts or colic.*
Bauckie-bird, *the bat.*
Baudrons, *a cat.*
Bauks, *cross-beams.*
Bauk-en', *end of a bank or cross-beam.*
Bauld, *bold.*
Baumy, *balmy.*
Bawk, *a ridge left untilled.*
Baws'nt, *having a white stripe down the face.*
Bawtie, *a familiar name for a dog.*
Be't, *be it.*
Bear, *barley.*
Beets, *adds fuel to fire, incites.*
Befa', *befall.*
Behint, *behind.*
Belang, *belong to.*
Beld, *bald.*
Bellyfu', *bellyfull.*
Belyve, *by-and-by.*
Ben, *the inner or best room of a cottage.*

Benmost bore, *the innermost recess, or hole.*
Bethankit, *the grace after meat.*
Beuk, *a book.* Devil's pictur'd beuks, *cards.*
Bicker, *a wooden bowl,* or *a short race.*
Bid, *to wish or ask.*
Bide, *to stand, to endure.*
Biel, *a habitation.*
Bield, *shelter.*
Bien (of a person) *well-to-do;* (of a place) *comfortable.*
Big, *to build.*
Biggin, *building.*
Bill, *a bull.*
Billie, *a comrade, fellow, young man.*
Bings, *heaps.*
Birk, *the birch.*
Birken-shaw, *a small birch-wood.*
Birkie, *a lively, young, forward fellow.*
Birring, *whirring.*
Birses, *bristles.*
Bit, *crisis;* also, *little.*
Bizzard gled, *a kite.*
Bizz, *a bustling haste.*
Bizzy, *busy.*
Bizzies, *buzzes.*
Black Bonnet, *the elder.*
Blae, *blue, sharp, keen.*
Blastie, *a term of contempt.*
Blastit, *blasted, withered.*
Blate, *shamefaced, sheepish.*
Blather, *bladder.*
Blaud, *to slap; a quantity of anything.*
Blaudin', *pelting or beating.*
Blaw, *to blow, to brag.*
Blawn, *blown.*
Bleerit, *bleared.*
Bleeze, *a blaze.*
Bleezin, *blazing.*
Blellum, *an idle talking fellow.*
Blether, *the bladder, nonsense.*
Blethers, *nonsense.*
Bleth'rin, *talking idly.*
Blin', *blind.*
Blink, *a short time, a look.*
Blinks, *looks smilingly.*

Glossary

Blinkers, *a term of contempt, pretty girls.*

Blinkin, *smirking.*

Blitter, *the mire snipe.*

Blue-gown, *one of those beggars who get annually on the king's birthday a blue cloak or gown with a badge, a beggar, a bedesman.*

Blude, *blood.*

Bluid, *blood.*

Blume, *bloom.*

Bluntie, *a stupid person.*

Blypes, *peelings.*

Bocked, *vomited.*

Boddle, *a small coin, a halfpenny.*

Bogles, *hobgoblins.*

Bonnie, *beautiful.*

Bonnocks, *thick cakes of oatmeal bread.*

Boord, *board.*

Boortrees, *elder bushes.*

Boost, *must needs.*

Bore, *a hole or rent.*

Bouk, *a corpse.*

Bouses, *drinks.*

Bow-hough'd, *crook-thighed.*

Bow-kail, *cabbage.*

Bow't, *crooked.*

Brae, *the slope of a hill.*

Braid, *broad.*

Braid-claith, *broad-cloth.*

Braid Scots, *broad Scotch.*

Braik, *a harrow to break the clods.*

Braing't, *rushed forward.*

Brak, *did break.*

Brak's, *broke his.*

Brankie, *well attired.*

Branks, *a kind of wooden curb for horses.*

Brany, *brandy.*

Brash, *a sudden short illness.*

Brats, *clothes, aprons.*

Brattle, *a shore race.*

Braw, *handsome, gaily dressed.*

Brawly, *perfectly.*

Braxies, *sheep which have died of a disease called 'braxy.'*

Breastie, *dim. of breast.*

Breastit, *did spring up or forward.*

Brechan, *a horse-collar.*

Breckan, *fern.*

Bree, *juice, liquid.*

Breeks, *breeches.*

Brent, *high, smooth, unwrinkled.*

Brief, *a writing.*

Brig, *bridge.*

Brither, *brother.*

Brithers, *brothers.*

Brock, *a badger.*

Brogue, *a trick.*

Broo, *water, broth.*

Brooses, *races at country weddings who shall first reach the bridegroom's house on returning from church.*

Browst, *as much malt liquor as is brewed at a time.*

Browster-wives, *ale-house wives.*

Brugh, *burgh.*

Brulzie, *a broil.*

Brunstane, *brimstone.*

Brunt, *burned.*

Brust, *burst.*

Buckie, *dim of buck.*

Buckskin, *an inhabitant of Virginia.*

Buff, *to beat.*

Bughtin-time, *the time of collecting the ewes in the pens to be milked.*

Buirdly, *strong, well-knit.*

Buke, *book.*

Bum, *to hum.*

Bum-clock, *a beetle.*

Bumming, *humming.*

Bummle, *a blunderer.*

Bunker, *a seat in a window.*

Burdies, *damsels.*

Bure, *bore, did bear.*

Burns, *streams.*

Burnie, *streamlet.*

Burnewin, *i.e. burn the wind, a blacksmith.*

Bur-thistle, *the spear-thistle.*

Busking, *dressing, decorating.*

Buskit, *dressed.*

Busks, *adorns.*

Buss, *a bush.*

Bussle, *a bustle.*

But, *without, or wanting.*

But an' ben, *kitchen and parlour.*

By, *past, apart.*
By attour, *in the neighbourhood,*
   outside.
Byke, *a bee-hive.*
Byre, *cowshed.*

Ca', *to drive; a call.*
Ca'd, *named, driven; calved.*
Ca't, *called.*
Ca'throu', *to push forward.*
Cadger, *a carrier or travelling*
   dealer.
Cadie, *a fellow.*
Caff, *chaff.*
Cairds, *tinkers.*
Calf-ward, *a small inclosure for calves.*
Callans, *boys.*
Caller, *fresh.*
Callet, *a trull.*
Cam, *came.*
Cankert, *cankered.*
Cankrie, *cankered.*
Canna, *cannot.*
Cannie, *carefully, softly.*
Cantie, *cheerful, lively.*
Cantrip, *a charm, a spell.*
Cape-stane, *cope-stone.*
Carl, *a carle, a man.*
Carlin, *an old woman.*
Cartes, *cards for playing.*
Cartie, dim. of *cart.*
Caudrons, *cauldrons.*
Cauf, *a calf.*
Cauk and keel, *chalk and ruddle.*
Cauld, *cold.*
Caups, *wooden bowl.*
Causey, *causeway.*
Cavie, *a hen-coop.*
Chamer, *chamber.*
Change-house, *a tavern.*
Chap, *a fellow.*
Chapman, *a pedlar.*
Chaup, *a blow.*
Cheek for chow, *cheek for jowl.*
Cheep, *chirp.*
Chiels, *young fellows.*
Chimla, *chimney.*
Chittering, *shivering with cold.*

Chows, *chews.*
Chuckie, dim. of *chuck.*
Christendie, *Christendom.*
Chuffie, *fat-faced.*
Clachan, *a hamlet.*
Claise, *clothes.*
Claith, *cloth.*
Claithing, *clothing.*
Claiver, *to talk idly or foolishly.*
Clamb, *clomb.*
Clankie, *a sharp stroke.*
Clap, *a clapper.*
Clark, *clerky, scholarly.*
Clarkit, *wrote.*
Clarty, *dirty.*
Clash, *gossip; to talk.*
Clatter, *to talk idly.*
Claught, *clutched.*
Claughtin, *catching at anything*
   greedily.
Claut, *to snatch at, to lay hold of a*
   quantity scraped together.
Claver, *clover.*
Clavers, *idle stories.*
Claw, *scratch.*
Cleckin, *a brood.*
Cleed, *to clothe.*
Cleeding, *clothing.*
Cleek, *to seize.*
Cleekit, *linked themselves.*
Clegs, *gad-flies.*
Clink, *to rhyme; money.*
Clinkin, *sitting down neatly.*
Clinkumbell, *the church bell-ringer.*
Clips, *shears.*
Clishmaclaver, *idle talk.*
Clockin-time, *hatching-time.*
Cloot, *the hoof.*
Clootie, *Satan.*
Clours, *bumps or swellings after a blow.*
Clouts, *clothes.*
Clout, *patch.*
Clud, *a cloud.*
Coble, *a fishing-boat.*
Cock, *to erect.*
Cocks, *good fellows.*
Cod, *a pillow.*
Co'er, *to cover.*

Coft, *bought.*
Cog, *a wooden dish.*
Coggie, dim. of *cog.*
Coila, *from* Kyle, *a district of* Ayrshire.
Collie, *a sheep dog.*
Collieshangie, *an uproar, a quarrel.*
Commans, *commandments.*
Compleenin, *complaining.*
Cood, *the cud.*
Coofs, *fools, ninnies.*
Cookit, *appeared and disappeared,* or *peeped.*
Coost, *did cast.*
Cootie, *a kind of large spoon, or spade;* also, *feathered at the ankles.*
Corbies, *crows.*
Corn't, *fed with oats.*
Corss, *the market-cross.*
Couldna, *could not.*
Countra, *country.*
Couthie, *kindly, loving, comfortable.*
Cowp, *to tumble over.*
Cowpit, *tumbled.*
Cow'rin, *cowering.*
Cowr, *to cower.*
Cour, *to cower.*
Cowte, *a colt.*
Crack, *a story or harangue, talk.*
Crackin, *conversing, gossiping.*
Craft, *a croft.*
Craig, *the throat.*
Craigs, *crags.*
Craigy, *craggy.*
Craiks, *landrails.*
Crambo-clink, *rhymes, or doggerel verses crammed together.*
Crambo-jingle, *rhymes.*
Crankous, *fretful.*
Cranreuch, *hoar frost.*
Crap, *crop.*
Craw, *to crow.*
Creel, *a basket.*
Creepie-chair, *the chair or stool of repentance.*
Creeshie, *greasy.*
Crocks, *old sheep.*
Croods, *coos.*

Crooded, *cooed.*
Cronie, *an intimate comrade.*
Croon, *a groaning or murmuring sound.*
Crouchie, *crook-backed.*
Crouse, *brisk and bold.*
Crowdie, *porridge.*
Crowdie-time, *breakfast-time.*
Crummock, *a staff with a crooked head.*
Crump, *crisp or crumbly.*
Crunt, *a blow on the head with a cudgel.*
Cuddle, *to fondle.*
Cuifs, *blockheads, ninnies.*
Cummock, *a staff with a crooked head.*
Curch, *a female head-dress.*
Curchie, *a curtsy.*
Curmurring, *rumbling.*
Curpin, *the crupper.*
Curple, *the crupper.*
Cushats, *wood pigeons.*
Custock, *the heart of a stalk of cabbage.*
Cutty, *short.*

Daddie, *father.*
Daes't, *stupified, dazed.*
Daffin, *merriment.*
Daft, *foolish, sportive.*
Dails, *deals of wood.*
Daimen-icker, *an occasional ear of corn.*
Damies, dim. of *dames.*
Dam, *water.*
Dang, *knocked, pushed.*
Danton, *to subdue.*
Darklins, *darkling.*
Daud, *a lump; to knock.*
Daudin', *pelting.*
Dauntingly, *dauntlessly.*
Daur, *to dare.*
Daurna, *dare not.*
Daut, *to fondle, to doat on.*
Daw, *to dawn.*
Dawtit, *fondled, caressed.*
Daurg, *a day's work.*
Daviely, *spiritless.* [Dowiely.]

Davie's, *King David's*.
Dead-sweer, *extremely reluctant*.
Deave, *to deafen*.
Deils, *devils*.
Deil ma care, *devil may care, no matter for all that*.
Deil haet, *devil a thing; devil have it!*.
Deleerit, *delirious*.
Delvin, *delving*.
Descrive, *to describe*.
Deservin't, *deserving of it*.
Deuk, *a duck*.
Devel, *a stunning blow*.
Diddle, *to jog, or fiddle*.
Differ, *difference*.
Dight, *cleaned from chaff, to wipe away*.
Din, *dun in colour*.
Ding, *to surpass, to beat*.
Dink, *neat, trim*.
Dinna, *do not* .
Dirl, *a thrilling blow*.
Dizzen, *a dozen*.
Dochter, *daughter*.
Doited, *stupefied*.
Donsie, *stupid, unmanageable*.
Dooked, *ducked*.
Dool, *sorrow*.
Doolfu', *sorrowful*.
Doos, *pigeons*.
Dorty, *saucy, sullen*.
Douce, *grave, sober, modest, gentle*.
Doucely, *soberly*.
Doudled, *dandled*.
Dought, *could, might*.
Dought na, *did not*, or *did not choose to*.
Doup, *the backside, the bottom*.
Dour, *stubborn*.
Dow, *do. can*.
Dowff, *pithless, dull*.
Dowie, *faded or worn with sorrow, sad*.
Downa bide, *cannot stand*.
Downa do, *impotence*.
Doylt, *stupid*.
Doytin, *walking stupidly*.
Dozen'd, *impotent, torpid or benumbed*.

Draiglit, *draggled*.
Drants, *sullen fits*.
Drap, *drop, a small quantity*.
Drappie, dim. of *drap*.
Drapping, *dropping*.
Draunting, *drawling, of a slow enunciation*.
Dree, *to endure*.
Dreeping, *dripping*.
Dreigh, *tedious and slow*.
Driddle, *to play on the fiddle without skill*.
Drift, *a drove*. Fell aff the drift, *wandered from his companions*.
Droddum, *the breech*.
Drone, *the bagpipe*.
Droop-rumpl't, *that drops at the crupper*.
Drouk, *to drench*.
Droukit, *wet, drenched*.
Drouth, *thirst*.
Drouthy, *thirsty*.
Druken, *drunken*.
Drumly, *muddy*.
Drummock, *meal and water mixed raw*.
Drunt, *pet, sullen humour*.
Dry, *thirsty*.
Dubs, *puddles*.
Duds, *garments*.
Duddie, *ragged*.
Duddies, *garments*.
Dung, *knocked, exhausted*.
Dunted, *beat, thumped*.
Dunts, *blows, knocks*.
Durk, *a dirk*.
Dusht, *pushed*.
Dwalling, *dwelling*.
Dwalt, *dwelt*.
Dyvors, *bankrupts, disreputable fellows*.

Earns, *eagles*.
Eastlin, *eastern*.
Ee, *eye; to watch*.
Een, *eyen*.
E'e brie, *the eyebrow*.
E'en, *evening*.

E'enins, *evenings.*
Eerie, *having or producing a super-stitious feeling of dread; dismal.*
Eild, *age.*
Eke, *also.*
Elbucks, *elbows.*
Eldritch, *elvish; strange, wild, hideous.*
Eleckit, *elected.*
Eller, *an elder.*
En', *end.*
Enbrugh, *Edinburgh.*
Em'brugh, *Edinburgh.*
Enow, *enough.*
Erse, *Gaelic.*
Ether-stane, *adder-stone.*
Ettle, *design.*
Expeckit, *expected.*
Eydent, *diligent.*

Fa', *lot; also, have as one's lot, obtain.*
Faddom't, *fathomed.*
Fae, *foe.*
Faem, *foam.*
Faikit, *bated, forgiven, excused.*
Failins, *failings.*
Fair-fa', *may good befall!*
Fairin, *a present, a reward.*
Fairly, *entirely, completely.*
Fallow, *a fellow.*
Fa'n or fa'en, *have fallen.*
Fan, *found.*
Fand, *found.*
Farls, *cakes of oat-bread.*
Fash, *trouble myself.*
Fash your thumb, *trouble yourself in the least.*
Fashous, *troublesome.*
Fasten-een, *Fasten's-even (before Lent).*
Fatt'rels, *ribbon-ends.*
Faught, *a fight.*
Fauld, *a fold.*
Faulding, *folding.*
Faulding slap, *the gate of the fold.*
Fause, *false.*
Faut, *fault.*
Fautor, *a transgressor.*
Fawsont, *seemly, respectably.*

Fearfu', *fearful.*
Feat, *spruce.*
Fecht, *to fight.*
Feck, *the greater portion.*
Feckly, *mostly.*
Fecket, *an under waistcoat with sleeves.*
Feckless, *powerless, without effect.*
Feg, *a fig.*
Feide, *feud.*
Fell, *the flesh immediately under the skin; keen, biting; tasty.*
Fen, *a shift, provision.*
Fend, *to keep off, to live comfortably.*
Ferlie, *wonder.*
Fetch't, *pulled by fits and starts.*
Fey, *fated.*
Fidge, *to fidget.*
Fidgin-fain, *fidgetting with eagerness.*
Fiel, *soft, smooth.*
Fient, *fiend.* The fient a, *the devil a.*
Fier, *healthy, sound; brother, friend.*
Fiere, *companion.*
Fillie, *a filly.*
Fin', *find.*
Fissle, *bustle or rustle.*
Fit, *foot.*
Fittie-lan, *the near horse of the hinder-most pair in the plough.*
Fizz, *to make a hissing noise like fer-mentation.*
Flaffin, *flapping, fluttering.*
Flae, *a flea.*
Flang, *did fling or caper.*
Flannen, *flannel.*
Fleech'd, *supplicated, flattered.*
Flee, *a fly.*
Fleesh, *a fleece.*
Fleg, *a fright, a random stroke.*
Fleth'rin, *flattering.*
Flewit, *a sharp blow.*
Fley'd, *scared.*
Flichterin', *fluttering.*
Flinders, *shreds.*
Flinging, *dancing wildly.*
Flingin-tree, *a flail.*
Fliskit, *fretted and capered.*
Flittering, *fluttering.*

Flyte, *to scold.*
Fodgel, *squat, plump.*
Foor, *fared, went.*
Foord, *a ford.*
Foorsday, *Thursday.*
Forbears, *forefathers.*
Forbye, *besides.*
Forfairn, *worn out, jaded.*
Forfoughten, *fatigued.*
Forgather, *meet, fall in with.*
Forgie, *forgive.*
Forjesket, *jaded with fatigue.*
Forrit, *forward.*
Fother, *fodder.*
Fou, *full, tipsy.*
Foughten, *troubled.*
Fouth, *abundance.*
Fow, *full measure of corn, bushel.*
Frae, *from.*
Freath, *to froth.*
Fremit, *strange, foreign.*
Frien', *friend.*
Fu', *full.*
Fud, *hare's tail.*
Fufft, *puffed, blew.*
Furder, *furtherance, success.*
Furms, *wooden forms or seats.*
Furr-ahin, *the hindmost horse on the right hand of the plough.*
Furrs, *furrows.*
Fushionless, *pithless.*
Fy, *an exclamation of haste.*
Fyke, *trouble, fuss.*
Fyle, *to soil or dirty.*

Gab, *the mouth; to prate.*
Gae, *go, gave.*
Gaed, *went.*
Gaets, *manners,* or *ways.*
Gairs, *'purple patches'.*
Gane, *gone.*
Gang, *to go.*
Gangrel, *vagrant.*
Gar, *to make.*
Garten, *garter.*
Gash, *sagacious.*
Gashin, *conversing.*
Gat, *got.*

Gate, *manner, way or road.*
Gatty, *swelled.*
Gaucie, *large, bushy, full, stately.*
Gaud, *the plough shaft.*
Gaudsman, *a ploughboy, the boy who drives the horses in the plough.*
Gaun, *going.*
Gaunted, *yawned.*
Gawcie, *jolly, large, flourishing.*
Gawkies, *foolish persons.*
Gawn, *Gavin.*
Gaylies, *pretty well.*
Gear, *wealth, goods.*
Geck, *to toss the head in scorn.*
Geds, *pike.*
Genty, *slender.*
Geordie, *George.* The yellow letter'd Geordie, *a guinea.*
Get, *child.*
Ghaists, *ghosts.*
Gie, *give.*
Gied, *gave.*
Gien, *given.*
Gi'en, *given.*
Gies, *give us.*
Gif, *if.*
Giftie. dim. of *gift.*
Giglets, *laughing children.*
Gillie, dim. of *gill.*
Gilpey, *a young person.*
Gimmer, *a ewe two years old.*
Gin, *if.*
Girdle, *a circular plate of iron for toasting cakes on the fire.*
Girn, *to grin.*
Girrs, *hoops.*
Gizz, *a wig.*
Glaikit, *thoughtless, giddy.*
Glaizie, *smooth, glossy.*
Glamour, *effect of a charm.*
Glaum'd, *grasped.*
Gled, *a kite.*
Gleed, *a live coal.*
Gleg, *sharp; cleverly, swiftly.*
Gleib, *a gleb or portion.*
Glib-gabbet, *that speaks smoothly and readily.*
Glinted, *glanced.*

Glossary

Gloamin, *twilight.*
Gloamin-shot, *a twilight interview.*
Glowrin, *staring.*
Glowr'd, *looked earnestly, stared.*
Glunch, *a frown.*
Goavan, *moving and looking vacantly.*
Gotten, *got.*
Gowan, *the daisy.*
Gowd, *gold.*
Gowden, *golden.*
Gowff'd, *golfed.*
Gowk, *a fool.*
Gowling, *howling.*
Graff, *a grave.*
Grained, *groaned.*
Graip, *a pronged instrument.*
Graith, *harness accoutrements.*
Granes, *groans.*
Grannie, *grandmother.*
Grape, *to grope.*
Grapit, *groped.*
Grat, *wept.*
Gree, *a prize; to agree.*
Gree't, *agreed.*
Greet, *to weep.*
Griens, *longs for.*
Grippet, *gripped, caught hold of.*
Grissle, *gristle.*
Grit, *great.*
Grozet, *a gooseberry.*
Grumphie, *the sow.*
Grun', *the ground.*
Grunstane, *a grindstone.*
Gruntle, *the countenance, a grunting noise.*
Grunzie, *the mouth.*
Grushie, *thick, of thriving growth.*
Grusome, *ill favoured.*
Grutten, *wept.*
Gudeen, *good even.*
Gudeman, *goodman.*
Gudes, *goods.*
Guid, *good.*
Guid-e'en, *good even.*
Guidfather, *father-in-law.*
Guidwife, *the mistress of the house, the landlady.*
Guid-willie, *hearty.*

Gully, *a large knife.*
Gulravage, *riotous and hasty.*
Gumlie, *muddy, discoloured.*
Gumption, *understanding.*
Gusty, *tasteful.*
Gutcher, *grandfather, goodsire.*

Ha', *hall.*
Haddin, *holding, inheritance.*
Hae, *have.*
Haffets, *the temples.*
Hafflins, *partly; also, growing lads.*
Hafflins-wise, *almost half.*
Hag, *a pit in mosses and moors.*
Haggis, *a kind of pudding boiled in the stomach of an ox or a sheep.*
Hain, *to spare, to save.*
Hain'd, *spared.*
Hairst, *harvest.*
Haith, *faith!*
Haivers, *idle talk.*
Hald, *an abiding-place.*
Hale, *whole, entire.*
Haly, *holy.*
Hallan, *a partition-wall in a cottage, hall-end.*
Hallions, *clowns, roysterers.*
Hallowmans, *the 31st of October.*
Hame, *home.*
Han', *hand.*
Han'afore, *the foremost horse on the left hand in the plough.*
Han'ahin, *the hindmost horse on the left hand in the plough.*
Hand-breed, *a hand-breadth.*
Hand-waled, *carefully selected by hand.*
Handless, *without hands, useless, awkward.*
Hangit, *hanged.*
Hansel, *a gift for a particular season, or the first money on any particular occasion.*
Hap, *to wrap.* Winter Hap, *winter clothing.*
Hap, *hop.*
Happer, *a hopper.*
Happing, *hopping.*

Hap-step-an'-lowp, *hop, step, and jump.*
Harkit, *hearkened.*
Harn, *coarse linen.*
Har'sts, *harvests.*
Hash, *a soft, useless fellow.*
Hash'd, *cut.*
Haslock, *the finest wool, being the lock that grows on the* hals *or throat.*
Hastit, *hasted.*
Haud, *to hold.*
Hauf, *the half.*
Haughs, *the low-lying lands on the border of a river.*
Hauns, *hands.*
Haurl, *to drag.*
Haurlin, *peeling, dragging off.*
Hauver, *coarsely ground.*
Havins, *good manners.*
Hav'rel, *half-witted.*
Hawkie, *a cow, properly one with a white face.*
Healsome, *wholesome.*
Heapit, *heaped.*
Hearin', *hearing.*
Hearse, *hoarse.*
Hech, *an exclamation of surprise and grief.*
Hecht, *foretold, offered.*
Hechtin', *making to pant.*
Heckle, *a comb used in dressing hemp, flax, &c.*
Heels-o'er gowdy, *head-over-heels.*
Heeze, *to elevate, to hoist.*
Heft, *haft.*
Hellim, *the helm.*
Hen-broo, *hen-broth.*
Herriet, *harried.*
Herryment, *plundering, devastation.*
Hersel, *herself.*
Het, *hot.*
Heugh, *pit or ravine.*
Heuk, *a reaping-hook.*
Hich, *high.*
Hidin', *hiding.*
Hie, *high.*
Hilch, *to hobble.*
Hilchin, *halting.*

Hill-tap, *hill-top.*
Hiltie-skiltie, *helter-skelter.*
Himsel, *himself.*
Hiney, *honey.*
Hing, *to hang.*
Hirples, *walks as if crippled.*
Hissel, hirsel, *as many cattle or sheep as one person can attend.*
Histie, *dry, barren.*
Hitch, *a loop or knot.*
Hizzies, *young women.*
Hoast, *a cough.*
Hoddin, *jogging, plodding.*
Hoggie, *a young sheep one year old.*
Hog-score, *a line drawn across the rink in the game of curling.*
Hog-shouther, *a kind of horse-play by justling with the shoulder.*
Hol't, *holed, perforated.*
Hoodie-craw, *the hooded crow.*
Hool, *the outer skin or case.*
Hoolie! *stop! cautiously! softly!*
Hoord, *hoard.*
Hoordet, *hoarded.*
Horn, *a spoon or a comb made of horn.*
Hornie, *Satan.*
Host or hoast, *a cough.*
Hostin, *coughing.*
Hotch'd, *fidgetted.*
Houghmagandie, *fornication.*
Houlets, *owls.*
Hov'd, *swelled.*
Howdie, *a midwife.*
Howe, *hollow.*
Howe-backit, *sunk in the back.*
Howes, *hollows.*
Howkit, *digged, dug up.*
Hoyse, *hoist.*
Hoy't, *urged.*
Hoyte, *to move clumsily.*
Hughoc, *Hugh.*
Hunder, *a hundred.*
Hunkers, *the hams.*
Huntit, *hunted.*
Hurcheon, *a hedgehog.*
Hurchin, *an urchin.*
Hurdies, *hips.*

Hurl, *to wheel* or *whirl*.
Hushion, *stocking-leg, worn on the arm*.
Hyte, *mad*.

Icker, *an ear of corn*.
Ier'oe, *a great-grandchild*.
Ilk, *each*.
Ilka, *every*.
Ill o't, *bad at it*.
Ill-willie, *ill-natured*.
Indentin, *indenturing*.
Ingine, *genius, ingenuity*.
Ingle-cheek, *the fireside*.
Ingle-lowe, *the household fire*.
I'se, *I shall* or *will*.
Isna, *is not*.
Ither, *other*.
Itsel, *itself*.

Jad, *a jade, a wild young woman*.
Janwar, *January*.
Jauk, *to dally, to trifle*.
Jaukin, *trifling, dallying*.
Jauner, *foolish talk*.
Jaups, *splashes*.
Jillet, *a jilt*.
Jimp, *slender*.
Jimply, *neatly*.
Jink, *to dodge*.
Jinker, *that turns quickly*.
Jinkers, *gay, sprightly girls*.
Jinkin, *dodging*.
Jirkinet, *an outer jacket or jerkin worn by women*.
Jirt, *a jerk; to squirt*.
Jo, *sweetheart, joy*.
Joctelegs, *clasp-knives*.
Joes, *lovers*.
Jorum, *the jug*.
Jouk, *to duck, to make obeisance*.
Jow, *to swing and ring*.
Jumpit, *jumped*.
Jundie, *to justle*.

Kaes, *daws*.
Kail, *broth*.
Kail-blade, *the leaf of the colewort*.

Kail-runt, *the stem of the colewort*.
Kain, *farm produce paid as rent*.
Kebars, *rafters*.
Kebbuck, *a cheese*.
Keckle, *to cackle, to laugh*.
Keekin'-glass, *a looking-glass*.
Keeks, *peeps*.
Keepit, *kept*.
Kelpies, *water-spirits*.
Ken, *know*.
Ken'les, *kindles*.
Kenn'd, *known*.
Kennin, *a little bit*.
Kent, *knew*.
Kep, *to catch anything when falling*.
Ket, *a fleece*.
Kiaugh, *anxiety, cark*.
Kilbagie, *the name of a certain kind of whisky*.
Kilt, *to tuck up*.
Kimmer, *a married woman, a gossip*.
Kin', *kind*.
King's-hood, *a part of the entrails of an ox*.
Kintra, *country*.
Kintra cooser, *a country stallion*.
Kirn, *a churn*.
Kirns, *harvest-homes*.
Kirsen, *to christen*.
Kist, *a chest*.
Kitchen, *anything that eats with bread to serve for a relish*.
Kitchens, *seasons. makes palatable*.
Kittle, *to tickle; ticklish, difficult*.
Kittlin, *a kitten*.
Kiutlin, *fondling*.
Knaggie, *like knags. or points of rock*.
Knappin-hammers, *hammers for breaking stones*.
Knowe, *a knoll*.
Knurlin, *a dwarf, knotted, gnarled*.
Kye, *cows*.
Kytes, *bellies*.
Kythe, *discover, appear*.

Laddie, *a lad*.

Lade, *a load.*
Laggen, *the angle between the side and bottom of a wooden dish.*
Laigh, *low.*
Laik, *lack.*
Lair, *lore.*
Lairing, *sticking in mire or mud.*
Laith, *loth.*
Laithfu', *bashful.*
Lallan, *lowland.*
Lampit, *limpet.*
Lan', *land, estate.*
Lane, *alone.*
Lanely, *lonely.*
Lang, *long.*
Lap, *did leap.*
Lave, *the rest.*
Lav'rocks, *larks.*
Lawin, *shot, reckoning, bill.*
Lawlan', *lowland.*
Lea'e, *leave.*
Leal, *true, loyal.*
Lea' rig, *a grassy ridge.*
Lear, *lore, learning.*
Lee-lang, *live-long.*
Leesome, or lo'esome, *pleasant.*
Leeze me, *leif (or dear) is to me; mine above everything else be.*
Leister, *a three-barbed instrument for sticking fish.*
Len', *lend.*
Leugh, *laughed.*
Leuk, *look, appearance.*
Libbet, *gelded.*
Licket, *beating.*
Licks, *a beating.*
Liein, *telling lies.*
Lien, *lain.*
Lift, *heaven, a large quantity.*
Lightly, *to undervalue, to slight.*
Lilt, *sing.*
Limmer, *a woman of loose manners or morals.*
Limpit, *limped.*
Lin, *a waterfall.*
Linket, *tripped deftly.*
Linkin, *tripping.*

Linn, *a waterfall.*
Lint, *flax.*
Linties, *linnets.*
Lippened, *trusted.*
Loan, *lane.*
Lo'ed, *loved.*
Lon'on, *London.*
Loof, *palm of the hand.*
Loosome, *lovesome.*
Loot, *did let.*
Looves, *palms.*
Losh, *a petty oath.*
Lough, *a lake.*
Louns, *fellows, rascals.*
Loup, *to leap.*
Lowe, *flame.*
Lowan, *flaming.*
Lowin, *blazing.*
Lowpin, *leaping.*
Lowping, *leaping.*
Lowse, *to loosen.*
Luckie, *a designation applied to an elderly woman.*
Lug, *the ear.*
Lugget, *eared.*
Luggies, *small wooden dishes with straight handles.*
Luke, *look.*
Lum, *the chimney.*
Lunardie, *a bonnet called after Lunardi, the aëronaut.*
Lunt, *a column of smoke.*
Luntin, *smoking.*
Luve, *love.*
Luvers, *lovers.*
Lyart, *grey.*
Lynin, *lining.*

Maf, *more.*
Mair, *more.*
Maist, *almost.*
Mak, *make.*
Mailie, *Molly.*
Mailins, *farms.*
Mang, *among.*
Manteels, *mantles.*
Mashlum, *mixed corn.*

Maskin-pat, *a tea-pot.*
Maukin, *a hare.*
Maun, *must.*
Maunna, *must not.*
Maut, *malt.*
Mavis, *the thrush.*
Mawin, *mowing.*
Mawn, *a basket; mown.*
Meere, *a mare.*
Meikle, *as much.*
Melder, *corn sent to the mill to be ground.*
Mell, *to meddle.*
Melvie, *to soil with mud.*
Men', *mend.*
Mense, *good manners.*
Mess John, *the clergyman.*
Messin, *a dog of mixed breeds.*
Midden, *the dunghill.*
Midden-creels, *dunghill baskets.*
Midden-hole, *the dunghill.*
Mim, *prim.*
Mim-mou'd, *prim-mouthed.*
Min', *remembrance.*
Min', *mind.*
Minnie, *mother.*
Mirk, *night; murky.*
Misca'd, *abused.*
Misguidin', *misguiding.*
Mishanter, *misfortune, disaster.*
Mislear'd, *mischievous; ill-bred.*
Mist, *missed.*
Misteuk, *mistook.*
Mither, *mother.*
Mixtie-maxtie, *confusedly mixed.*
Moistify, *to make moist.*
Mony, *many.*
Mools, *the earth of graves.*
Moop, *to nibble, to keep company with.*
Moorlan', *moorland.*
Moss, *a moorass.*
Mou', *mouth.*
Moudieworts, *moles.*
Muckle, *great, big, much.*
Muslin-kail, *thin broth.*
Mutchkin, *an English pint.*

Mysel, *myself.*

Na', *not, no.*
Nae, *no.*
Naebody, *nobody.*
Naig, *a nag.*
Nane, *none.*
Nappy, *strong ale.*
Natch, *grip, hold.*
Neibors, *neighbours.*
Needna, *need not.*
Neist, *next.*
Neuk, *nook, corner.*
New-ca'd, *newly calved.*
Nick, *to break, to sever suddenly.*
Nickan, *cutting.*
Nicket, *caught, cut off.*
Nick-nackets, *curiosities.*
Nicks, *notches.*
Niest, *next.*
Nieve-fu', *a fist-full .*
Nieves, *fists.*
Niffer, *exchange.*
Nits, *nuts.*
Nocht, *nothing.*
Norland, *Northland.*
Nowte, *cattle.*

O', *of.*
O'erlay, *an outside cravat, muffler.*
O'erword, *refrain.*
Ony, *any.*
Orra, *superfluous, extra.*
O't, *of it.*
Ought, *aught, anything.*
Oughtlins, *anything in the least.*
Ourie, *shivering, drooping.*
Oursel, *ourselves.*
Out-cast, *a quarrel.*
Outler, *un-housed, outlying.*
Owre, *over, too.*
Owsen, *oxen.*

Pack an' thick, *on intimate terms, closely familiar.*
Packs, *twelve stones.*
Paidle, *to paddle.*

Paidles, *wanders about without aim.*
Painch, *paunch, stomach.*
Paitricks, *partridges.*
Pangs, *crams.*
Parishen, *the parish.*
Parritch, *porridge.*
Parritch-pats, *porridge-pots.*
Pat, *put; a pot.*
Pattle, *a plough-spade.*
Paughty, *haughty, petulant.*
Paukie, *cunning, sly.*
Pay't, *paid.*
Pechan, *the stomach.*
Pechin', *panting.*
Penny wheep, *small beer.*
Pettle, *a plough-spade.*
Phraisin, *flattering, coaxing.*
Pickle, *a small quantity.*
Pit, *put.*
Placads, *public proclamations.*
Plack, *an old Scotch coin, the third part of a Scotch penny, twelve of which make an English penny.*
Plaiden, *plaiding.*
Plenished, *stocked.*
Pleugh, *plough.*
Pliskie, *a mischievous trick.*
Pliver, *a plover.*
Plumpit, *plumped.*
Pocks, *wallets or bags.*
Poind, *to seize or distrain.*
Poortith, *poverty.*
Pou, *to pull; to gather.*
Pouk, *to pluck.*
Poupit, *the pulpit.*
Pouse, *push or thrust.*
Poussie, *a hare.*
Pouts, *chicks.*
Pouther'd, *powdered.*
Pouthery, *powdery.*
Pow, *the head, the poll.*
Pownie, *a pony.*
Powther, *powder.*
Pree, *to taste.*
Preen, *a pin.*
Prent, *print.*
Prie'd, *tasted.*
Prief, *proof.*
Priggin', *haggling.*

Primsie, *demure, prim.*
Propone, *to propose.*
Proveses, *provosts.*
Pu', *to pull.*
Puddock-stools, *toadstools.*
Puir, *poor.*
Pund, *pounds.*
Pyet, *the magpie.*
Pyke, *to pick.*
Pyles, *grains.*

Quaick, *quack.*
Quat, *quit, quitted.*
Quaukin', *quaking.*
Quean, *a young woman.*
Quey, *a young cow.*
Quo', *quoth.*

Rab, *Rob, Robert.*
Rad, *afraid.*
Rade, *rode.*
Ragweed, *the plant ragwort.*
Raibles, *rattles nonsense.*
Rair, *to roar.*
Raise, *rose.*
Raize, *to madden, to inflame.*
Ramblin, *rambling.*
Ramfeezl'd, *fatigued.*
Ramgunshock, *rugged.*
Ram-stam, *forward, precipitate.*
Randie, *quarrelsome.*
Randy, *a vixen.*
Ranting, *noisy, full of animal spirits.*
Rants, *jollifications.*
Rape, *a rope.*
Raploch, *a coarse cloth.*
Rask, *a rush.*
Rash-buss, *a bush of rushes.*
Rattan, *a rat.*
Rattons, *rats.*
Raucle, *rough, rash, sturdy.*
Raught, *reached.*
Raw, *a row.*
Rax, *to stretch.*
Ream, *cream.*
Rebute, *a rebut, a repulse, a rebuke.*
Rede, *counsel.*
Red-wud, *stark mad.*
Reekin, *smoking.*

Reekit, *smoked, smoky.*
Reeks, *smokes.*
Reestit, *smoke-dried; stood restive.*
Reif randies, *roysterers.*
Remead, *remedy.*
Remuve, *remove.*
Rew, *to take pity.*
Rickles, *stocks of grain.*
Rig, *a ridge.*
Riggin, *rafters.*
Rigwoodie, *withered, sapless.*
Rin, *run.*
Rink, *the course of the stones in curling.*
Rinnin, *running.*
Ripp, *a handful of unthrashed corn.*
Ripple, *weakness in the back and reins.*
Ripplin-kame, *a flax-comb.*
Riskit, *made a noise like the tearing of roots.*
Rive, *to burst or tear.*
Rock, *a distaff.*
Rockin, *a social gathering, the women spinning on the rock or distaff.*
Roon, *round.*
Roose, *to praise.*
Roosty, *rusty.*
Roun', *round.*
Roupet, *hoarse as with a cold.*
Routhie, *well filled, abundant.*
Rowes, *rolls.*
Rowte, *to low, to bellow.*
Rowth, *abundance.*
Rowtin, *lowing.*
Rozet, *rosin.*
Ruefu', *rueful.*
Rung, *a cudgel.*
Runkl'd, *wrinkled.*
Runts, *the stems of cabbage.*
Ryke, *reach.*

Sabs, *sobs.*
Sae, *so.*
Saft, *soft.*
Sair, *sore; to serve.*
Sairly, *sorely.*
Sair't, *served.*
Sang, *song.*

Sannock *or* Sawnie, *Alexander.*
Sark, *a shirt.*
Sarkit, *provided in shirts.*
Saugh, *the willow.*
Saul, *soul.*
Saunt, *saints.*
Saut, *salt.*
Saw, *to sow.*
Sawmont, *a salmon.*
Sax, *six.*
Scaith, *hurt.*
Scaur, *to scare.*
Scaur, *frightened.*
Scaud, *to scald.*
Scawl, *a scold.*
Scho, *she.*
Schoolin', *schooling, teaching.*
Scones, *barley cakes.*
Sconner, *to loathe; disgust.*
Scraichin, *screeching.*
Screed, *a tear, a rent; to repeat glibly.*
Scriechin', *screeching.*
Scrievin', *gliding easily.*
Scrimpit, *scanty.*
Scrimply, *sparingly.*
Scroggie, *covered with stunted shrubs.*
Sculdudd'ry, *fornication.*
Seizins, *investitures.*
Sel, *self.*
Sell't, *sold.*
Sen', *send.*
Set, *lot.*
Sets, *becomes, set off, starts.*
Settlin', *settling.*
Shachl't, *loose and ill-shaped.*
Shaird, *a shred.*
Shangan, *a cleft stick.*
Shanna, *shall not.*
Shaul, *shallow.*
Shaver, *a wag.*
Shavie, *a trick.*
Shaw, *show.*
Shaw'd, *showed.*
Shaws, *wooded dells.*
Sheep-shank, Wha thinks himsel nae sheep-shank bane, *who thinks himself no unimportant person.*
Sheers, *shears.*

Sheugh, *a trench or ditch.*
Sheuk, *shook.*
Shiel, *a shieling, a hut.*
Shill, *shrill.*
Shog, *a shock.*
Shools, *shovels.*
Shoon, *shoes.*
Shor'd, *threatened, offered.*
Shore, *to threaten or offer.*
Shouldna, *should not.*
Shouther, *shoulder.*
Shure, *did shear (corn).*
Sic, *such.*
Siker, *secure.*
Siclike, *suchlike.*
Sidelins, *sidelong.*
Siller, *money, silver.*
Simmer, *summer.*
Sin', *since.*
Sindry, *sundry.*
Singet, *singed.*
Singin', *singing.*
Sinn, *the sun.*
Sinny, *sunny.*
Sinsyne, *since then.*
Skaith, *hurt.*
Skaithing, *injuring.*
Skeigh, *high-mettled, disdainful, skittish.*
Skellum, *a worthless fellow.*
Skelp, *a slap; to run with a slapping vigorous sound of the feet on the ground.*
Skelpie-limmer, *a technical term in female scolding.*
Skinkin', *thin liquid.*
Skinklin, *glittering.*
Skirl, *to shriek.*
Sklent, *to slope, to strike obliquely, to lie.*
Sklented, *slanted.*
Sklentin, *slanting.*
Skouth, *range, scope.*
Skreech, *to scream.*
Skriegh, *to scream.*
Skyrin, *parti-coloured.*
Skyte, *a glancing sliding stroke.*
Slade, *slid.*
Slae, *the sloe.*

Slaps, *gaps or breaches.*
Slaw, *slow.*
Slee, *sly, clever.*
Sleeest, *slyest.*
Sleekit, *sleek.*
Slidd'ry, *slippery.*
Sloken, *to quench, to allay thirst.*
Slypet, *slipped, fell over slowly.*
Sma', *small.*
Smeddum, *dust, mettle, sense.*
Smeek, *smoke.*
Smiddy, *a smithy.*
Smoor'd, *smothered.*
Smoutie, *smutty.*
Smytrie, *a number huddled together, a smatter.*
Snash, *abuse, impertinence.*
Snaw broo, *melted snow.*
Snawy, *snowy.*
Sned, *to lop, to cut off.*
Snell, *bitter, biting.*
Sneeshin-mill, *a snuff-box.*
Snick, *the latchet of a door.*
Snirtle, *to laugh slily.*
Snool, *to cringe, to sneak, to snub.*
Snoov'd, *went smoothly.*
Snowkit, *snuffed.*
Sodger, *a soldier.*
Soger, *a soldier.*
Sonsie, *jolly, comely, plump.*
Soom, *to swim.*
Soor, *sour.*
Sootie, *sooty.*
Sough, *a heavy sigh.*
Souk, *a suck.*
Soupe, *a spoonful, a small quantity of anything liquid.*
Souple, *supple.*
Souter, *a shoemaker.*
Sowps, *spoonfuls.*
Sowth, *to whistle over a tune.*
Sowther, *to solder, to make up.*
Spae, *to prophesy.*
Spails, *chips of wood.*
Spairges, *dashes or scatters about.*
Spairin, *sparing.*
Spak, *spake.*
Spate, *a flood.*
Spavie, *spavin (a disease).*

Spean, *to wean.*
Speel, *to climb.*
Speer, *to inquire.*
Spence, *the country parlour.*
Spier, *to ask, to inquire.*
Spleuchan, *a tobacco-pouch.*
Splore, *a frolic.*
Sprackled, *clambered.*
Sprattle, *to struggle.*
Spring, *a quick air in music, a Scottish reel.*
Spritty, *full of rushes or reed-grasses.*
Sprush, *spruce.*
Spunk, *fire, mettle.*
Spunkie, *full of spirit, mettlesome.*
Spunkies, *Wills-o'-the-wisp.*
Spurtle, *a stick with which porridge, broth, &c. are stirred.*
Squattle, *to sprawl.*
Stacher'd, *staggered, walked unsteadily.*
Stack, *stuck.*
Staig, *a horse two years old.*
Stan', *stand.*
Stanes, *stones.*
Stang, *to sting.*
Stank, *a pool of stagnant water.*
Stap, *to stop.*
Stark, *strong, hardy.*
Starns, *stars.*
Staukin, *stalking.*
Staw, *to steal, to surfeit.*
Stechin, *cramming.*
Steek, *to close.*
Steeks, *stitches.*
Steer, *to molest, to stir up.*
Steeve, *firm.*
Stells, *stills—commonly illicit.*
Sten, *a leap or bound.*
Stents, *assessments, dues.*
Steyest, *steepest.*
Stibble, *stubble.*
Stibble-rig, *the reaper in harvest who takes the lead, a stubble-ridge.*
Stick-an-stowe, *totally, altogether.*
Stilt, *halt.*
Stimpart, *an eighth part of a Winchester bushel, half a peck.*
Stirk, *a cow or bullock a year or two old.*

Stockins, *stockings.*
Stockit, *stocked.*
Stocks, *plants of cabbage.*
Stoitered, *staggered.*
Stoor, *strong, harsh, deep.*
Stoppit, *stopped.*
Stot, *an ox.*
Stoure, *dust, dust blown on the wind, battle or confusion.*
Stown, *stolen.*
Stownlins, *by stealth.*
Stowrie, *dusty.*
Stoyte, *to stumble.*
Strade, *strode.*
Strae, a fair strae-death, *a natural death in bed.*
Straik, *to stroke.*
Straikit, *stroked.*
Strak, *struck.*
Strang, *strong.*
Strappin, *strapping.*
Straught, *straight.*
Streekit, *stretched.*
Striddle, *to straddle.*
Stringin, *stringing.*
Stroan't, *pissed.*
Studdie, *a stithy.*
Stumpie, *dim. of stump, a short quill.*
Strunt, *spirituous liquor of any kind; to strut.*
Stuff, *corn.*
Sturt, *trouble, stir, disturbance.*
Sturtin, *frighted.*
Styme, *see a styme, see in the least.*
Sucker, *sugar.*
Sud, *should.*
Sugh, *a rushing sound.*
Sumphs, *stupid fellows.*
Sune, *soon.*
Suthron, *Southern, English.*
Swaird, *sward.*
Swall'd, *swelled.*
Swank, *thin, agile, vigorous.*
Swankies, *strapping young fellows.*
Swap, *an exchange.*
Swarf, *to swoon.*
Swat, *did sweat.*
Swatch, *sample.*

Swats, *new ale.*
Swearin', *swearing.*
Sweatin, *sweating.*
Swinge, *to lash.*
Swirl, *a curve.*
Swith, *swift, suddenly.*
Swither, *hesitation.*
Swoor, *swore.*
Sybow, *a thick-necked onion.*
Syne, *since, then.*

Tack, *possession, lease.*
Tackets, *hob-nails.*
Tae, *toe.* Three-tae'd, *three-toed.*
Taed, *a toad.*
Taen, *taken.*
Tairge, *to task severely.*
Tak, *to take.*
Tald, *told.*
Tane, *the one.*
Tangs, *tongs.*
Tapetless, *heedless, foolish, pith-less.*
Tapmost, *topmost.*
Tappit hen, *a quart measure.*
Taps, *tops.*
Tapsalteerie, *topsy-turvy.*
Tarrow, *to murmur.*
Tarry-breeks, *a sailor.*
Tassie, *a goblet or cup.*
Tauld, *told.*
Tawie, *that allows itself peaceably to be handled.*
Tawpies, *foolish young persons.*
Tawted, *matted.*
Teats, *small quantities.*
Teen, *sorrow.*
Tell'd, *told.*
Tellin', *telling.*
Temper-pin, *the wooden pin used for tempering or regulating the motion of a spinning-wheel.*
Tent, *to take heed, mark.*
Tentie, *heedful.*
Teughly, *toughly.*
Teuk, *took.*
Thack, *thatch.*
Thae, *these.*
Thairm, *fiddlestrings, intestines.*

Theekit, *thatched, covered up.*
Thegither, *together.*
Themsels, *themselves.*
Thieveless, *without an object, trifling, impotent.*
Thigger, *beggar.*
Thir, *these.*
Thril'd, *thrilled, bound.*
Thole, *to suffer, to endure.*
Thou's, *thou art.*
Thowes, *thaws.*
Thowless, *slack, lazy.*
Thrang, *busy; a crowd.*
Thrapple, *the throat.*
Thrave, *twenty-four sheaves of corn, making two shocks.*
Thraw, *to sprain or twist, to cross or contradict.*
Thrawin, *twisting.*
Thrawn, *twisted.*
Thraws, *throes.*
Threap, *to assert.*
Thretteen, *thirteen.*
Thretty, *thirty.*
Thrissle, *the thistle.*
Throwther, *mixed, pell-mell.*
Thuds, *that makes a loud intermittent noise, resounding blows.*
Thummart, *the polecat.*
Thumpit, *thumped.*
Thysel', *thyself.*
Tidins, *tidings.*
Till, *to.*
Till't, *to it.*
Timmer, *timber.*
Timmer-propt, *timber-propped.*
Tine, *to lose or be lost.*
Tint, *lost.*
Tint as win, *lost as won.*
Tinkler, *a tinker.*
Tips, *rams.*
Tippence; *twopence.*
Tirl, *to strip or uncover.*
Tirl'd, *rasped (knocked).*
Tirlin, *unroofing.*
Tither, *the other.*
Tittlin, *whispering and laughing.*
Tocher, *marriage-portion.*
Todlin', *walking unsteadily or softly like an infant.*

Tods, *foxes.*
Toom, *empty.*
Toop, *a ram.*
Toun, *a hamlet, a farm-house.*
Tout, *the blast of a horn or trumpet.*
Touzie, *rough, shaggy.*
Touzle *to rumple.*
Tow, *a rope.*
Towmond, *a twelvemonth.*
Toy, *a fashion of female head-dress.*
Toyte, *to totter.*
Transmugrify'd, *metamorphosed.*
Trashtrie, *trash.*
Treadin', *treading.*
Trews, *trousers.*
Trickie, *tricksy.*
Trig, *spruce, neat.*
Trinkling, *trickling.*
Troggin, *wares sold by wandering merchants or cadgers.*
Troke, *to exchange, to deal with.*
Trottin', *trotting.*
Trow't, *believed.*
Trowth! *in truth!*
Tulzie, *a quarrel.*
Tup, *a ram.*
Twa, *two.*
Twa-fauld, *twofold.*
Twa-three, *two or three.*
Twal, *twelve.*
Twalt, *the twelfth.*
Twang, *twinge.*
Twined, *reft, separated from.*
Twins, *bereaves, takes away from.*
Twistle, *a twist.*
Tyke, *a vagrant dog.*
Tyne, *to lose.*
Tysday 'teen, *Tuesday at evening.*

Unchancy, *dangerous.*
Unco, *very, great, extreme, strange.*
Uncos, *strange things, news of the country-side.*
Unkenn'd, *unknown.*
Unsicker, *unsecure.*
Unskaith'd, *unhurt.*
Upo', *upon.*
Upon't, *upon it.*

Vap'rin, *vapouring.*
Vauntie, *proud, in high spirits.*
Vera, *very.*
Viewin, *viewing.*
Virls, *rings.*
Vittel, *victual, grain.*
Vittle, *victual.*
Vogie, *proud, well-pleased.*
Vow, *an interjection of admiration or surprise.*

Wa', *a wall.*
Wa'-flower, *the wallflower.*
Wab, *a web.*
Wabster, *a weaver.*
Wad, *would; a wager; to wed.*
Wad a haen, *would have had.*
Wadna, *would not.*
Wadset, *a mortgage.*
Wae, *sorrowful.*
Wae days, *woful days.*
Waefu', *woful.*
Waes me, *woe's me.*
Waesucks! *alas!*
Wae worth, *woe befall.*
Waft, *the cross thread that goes from the shuttle through the web.*
Waifs, *stray sheep.*
Wair't, *spend it.*
Wal'd, *chose.*
Wale, *choice.*
Walie, *ample, large.*
Wallop in a tow, *to hang one's self.*
Wame, *the belly.*
Wamefou, *bellyful.*
Wan, *did win, earned.*
Wanchancie, *unlucky.*
Wanrestfu', *restless.*
War'd, *spent, bestowed.*
Ware, *to spend.*
Wark, *work.*
Wark-lume, *tool.*
Warks, *works.*
Warld, *world.*
Warlock, *wizard.*
Warly, *worldly.*
Warran', *warrant.*
Warsle, *to wrestle.*

Warst, *worst.*
Warstl'd, *wrestled.*
Wasna, *was not.*
Wast, *west.*
Wastrie, *prodigality, riot.*
Wat, *wet; wot, know.*
Wat na, *wot not.*
Waterbrose, *meal and water.*
Wattle, *twisted wands.*
Wauble, *to wabble.*
Waught, *a big drink.*
Waukening, *awakening.*
Waukens, *wakens.*
Waukit, *thickened with toil.*
Waukrife, *wakeful.*
Wauks, *awakes.*
Waur, *to fight, to defeat; worse.*
Waur't, *worsted.*
Weans, *children.*
Weason, *the weasand.*
Wee, *little.*
   A wee, *a short period of time.*
   A week a-back, *a small space be-
     hind.*
Weel, *well.*
Weel-gaun, *well-going.*
Weel-kent, *well known.*
Weet, *wet.*
We'se, *we shall or will.*
Westlin, *western.*
Wha, *who.*
Wha t'er, *whoever.*
Whaizle, *to wheeze.*
Whalpit, *whelped.*
Wham, *whom.*
Whan, *when.*
Whang, *a large slice.*
Whar, *where.*
Whare, *where.*
Wha's, *whose.*
Whase, *whose.*
Whatfor no? *for what reason not?*
Whatt, *did whet or cut.*
Whaup, *a curlew.*
Whaur'll, *where will.*
Whiddin, *running as a hare.*
Whigmaleeries, *crochets.*

Whingin', *crying, complaining,
   fretting.*
Whins, *furze bushes.*
Whirlygigums, *useless ornaments.*
Whisht, *peace.*
Whiskit, *whisked.*
Whissle, *whistle.*
Whistle, *the throat.*
Whitter, *a hearty draught of liquor.*
Whun-stane, *whinstone, granite.*
Whup, *a whip.*
Whyles, *sometimes.*
Wi', *with.*
Wick, *a term in curling.*
Widdle, *a struggle or bustle.*
Wiel, *a small whirlpool.*
Wifie, *dim. of wife.*
Wight, *strong, powerful.*
Wil' cat, *the wild cat.*
Willow wicker, *the smaller species of
   willow.*
Willyart, *wild, strange.*
Wimplin, *flowing, meandering.*
Wimpl't, *wimpled.*
Win', *wind.*
Winkin, *winking.*
Winna, *will not.*
Winnock-bunker, *a seat in a
   window.*
Winnocks, *windows.*
Wins, *winds.*
Win't, *did wind.*
Wintle, *a staggering motion.*
Wintles, *struggles.*
Winze, *a curse.*
Wiss, *wish.*
Witha', *withal.*
Withoutten, *without.*
Wonner, *a wonder.*
Wons, *dwells.*
Woo', *wool.*
Woodie, *the gallows, a withe.*
Wooer-babs, *garters tied above the
   calf of the leg with two loops.*
Wordie, *dim. of word.*
Wordy, *worthy.*
Worl', *world.*

Worset, *worsted.*
Wow, *an exclamation of surprise or wonder.*
Wrang, *wrong.*
Wreeths, *wreaths.*
Wud, *mad.*
Wumble, *a wimble or anger.*
Wyle, *to beguile, to decoy.*
Wyliecoat, *a flannel vest.*
Wyling, *beguiling.*
Wyte, *to blame.*

Yard, *a garden.*
Yaud, *a worn-out horse.*
Yealings, *coevals.*
Yell, *barren, giving no milk.*
Yerd, *yard.*

Yerket, *jerked, lashed.*
Yerl, *an earl.*
Ye'se, *you shall or will.*
Yestreen, *yesternight.*
Yetts, *gates.*
Yeukin, *itching.*
Yeuks, *itches.*
Yill, *ale.*
Yill-caup, *ale-mug.*
Yird, *earth.*
Yirth, *the earth.*
Yokin, *yoking, a bout, set to.*
Yont, *beyond.*
Yoursel, *yourselves, yourself.*
Yowes, *ewes.*
Yowie, *pet ewe.*
Yule, *Christmas.*